♥ Alice IN THE COUNTRY OF Hearts

Volume 3

Created by
QuinRose X Soumei Hoshino

TOKYOPOP®

HAMBURG // LONDON // LOS ANGELES // TOKYO

Alice in the Country of Hearts Volume 3
Created by QuinRose X Soumei Hoshino

Translation - Angela Liu
English Adaptation - Lianne Sentar
Copy Editor - Daniella Orihuela-Grober
Retouch and Lettering - Star Print Brokers
Production Artist - Rui Kyo
Graphic Designer - Al-Insan Lashley

Editor - Cindy Suzuki
Print Production Manager - Lucas Rivera
Managing Editor - Vy Nguyen
Senior Designer - Louis Csontos
Art Director - Al-Insan Lashley
Director of Sales and Manufacturing - Allyson De Simone
Associate Publisher - Marco F. Pavia
President and C.O.O. - John Parker
C.E.O. and Chief Creative Officer - Stu Levy

A **TOKYOPOP** Manga

TOKYOPOP Inc.
5900 Wilshire Blvd. Suite 2000
Los Angeles, CA 90036

E-mail: info@TOKYOPOP.com
Come visit us online at www.TOKYOPOP.com

ISBN: 978-1-4278-1818-8

First TOKYOPOP printing: June 2010
10 9 8 7 6 5 4
Printed in the USA

Alice in the Country of Hearts

ハートの国のアリス

~ Wonderful Wonder World ~

3

QuinRose ✕ Soumei Hoshino

ハートの国のアリス
～ Wonderful Wonder World ～

3

C O N T E N T S

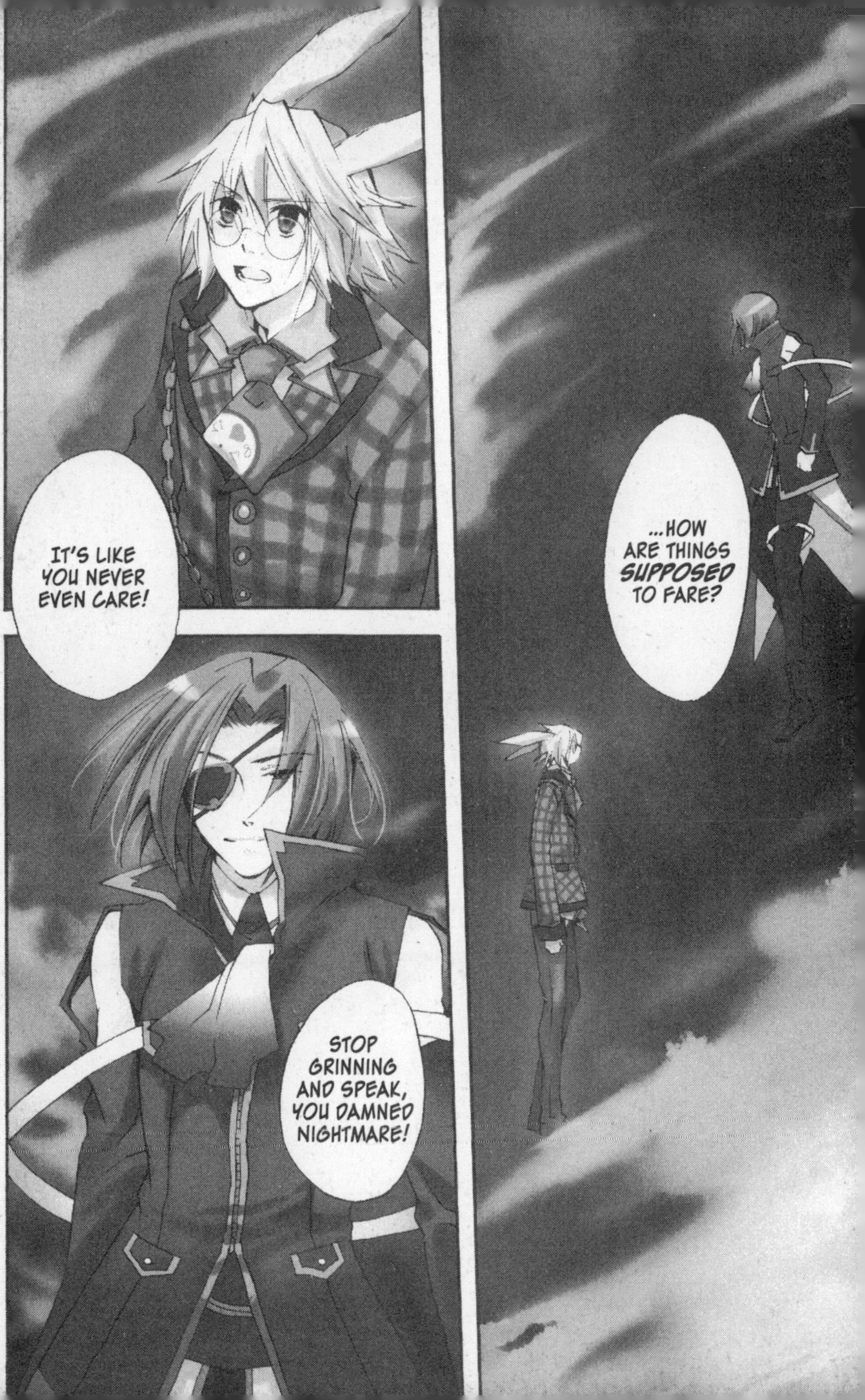
...HOW ARE THINGS *SUPPOSED* TO FARE?
IT'S LIKE YOU NEVER EVEN CARE!
STOP GRINNING AND SPEAK, YOU DAMNED NIGHTMARE!

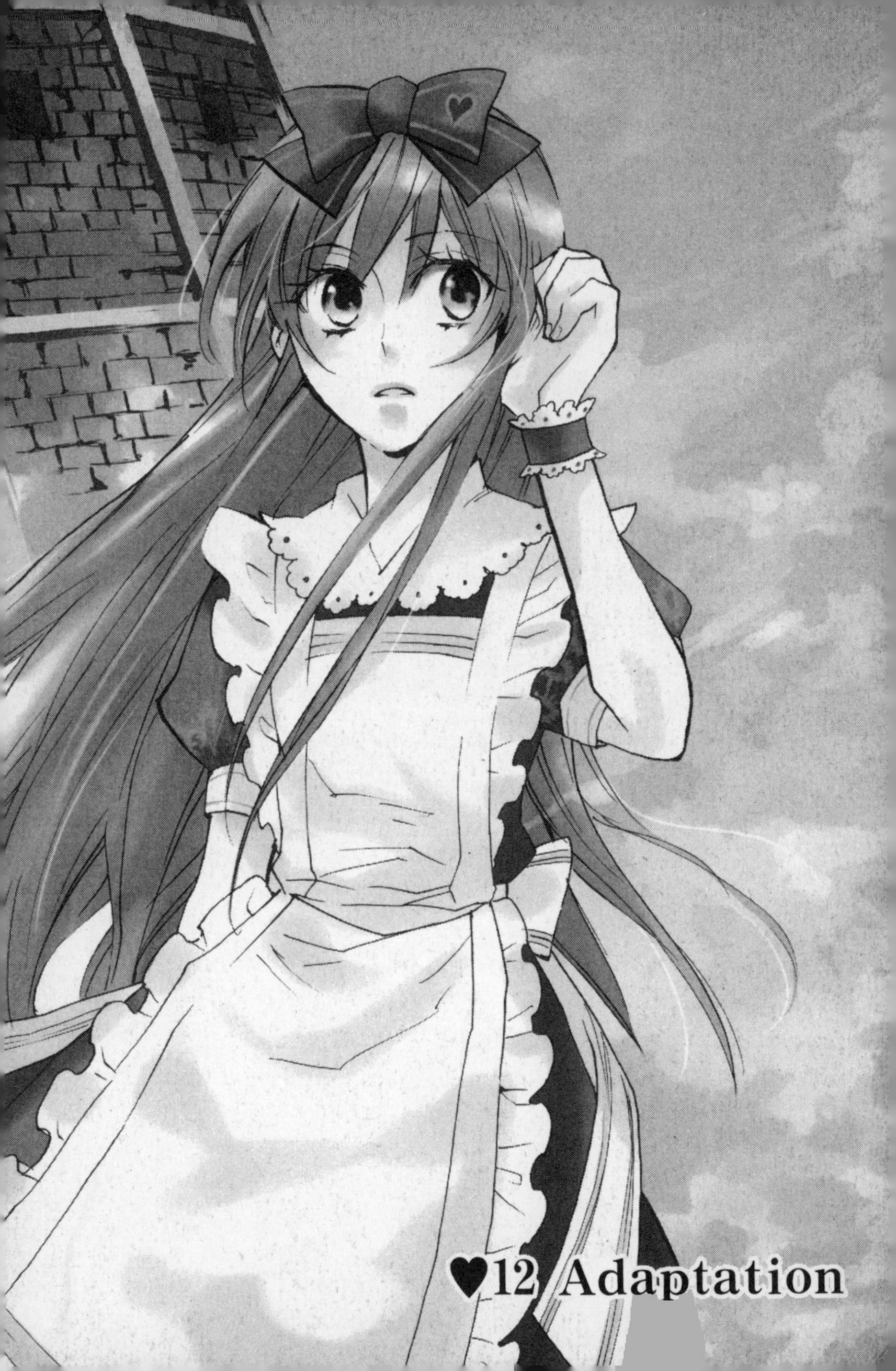
♥12 Adaptation

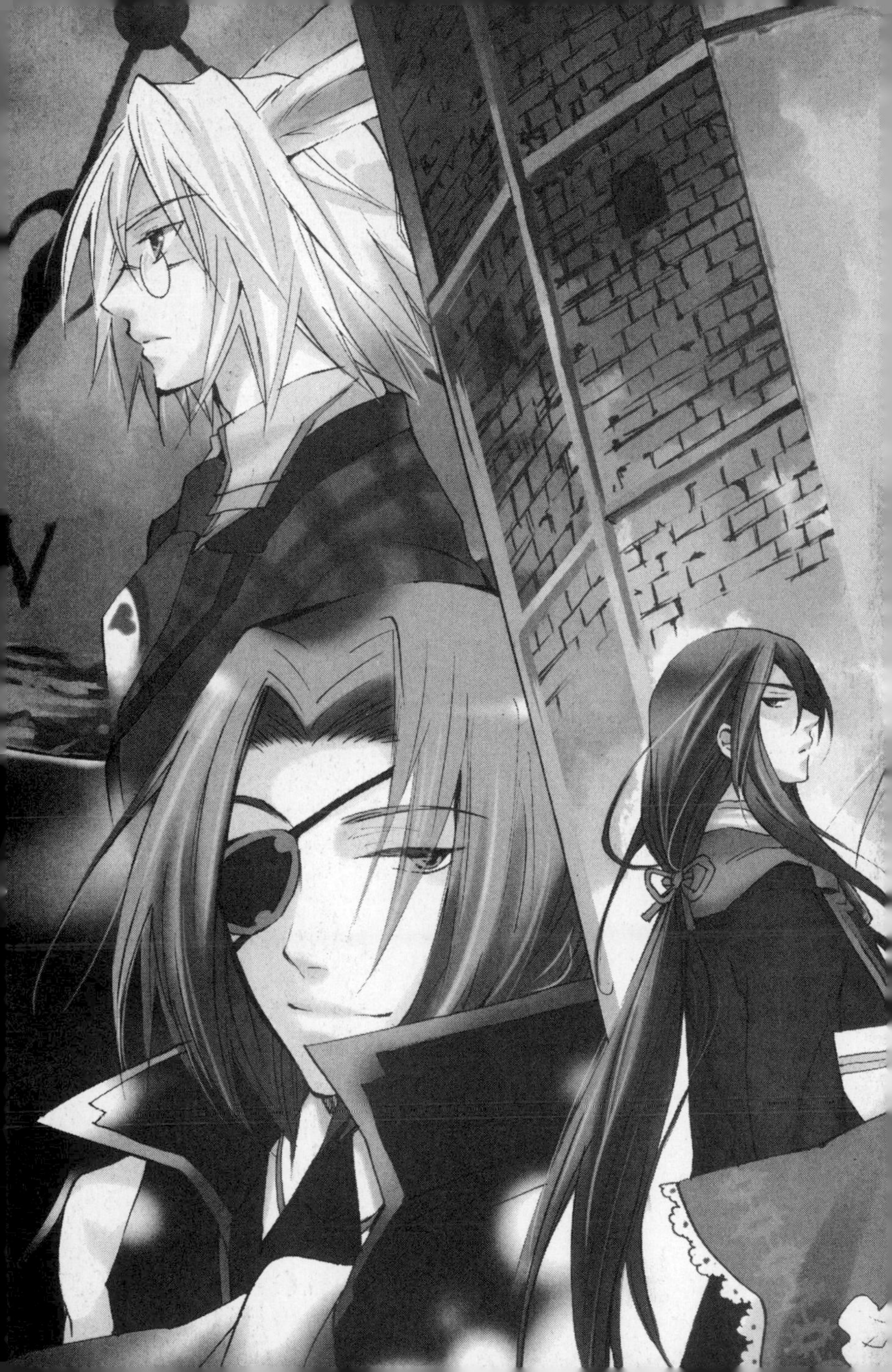

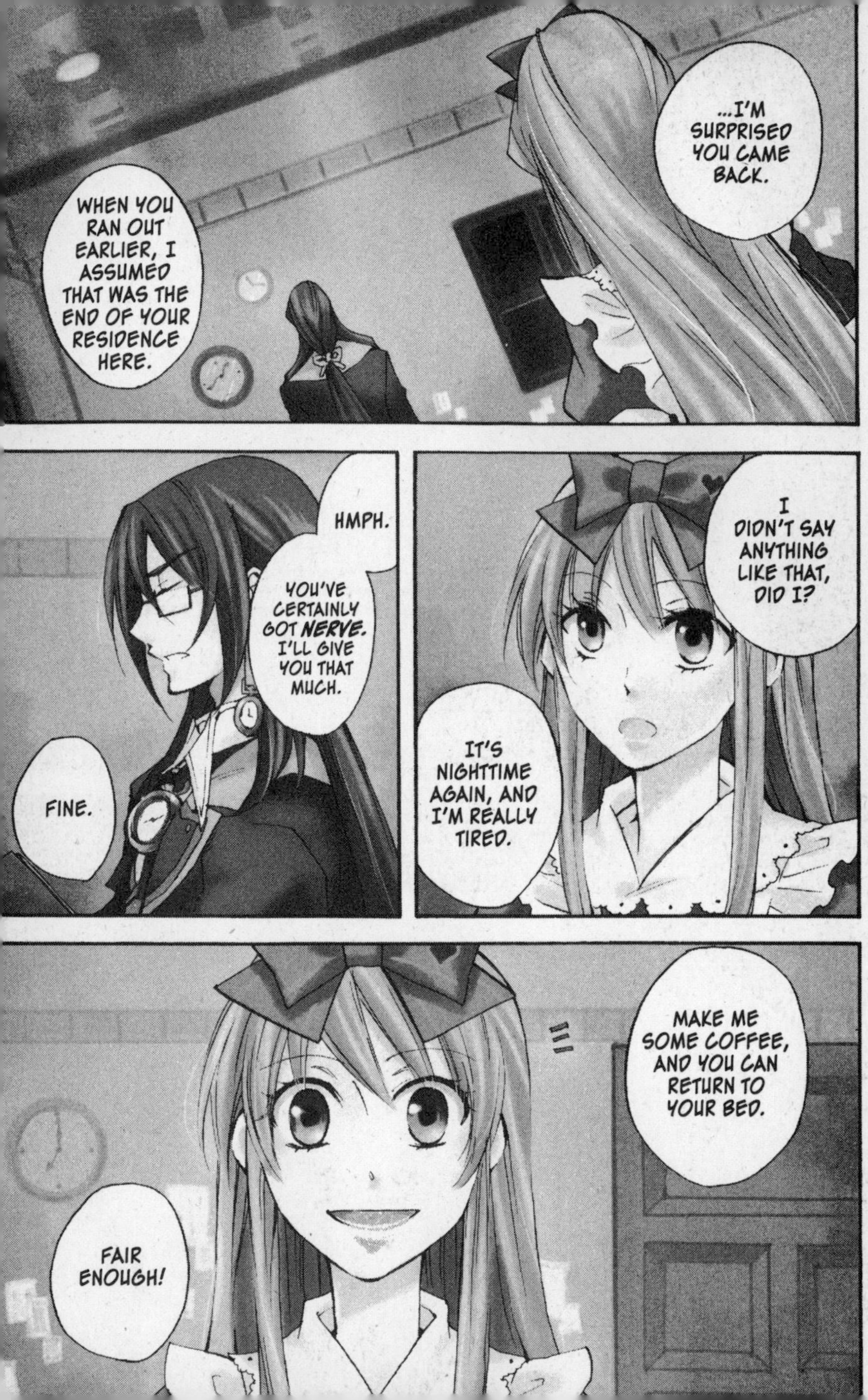
...I'M SURPRISED YOU CAME BACK.
WHEN YOU RAN OUT EARLIER, I ASSUMED THAT WAS THE END OF YOUR RESIDENCE HERE.
I DIDN'T SAY ANYTHING LIKE THAT, DID I?
IT'S NIGHTTIME AGAIN, AND I'M REALLY TIRED.
HMPH.
YOU'VE CERTAINLY GOT **NERVE.** I'LL GIVE YOU THAT MUCH.
FINE.
MAKE ME SOME COFFEE, AND YOU CAN RETURN TO YOUR BED.
FAIR ENOUGH!

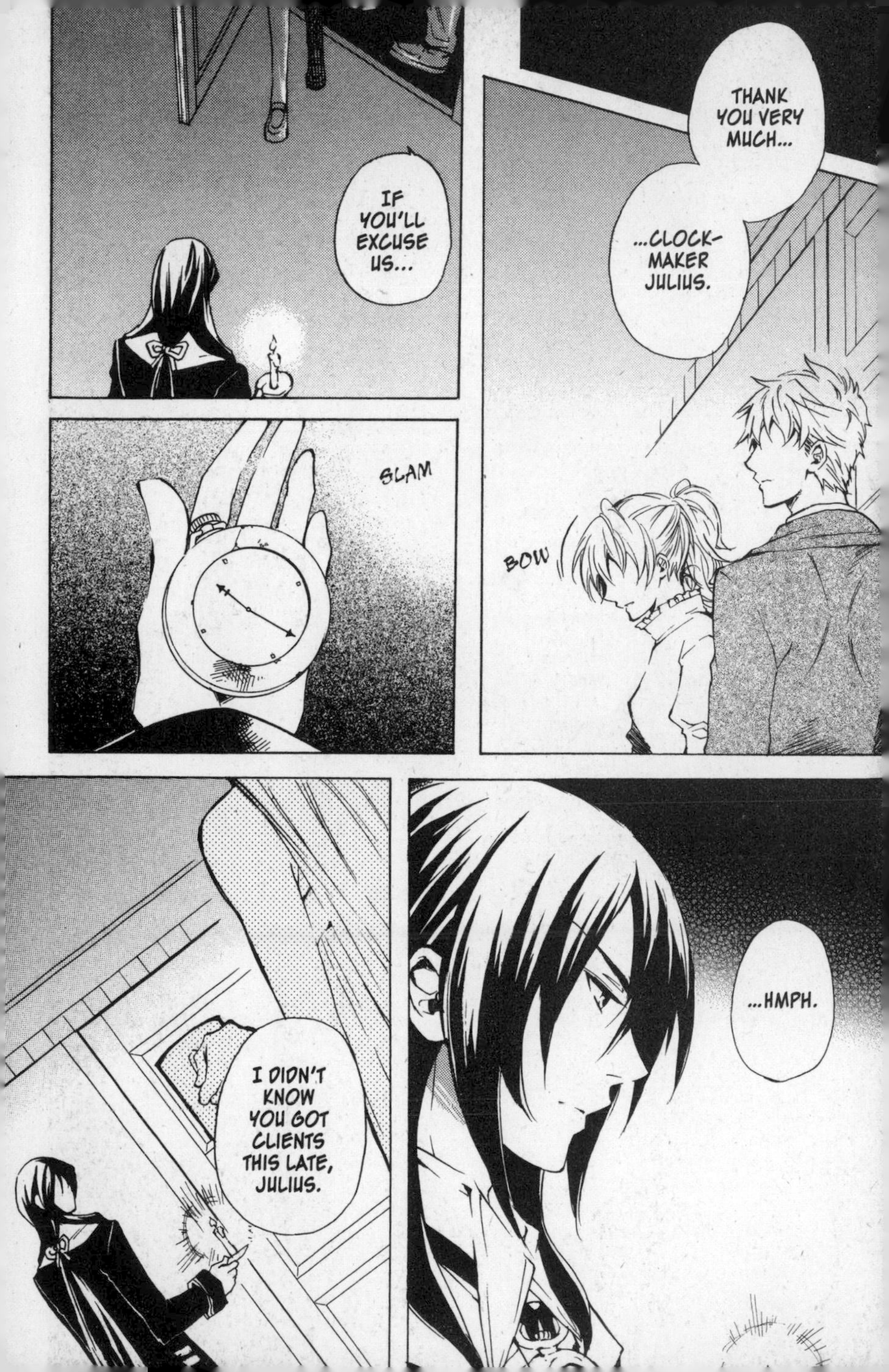
THANK YOU VERY MUCH...
...CLOCK-MAKER JULIUS.
BOW
IF YOU'LL EXCUSE US...
SLAM
...HMPH.
I DIDN'T KNOW YOU GOT CLIENTS THIS LATE, JULIUS.

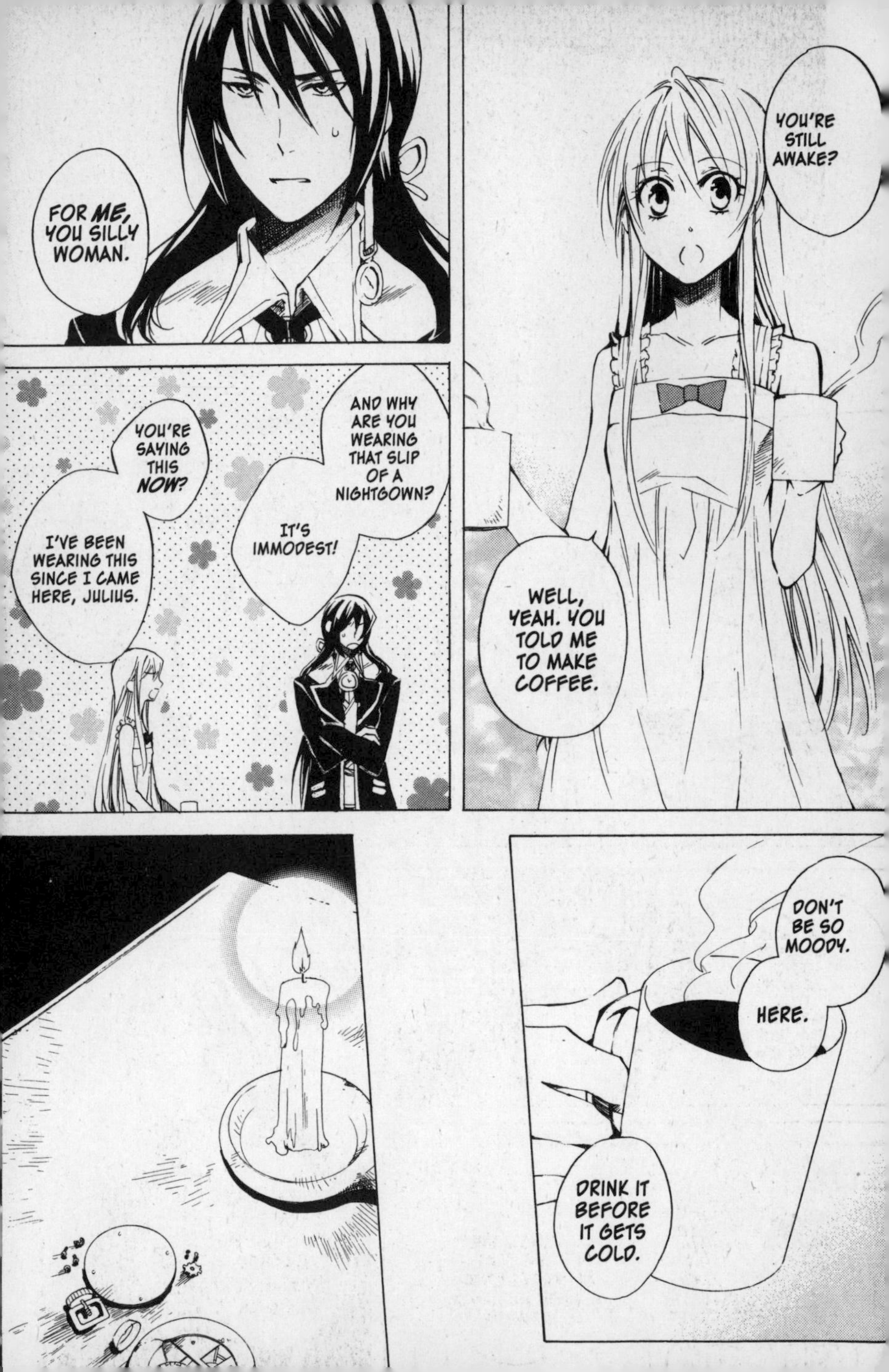
YOU'RE STILL AWAKE?
WELL, YEAH. YOU TOLD ME TO MAKE COFFEE.
FOR ME, YOU SILLY WOMAN.
AND WHY ARE YOU WEARING THAT SLIP OF A NIGHTGOWN?
IT'S IMMODEST!
YOU'RE SAYING THIS NOW?
I'VE BEEN WEARING THIS SINCE I CAME HERE, JULIUS.
DON'T BE SO MOODY.
HERE.
DRINK IT BEFORE IT GETS COLD.

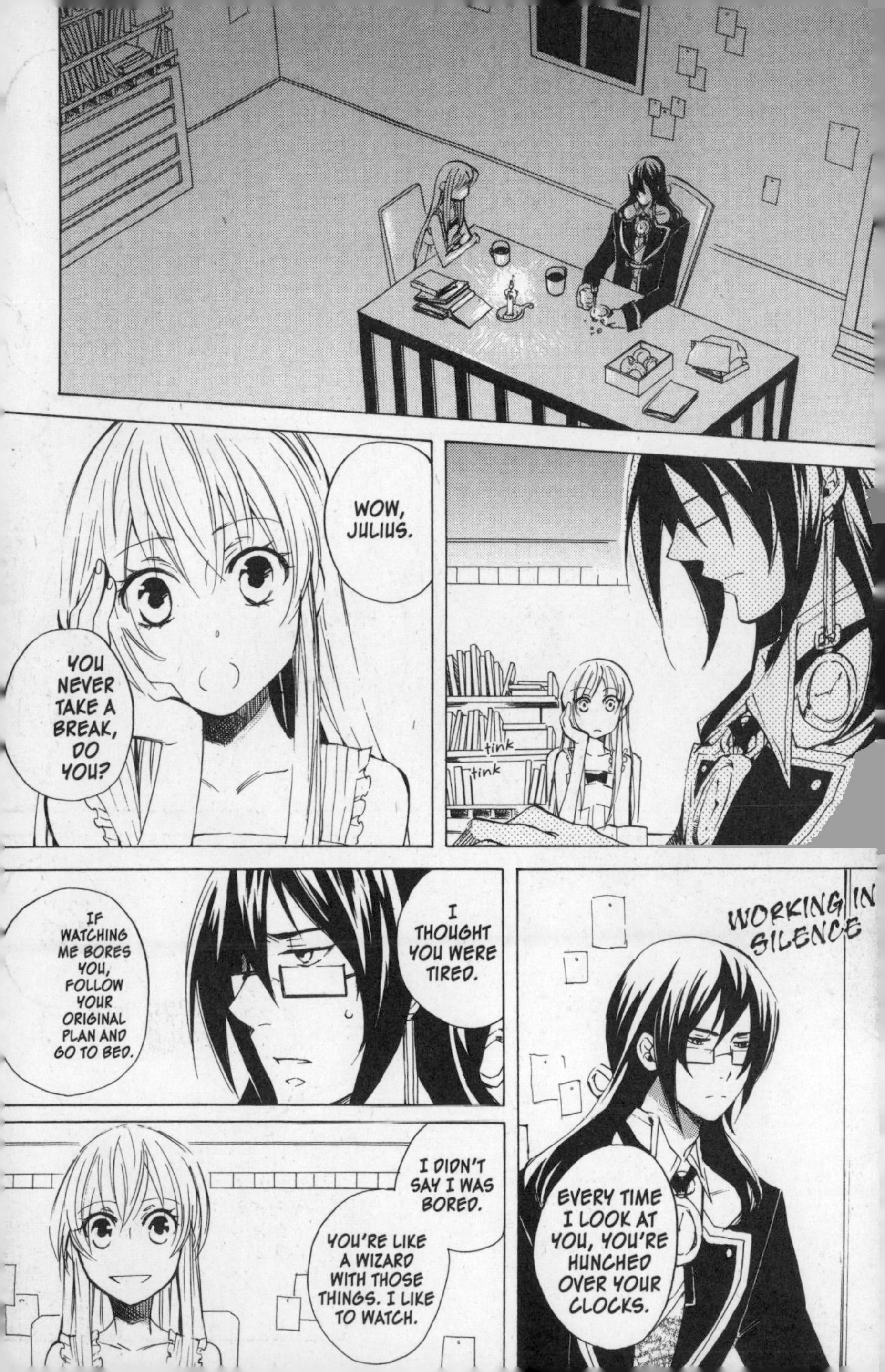
tink
tink
WOW, JULIUS.
YOU NEVER TAKE A BREAK, DO YOU?
WORKING IN SILENCE
EVERY TIME I LOOK AT YOU, YOU'RE HUNCHED OVER YOUR CLOCKS.
I THOUGHT YOU WERE TIRED.
IF WATCHING ME BORES YOU, FOLLOW YOUR ORIGINAL PLAN AND GO TO BED.
I DIDN'T SAY I WAS BORED.
YOU'RE LIKE A WIZARD WITH THOSE THINGS. I LIKE TO WATCH.

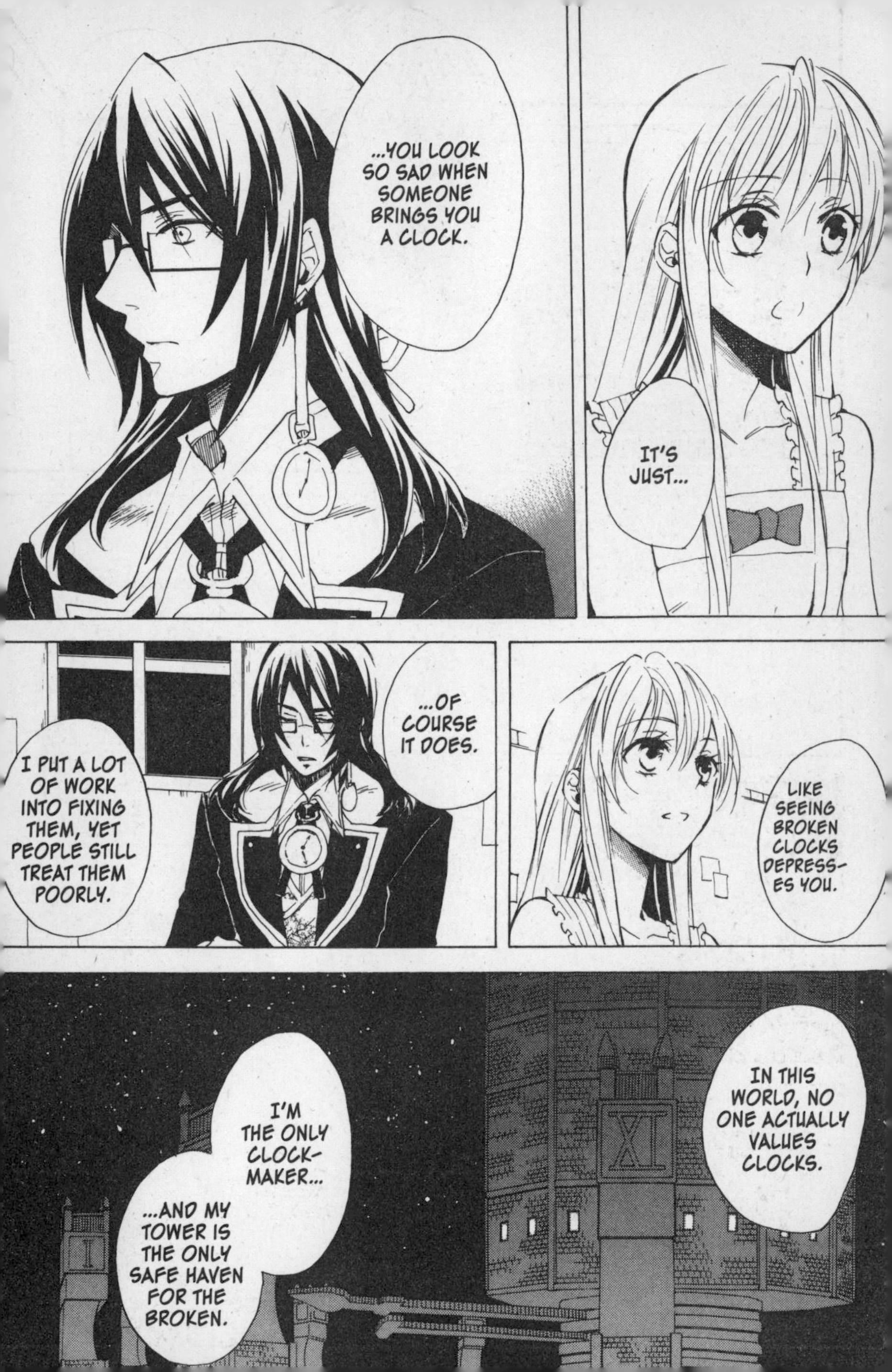
IT'S JUST...
...YOU LOOK SO SAD WHEN SOMEONE BRINGS YOU A CLOCK.
LIKE SEEING BROKEN CLOCKS DEPRESSES YOU.
...OF COURSE IT DOES.
I PUT A LOT OF WORK INTO FIXING THEM, YET PEOPLE STILL TREAT THEM POORLY.
IN THIS WORLD, NO ONE ACTUALLY VALUES CLOCKS.
I'M THE ONLY CLOCK-MAKER...
...AND MY TOWER IS THE ONLY SAFE HAVEN FOR THE BROKEN.

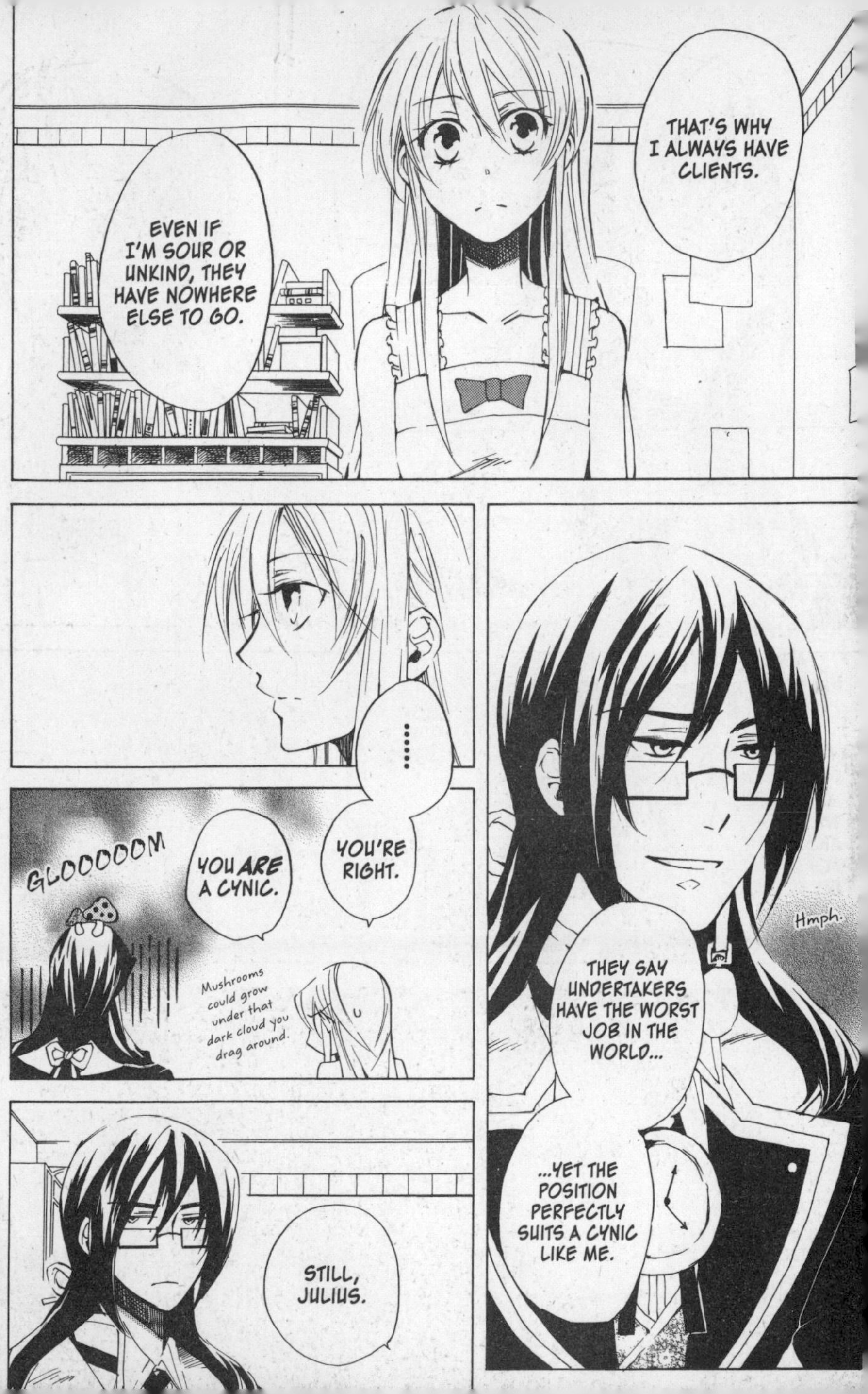
THAT'S WHY I ALWAYS HAVE CLIENTS.
EVEN IF I'M SOUR OR UNKIND, THEY HAVE NOWHERE ELSE TO GO.
Hmph.
THEY SAY UNDERTAKERS HAVE THE WORST JOB IN THE WORLD...
...YET THE POSITION PERFECTLY SUITS A CYNIC LIKE ME.
......
YOU'RE RIGHT.
YOU **ARE** A CYNIC.
GLOOOOOM
Mushrooms could grow under that dark cloud you drag around.
STILL, JULIUS.

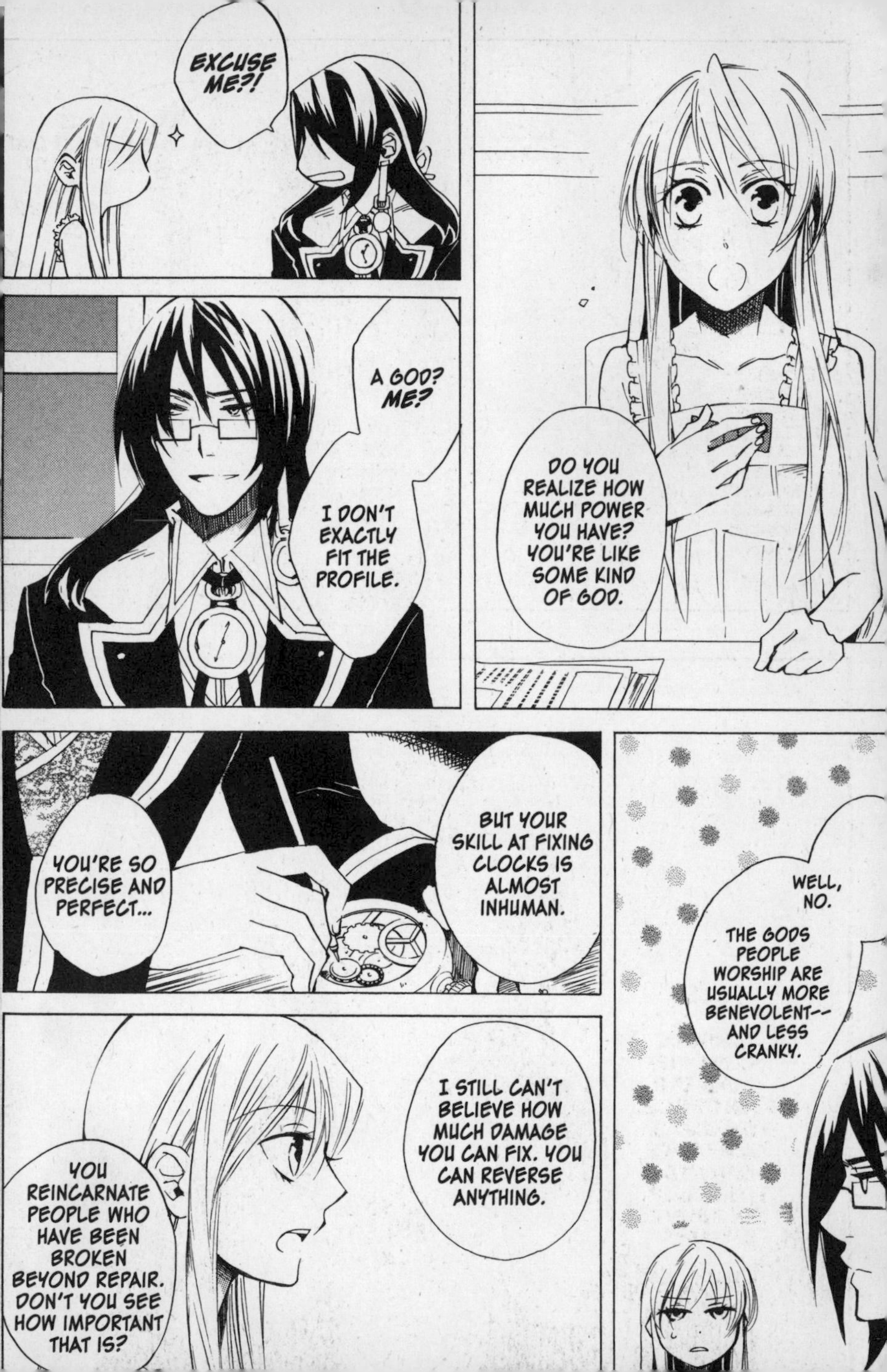
DO YOU REALIZE HOW MUCH POWER YOU HAVE? YOU'RE LIKE SOME KIND OF GOD.
EXCUSE ME?!
A GOD? ME?
I DON'T EXACTLY FIT THE PROFILE.
WELL, NO.
THE GODS PEOPLE WORSHIP ARE USUALLY MORE BENEVOLENT--AND LESS CRANKY.
BUT YOUR SKILL AT FIXING CLOCKS IS ALMOST INHUMAN.
YOU'RE SO PRECISE AND PERFECT...
I STILL CAN'T BELIEVE HOW MUCH DAMAGE YOU CAN FIX. YOU CAN REVERSE ANYTHING.
YOU REINCARNATE PEOPLE WHO HAVE BEEN BROKEN BEYOND REPAIR. DON'T YOU SEE HOW IMPORTANT THAT IS?

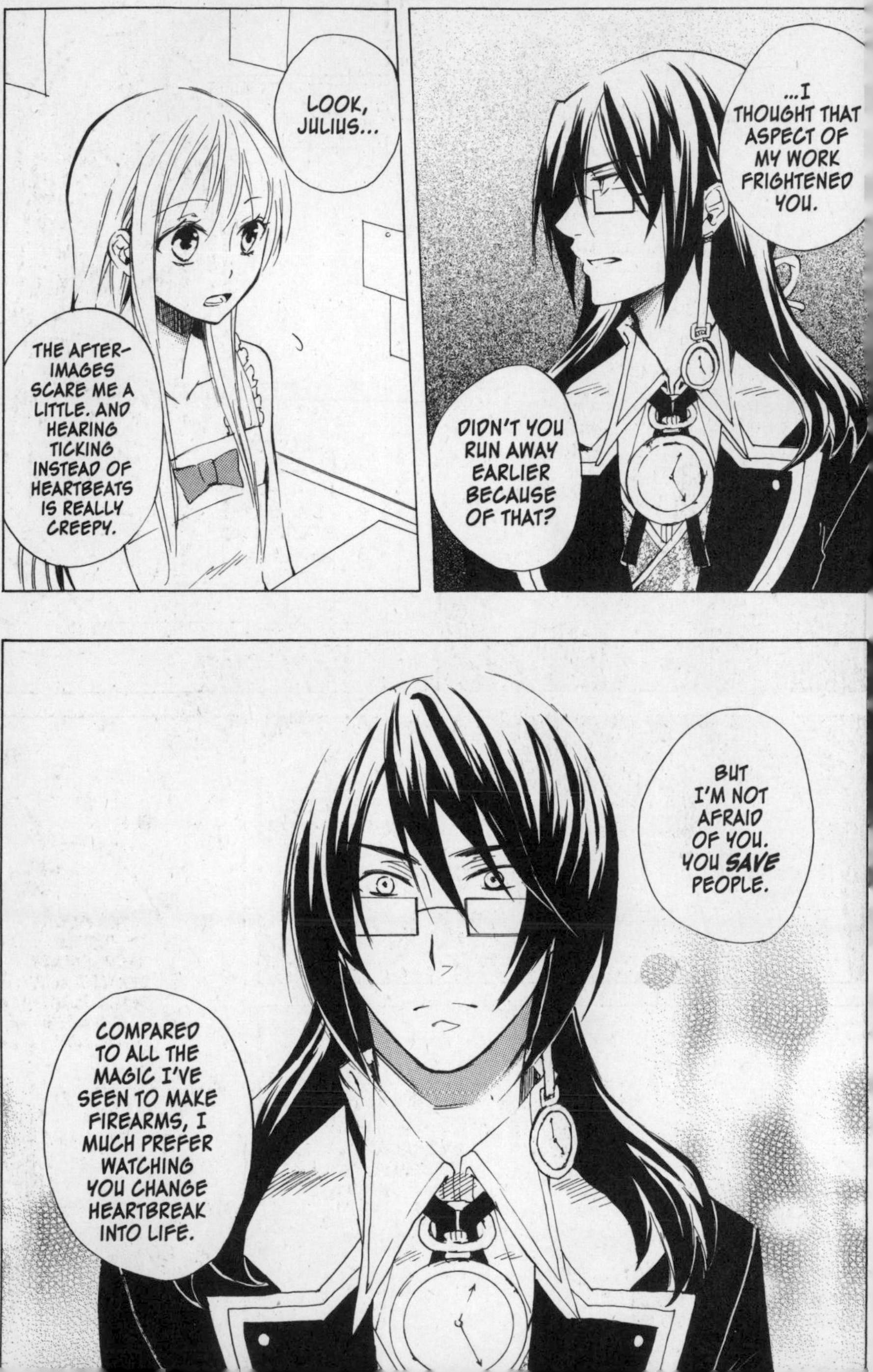
...I THOUGHT THAT ASPECT OF MY WORK FRIGHTENED YOU.
DIDN'T YOU RUN AWAY EARLIER BECAUSE OF THAT?
LOOK, JULIUS...
THE AFTER-IMAGES SCARE ME A LITTLE. AND HEARING TICKING INSTEAD OF HEARTBEATS IS REALLY CREEPY.
BUT I'M NOT AFRAID OF YOU. YOU *SAVE* PEOPLE.
COMPARED TO ALL THE MAGIC I'VE SEEN TO MAKE FIREARMS, I MUCH PREFER WATCHING YOU CHANGE HEARTBREAK INTO LIFE.

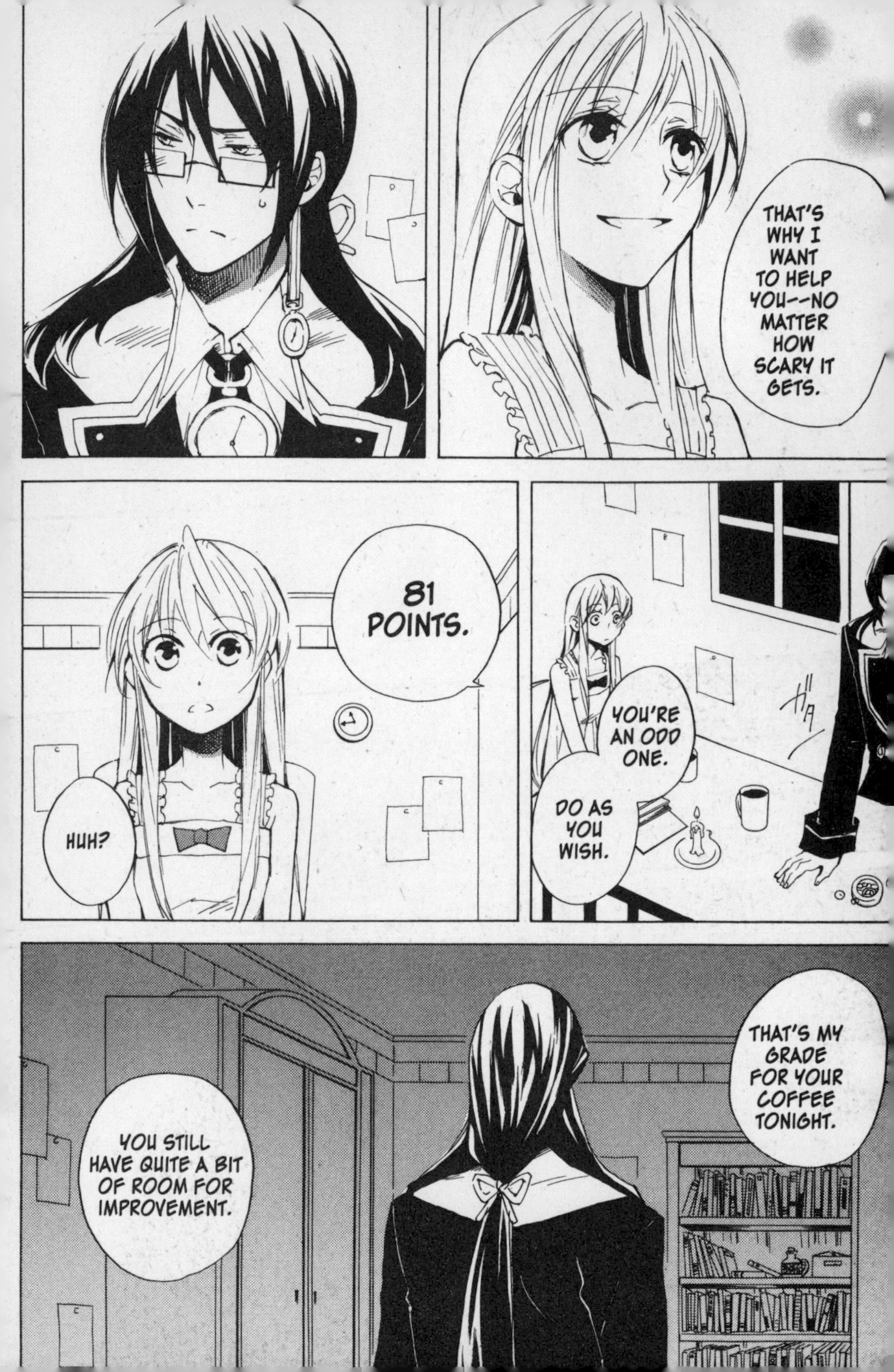
THAT'S WHY I WANT TO HELP YOU--NO MATTER HOW SCARY IT GETS.
YOU'RE AN ODD ONE.
DO AS YOU WISH.
ガタ
81 POINTS.
HUH?
THAT'S MY GRADE FOR YOUR COFFEE TONIGHT.
YOU STILL HAVE QUITE A BIT OF ROOM FOR IMPROVEMENT.

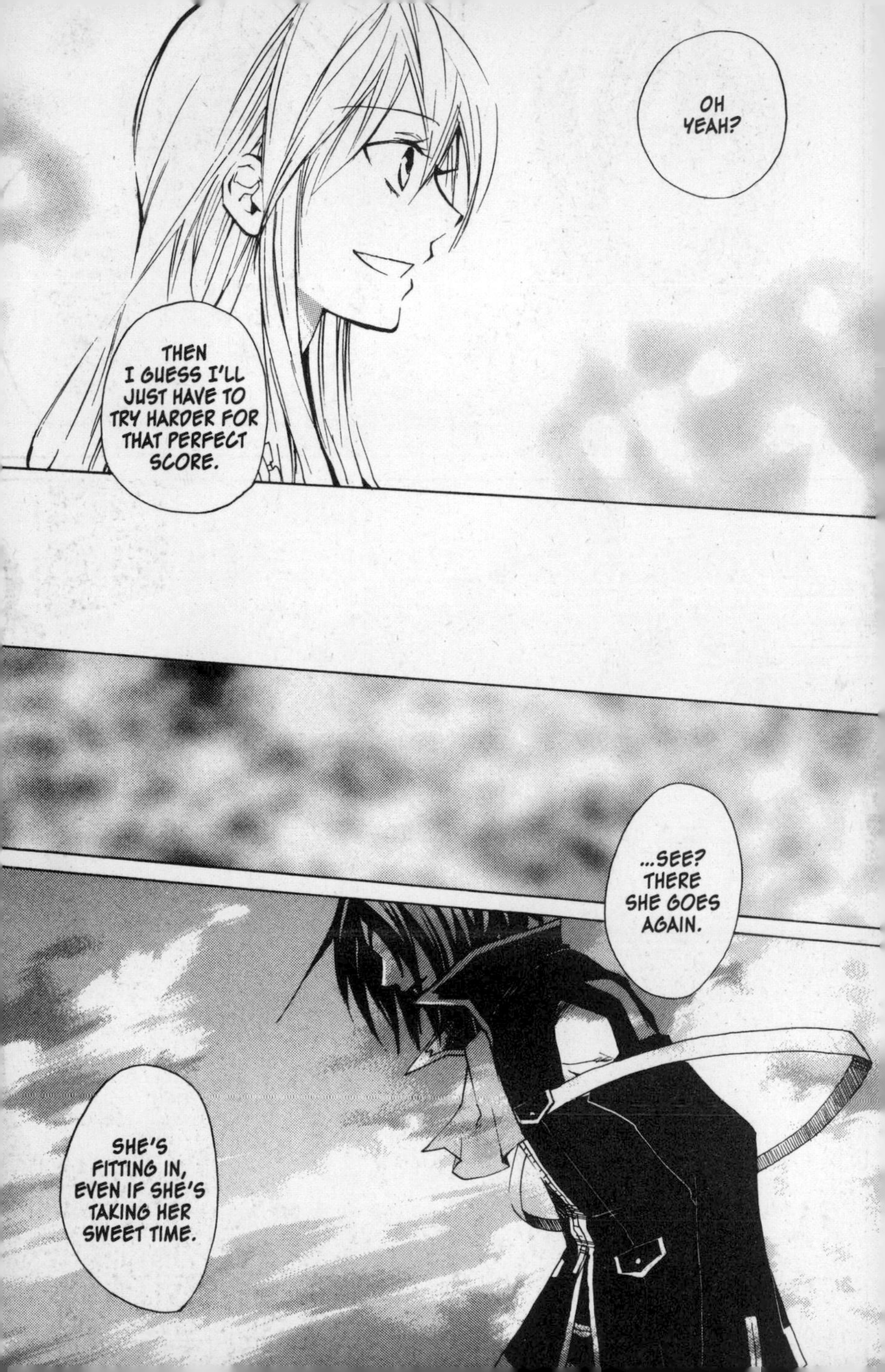
OH YEAH?
THEN I GUESS I'LL JUST HAVE TO TRY HARDER FOR THAT PERFECT SCORE.
...SEE? THERE SHE GOES AGAIN.
SHE'S FITTING IN, EVEN IF SHE'S TAKING HER SWEET TIME.

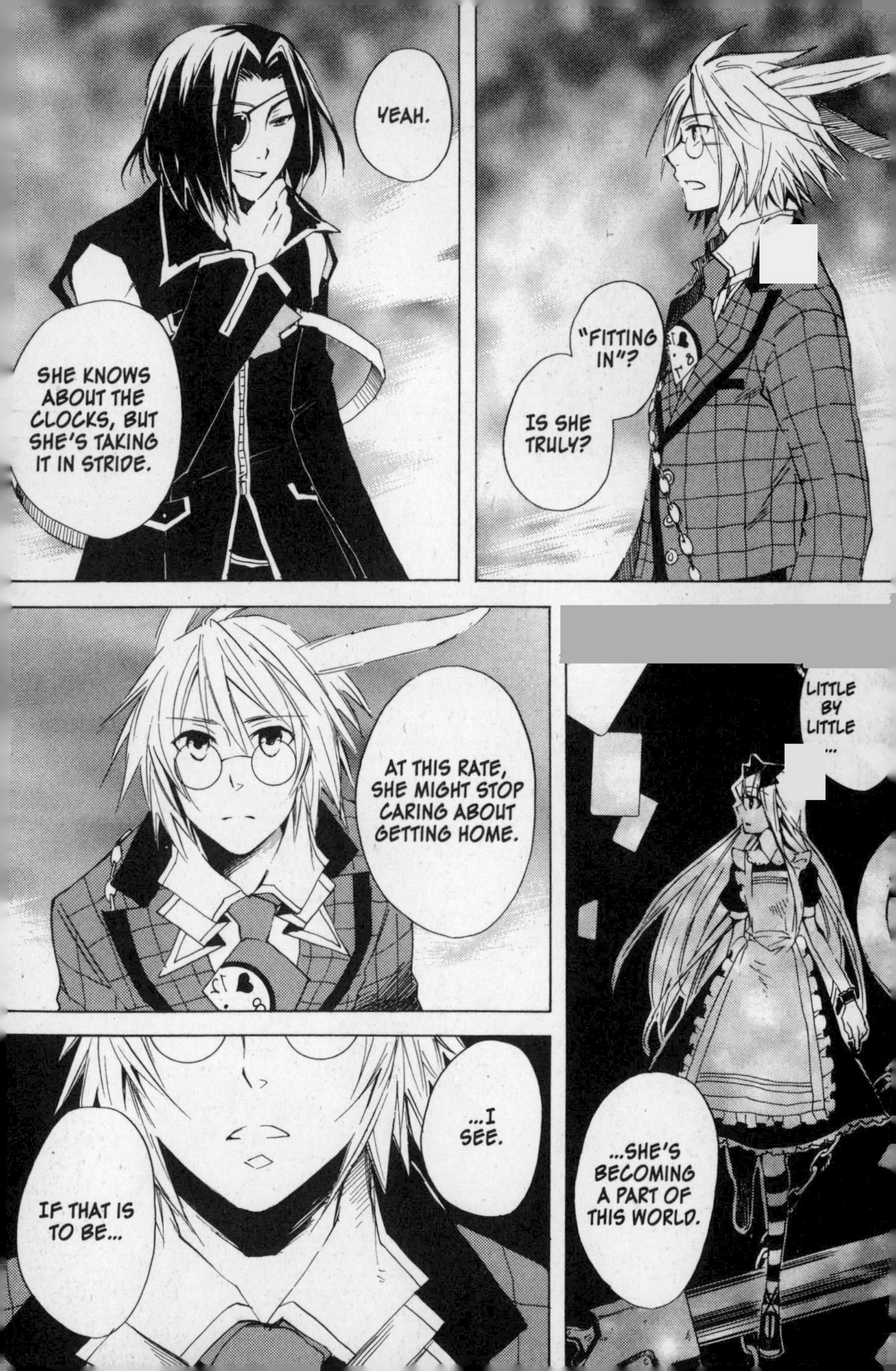
"FITTING IN"?
IS SHE TRULY?
YEAH.
SHE KNOWS ABOUT THE CLOCKS, BUT SHE'S TAKING IT IN STRIDE.
LITTLE BY LITTLE...
...SHE'S BECOMING A PART OF THIS WORLD.
AT THIS RATE, SHE MIGHT STOP CARING ABOUT GETTING HOME.
...I SEE.
IF THAT IS TO BE...

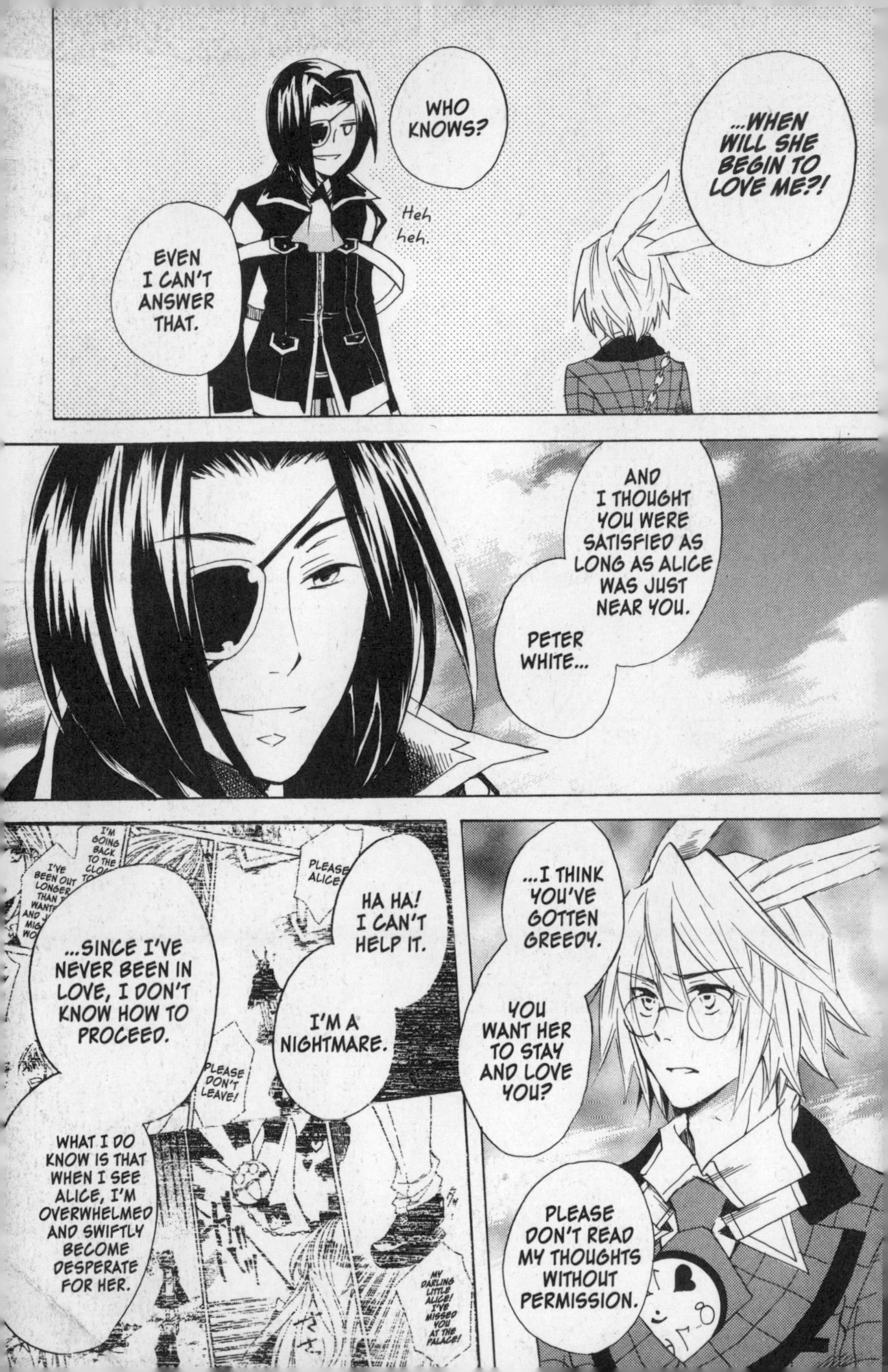
...WHEN WILL SHE BEGIN TO LOVE ME?!
WHO KNOWS?
Heh heh.
EVEN I CAN'T ANSWER THAT.
AND I THOUGHT YOU WERE SATISFIED AS LONG AS ALICE WAS JUST NEAR YOU.
PETER WHITE...
...I THINK YOU'VE GOTTEN GREEDY.
YOU WANT HER TO STAY AND LOVE YOU?
PLEASE DON'T READ MY THOUGHTS WITHOUT PERMISSION.
HA HA! I CAN'T HELP IT.
I'M A NIGHTMARE.
...SINCE I'VE NEVER BEEN IN LOVE, I DON'T KNOW HOW TO PROCEED.
WHAT I DO KNOW IS THAT WHEN I SEE ALICE, I'M OVERWHELMED AND SWIFTLY BECOME DESPERATE FOR HER.
PLEASE DON'T LEAVE!
MY DARLING LITTLE ALICE! I'VE MISSED YOU AT THE PALACE!

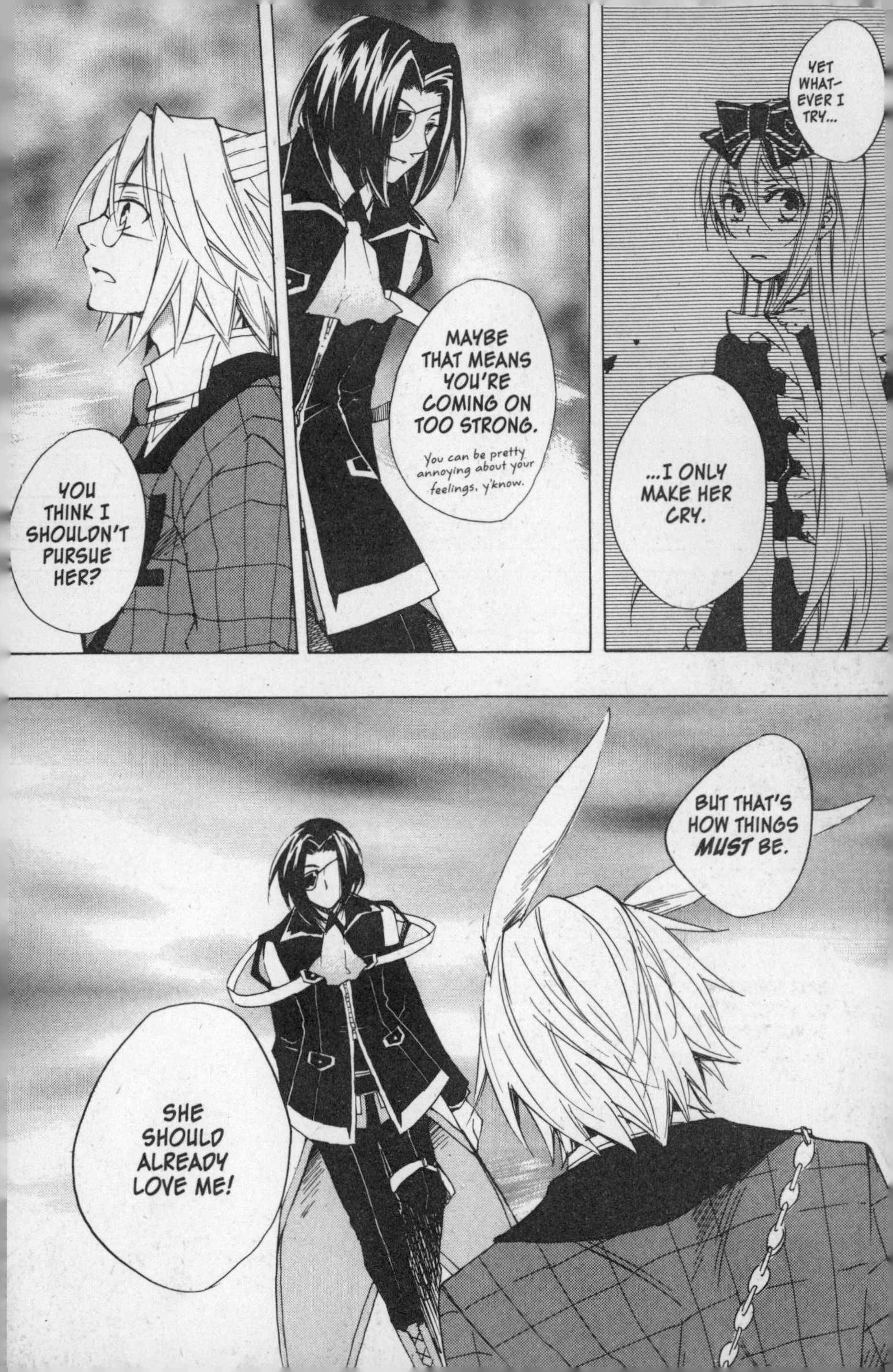
YET WHATEVER I TRY...
...I ONLY MAKE HER CRY.
MAYBE THAT MEANS YOU'RE COMING ON TOO STRONG.
You can be pretty annoying about your feelings, y'know.
YOU THINK I SHOULDN'T PURSUE HER?
BUT THAT'S HOW THINGS *MUST* BE.
SHE SHOULD ALREADY LOVE ME!

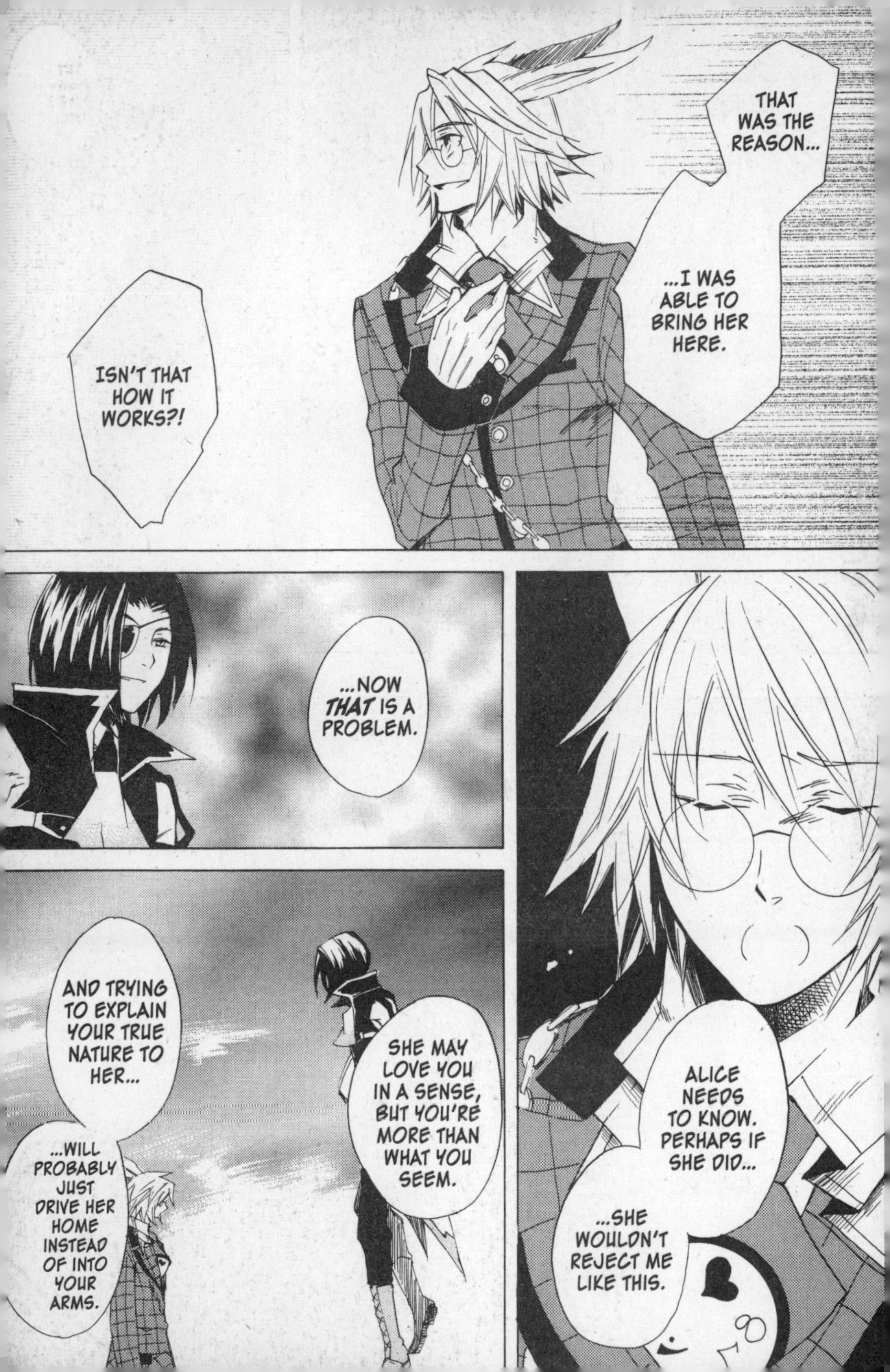
THAT WAS THE REASON...
...I WAS ABLE TO BRING HER HERE.
ISN'T THAT HOW IT WORKS?!
ALICE NEEDS TO KNOW. PERHAPS IF SHE DID...
...SHE WOULDN'T REJECT ME LIKE THIS.
...NOW *THAT* IS A PROBLEM.
SHE MAY LOVE YOU IN A SENSE, BUT YOU'RE MORE THAN WHAT YOU SEEM.
AND TRYING TO EXPLAIN YOUR TRUE NATURE TO HER...
...WILL PROBABLY JUST DRIVE HER HOME INSTEAD OF INTO YOUR ARMS.

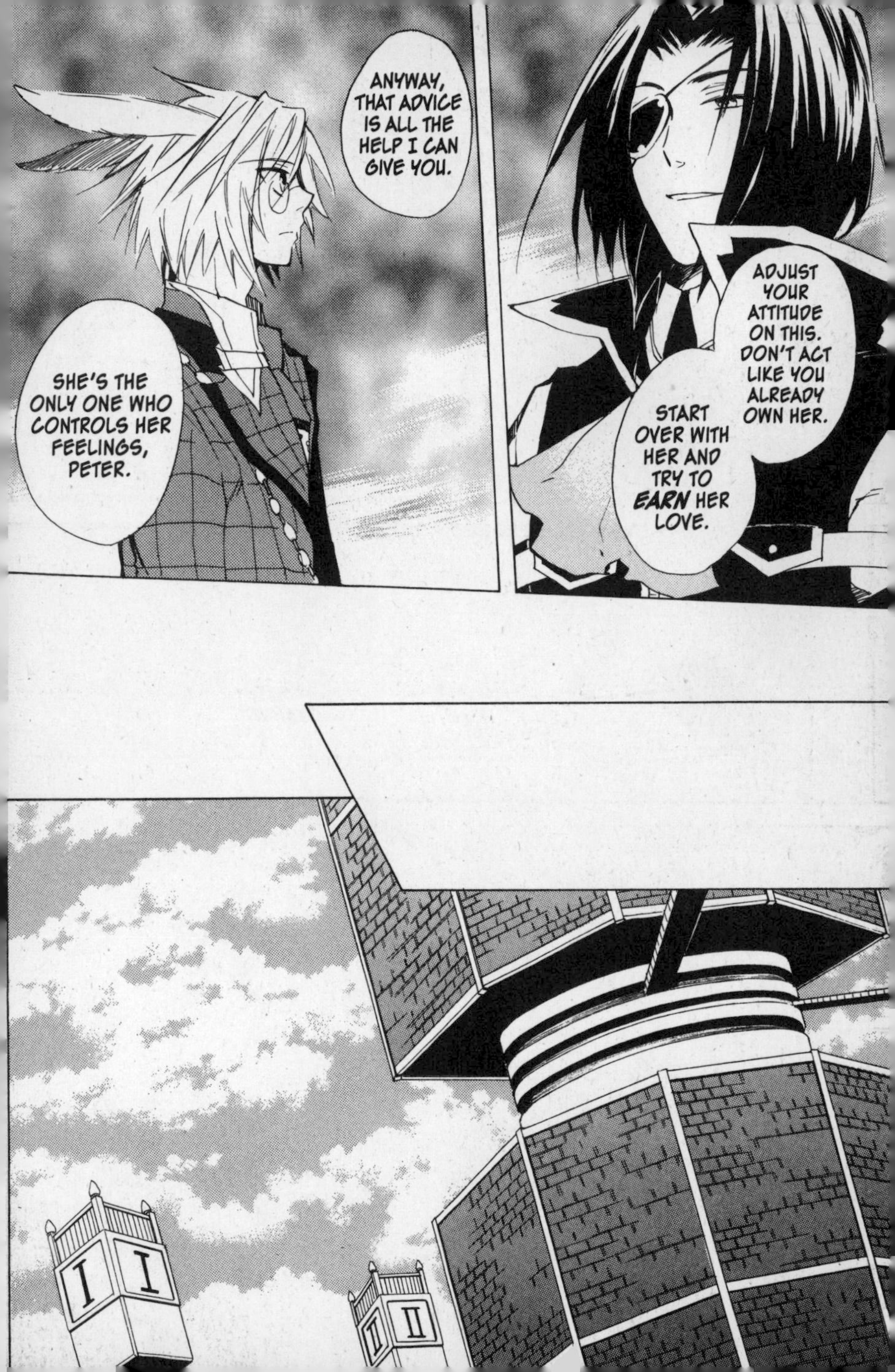
ADJUST YOUR ATTITUDE ON THIS. DON'T ACT LIKE YOU ALREADY OWN HER.
START OVER WITH HER AND TRY TO **EARN** HER LOVE.
ANYWAY, THAT ADVICE IS ALL THE HELP I CAN GIVE YOU.
SHE'S THE ONLY ONE WHO CONTROLS HER FEELINGS, PETER.
I
II

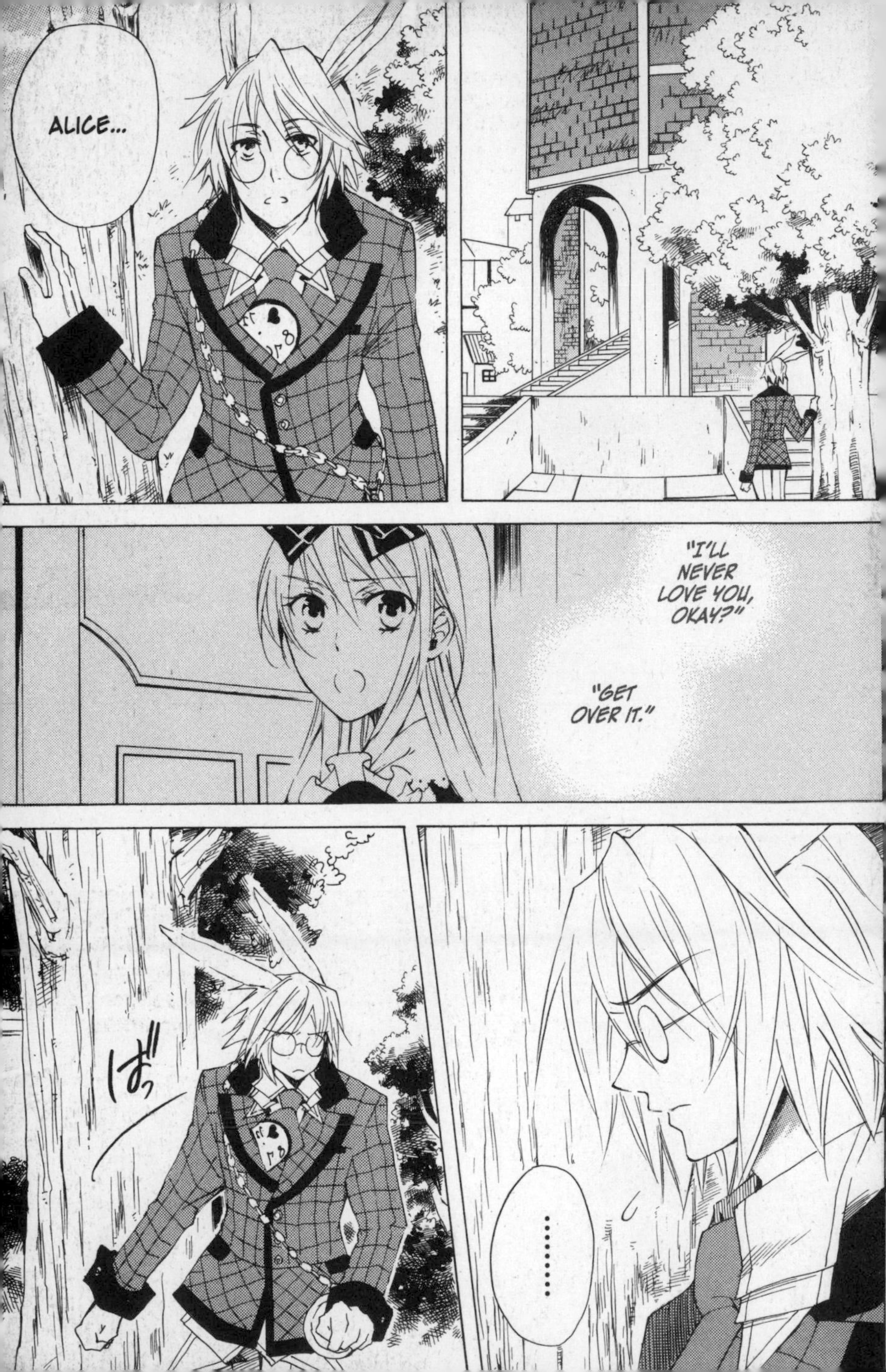
ALICE...
"I'LL NEVER LOVE YOU, OKAY?"
"GET OVER IT."
......
ばっ

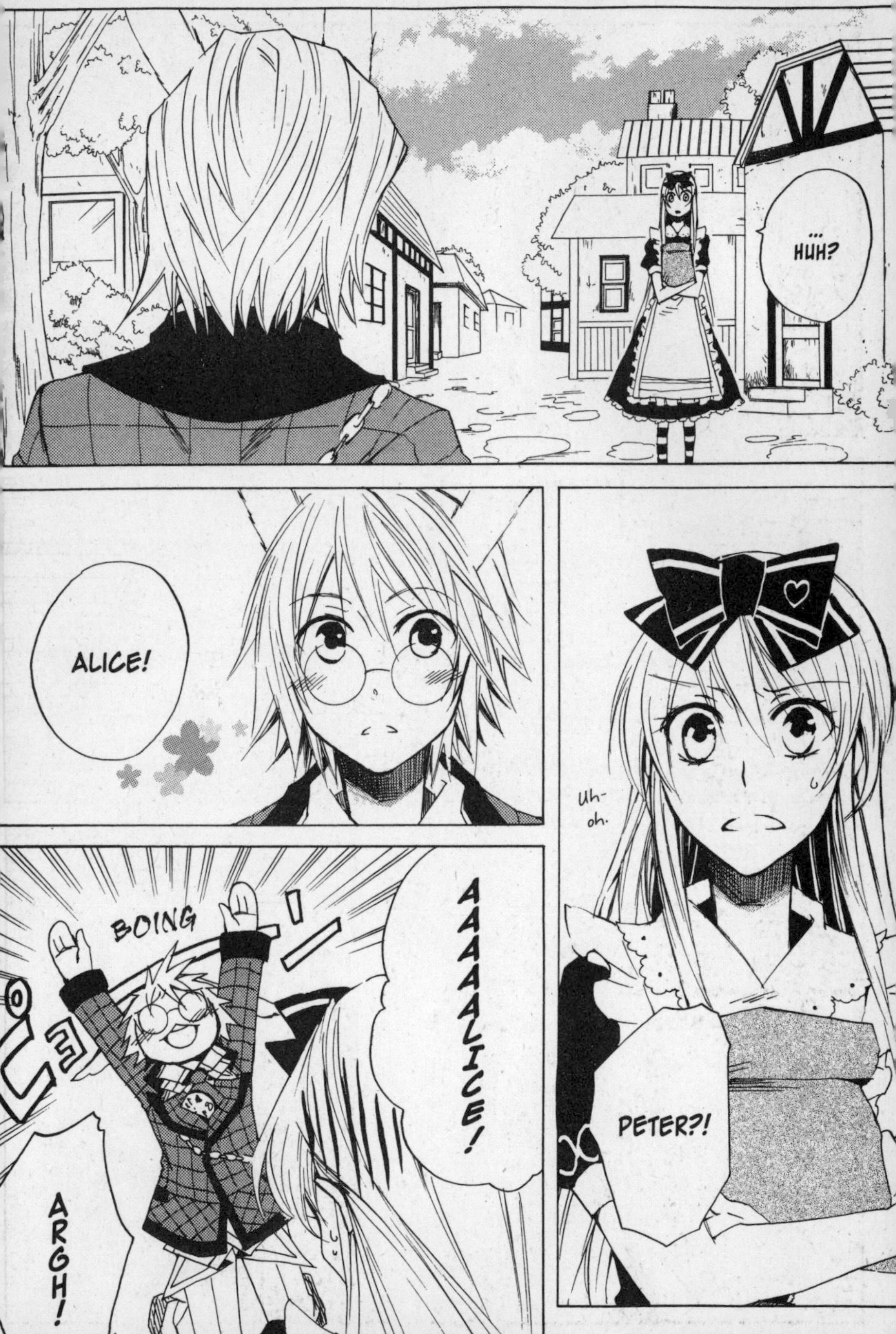

...HUH?
Uh-oh.
PETER?!
ALICE!
AAAAALICE!
BOING
ARGH!

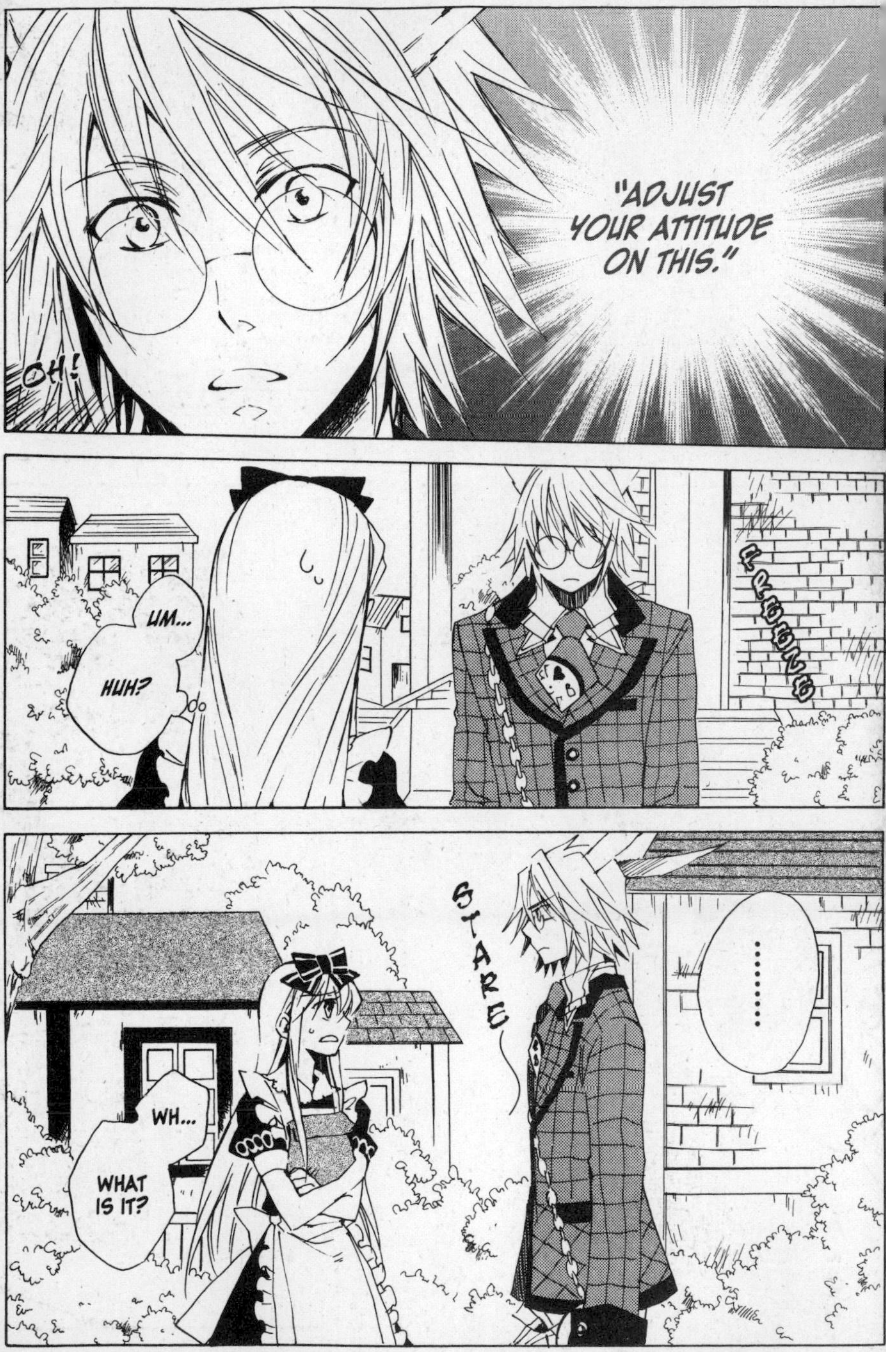
"ADJUST YOUR ATTITUDE ON THIS."
OH!
UM...
HUH?
......
STARE
WH...
WHAT IS IT?

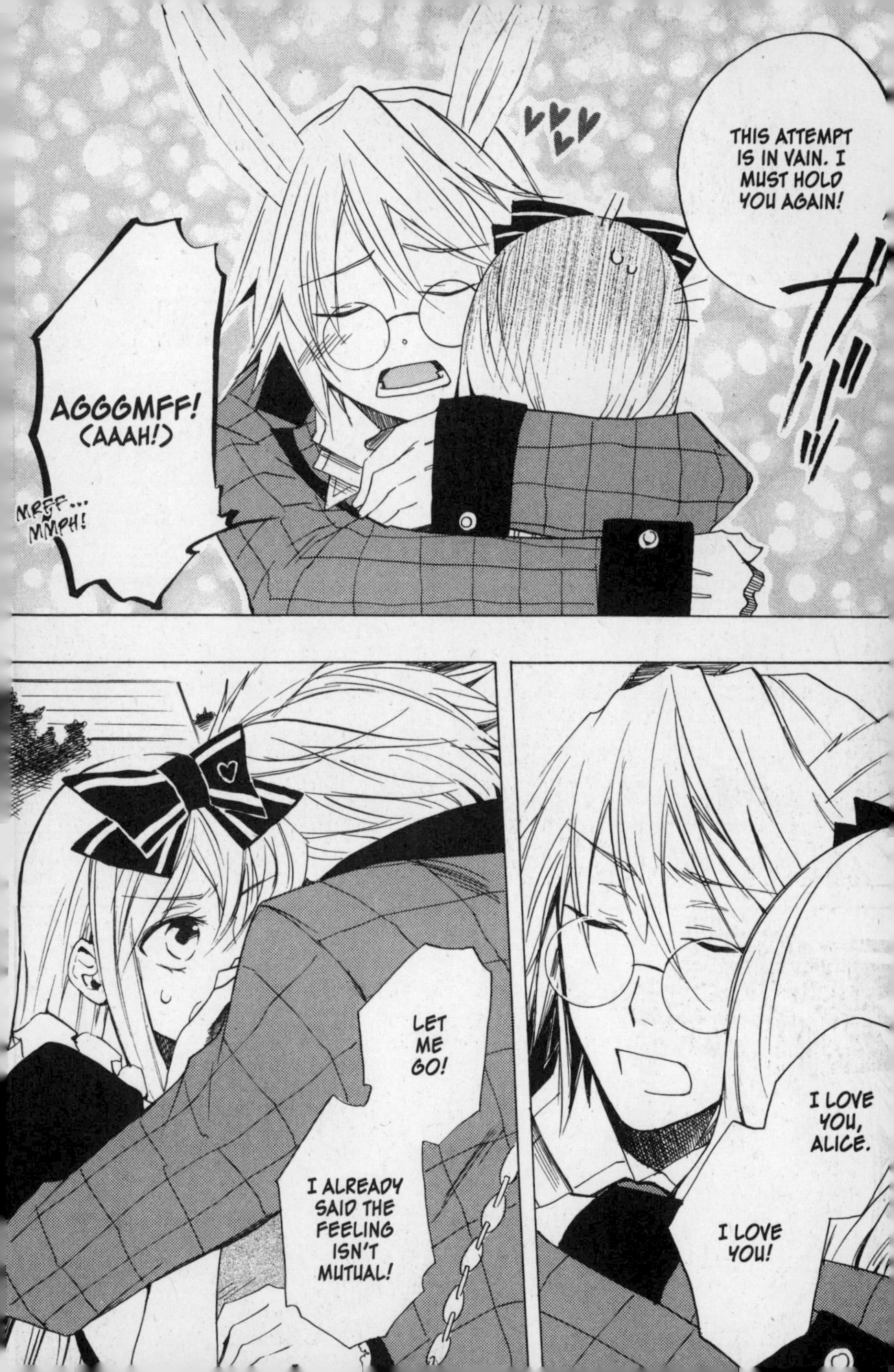
THIS ATTEMPT IS IN VAIN. I MUST HOLD YOU AGAIN!
AGGGMFF! (AAAH!)
MRFF... MMPH!
I LOVE YOU, ALICE.
I LOVE YOU!
LET ME GO!
I ALREADY SAID THE FEELING ISN'T MUTUAL!

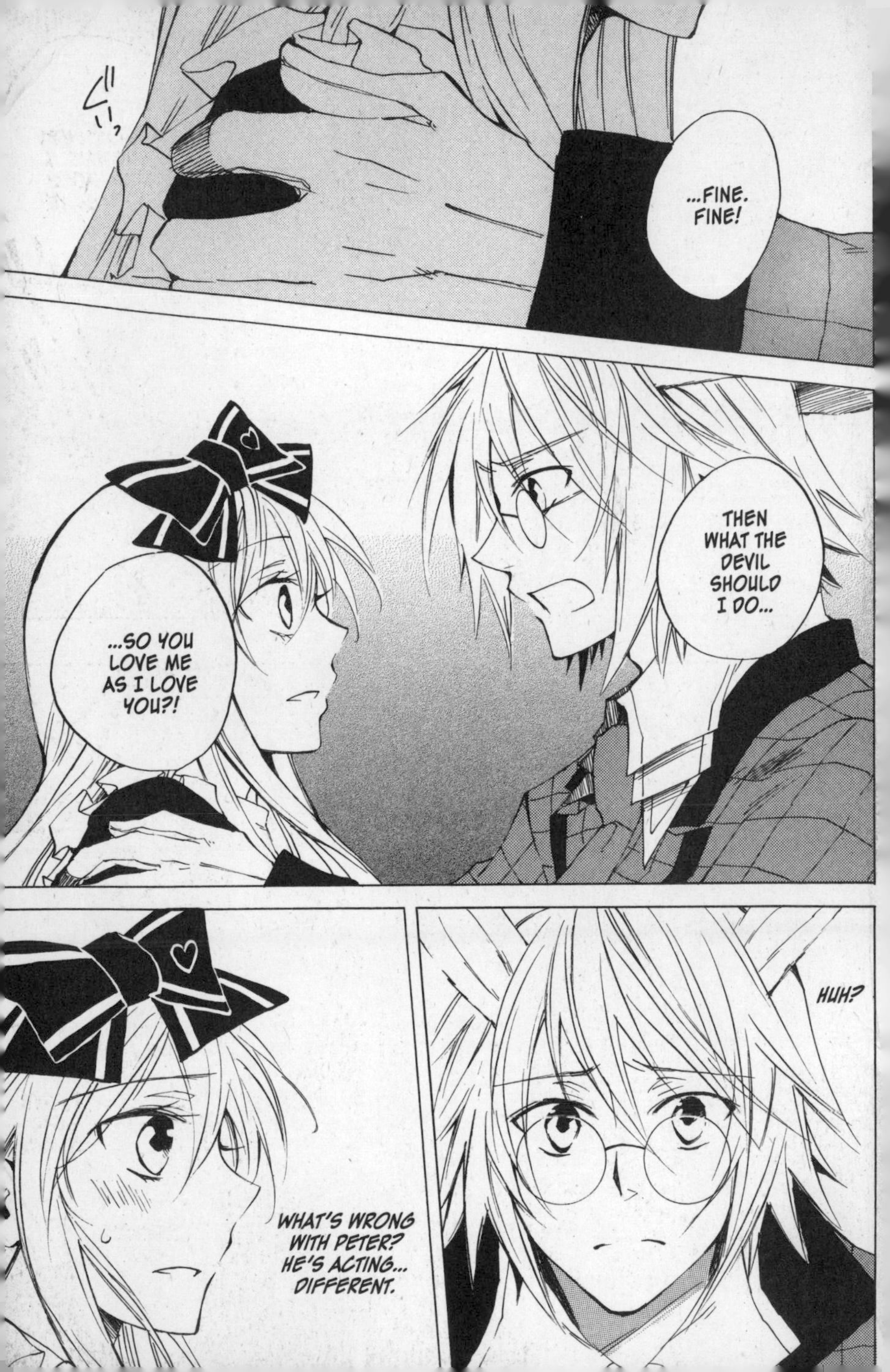
...FINE. FINE!
THEN WHAT THE DEVIL SHOULD I DO...
...SO YOU LOVE ME AS I LOVE YOU?!
HUH?
WHAT'S WRONG WITH PETER? HE'S ACTING... DIFFERENT.

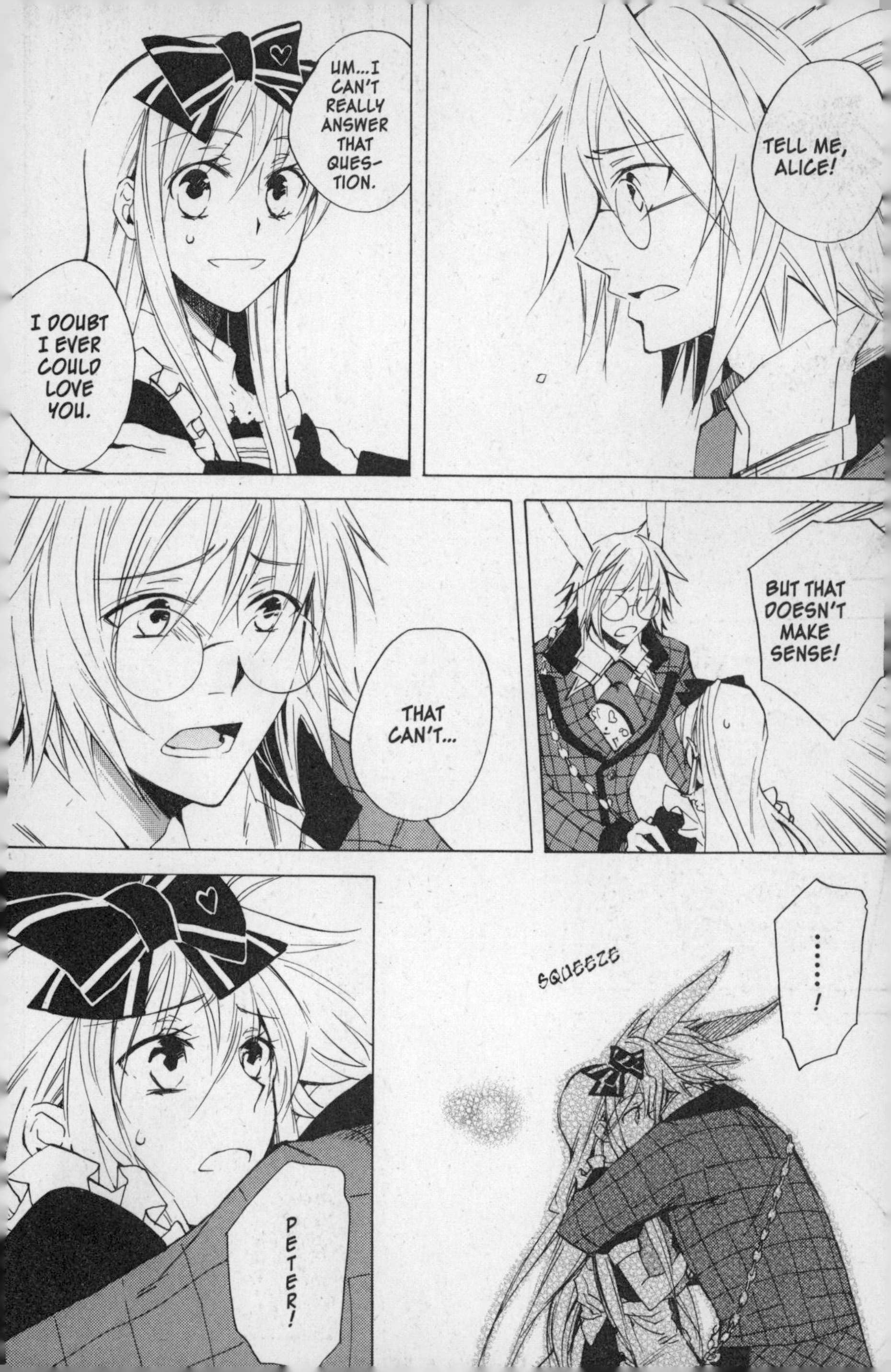
TELL ME, ALICE!
UM...I CAN'T REALLY ANSWER THAT QUES-TION.
I DOUBT I EVER COULD LOVE YOU.
BUT THAT DOESN'T MAKE SENSE!
THAT CAN'T...
......!
SQUEEZE
PETER!

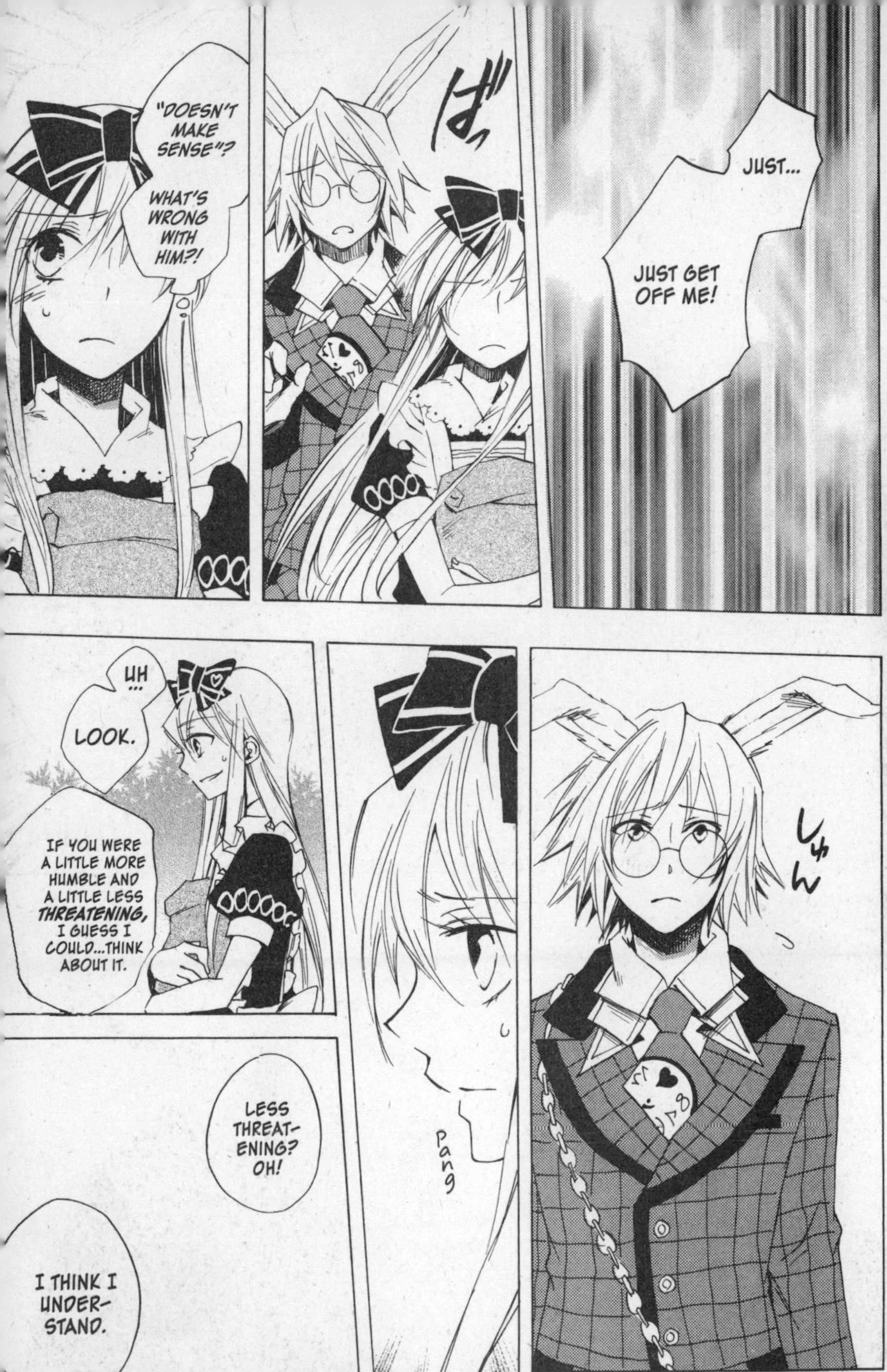
JUST...
JUST GET OFF ME!
ばっ
"DOESN'T MAKE SENSE"?
WHAT'S WRONG WITH HIM?!
しゅん
Pang
UH...
LOOK.
IF YOU WERE A LITTLE MORE HUMBLE AND A LITTLE LESS *THREATENING,* I GUESS I COULD...THINK ABOUT IT.
LESS THREAT-ENING? OH!
I THINK I UNDER-STAND.

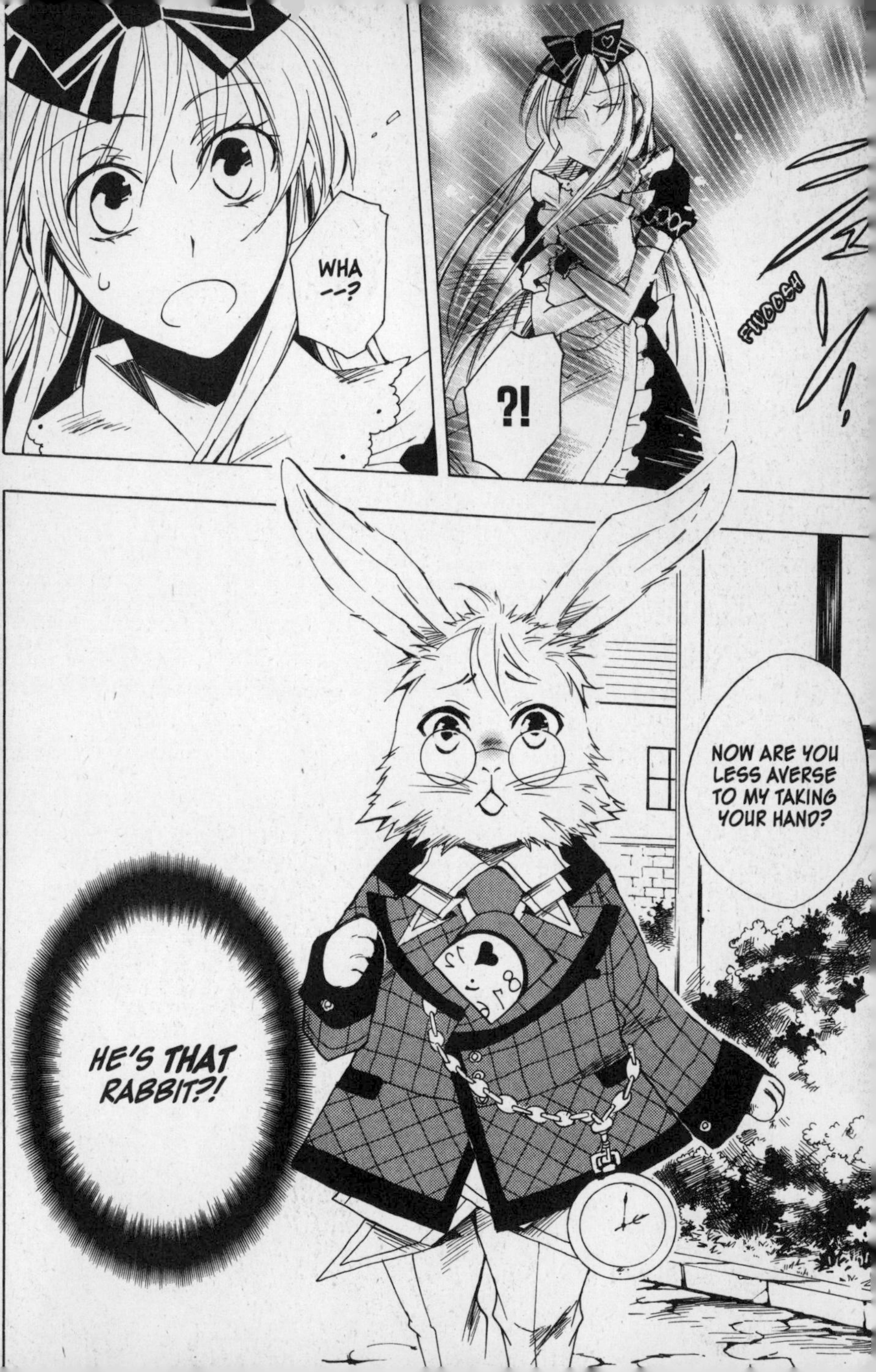
FWOOSH
?!
WHA --?
NOW ARE YOU LESS AVERSE TO MY TAKING YOUR HAND?
HE'S THAT RABBIT?!

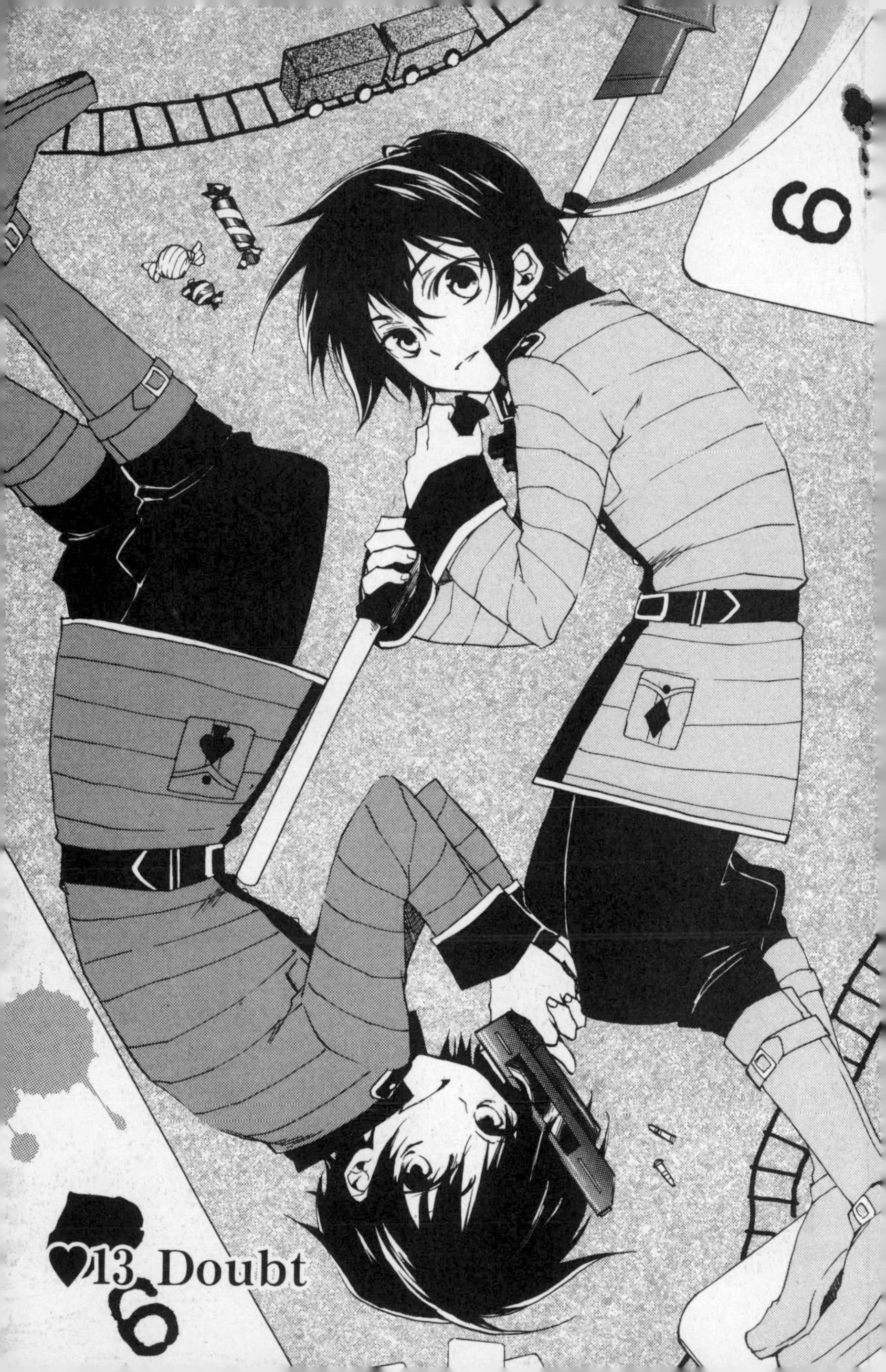
♥13 Doubt

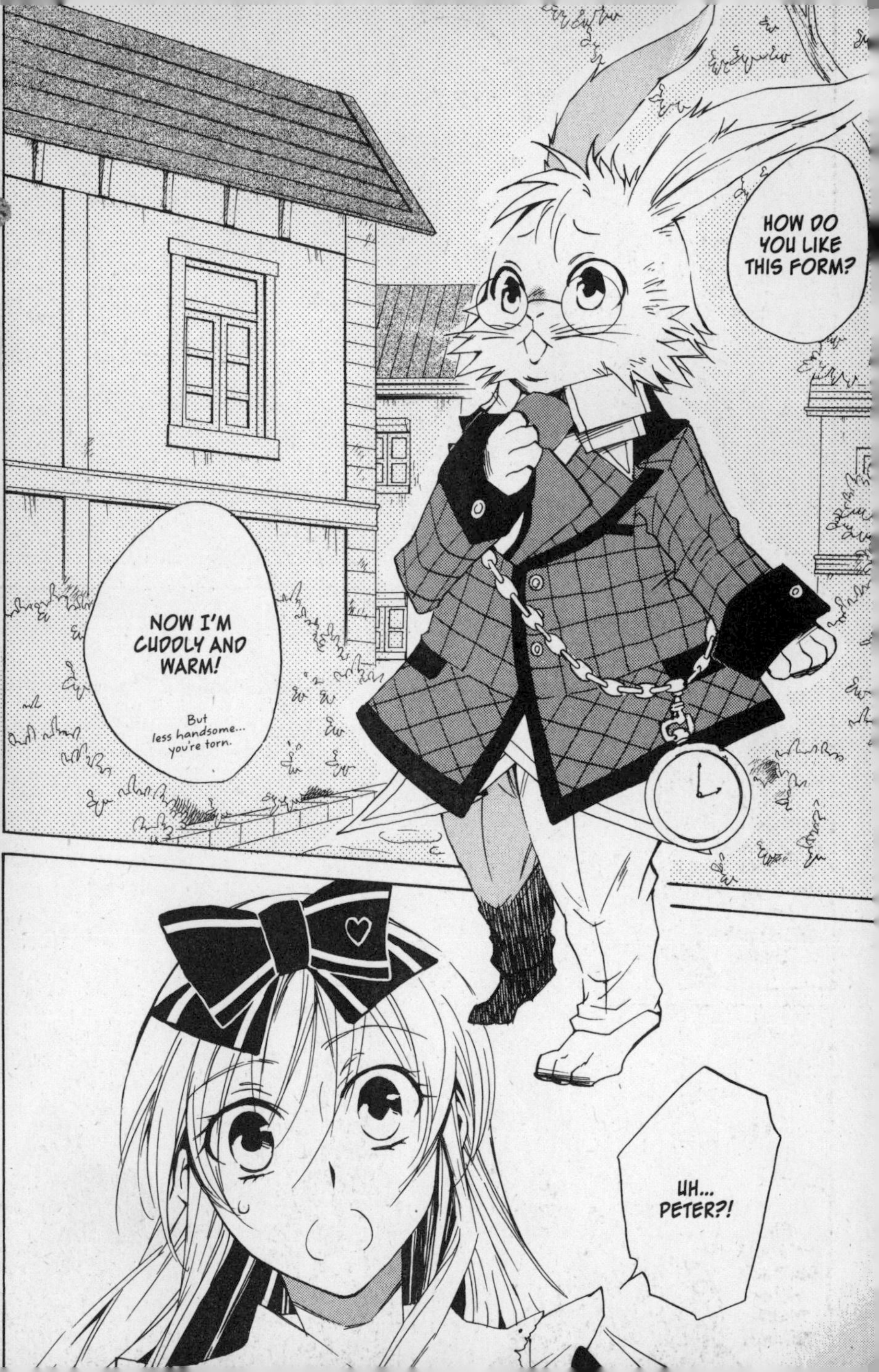
HOW DO YOU LIKE THIS FORM?
NOW I'M CUDDLY AND WARM!
But less handsome... you're torn.
UH... PETER?!

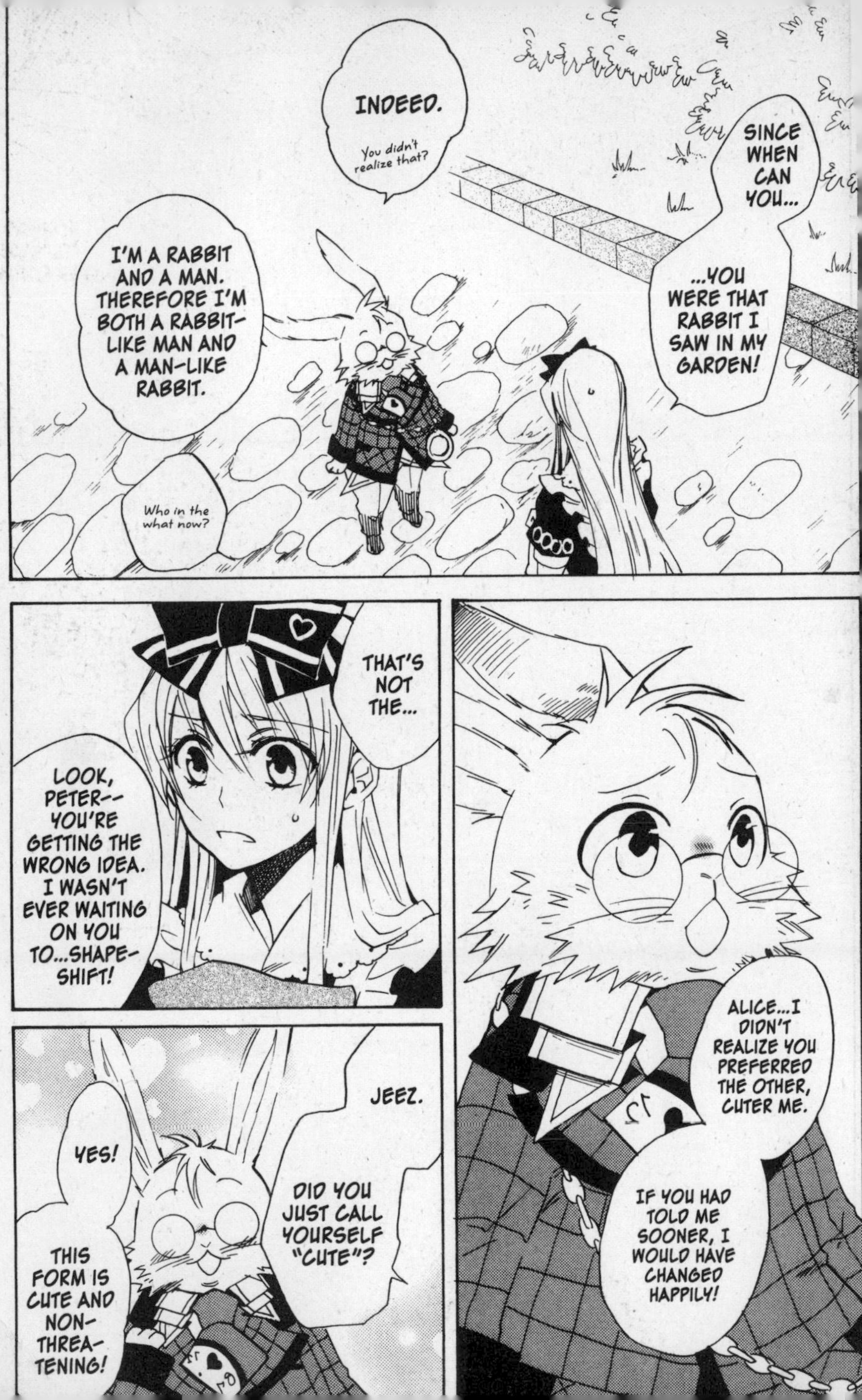
SINCE WHEN CAN YOU...
...YOU WERE THAT RABBIT I SAW IN MY GARDEN!
INDEED.
You didn't realize that?
I'M A RABBIT AND A MAN. THEREFORE I'M BOTH A RABBIT-LIKE MAN AND A MAN-LIKE RABBIT.
Who in the what now?
ALICE...I DIDN'T REALIZE YOU PREFERRED THE OTHER, CUTER ME.
IF YOU HAD TOLD ME SOONER, I WOULD HAVE CHANGED HAPPILY!
THAT'S NOT THE...
LOOK, PETER--YOU'RE GETTING THE WRONG IDEA. I WASN'T EVER WAITING ON YOU TO...SHAPE-SHIFT!
JEEZ.
DID YOU JUST CALL YOURSELF "CUTE"?
YES!
THIS FORM IS CUTE AND NON-THREA-TENING!

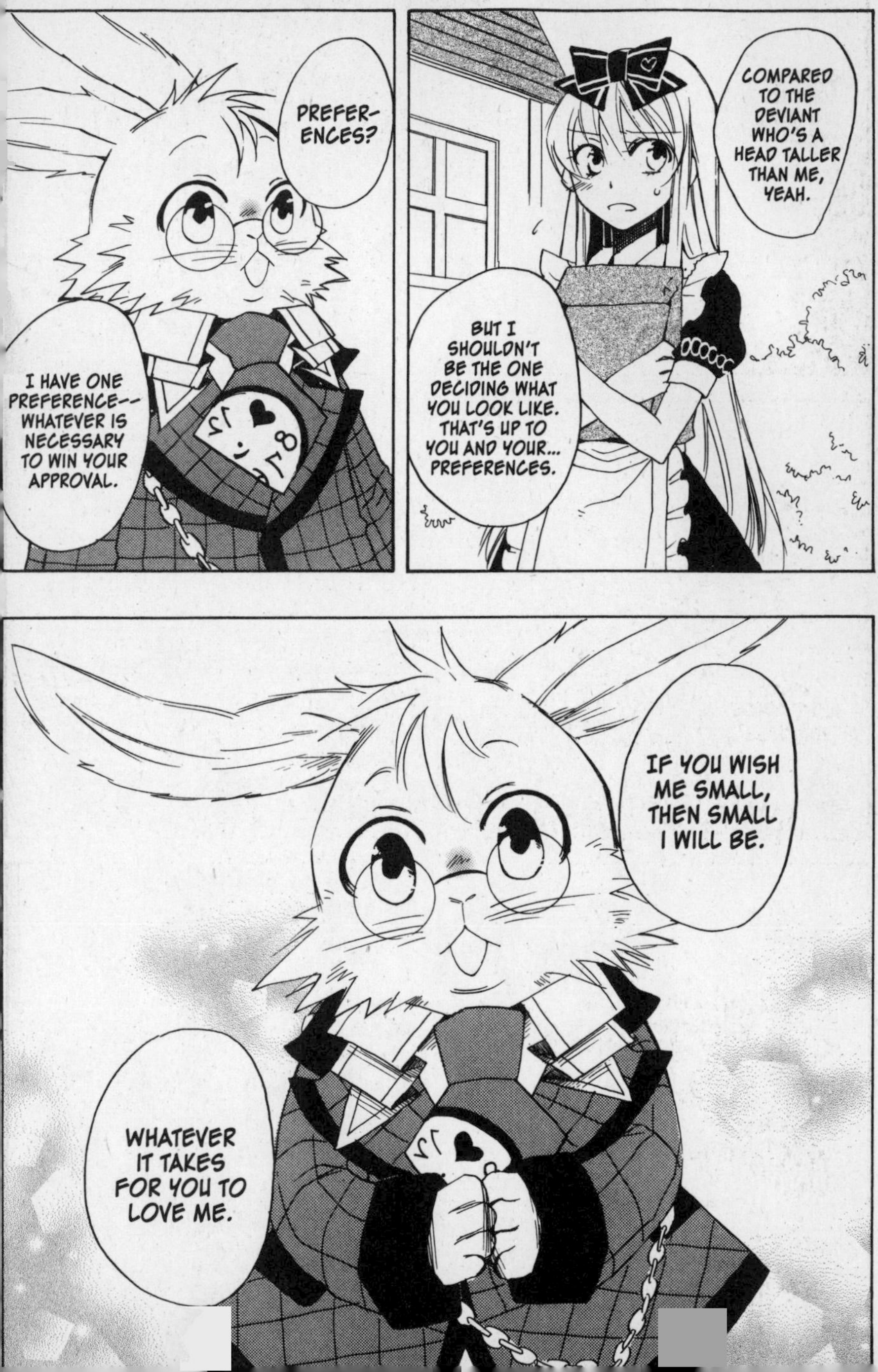
COMPARED TO THE DEVIANT WHO'S A HEAD TALLER THAN ME, YEAH.
BUT I SHOULDN'T BE THE ONE DECIDING WHAT YOU LOOK LIKE. THAT'S UP TO YOU AND YOUR... PREFERENCES.
PREFER-ENCES?
I HAVE ONE PREFERENCE-- WHATEVER IS NECESSARY TO WIN YOUR APPROVAL.
IF YOU WISH ME SMALL, THEN SMALL I WILL BE.
WHATEVER IT TAKES FOR YOU TO LOVE ME.

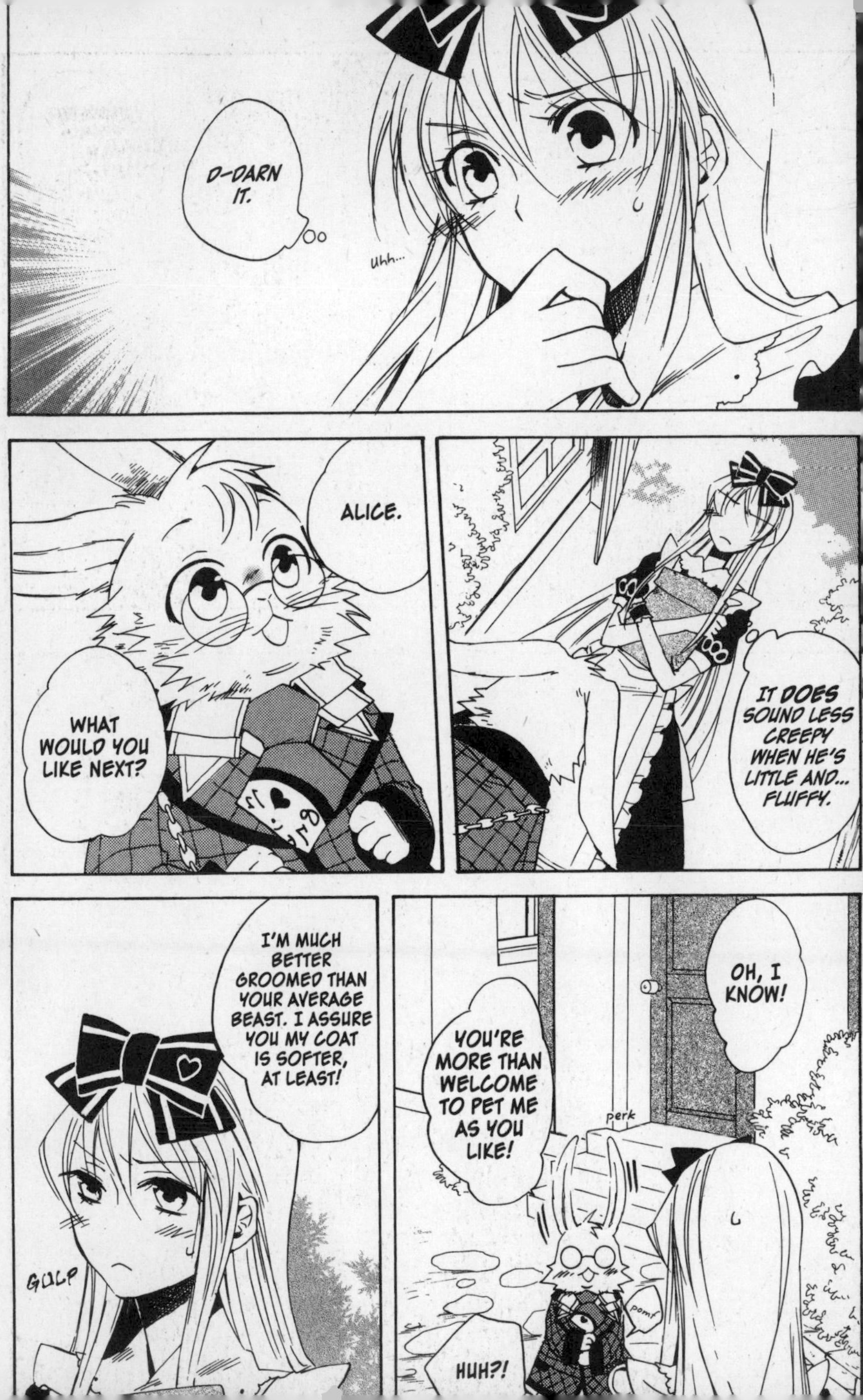
D-DARN IT.
Uhh...
IT DOES SOUND LESS CREEPY WHEN HE'S LITTLE AND... FLUFFY.
ALICE.
WHAT WOULD YOU LIKE NEXT?
OH, I KNOW!
YOU'RE MORE THAN WELCOME TO PET ME AS YOU LIKE!
perk
pomf
HUH?!
I'M MUCH BETTER GROOMED THAN YOUR AVERAGE BEAST. I ASSURE YOU MY COAT IS SOFTER, AT LEAST!
GULP

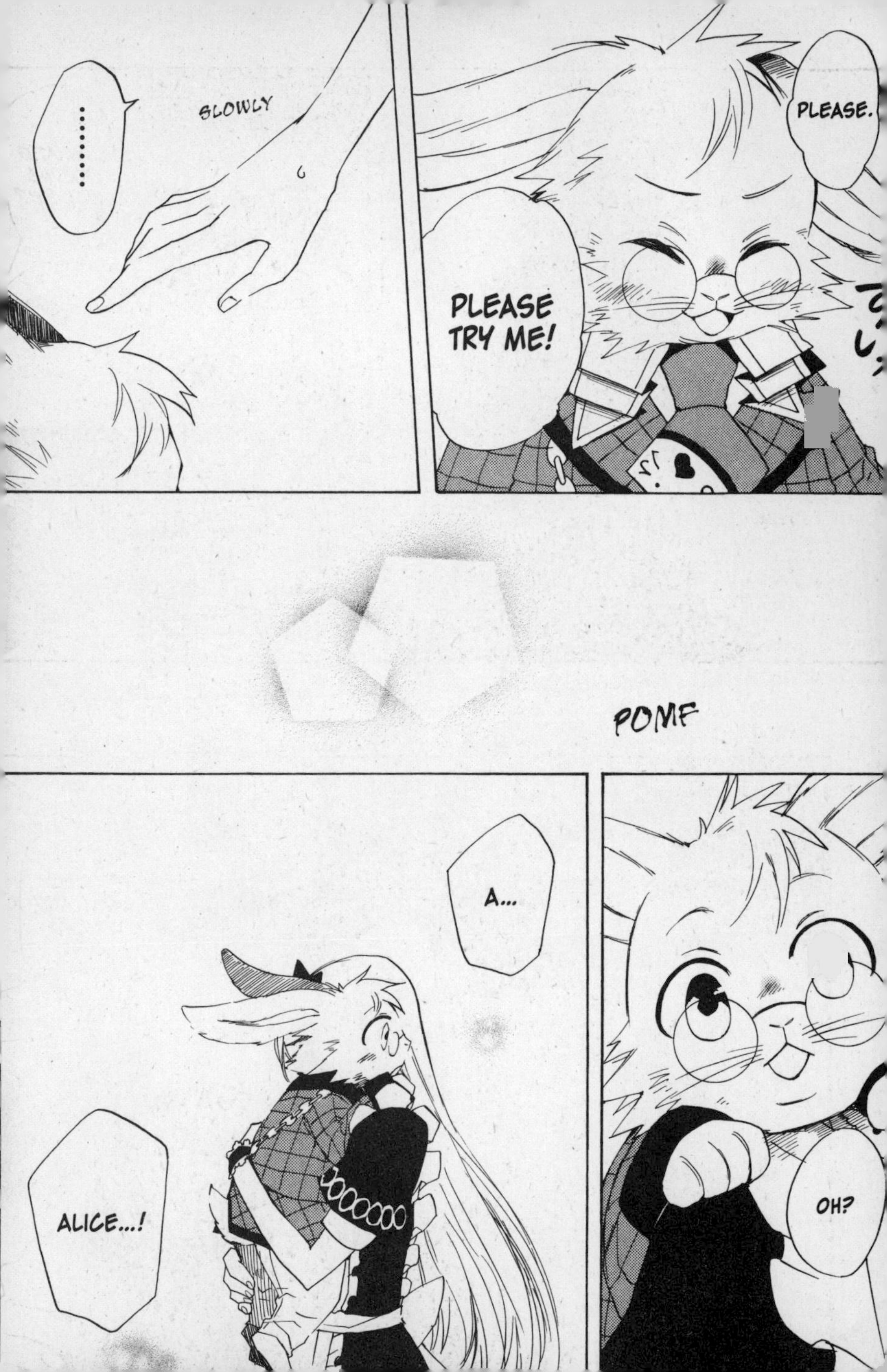
PLEASE.
PLEASE TRY ME!
SLOWLY
......
POMF
OH?
A...
ALICE...!

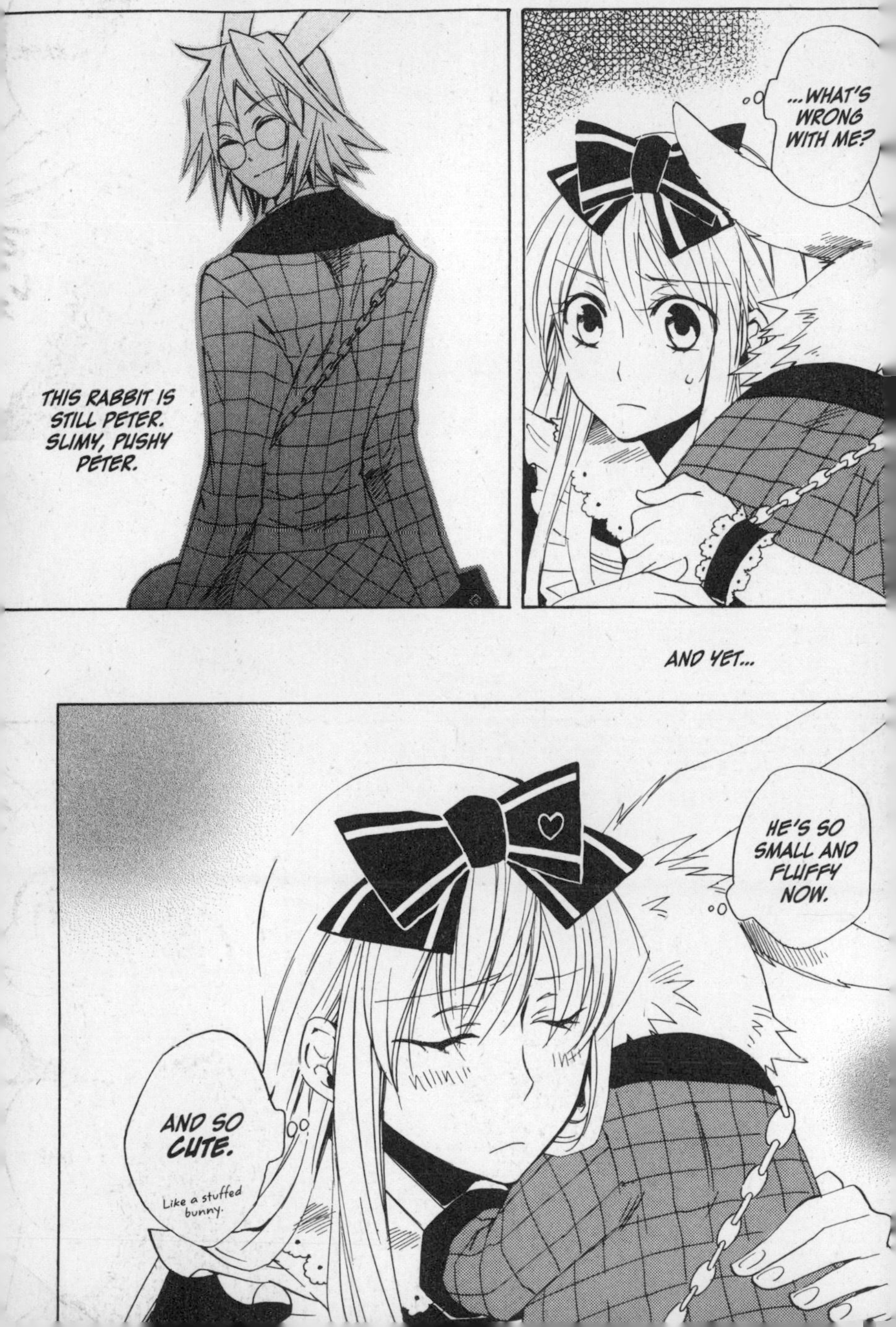
...WHAT'S WRONG WITH ME?
THIS RABBIT IS STILL PETER. SLIMY, PUSHY PETER.
AND YET...
HE'S SO SMALL AND FLUFFY NOW.
AND SO CUTE.
Like a stuffed bunny.

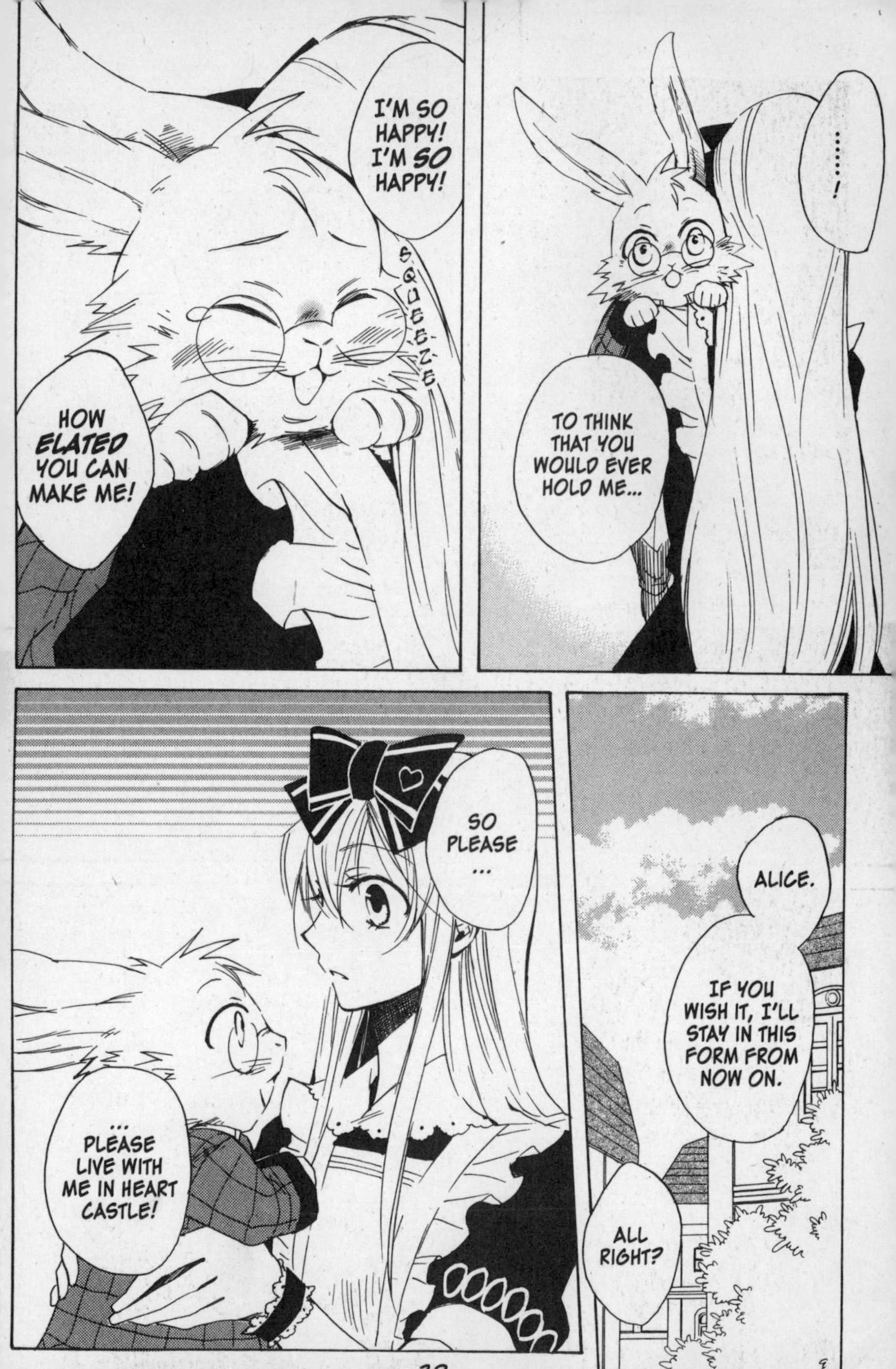
......!
TO THINK THAT YOU WOULD EVER HOLD ME...
I'M SO HAPPY! I'M SO HAPPY!
SQUEEZE
HOW ELATED YOU CAN MAKE ME!
ALICE.
IF YOU WISH IT, I'LL STAY IN THIS FORM FROM NOW ON.
ALL RIGHT?
SO PLEASE ...
... PLEASE LIVE WITH ME IN HEART CASTLE!

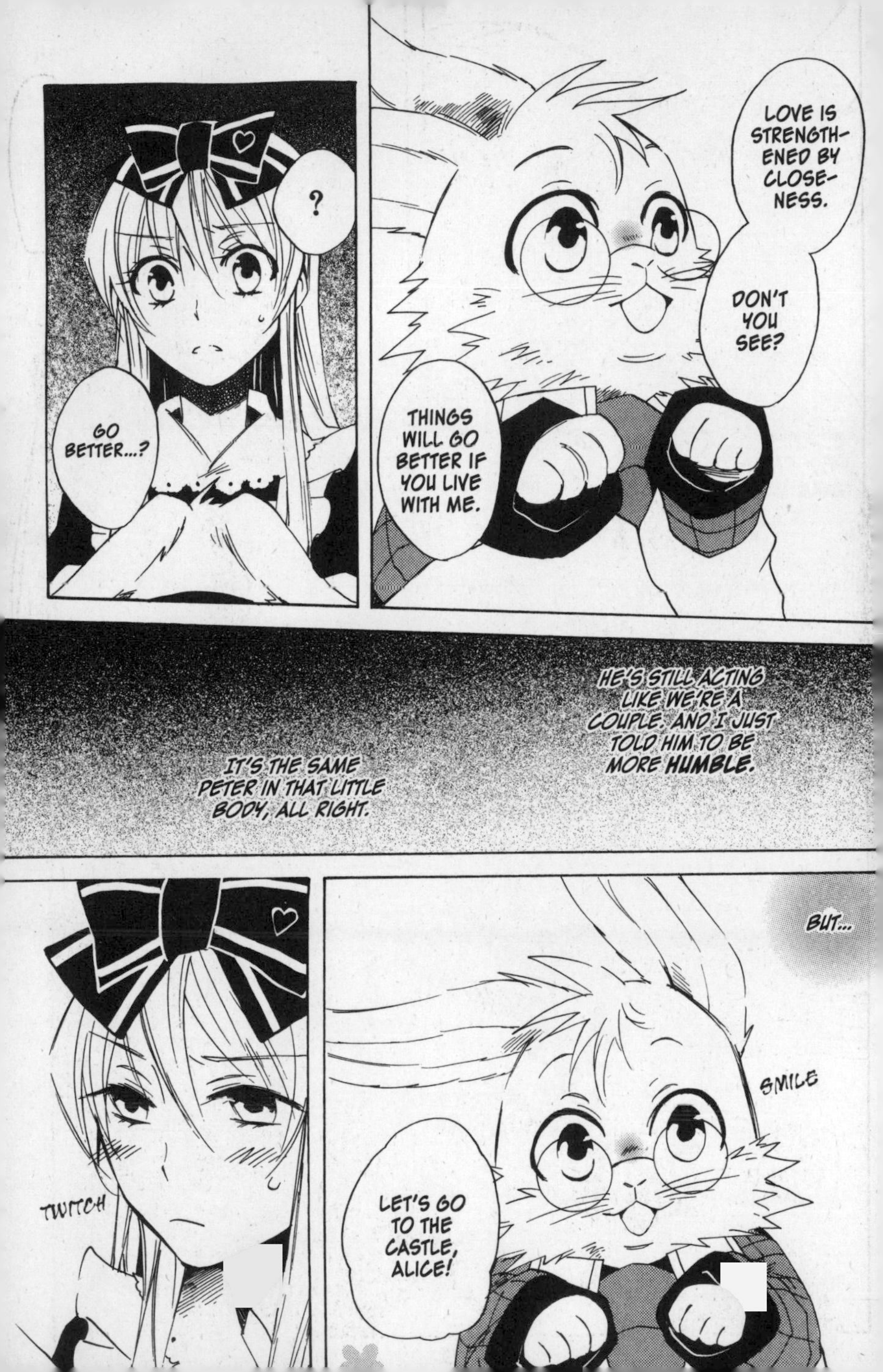
LOVE IS STRENGTH-ENED BY CLOSE-NESS.
DON'T YOU SEE?
THINGS WILL GO BETTER IF YOU LIVE WITH ME.
?
GO BETTER...?
HE'S STILL ACTING LIKE WE'RE A COUPLE. AND I JUST TOLD HIM TO BE MORE HUMBLE.
IT'S THE SAME PETER IN THAT LITTLE BODY, ALL RIGHT.
BUT...
SMILE
LET'S GO TO THE CASTLE, ALICE!
TWITCH

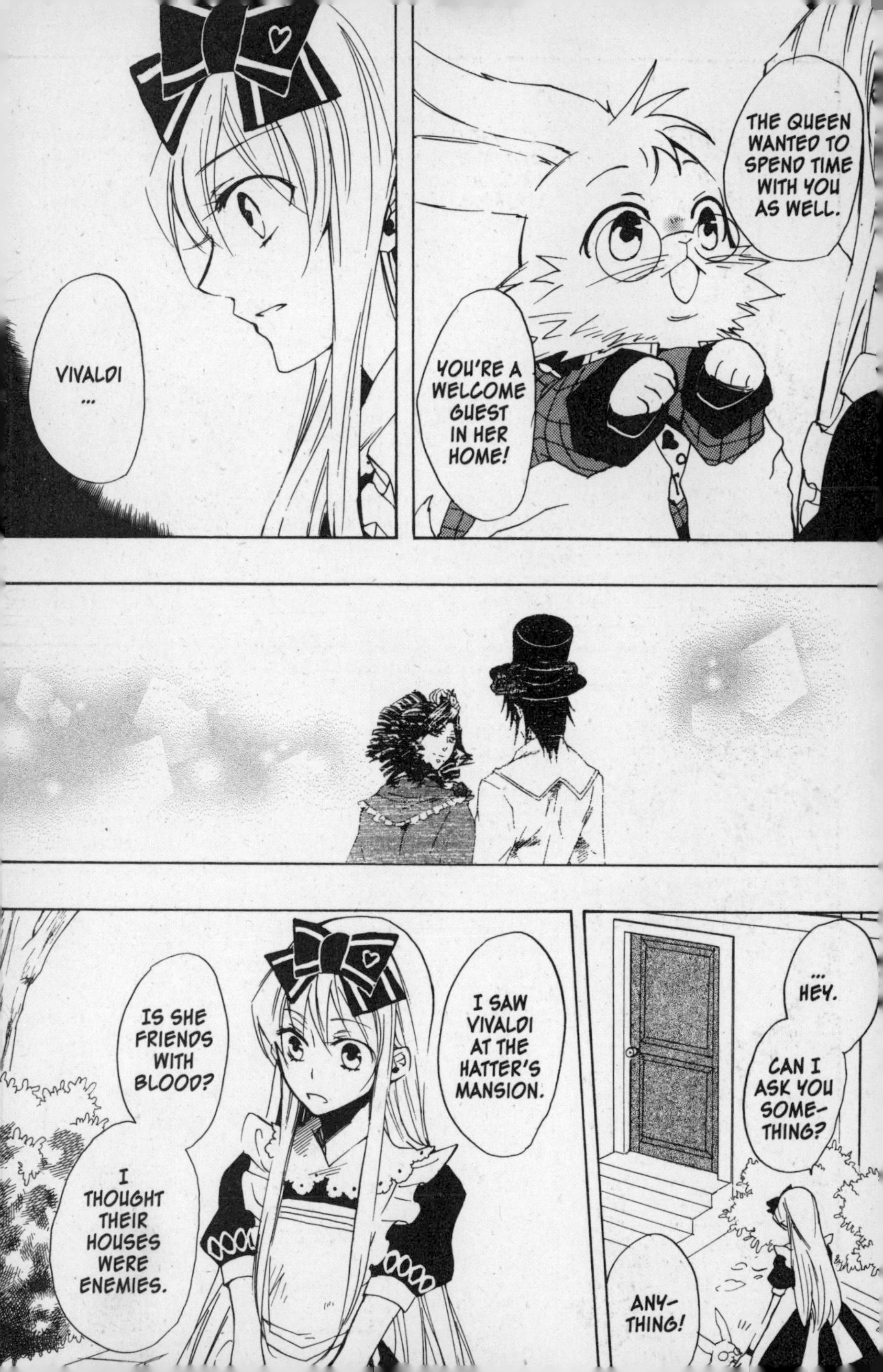
THE QUEEN WANTED TO SPEND TIME WITH YOU AS WELL.
YOU'RE A WELCOME GUEST IN HER HOME!
VIVALDI ...
... HEY.
CAN I ASK YOU SOME-THING?
ANY-THING!
I SAW VIVALDI AT THE HATTER'S MANSION.
IS SHE FRIENDS WITH BLOOD?
I THOUGHT THEIR HOUSES WERE ENEMIES.

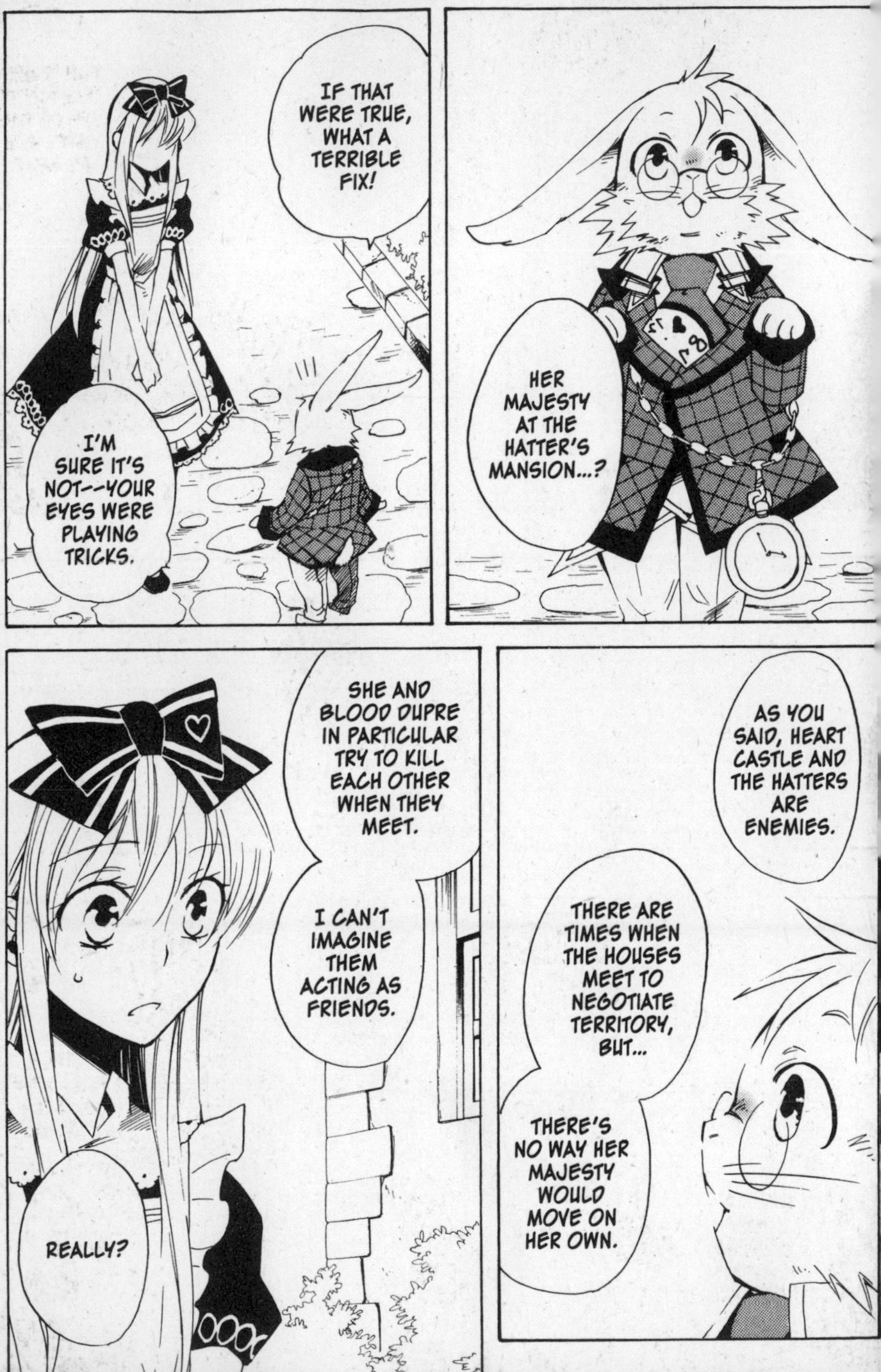
HER MAJESTY AT THE HATTER'S MANSION...?
IF THAT WERE TRUE, WHAT A TERRIBLE FIX!
I'M SURE IT'S NOT--YOUR EYES WERE PLAYING TRICKS.
AS YOU SAID, HEART CASTLE AND THE HATTERS ARE ENEMIES.
THERE ARE TIMES WHEN THE HOUSES MEET TO NEGOTIATE TERRITORY, BUT...
THERE'S NO WAY HER MAJESTY WOULD MOVE ON HER OWN.
SHE AND BLOOD DUPRE IN PARTICULAR TRY TO KILL EACH OTHER WHEN THEY MEET.
I CAN'T IMAGINE THEM ACTING AS FRIENDS.
REALLY?

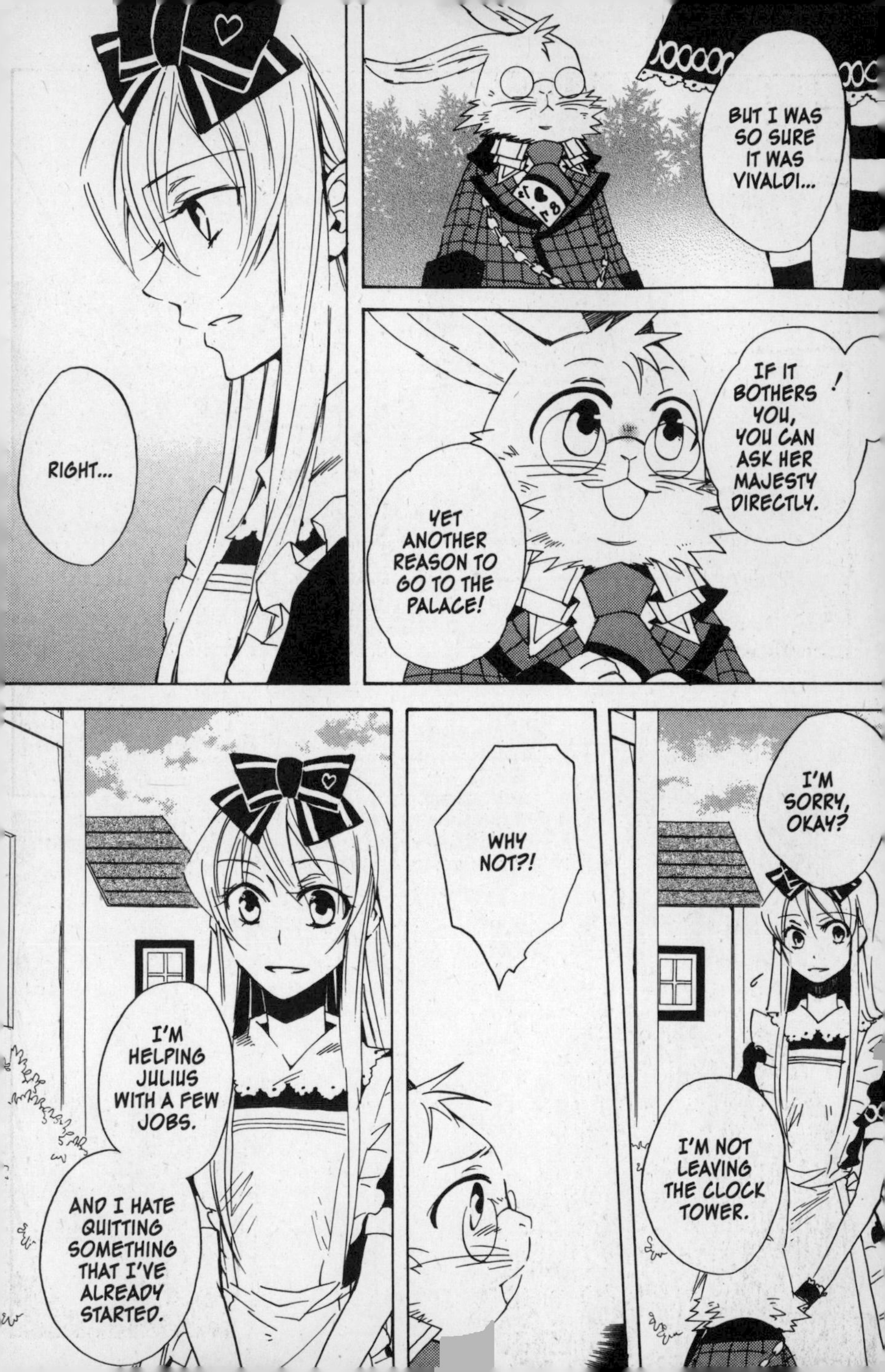
BUT I WAS SO SURE IT WAS VIVALDI...
IF IT BOTHERS YOU, YOU CAN ASK HER MAJESTY DIRECTLY.
!
YET ANOTHER REASON TO GO TO THE PALACE!
RIGHT...
I'M SORRY, OKAY?
I'M NOT LEAVING THE CLOCK TOWER.
WHY NOT?!
I'M HELPING JULIUS WITH A FEW JOBS.
AND I HATE QUITTING SOMETHING THAT I'VE ALREADY STARTED.

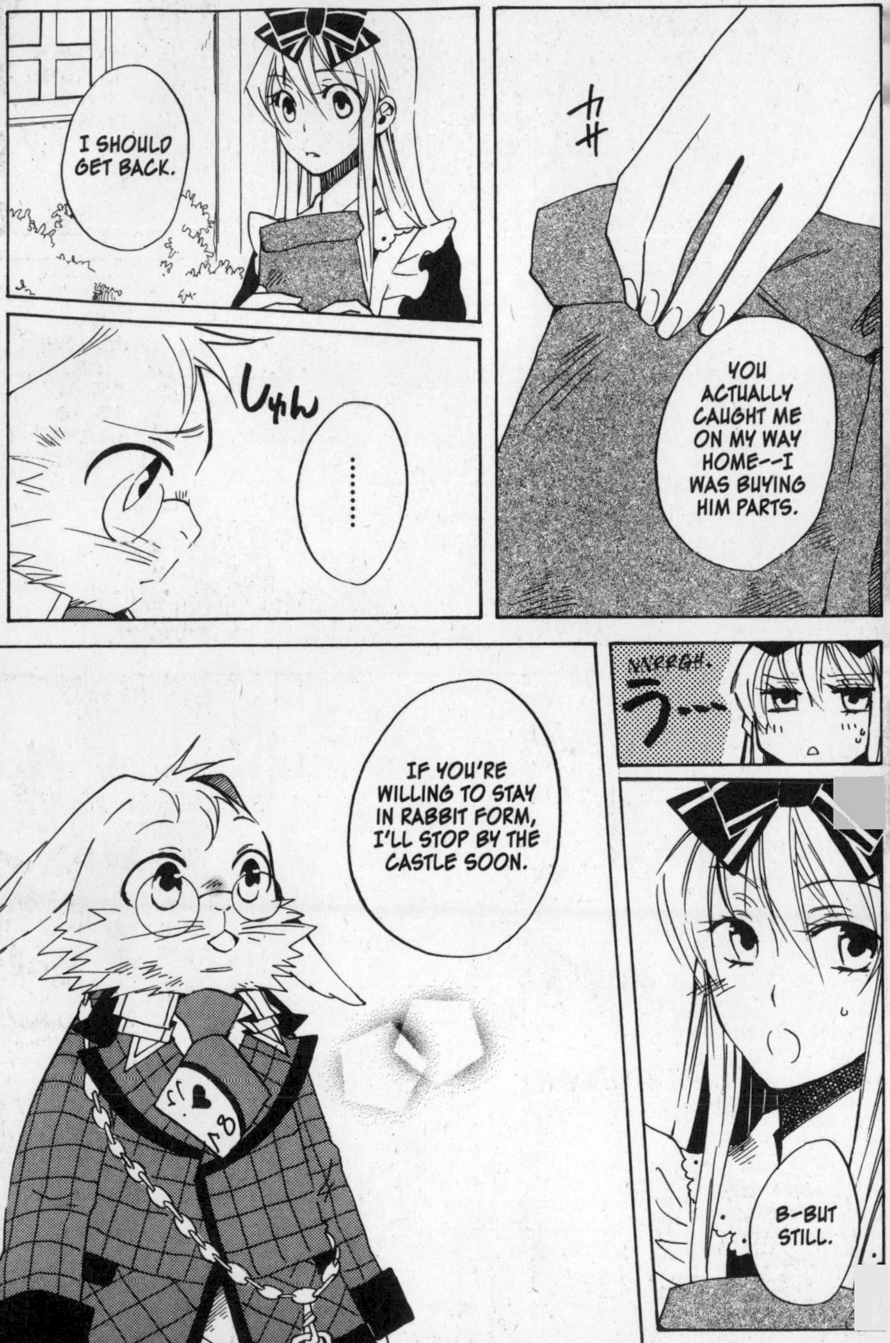
カサ
YOU ACTUALLY CAUGHT ME ON MY WAY HOME--I WAS BUYING HIM PARTS.
I SHOULD GET BACK.
しゅん
......
NARRGH.
う---
B-BUT STILL.
IF YOU'RE WILLING TO STAY IN RABBIT FORM, I'LL STOP BY THE CASTLE SOON.

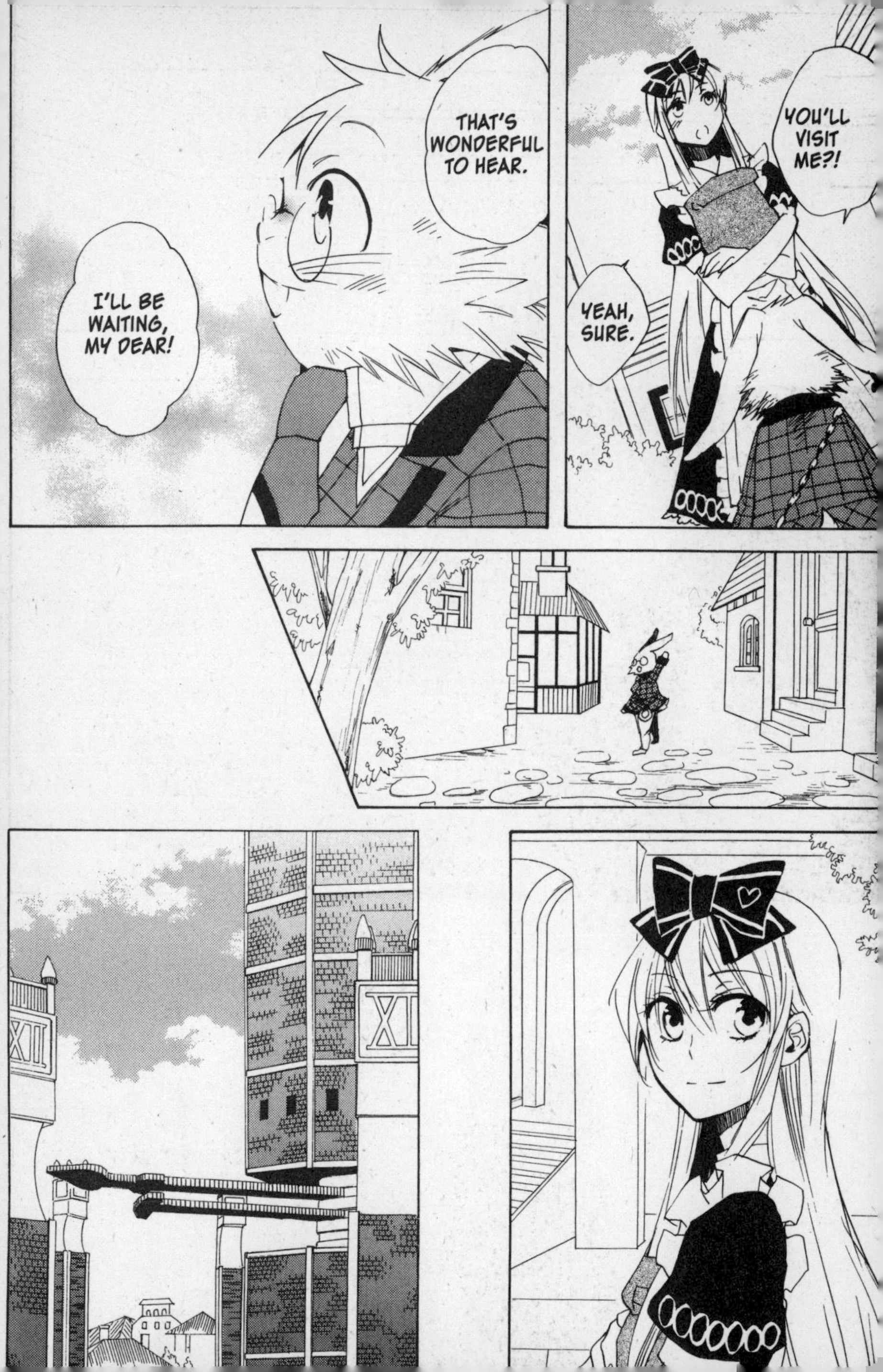
YOU'LL VISIT ME?!
YEAH, SURE.
THAT'S WONDERFUL TO HEAR.
I'LL BE WAITING, MY DEAR!

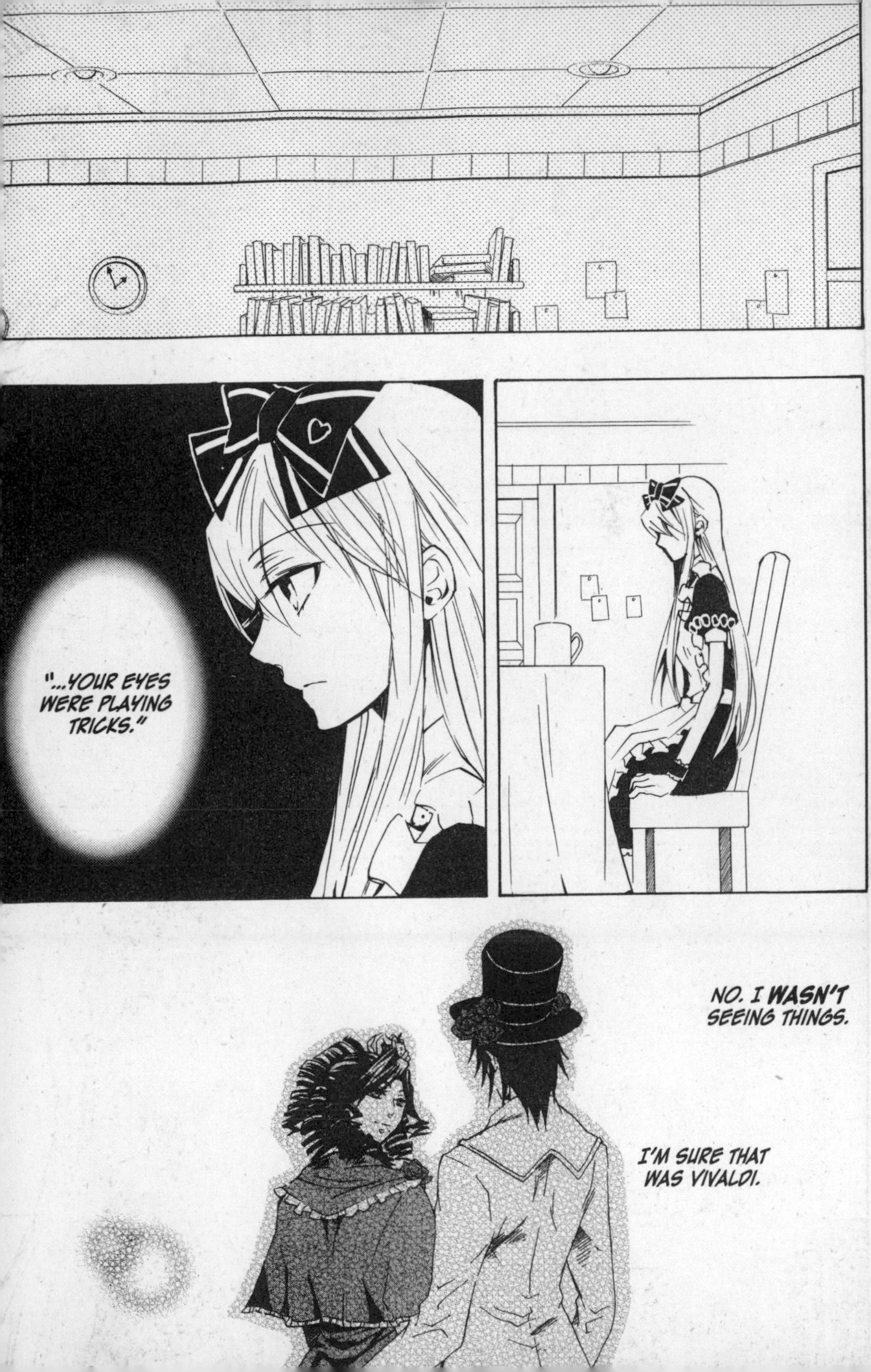
"...YOUR EYES WERE PLAYING TRICKS."
NO. I WASN'T SEEING THINGS.
I'M SURE THAT WAS VIVALDI.

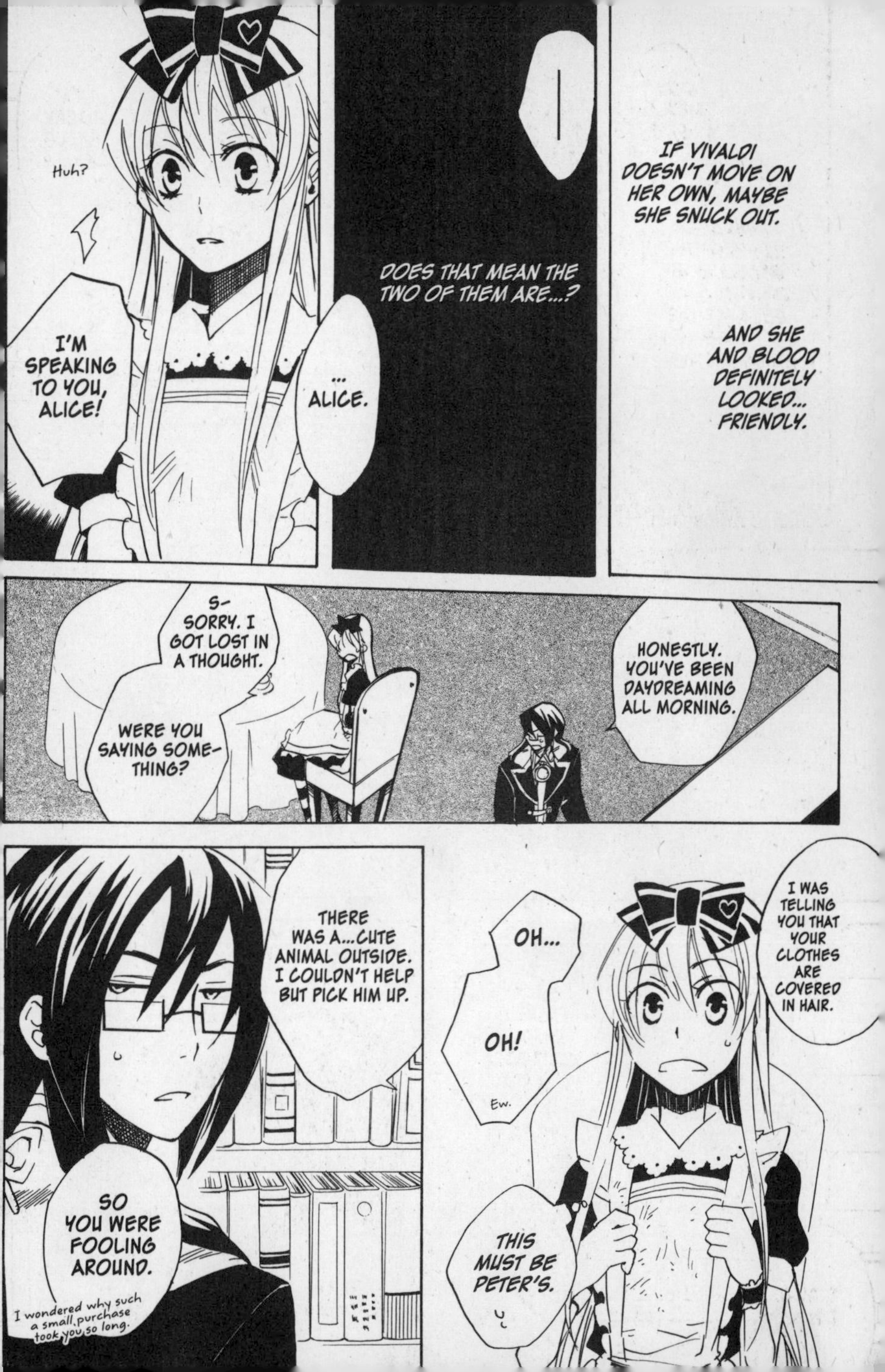
IF VIVALDI DOESN'T MOVE ON HER OWN, MAYBE SHE SNUCK OUT.
AND SHE AND BLOOD DEFINITELY LOOKED... FRIENDLY.
DOES THAT MEAN THE TWO OF THEM ARE...?
... ALICE.
I'M SPEAKING TO YOU, ALICE!
Huh?
HONESTLY. YOU'VE BEEN DAYDREAMING ALL MORNING.
S-SORRY. I GOT LOST IN A THOUGHT.
WERE YOU SAYING SOME-THING?
I WAS TELLING YOU THAT YOUR CLOTHES ARE COVERED IN HAIR.
OH...
OH!
Ew.
THIS MUST BE PETER'S.
THERE WAS A...CUTE ANIMAL OUTSIDE. I COULDN'T HELP BUT PICK HIM UP.
SO YOU WERE FOOLING AROUND.
I wondered why such a small purchase took you so long.

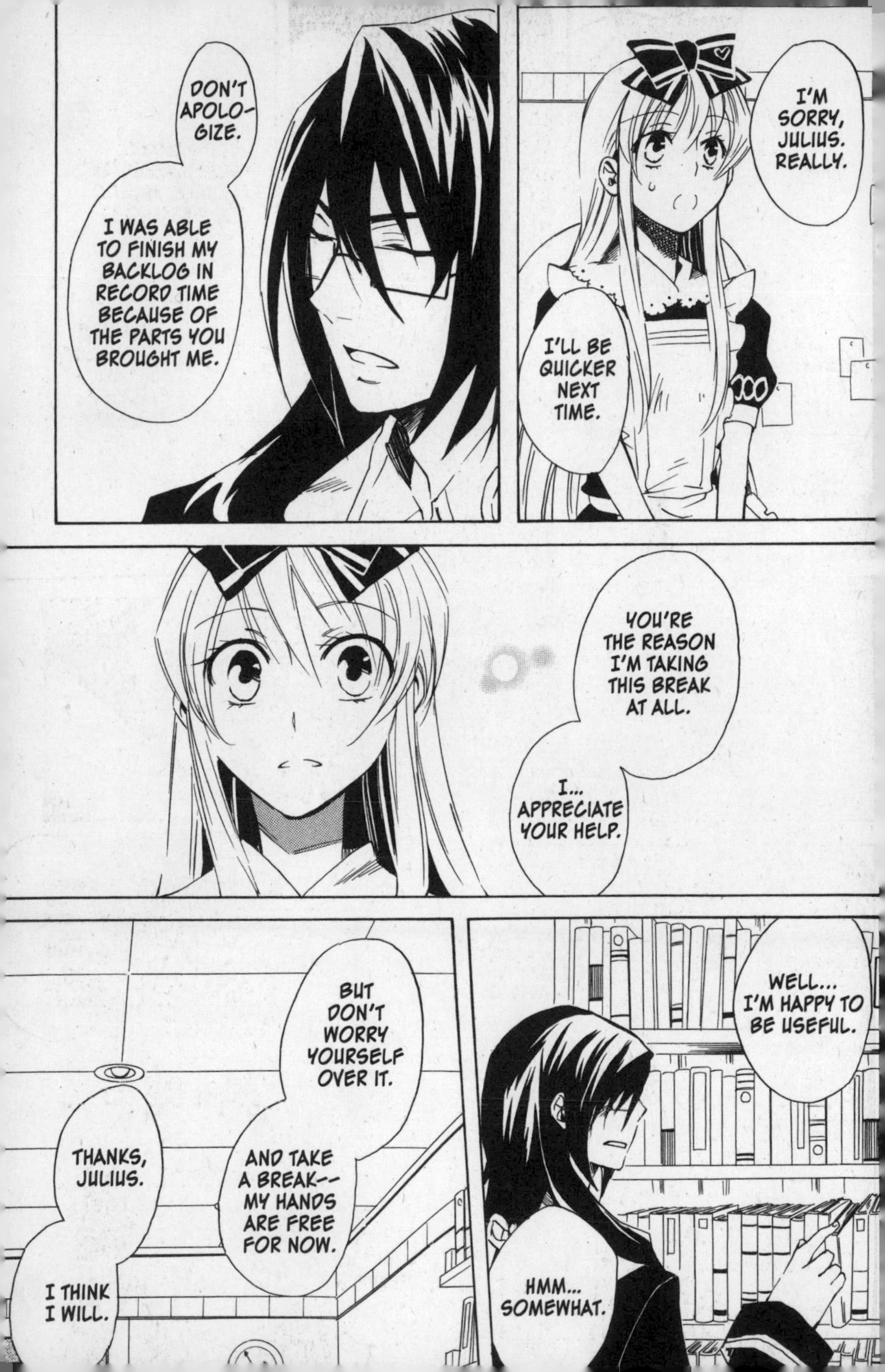
I'M SORRY, JULIUS. REALLY.
I'LL BE QUICKER NEXT TIME.
DON'T APOLOGIZE.
I WAS ABLE TO FINISH MY BACKLOG IN RECORD TIME BECAUSE OF THE PARTS YOU BROUGHT ME.
YOU'RE THE REASON I'M TAKING THIS BREAK AT ALL.
I... APPRECIATE YOUR HELP.
WELL... I'M HAPPY TO BE USEFUL.
HMM... SOMEWHAT.
BUT DON'T WORRY YOURSELF OVER IT.
AND TAKE A BREAK--MY HANDS ARE FREE FOR NOW.
THANKS, JULIUS.
I THINK I WILL.

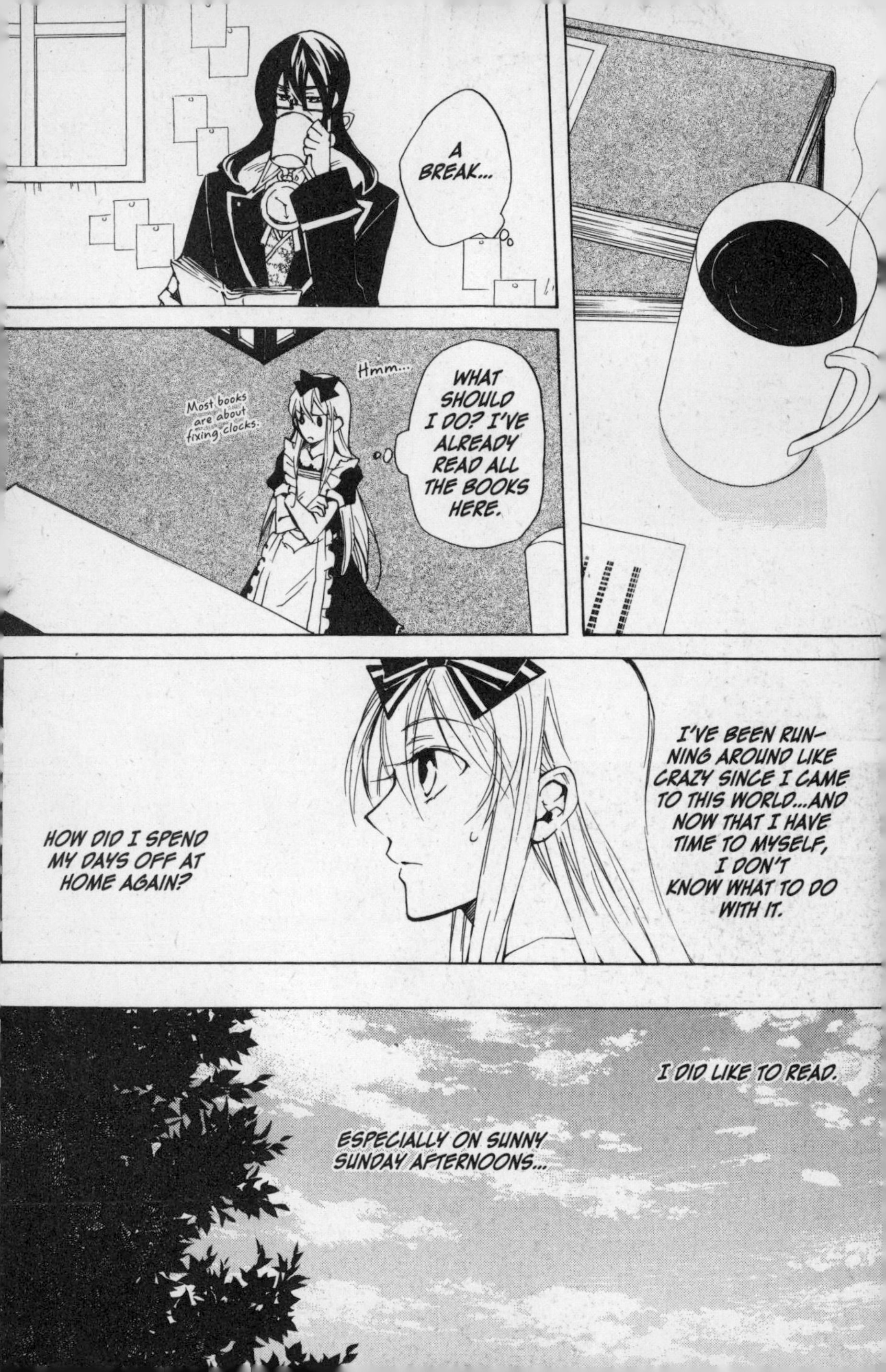
A BREAK...
WHAT SHOULD I DO? I'VE ALREADY READ ALL THE BOOKS HERE.
Hmm...
Most books are about fixing clocks.
I'VE BEEN RUN-NING AROUND LIKE CRAZY SINCE I CAME TO THIS WORLD...AND NOW THAT I HAVE TIME TO MYSELF, I DON'T KNOW WHAT TO DO WITH IT.
HOW DID I SPEND MY DAYS OFF AT HOME AGAIN?
I DID LIKE TO READ.
ESPECIALLY ON SUNNY SUNDAY AFTERNOONS...

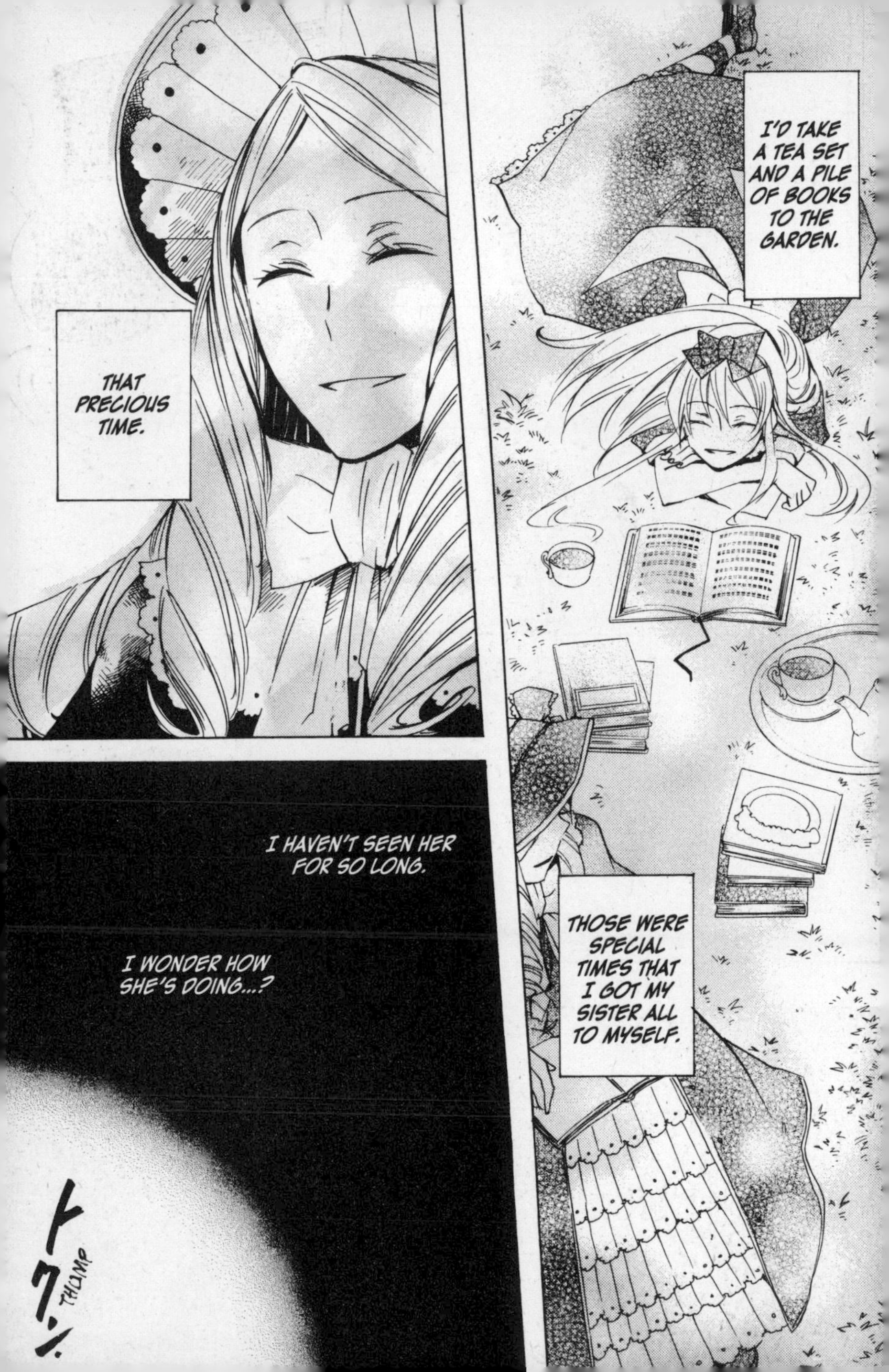
I'D TAKE A TEA SET AND A PILE OF BOOKS TO THE GARDEN.
THOSE WERE SPECIAL TIMES THAT I GOT MY SISTER ALL TO MYSELF.
THAT PRECIOUS TIME.
I HAVEN'T SEEN HER FOR SO LONG.
I WONDER HOW SHE'S DOING...?
トクン
THUMP

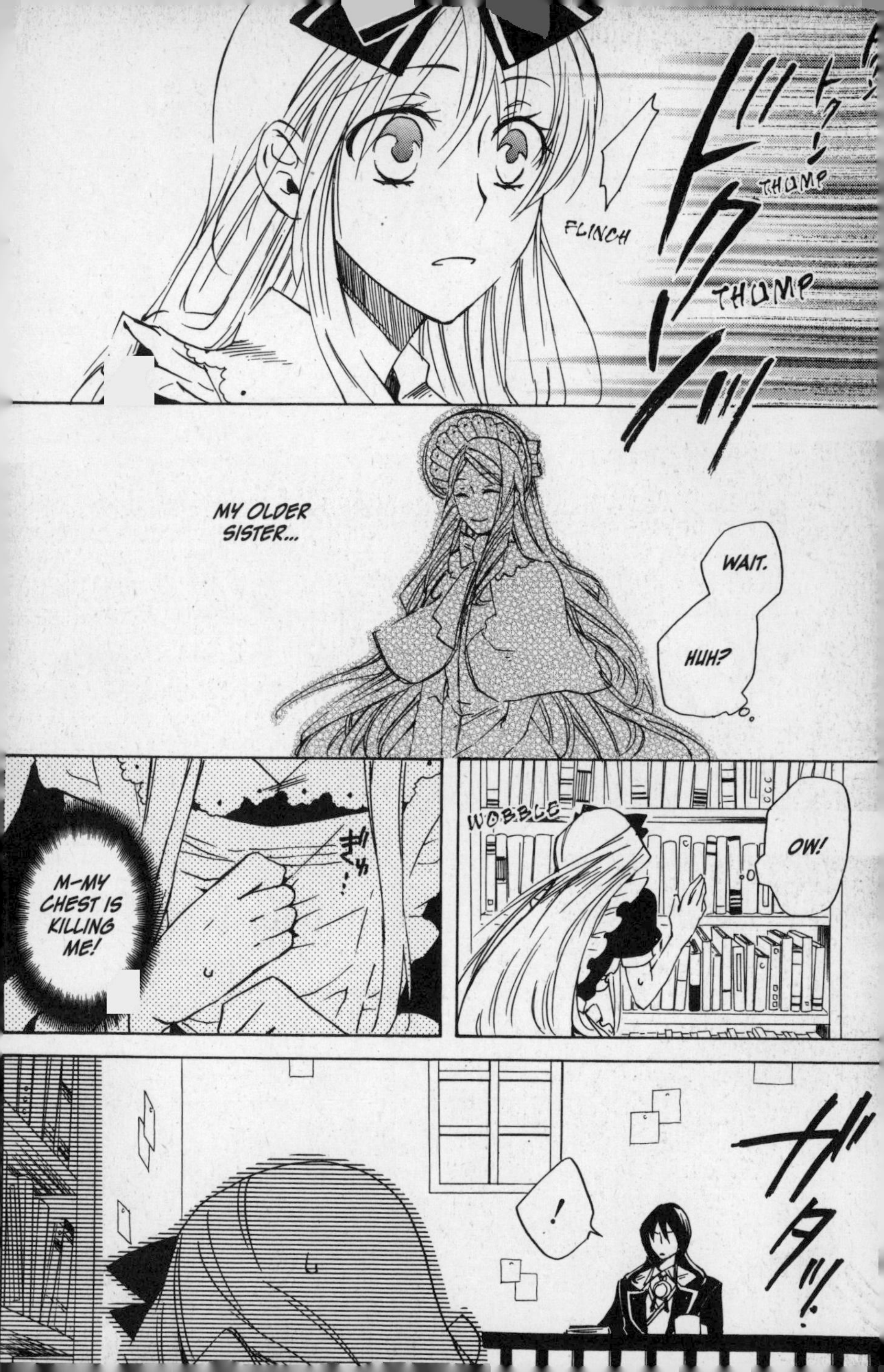
THUMP
THUMP
FLINCH
WAIT.
HUH?
MY OLDER SISTER...
OW!
WOBBLE
M-MY CHEST IS KILLING ME!
ガタッ!
!

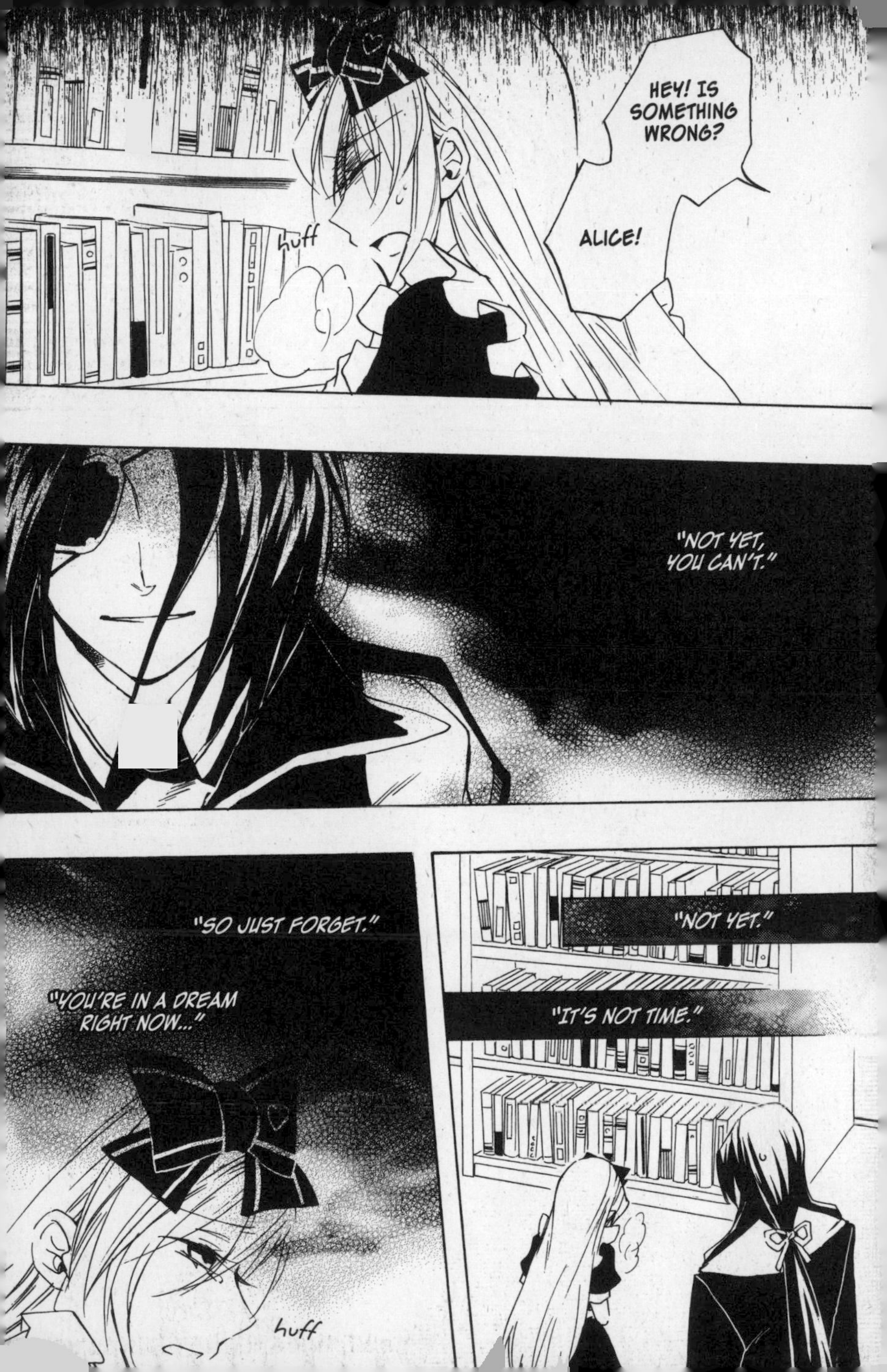
HEY! IS SOMETHING WRONG?
ALICE!
huff
"NOT YET, YOU CAN'T."
"NOT YET."
"IT'S NOT TIME."
"SO JUST FORGET."
"YOU'RE IN A DREAM RIGHT NOW..."
huff

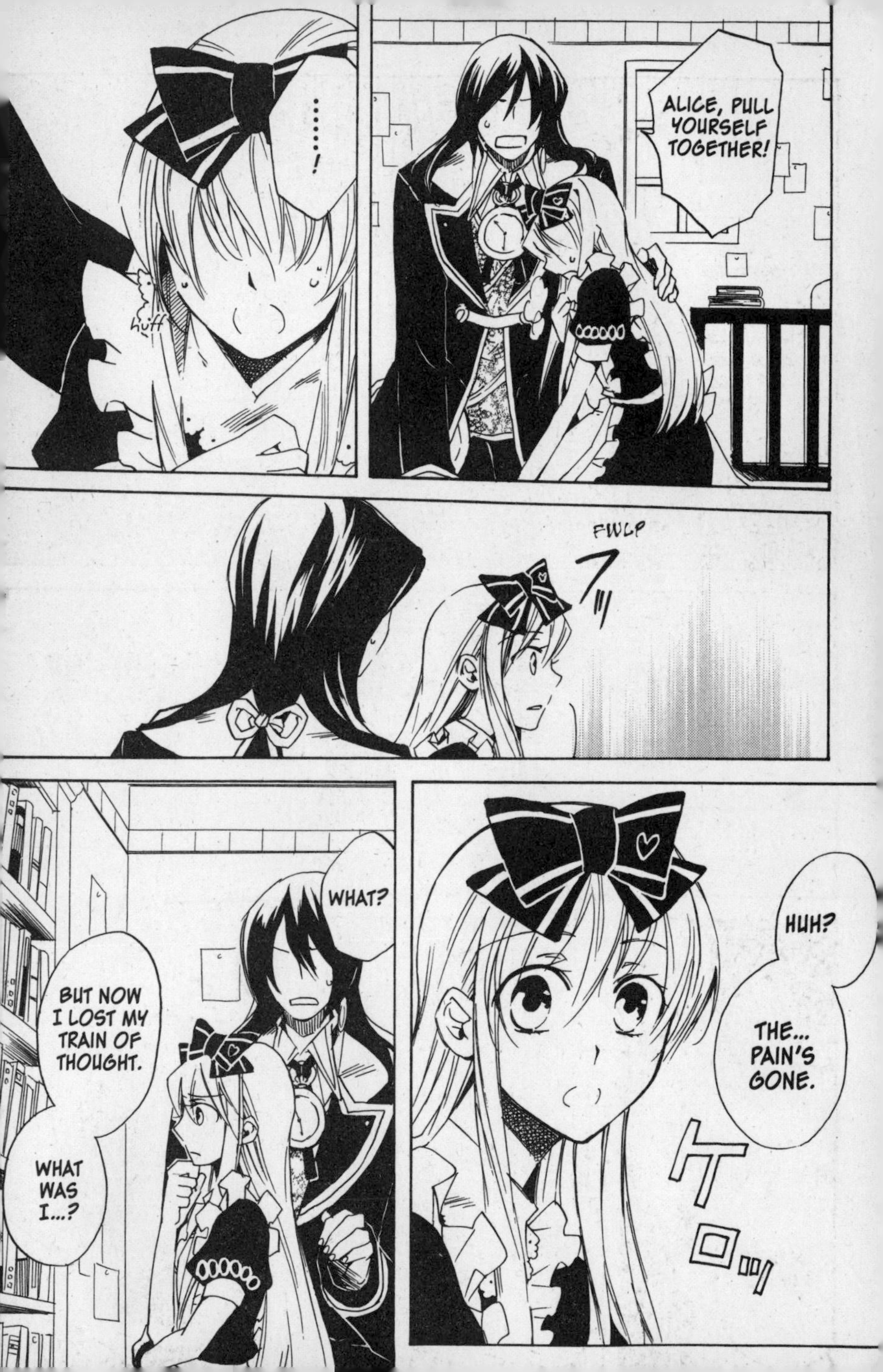
ALICE, PULL YOURSELF TOGETHER!
......!
huff
FWLP
フッ
HUH?
THE... PAIN'S GONE.
ケロッ
WHAT?
BUT NOW I LOST MY TRAIN OF THOUGHT.
WHAT WAS I...?

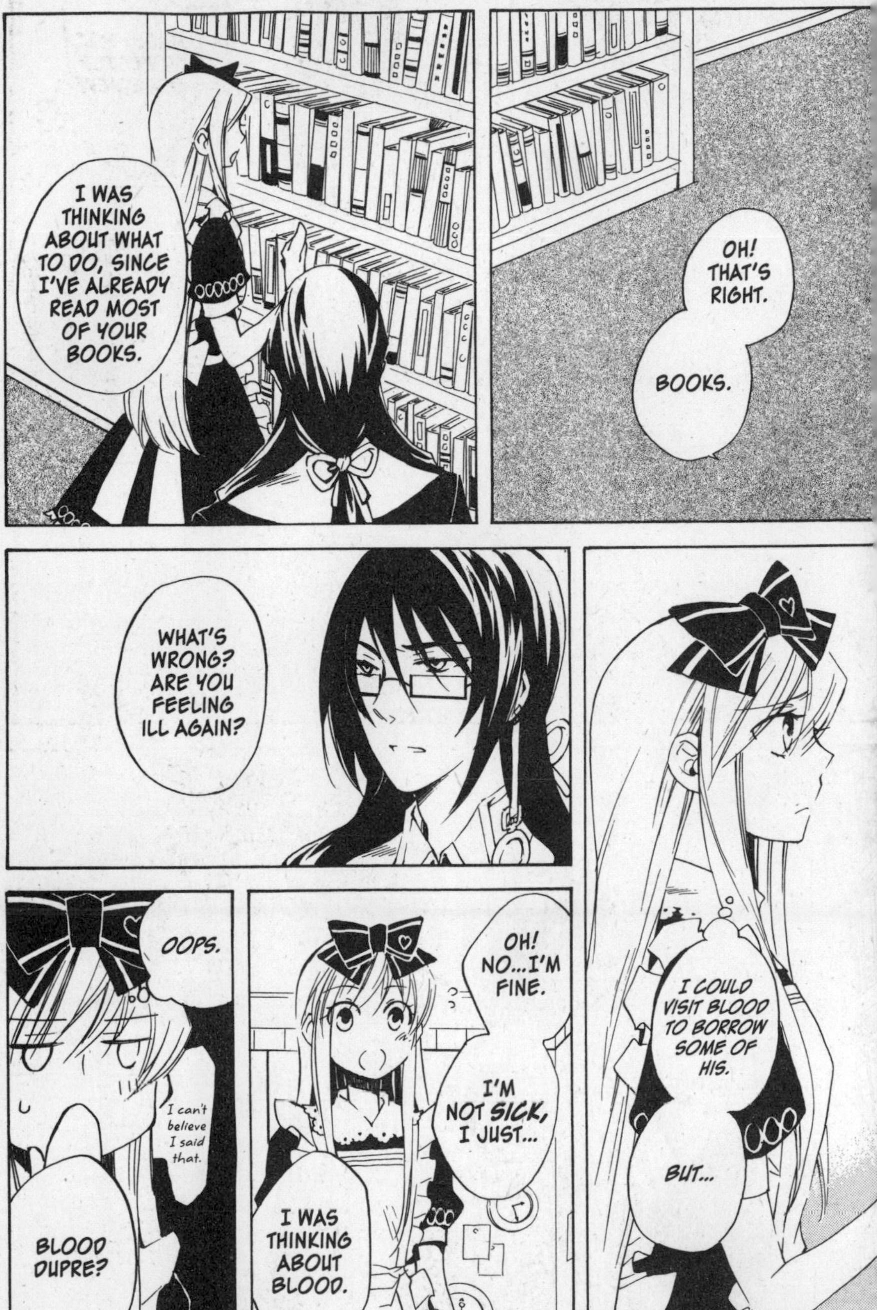
OH! THAT'S RIGHT.
BOOKS.
I WAS THINKING ABOUT WHAT TO DO, SINCE I'VE ALREADY READ MOST OF YOUR BOOKS.
I COULD VISIT BLOOD TO BORROW SOME OF HIS.
BUT...
WHAT'S WRONG? ARE YOU FEELING ILL AGAIN?
OH! NO...I'M FINE.
I'M NOT SICK, I JUST...
I WAS THINKING ABOUT BLOOD.
OOPS.
I can't believe I said that.
BLOOD DUPRE?

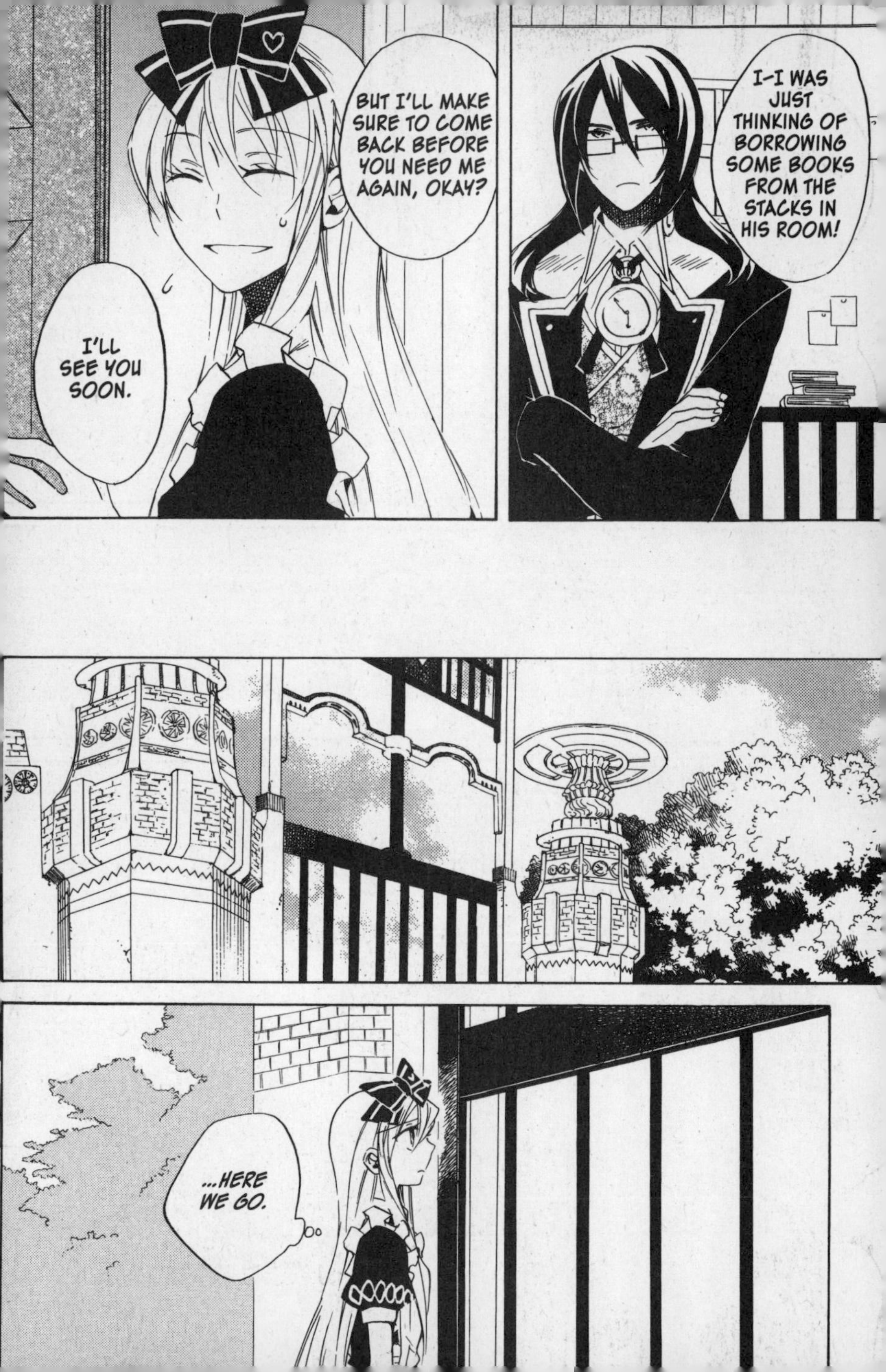
I-I WAS JUST THINKING OF BORROWING SOME BOOKS FROM THE STACKS IN HIS ROOM!
BUT I'LL MAKE SURE TO COME BACK BEFORE YOU NEED ME AGAIN, OKAY?
I'LL SEE YOU SOON.
...HERE WE GO.

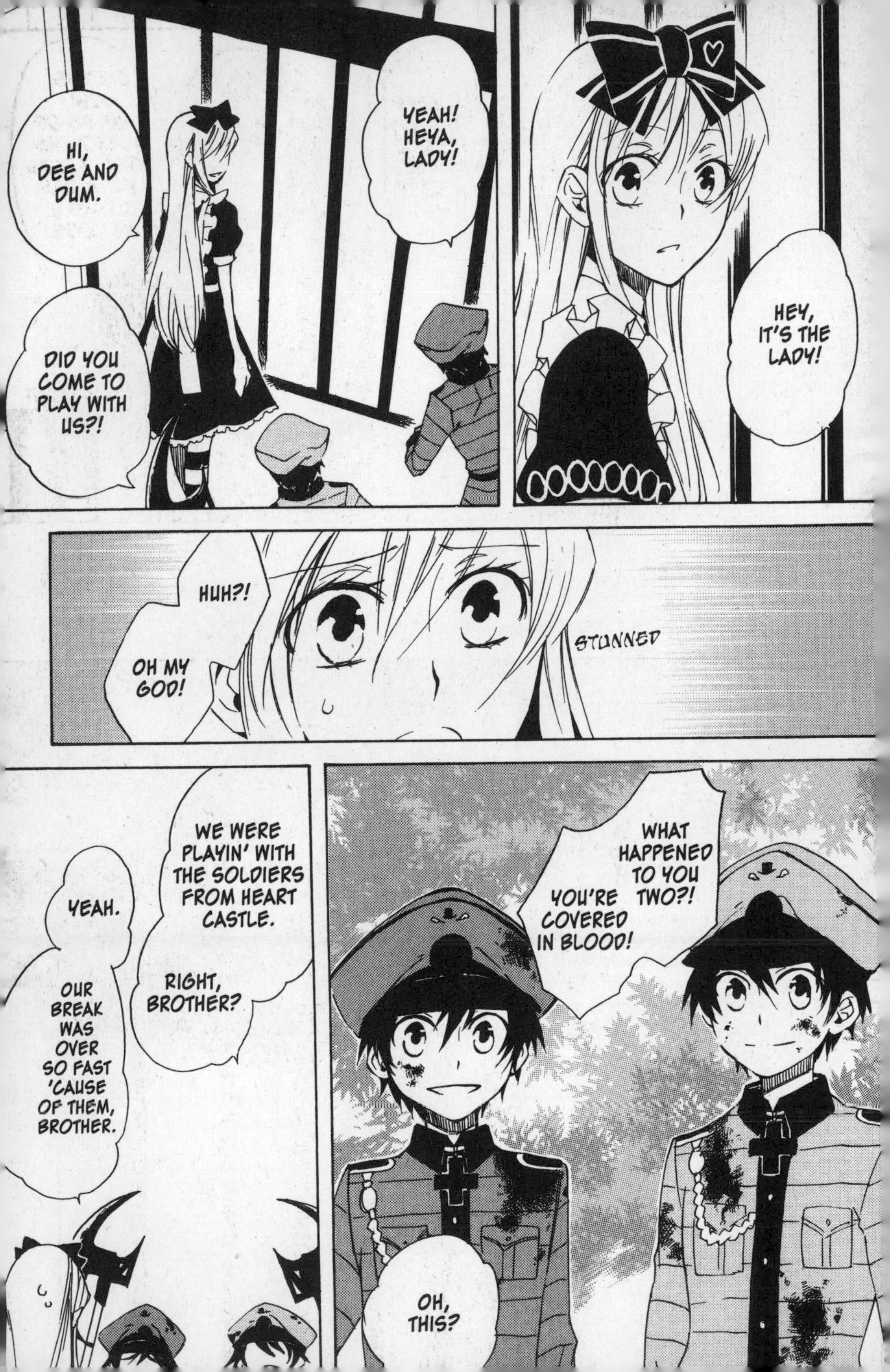

HEY, IT'S THE LADY!
YEAH! HEYA, LADY!
HI, DEE AND DUM.
DID YOU COME TO PLAY WITH US?!
HUH?!
OH MY GOD!
STUNNED
WHAT HAPPENED TO YOU TWO?!
YOU'RE COVERED IN BLOOD!
OH, THIS?
WE WERE PLAYIN' WITH THE SOLDIERS FROM HEART CASTLE.
RIGHT, BROTHER?
YEAH.
OUR BREAK WAS OVER SO FAST 'CAUSE OF THEM, BROTHER.

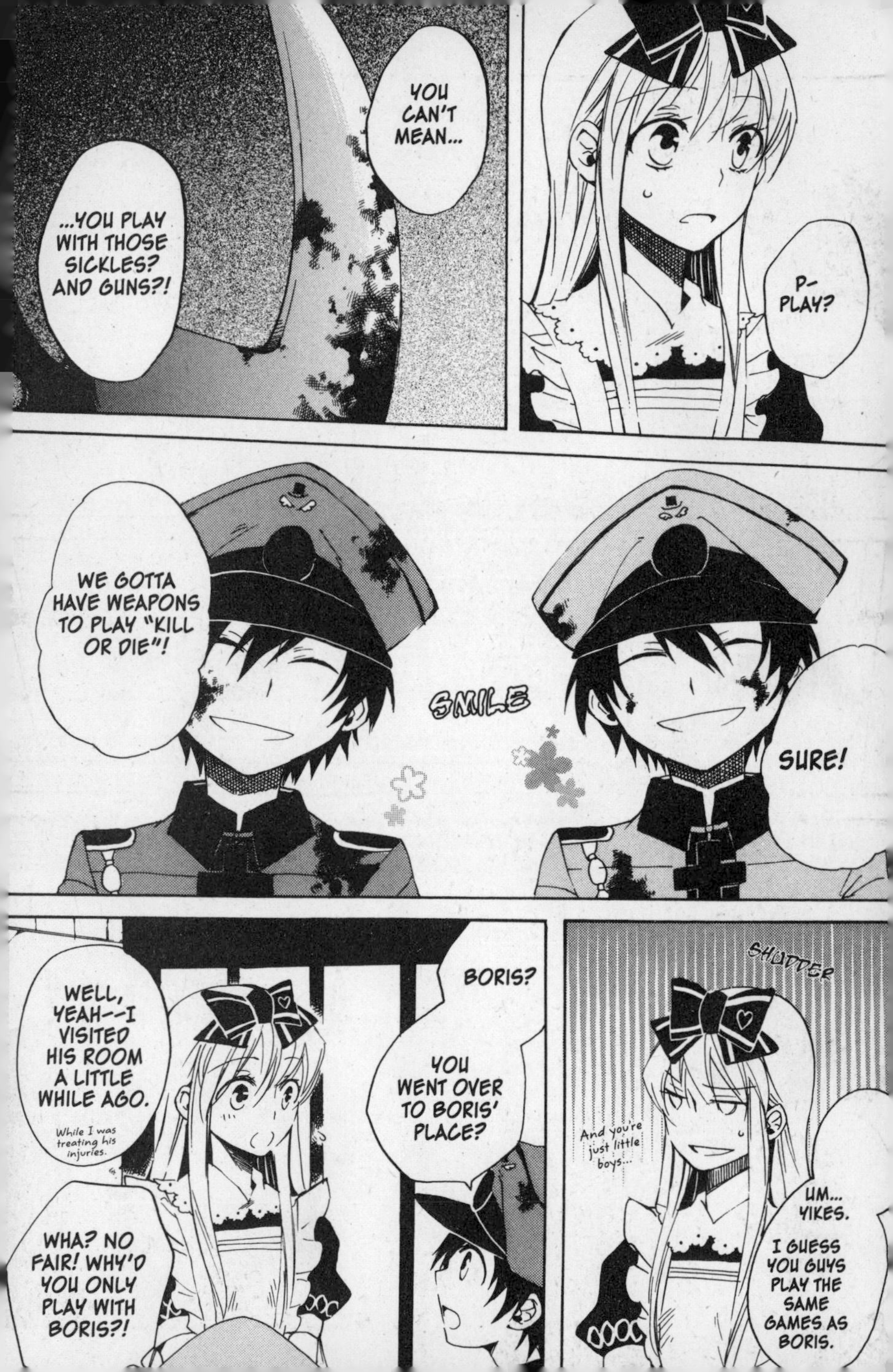
P-PLAY?
YOU CAN'T MEAN...
...YOU PLAY WITH THOSE SICKLES? AND GUNS?!
SURE!
SMILE
WE GOTTA HAVE WEAPONS TO PLAY "KILL OR DIE"!
SHUDDER
And you're just little boys...
UM... YIKES.
I GUESS YOU GUYS PLAY THE SAME GAMES AS BORIS.
BORIS?
YOU WENT OVER TO BORIS' PLACE?
WELL, YEAH--I VISITED HIS ROOM A LITTLE WHILE AGO.
While I was treating his injuries.
WHA? NO FAIR! WHY'D YOU ONLY PLAY WITH BORIS?!

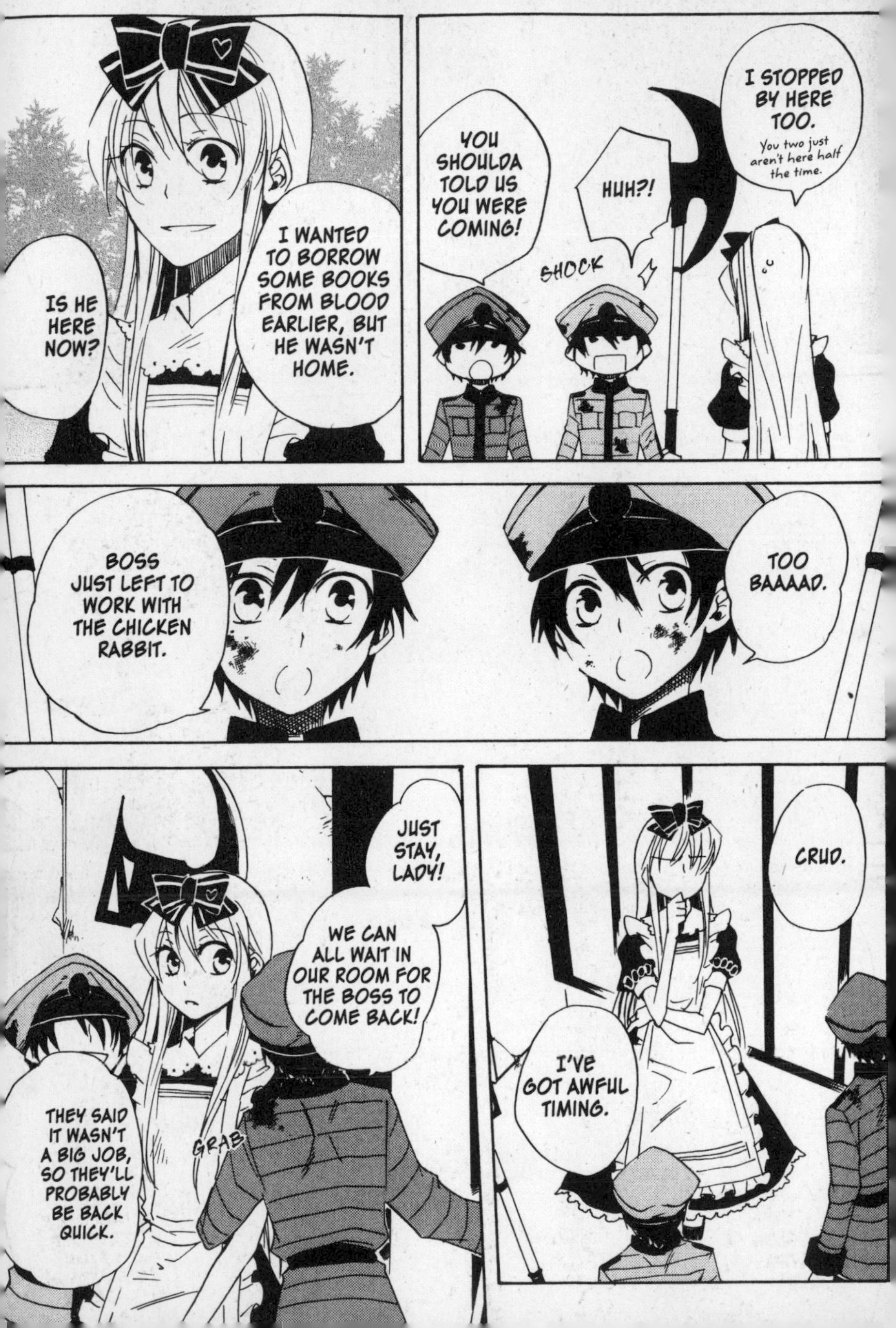
I STOPPED BY HERE TOO.
You two just aren't here half the time.
HUH?!
YOU SHOULDA TOLD US YOU WERE COMING!
SHOCK
I WANTED TO BORROW SOME BOOKS FROM BLOOD EARLIER, BUT HE WASN'T HOME.
IS HE HERE NOW?
TOO BAAAAD.
BOSS JUST LEFT TO WORK WITH THE CHICKEN RABBIT.
CRUD.
I'VE GOT AWFUL TIMING.
JUST STAY, LADY!
WE CAN ALL WAIT IN OUR ROOM FOR THE BOSS TO COME BACK!
GRAB
THEY SAID IT WASN'T A BIG JOB, SO THEY'LL PROBABLY BE BACK QUICK.

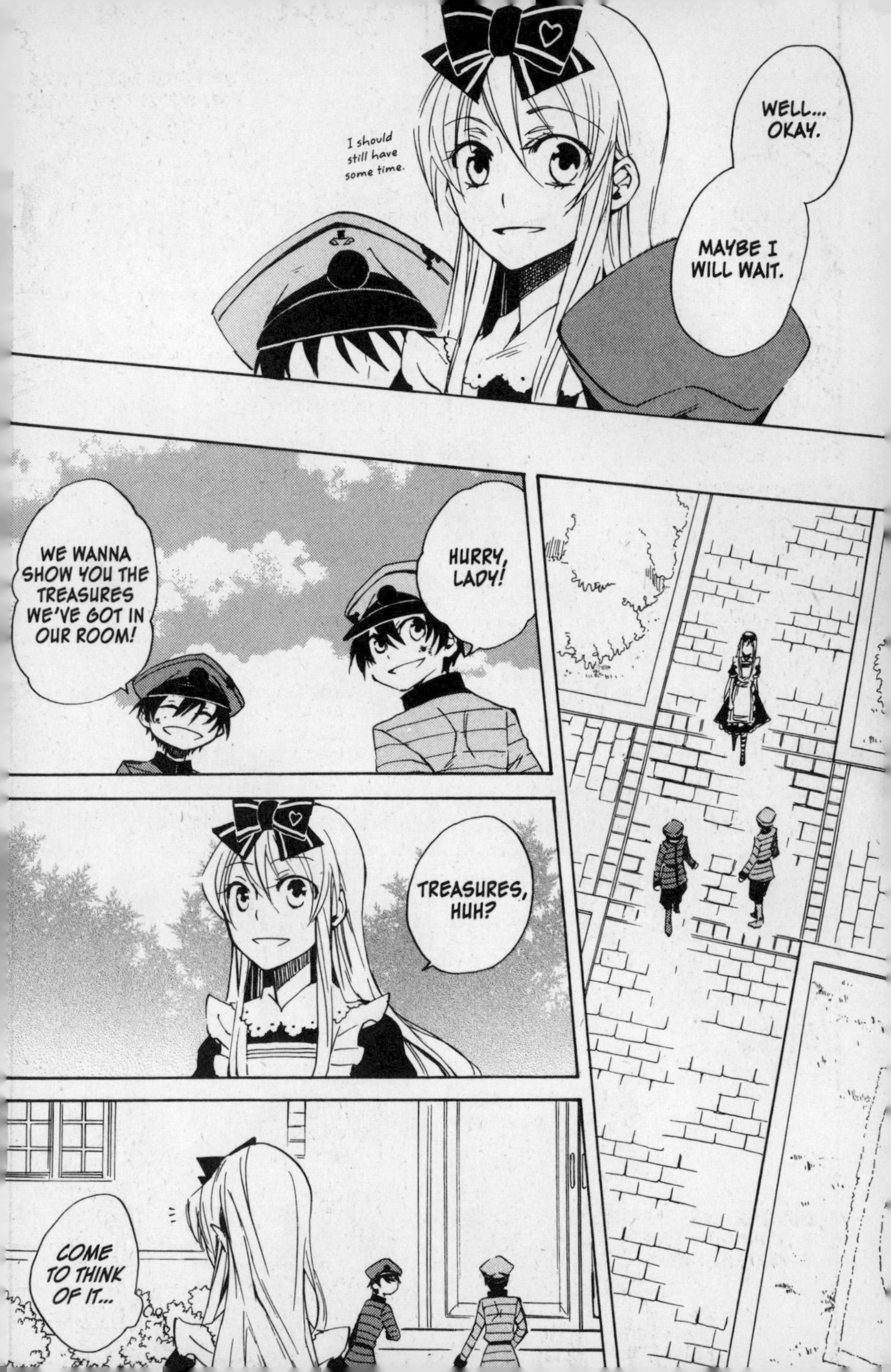
WELL... OKAY.
MAYBE I WILL WAIT.
I should still have some time.
HURRY, LADY!
WE WANNA SHOW YOU THE TREASURES WE'VE GOT IN OUR ROOM!
TREASURES, HUH?
COME TO THINK OF IT...

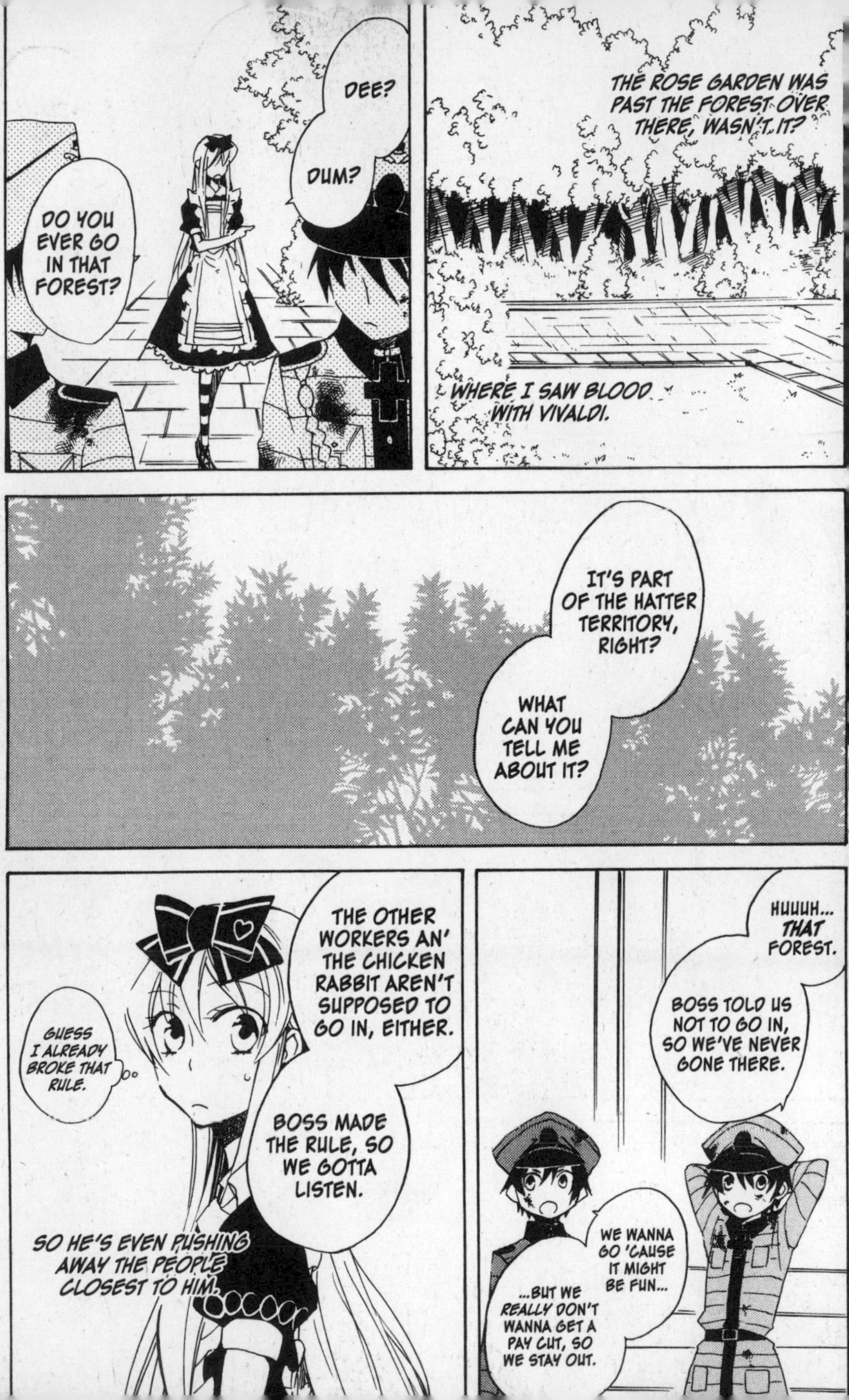
THE ROSE GARDEN WAS PAST THE FOREST OVER THERE, WASN'T IT?
WHERE I SAW BLOOD WITH VIVALDI.
DEE?
DUM?
DO YOU EVER GO IN THAT FOREST?
IT'S PART OF THE HATTER TERRITORY, RIGHT?
WHAT CAN YOU TELL ME ABOUT IT?
HUUUH... THAT FOREST.
BOSS TOLD US NOT TO GO IN, SO WE'VE NEVER GONE THERE.
WE WANNA GO 'CAUSE IT MIGHT BE FUN...
...BUT WE REALLY DON'T WANNA GET A PAY CUT, SO WE STAY OUT.
THE OTHER WORKERS AN' THE CHICKEN RABBIT AREN'T SUPPOSED TO GO IN, EITHER.
GUESS I ALREADY BROKE THAT RULE.
BOSS MADE THE RULE, SO WE GOTTA LISTEN.
SO HE'S EVEN PUSHING AWAY THE PEOPLE CLOSEST TO HIM.

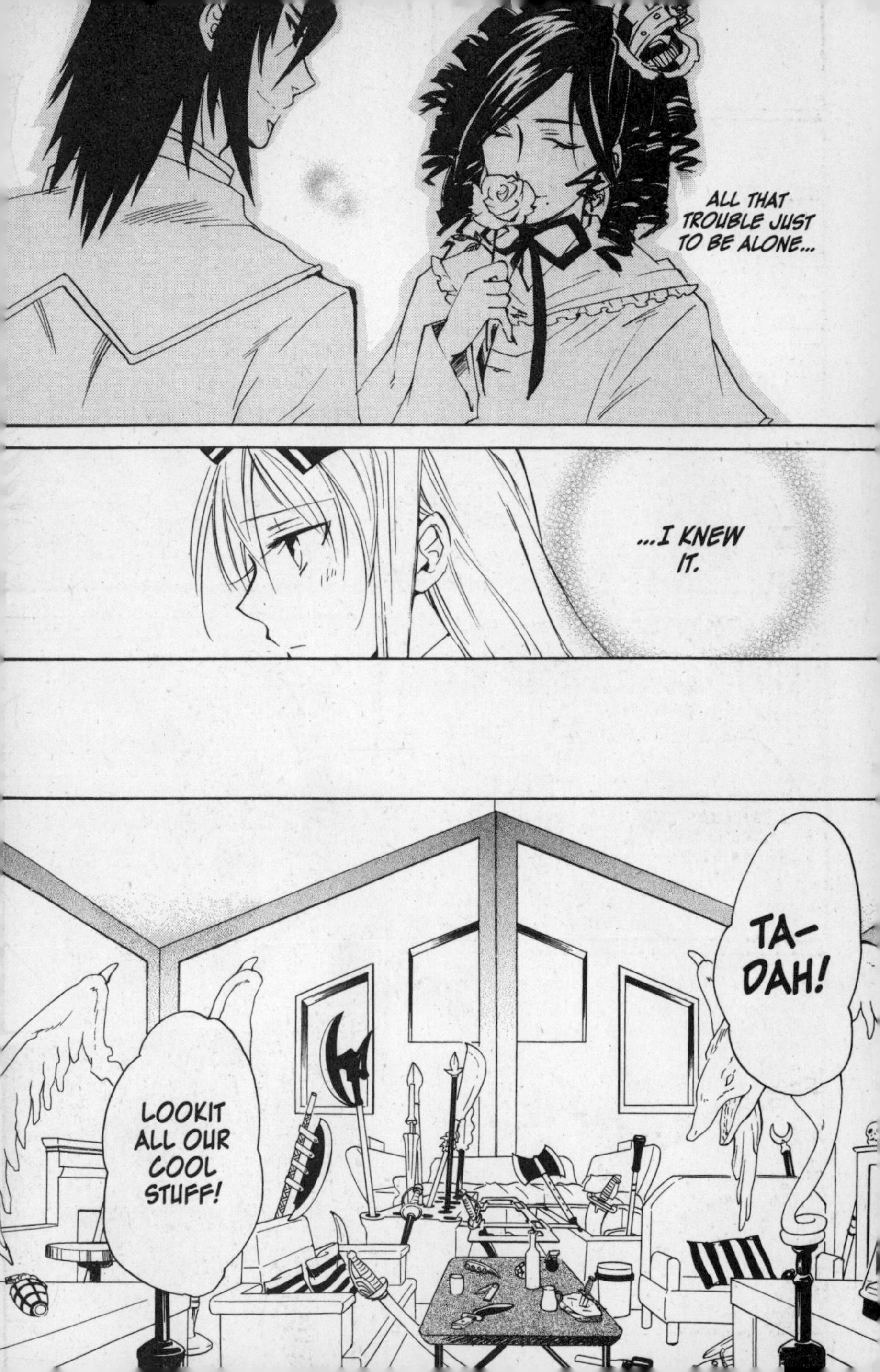
ALL THAT TROUBLE JUST TO BE ALONE...
...I KNEW IT.
TA-DAH!
LOOKIT ALL OUR COOL STUFF!

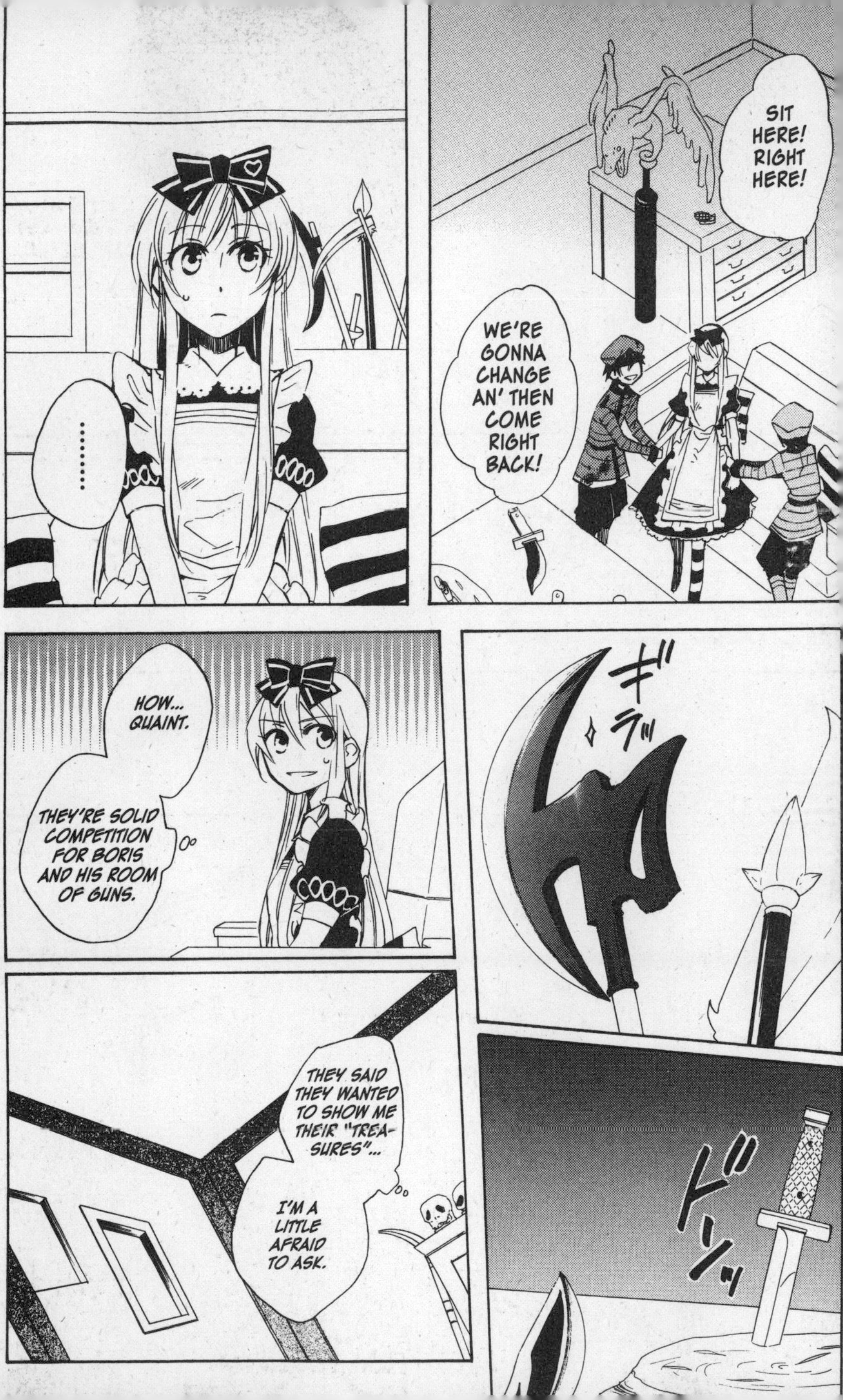
SIT HERE! RIGHT HERE!
WE'RE GONNA CHANGE AN' THEN COME RIGHT BACK!
......
ギラッ
HOW... QUAINT.
THEY'RE SOLID COMPETITION FOR BORIS AND HIS ROOM OF GUNS.
ドーンッ
THEY SAID THEY WANTED TO SHOW ME THEIR "TREA-SURES"...
I'M A LITTLE AFRAID TO ASK.

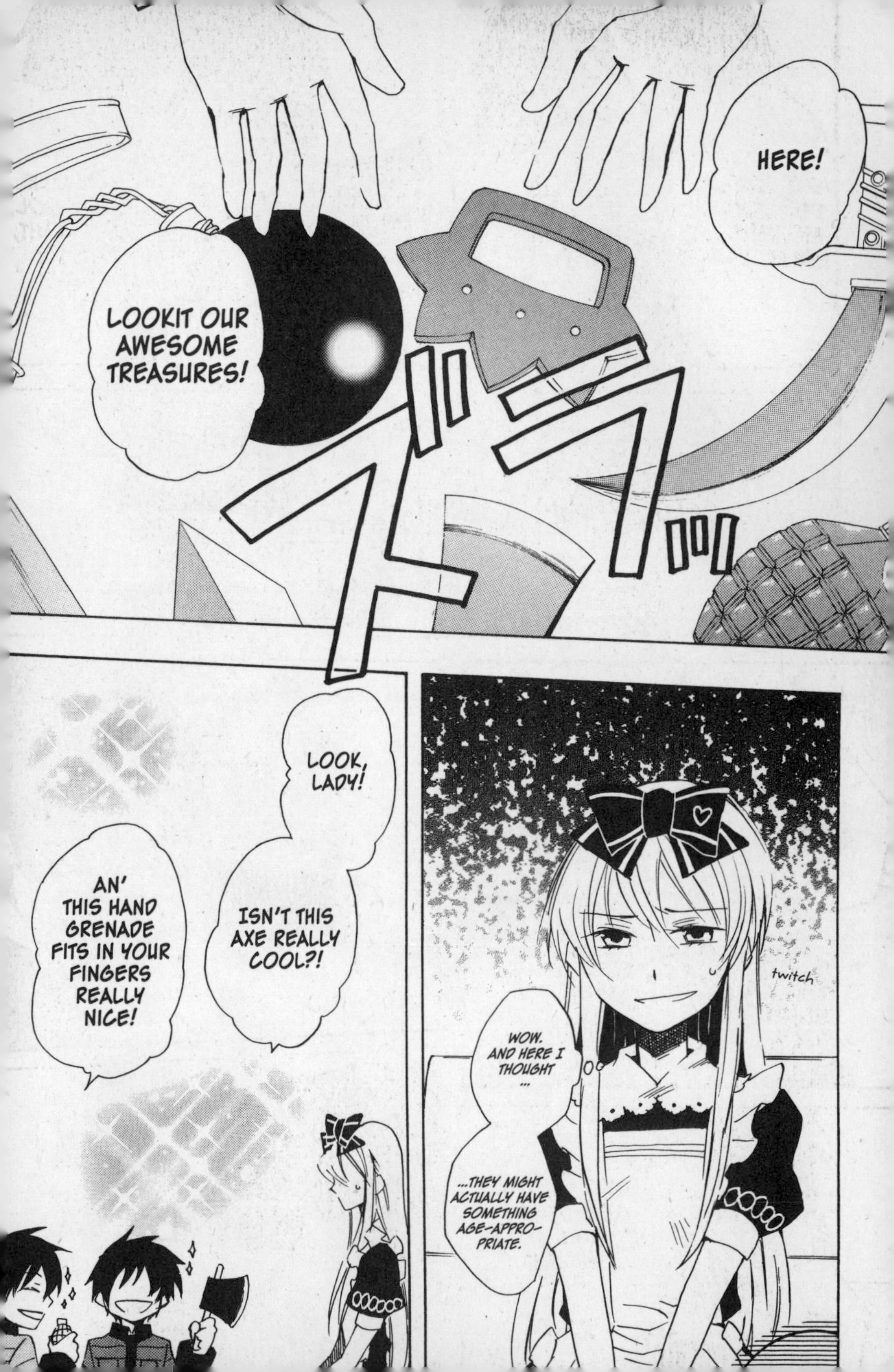
HERE!
LOOKIT OUR AWESOME TREASURES!
WOW. AND HERE I THOUGHT ...
twitch
...THEY MIGHT ACTUALLY HAVE SOMETHING AGE-APPROPRIATE.
LOOK, LADY!
ISN'T THIS AXE REALLY COOL?!
AN' THIS HAND GRENADE FITS IN YOUR FINGERS REALLY NICE!

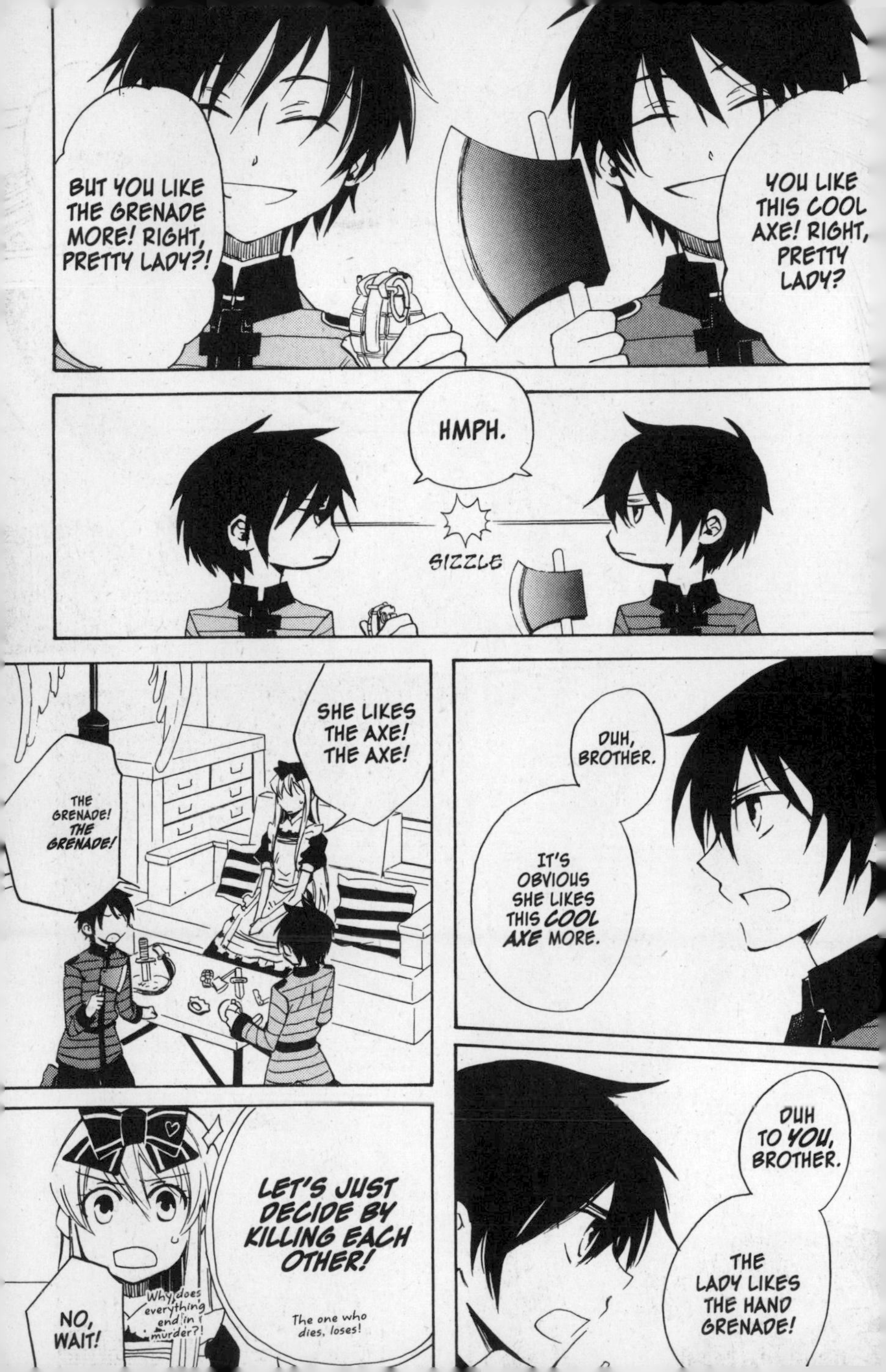
YOU LIKE THIS COOL AXE! RIGHT, PRETTY LADY?
BUT YOU LIKE THE GRENADE MORE! RIGHT, PRETTY LADY?!
HMPH.
SIZZLE
DUH, BROTHER.
IT'S OBVIOUS SHE LIKES THIS COOL AXE MORE.
SHE LIKES THE AXE! THE AXE!
THE GRENADE! THE GRENADE!
DUH TO YOU, BROTHER.
THE LADY LIKES THE HAND GRENADE!
LET'S JUST DECIDE BY KILLING EACH OTHER!
The one who dies, loses!
Why does everything end in murder?!
NO, WAIT!

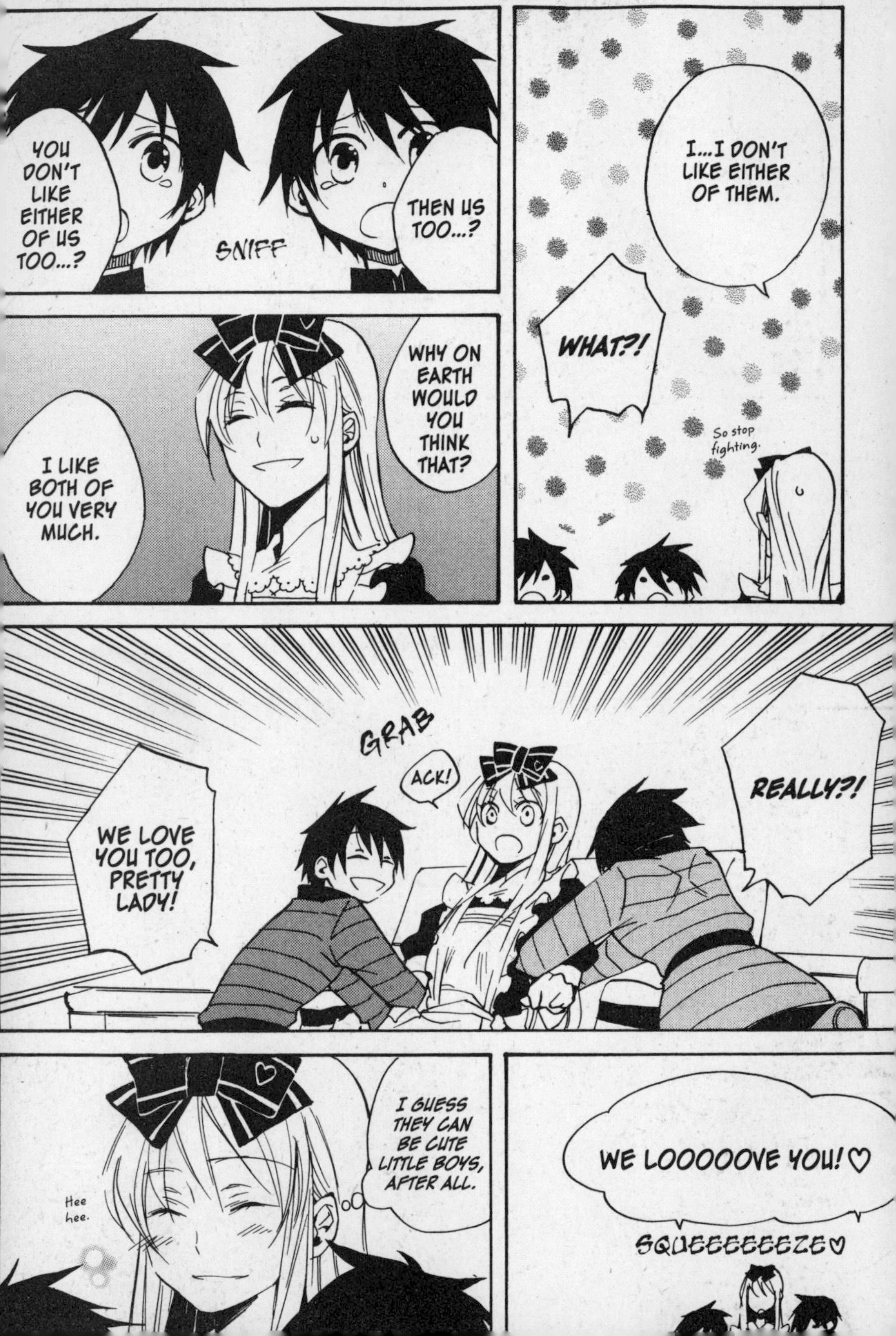
I...I DON'T LIKE EITHER OF THEM.
WHAT?!
So stop fighting.
THEN US TOO...?
SNIFF
YOU DON'T LIKE EITHER OF US TOO...?
WHY ON EARTH WOULD YOU THINK THAT?
I LIKE BOTH OF YOU VERY MUCH.
REALLY?!
ACK!
GRAB
WE LOVE YOU TOO, PRETTY LADY!
WE LOOOOOVE YOU! ♡
SQUEEEEEEEZE♡
I GUESS THEY CAN BE CUTE LITTLE BOYS, AFTER ALL.
Hee hee.

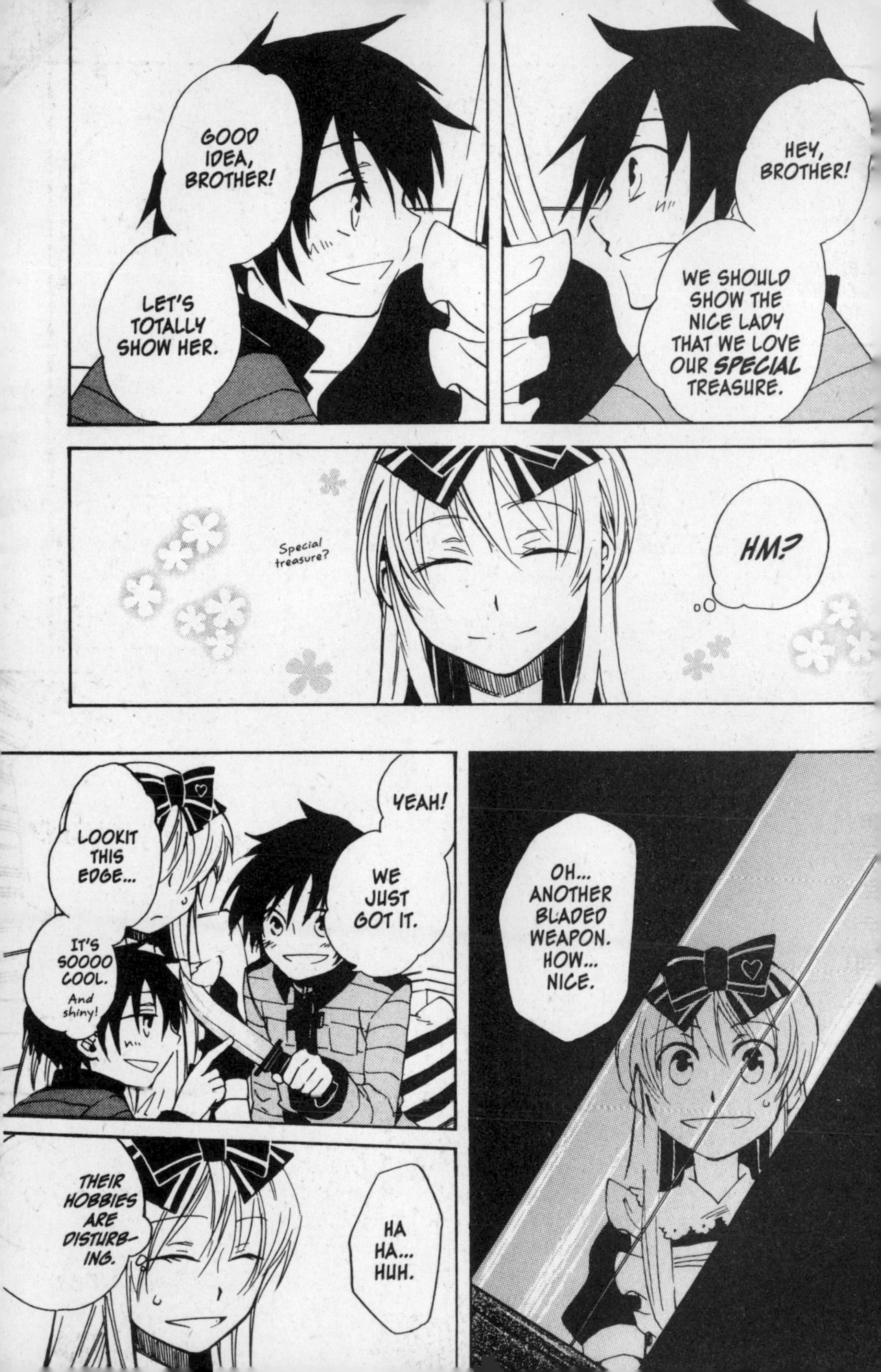
HEY, BROTHER!
WE SHOULD SHOW THE NICE LADY THAT WE LOVE OUR **SPECIAL** TREASURE.
GOOD IDEA, BROTHER!
LET'S TOTALLY SHOW HER.
HM?
Special treasure?
OH... ANOTHER BLADED WEAPON. HOW... NICE.
YEAH!
WE JUST GOT IT.
LOOKIT THIS EDGE...
IT'S SOOOO COOL.
And shiny!
HA HA... HUH.
THEIR HOBBIES ARE DISTURB-ING.

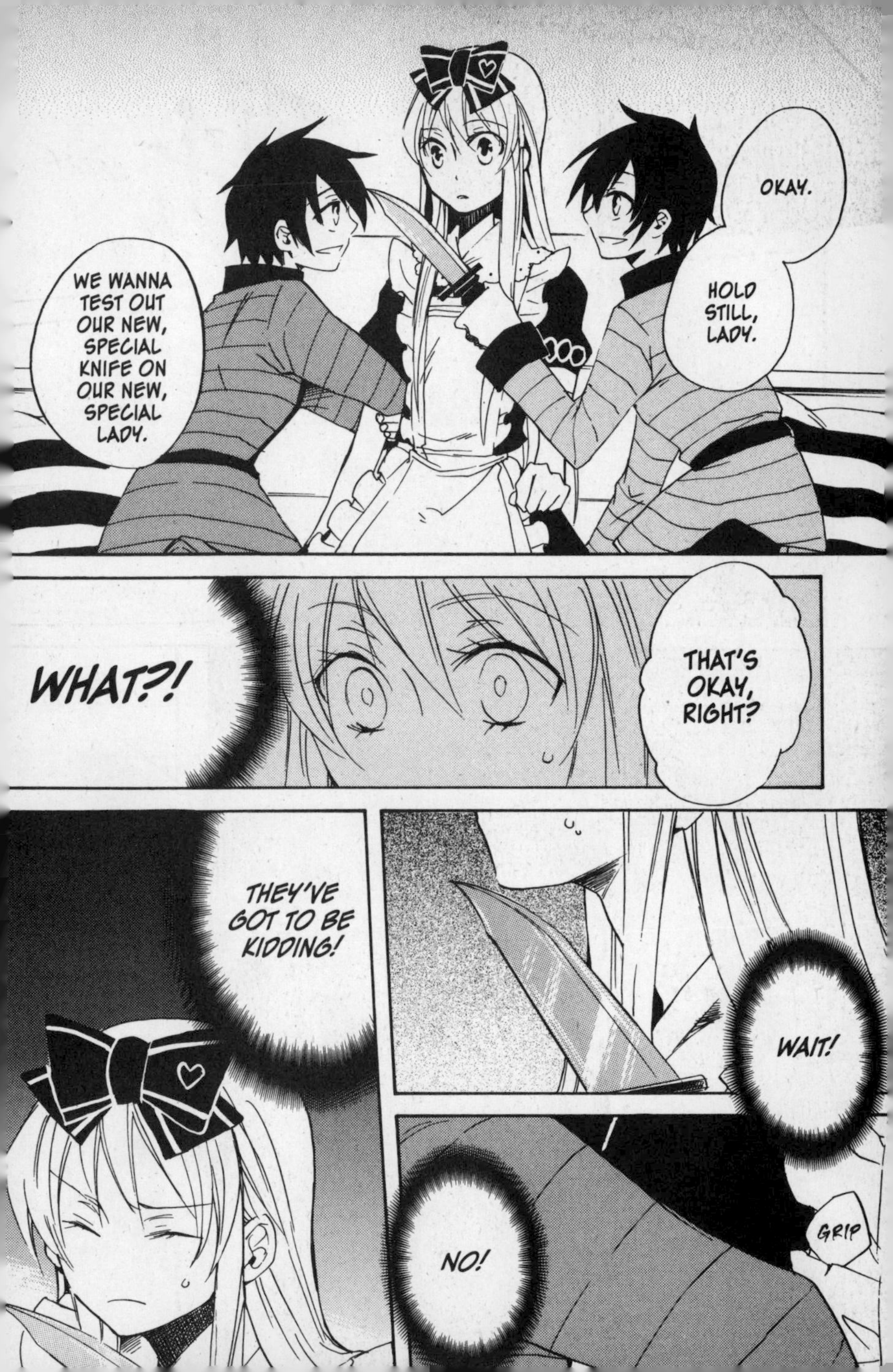
OKAY.
HOLD STILL, LADY.
WE WANNA TEST OUT OUR NEW, SPECIAL KNIFE ON OUR NEW, SPECIAL LADY.
THAT'S OKAY, RIGHT?
WHAT?!
WAIT!
GRIP
NO!
THEY'VE GOT TO BE KIDDING!

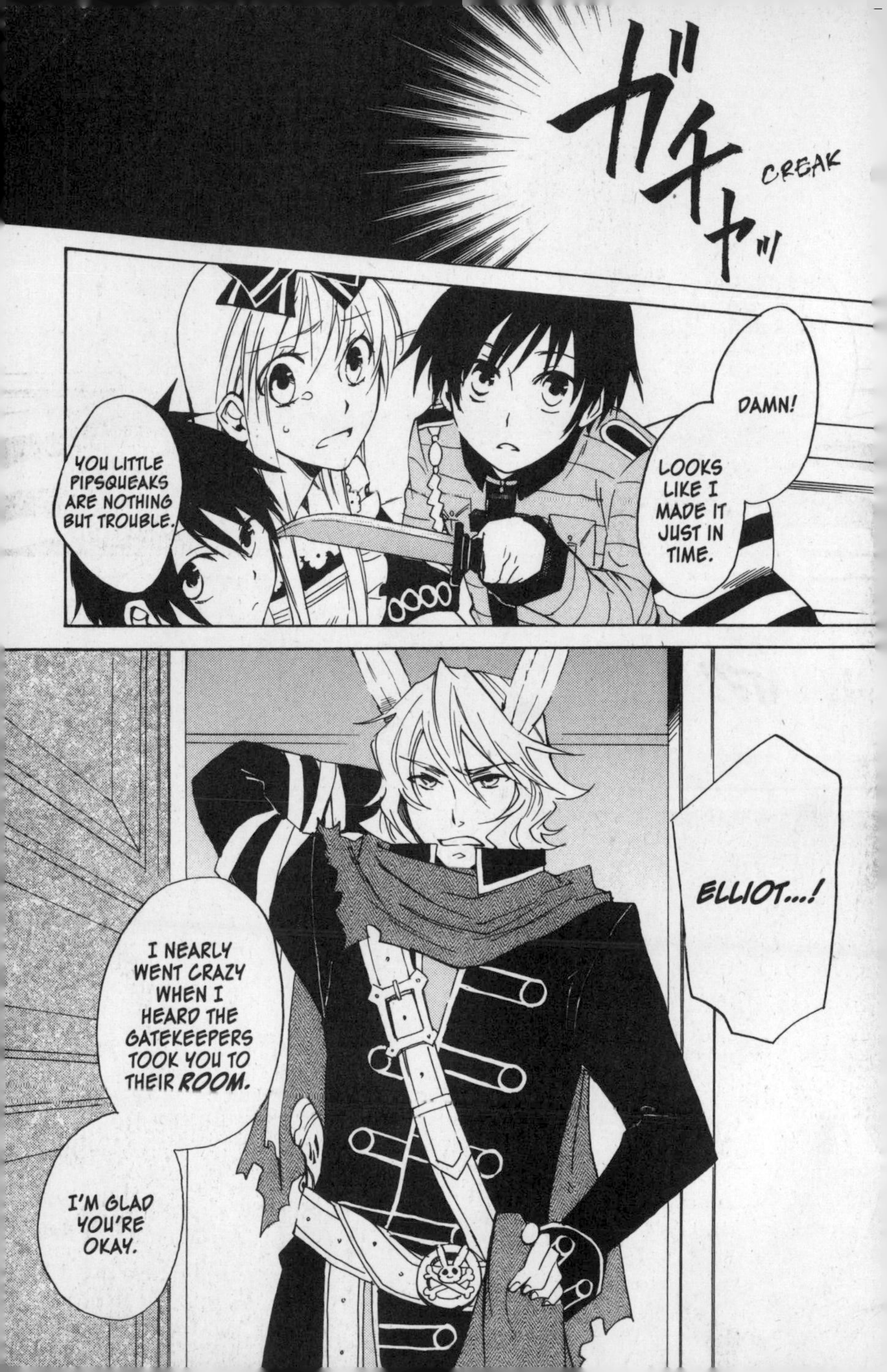
ガチャッ
CREAK
DAMN!
LOOKS LIKE I MADE IT JUST IN TIME.
YOU LITTLE PIPSQUEAKS ARE NOTHING BUT TROUBLE.
ELLIOT...!
I NEARLY WENT CRAZY WHEN I HEARD THE GATEKEEPERS TOOK YOU TO THEIR ROOM.
I'M GLAD YOU'RE OKAY.

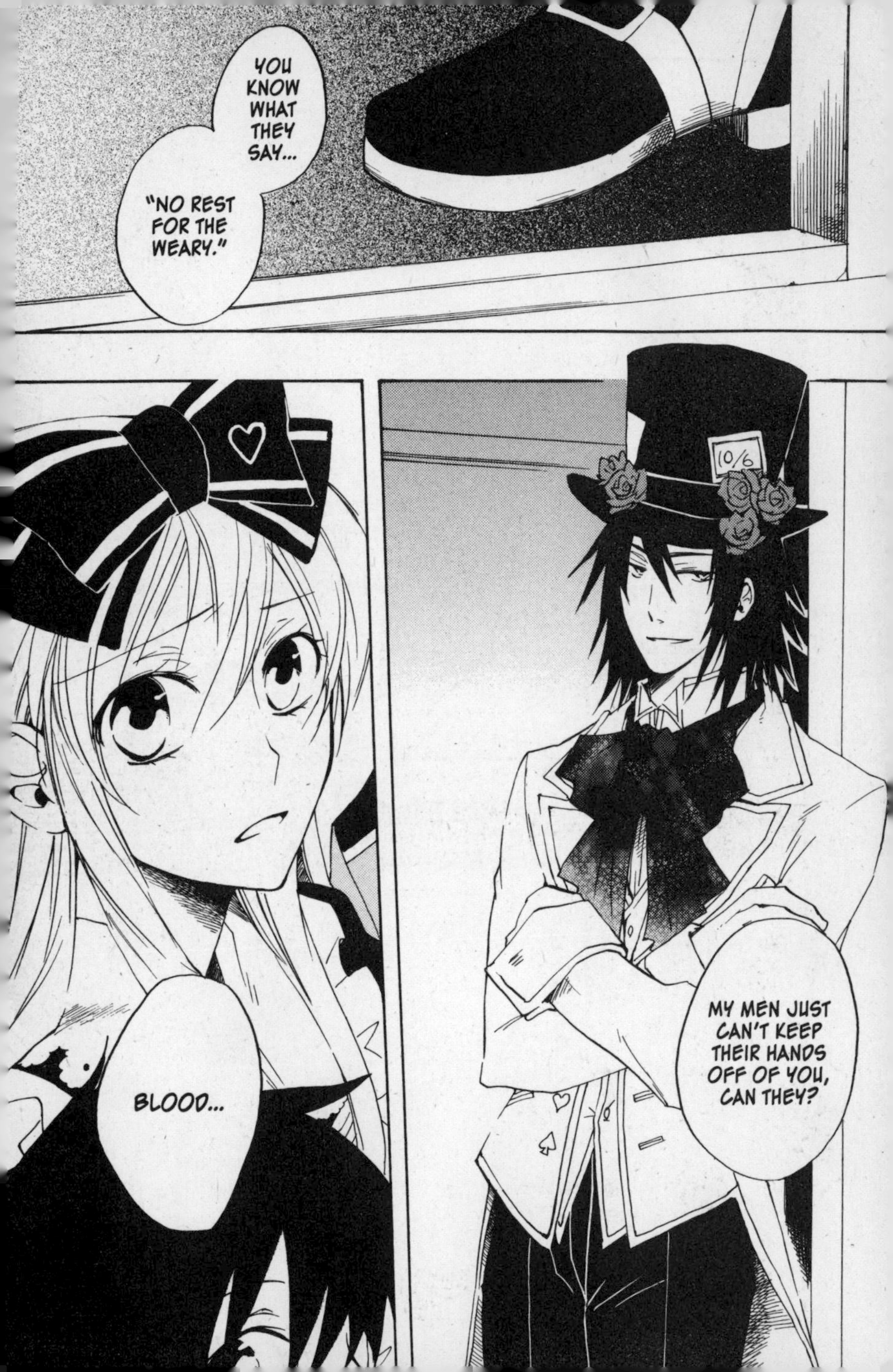
YOU KNOW WHAT THEY SAY...
"NO REST FOR THE WEARY."
MY MEN JUST CAN'T KEEP THEIR HANDS OFF OF YOU, CAN THEY?
BLOOD...

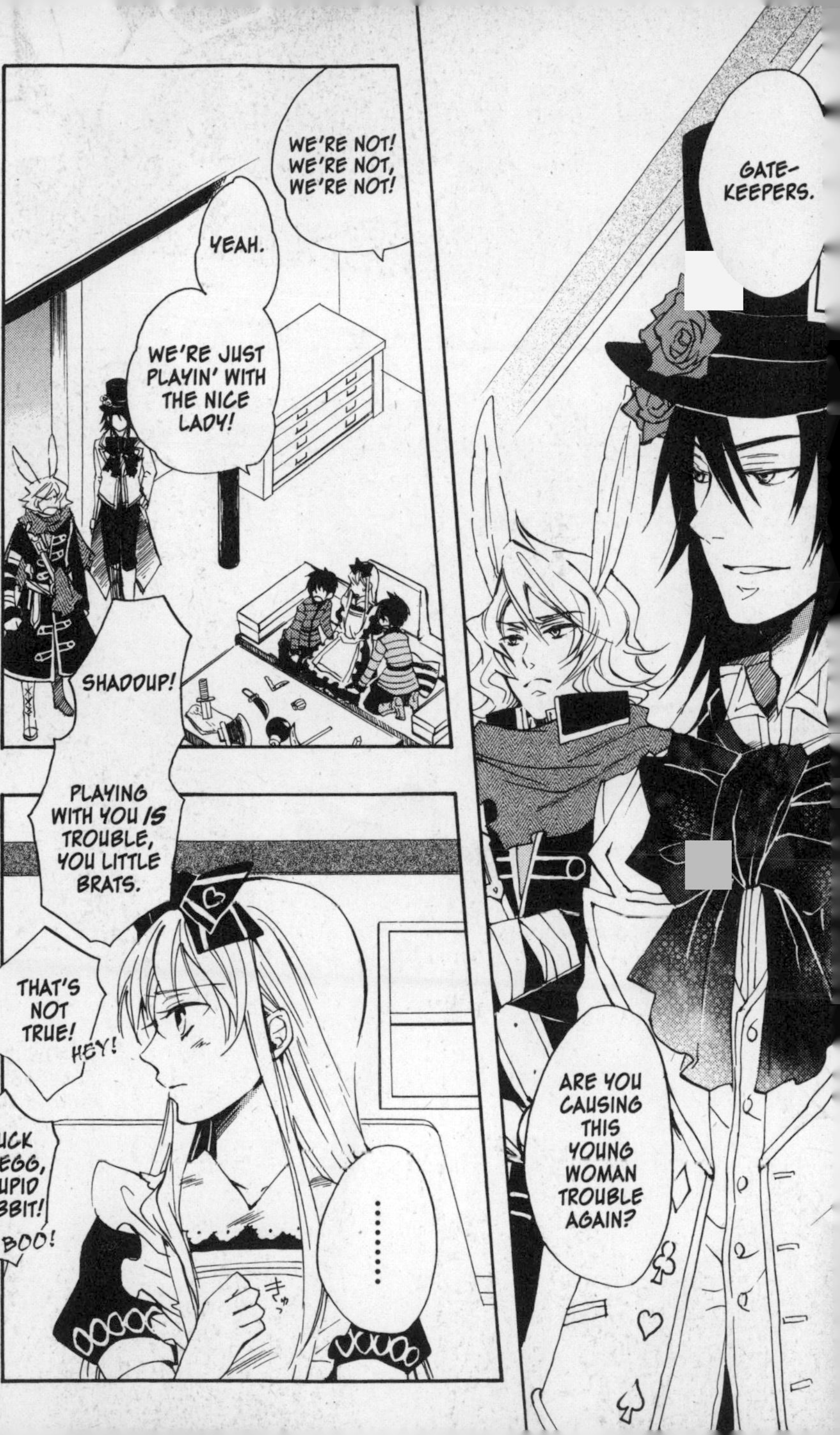
GATE-KEEPERS.
ARE YOU CAUSING THIS YOUNG WOMAN TROUBLE AGAIN?
WE'RE NOT! WE'RE NOT, WE'RE NOT!
YEAH.
WE'RE JUST PLAYIN' WITH THE NICE LADY!
SHADDUP!
PLAYING WITH YOU IS TROUBLE, YOU LITTLE BRATS.
THAT'S NOT TRUE!
HEY!
SUCK AN EGG, STUPID RABBIT!
BOO!
……
きゅっ

♥14 Disjointing Flower

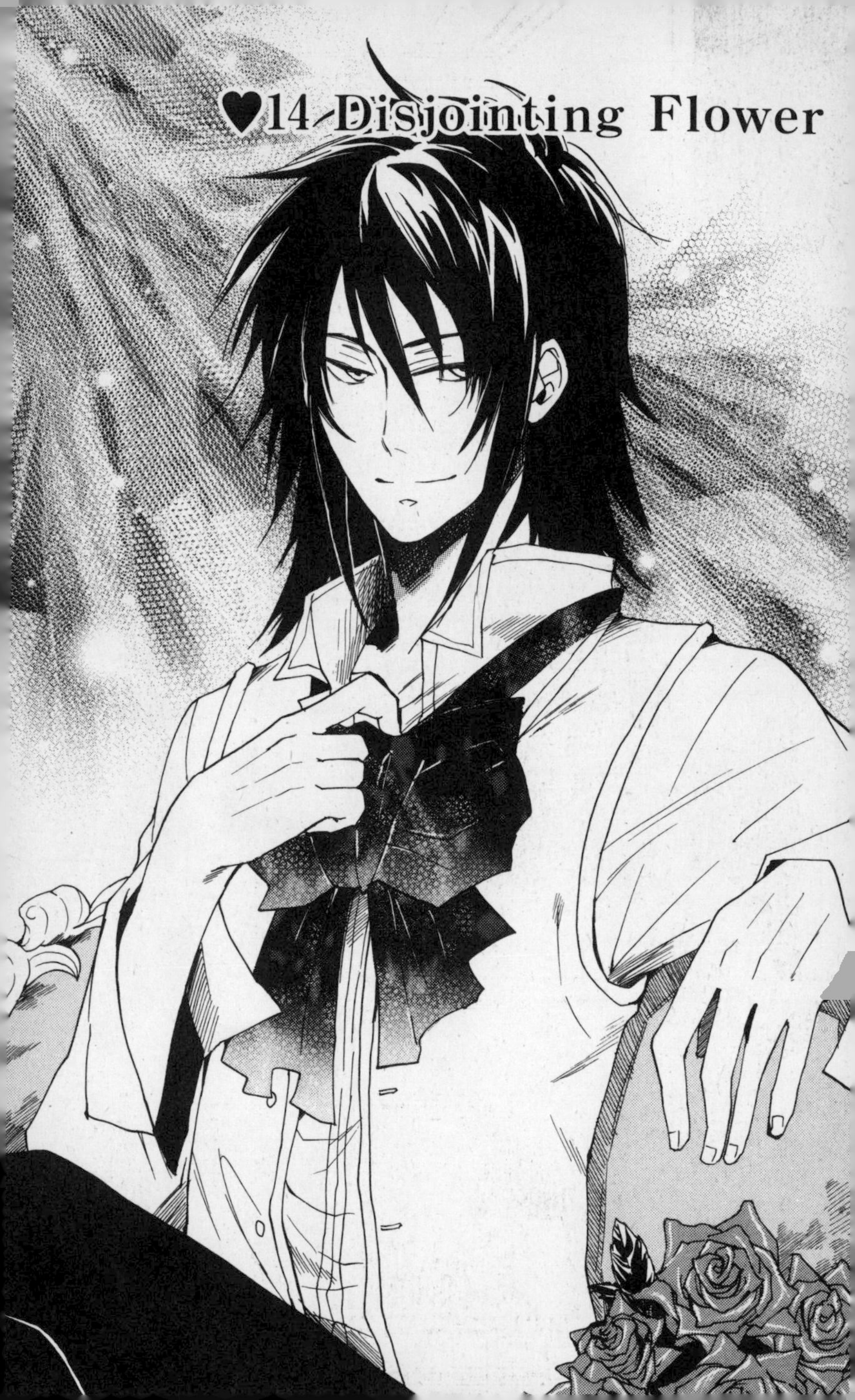

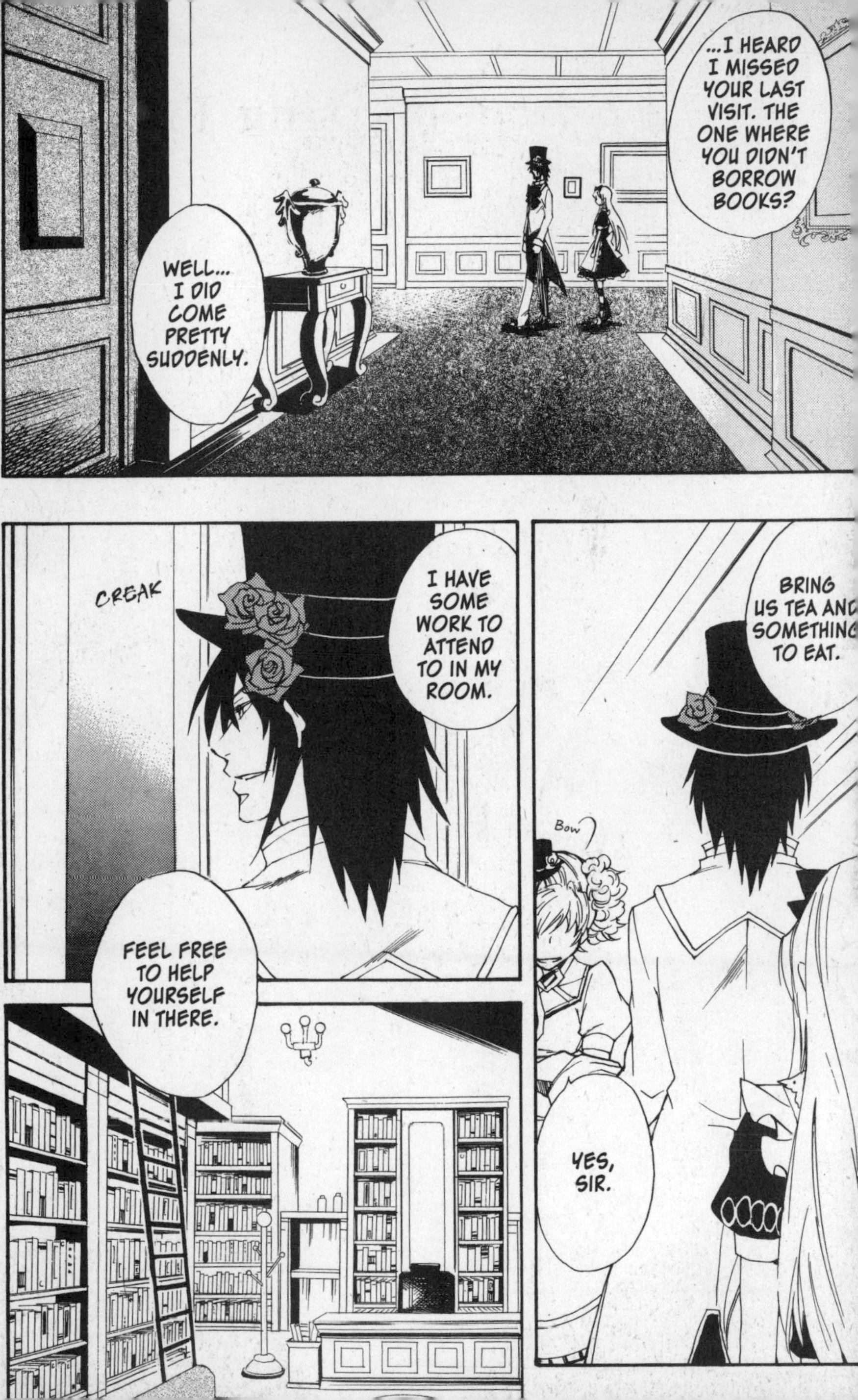
...I HEARD I MISSED YOUR LAST VISIT. THE ONE WHERE YOU DIDN'T BORROW BOOKS?
WELL... I DID COME PRETTY SUDDENLY.
BRING US TEA AND SOMETHING TO EAT.
Bow
YES, SIR.
I HAVE SOME WORK TO ATTEND TO IN MY ROOM.
CREAK
FEEL FREE TO HELP YOURSELF IN THERE.

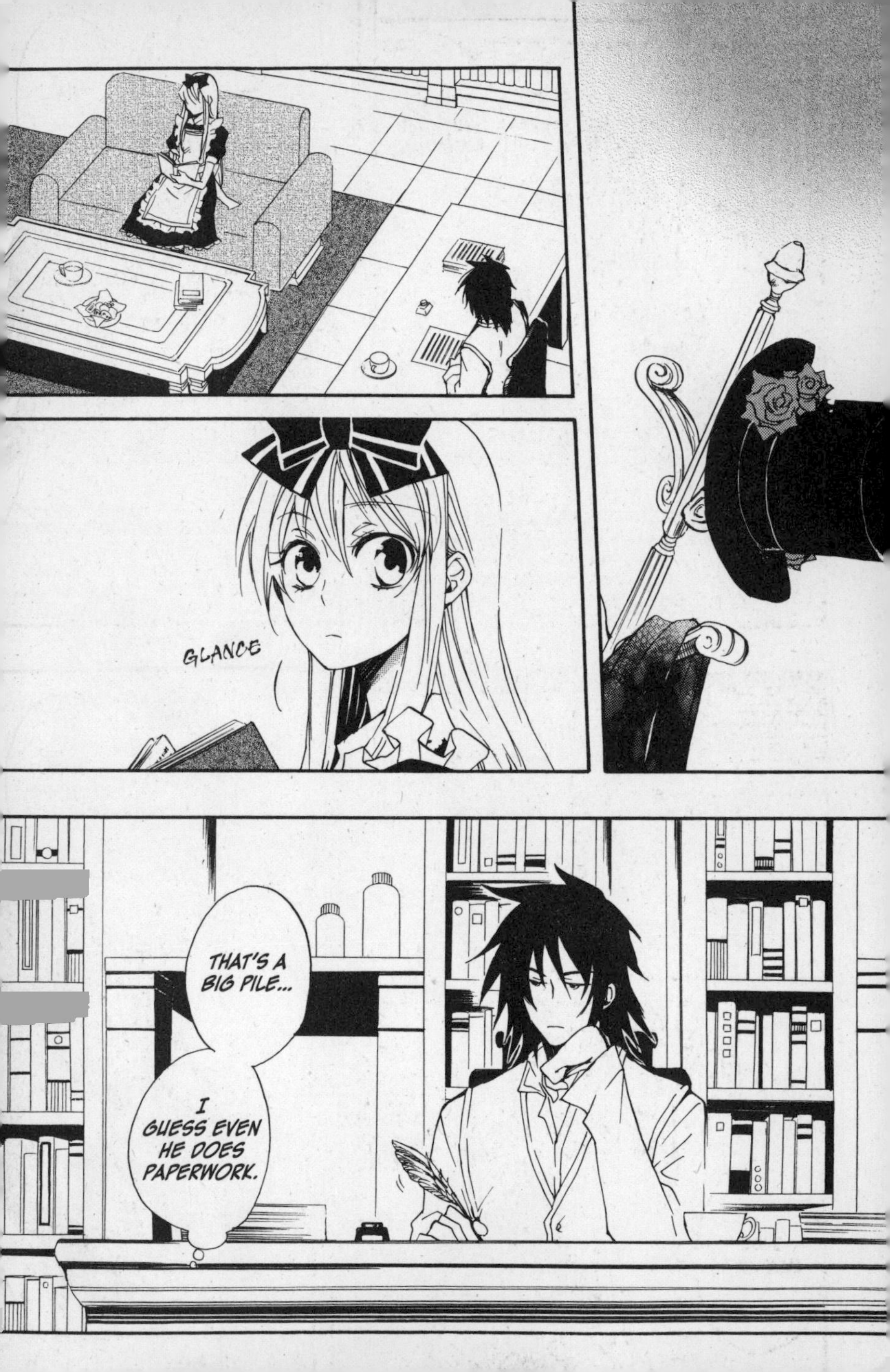
GLANCE
THAT'S A BIG PILE...
I GUESS EVEN HE DOES PAPERWORK.

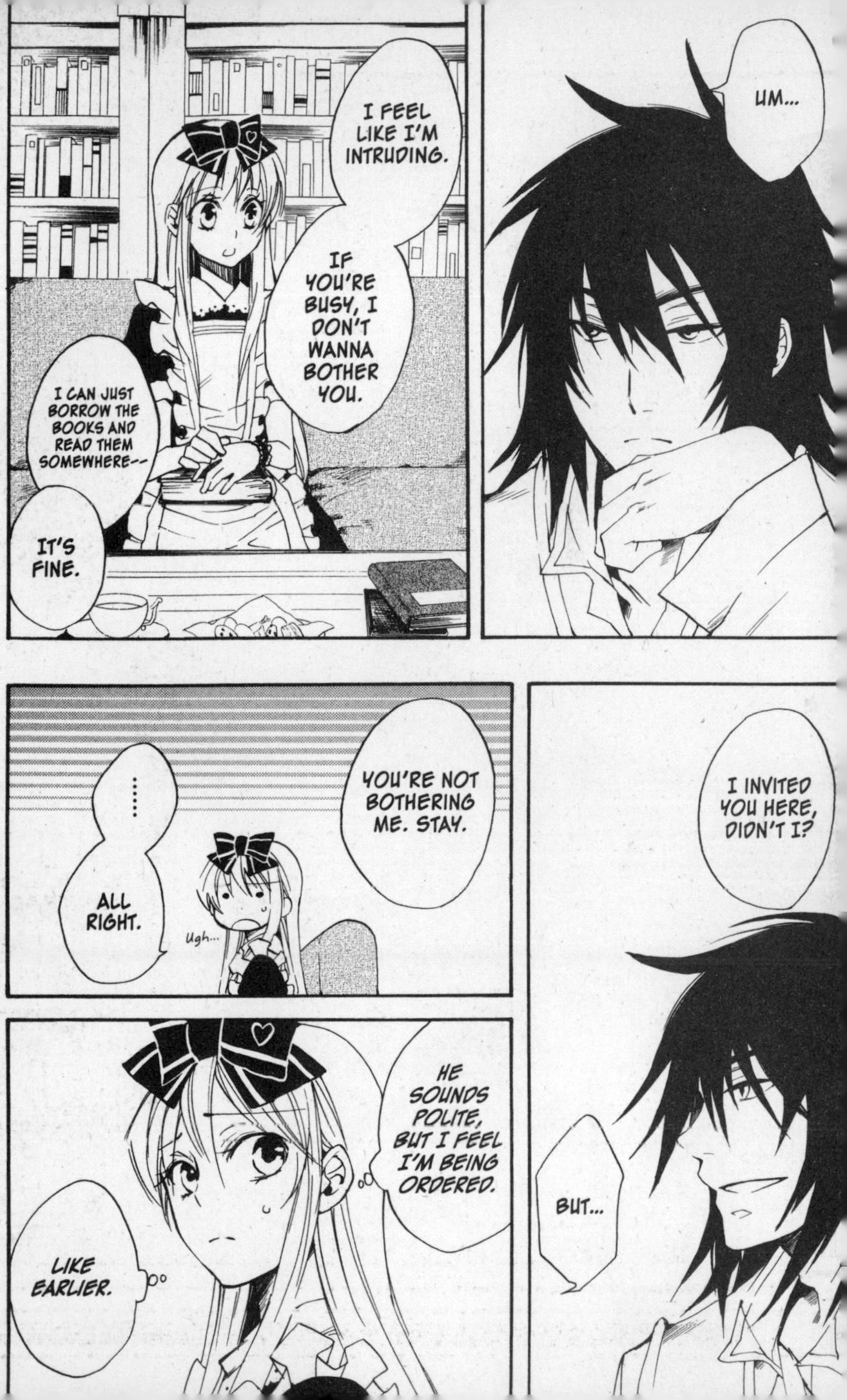
UM...
I FEEL LIKE I'M INTRUDING.
IF YOU'RE BUSY, I DON'T WANNA BOTHER YOU.
I CAN JUST BORROW THE BOOKS AND READ THEM SOMEWHERE--
IT'S FINE.
I INVITED YOU HERE, DIDN'T I?
BUT...
YOU'RE NOT BOTHERING ME. STAY.
......
ALL RIGHT.
Ugh...
HE SOUNDS POLITE, BUT I FEEL I'M BEING ORDERED.
LIKE EARLIER.

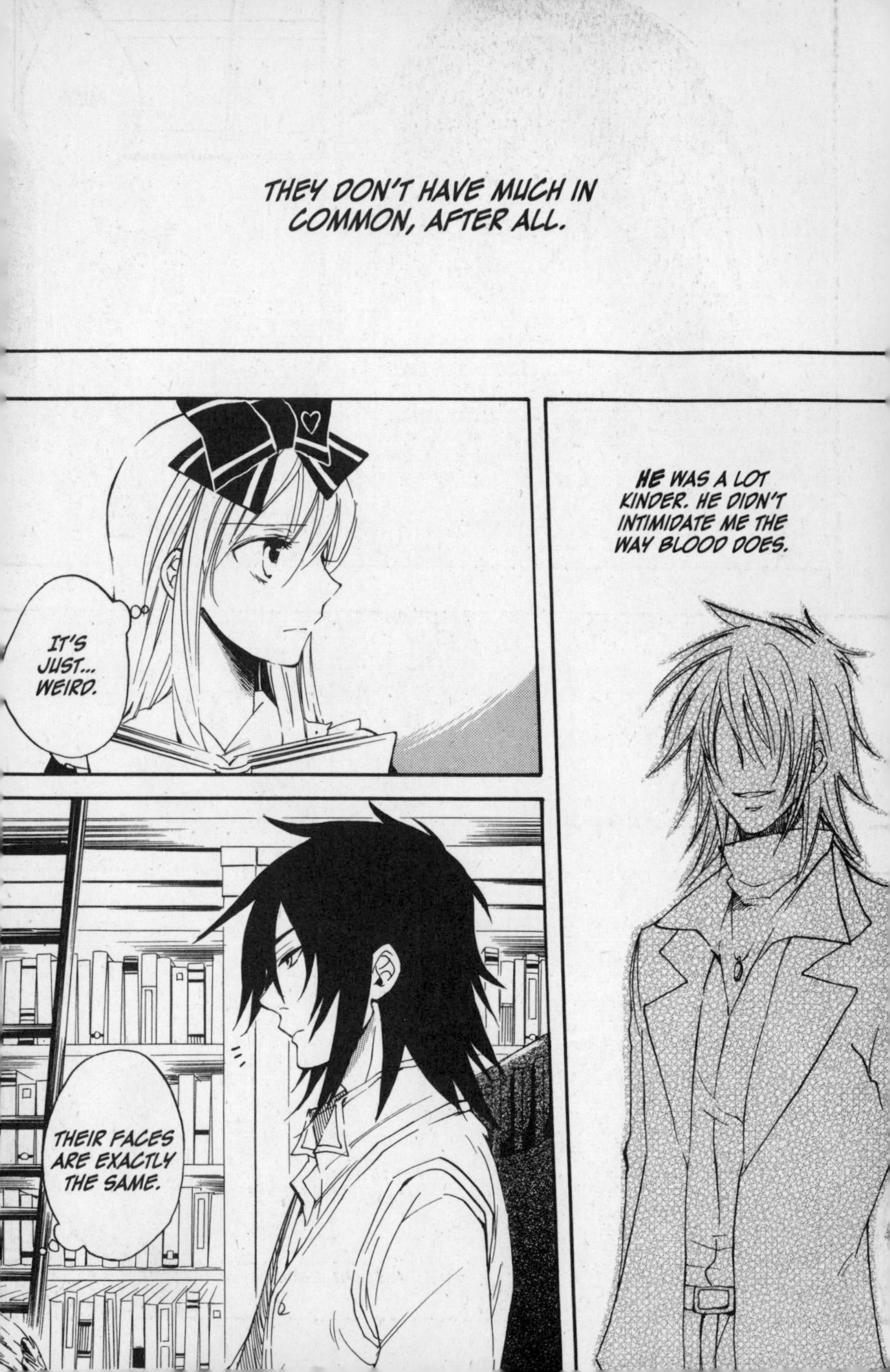
THEY DON'T HAVE MUCH IN COMMON, AFTER ALL.
HE WAS A LOT KINDER. HE DIDN'T INTIMIDATE ME THE WAY BLOOD DOES.
IT'S JUST... WEIRD.
THEIR FACES ARE EXACTLY THE SAME.

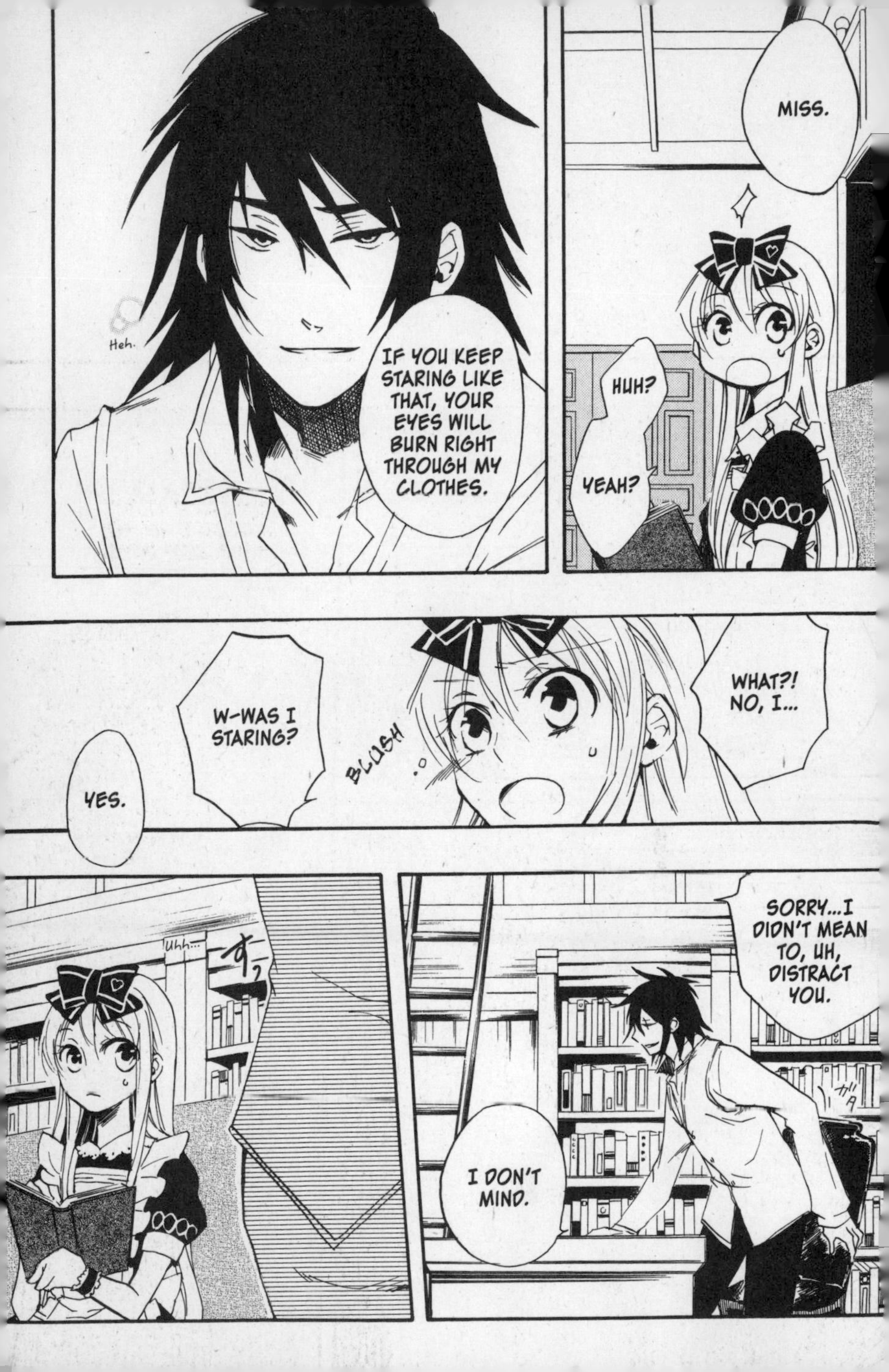
MISS.
HUH?
YEAH?
IF YOU KEEP STARING LIKE THAT, YOUR EYES WILL BURN RIGHT THROUGH MY CLOTHES.
Heh.
WHAT?! NO, I...
BLUSH
W-WAS I STARING?
YES.
SORRY...I DIDN'T MEAN TO, UH, DISTRACT YOU.
ガタ
I DON'T MIND.
す
Uhh...

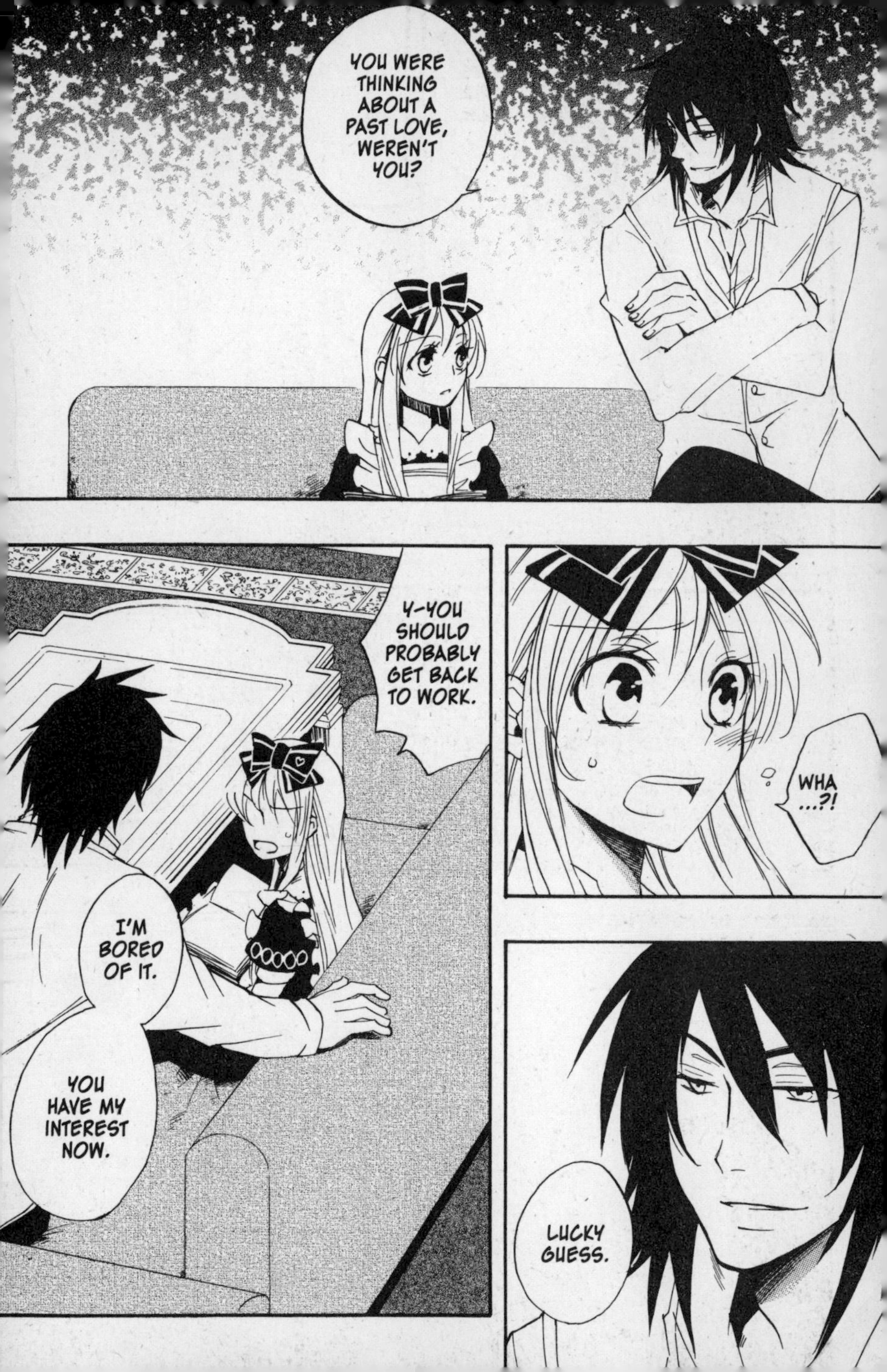
YOU WERE THINKING ABOUT A PAST LOVE, WEREN'T YOU?
WHA ...?!
LUCKY GUESS.
Y-YOU SHOULD PROBABLY GET BACK TO WORK.
I'M BORED OF IT.
YOU HAVE MY INTEREST NOW.

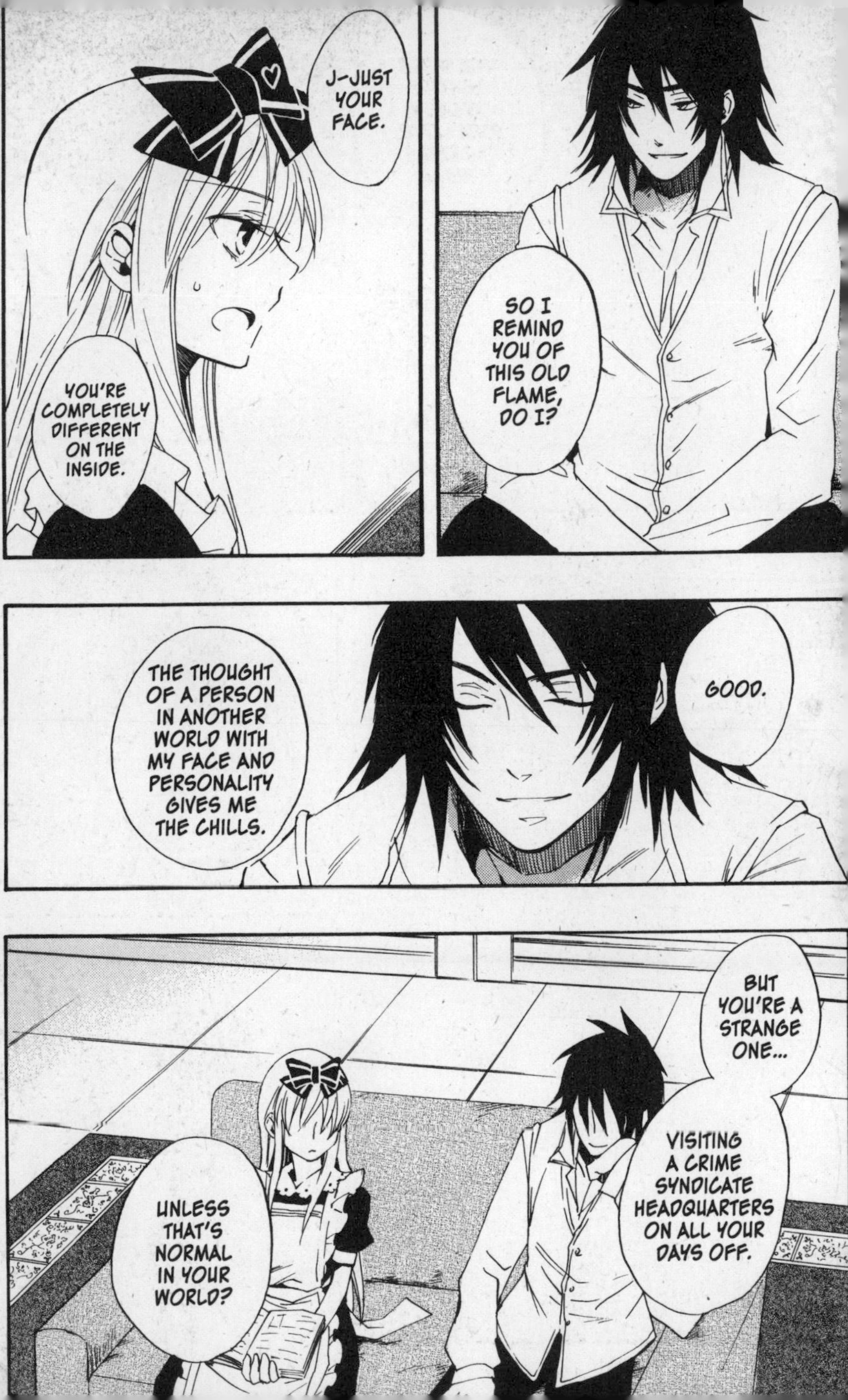
SO I REMIND YOU OF THIS OLD FLAME, DO I?
J-JUST YOUR FACE.
YOU'RE COMPLETELY DIFFERENT ON THE INSIDE.
GOOD.
THE THOUGHT OF A PERSON IN ANOTHER WORLD WITH MY FACE AND PERSONALITY GIVES ME THE CHILLS.
BUT YOU'RE A STRANGE ONE...
VISITING A CRIME SYNDICATE HEADQUARTERS ON ALL YOUR DAYS OFF.
UNLESS THAT'S NORMAL IN YOUR WORLD?

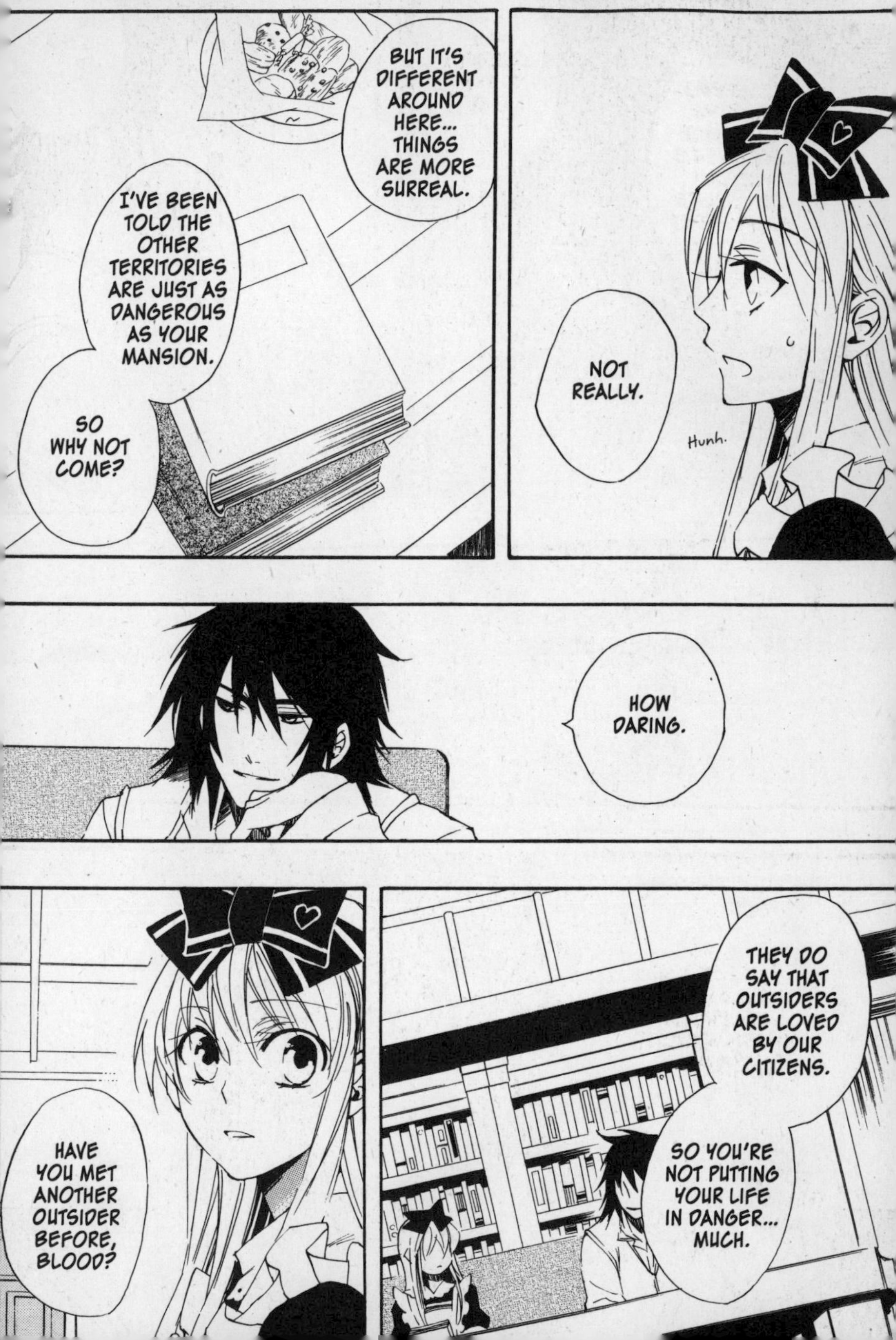
NOT REALLY.
Hunh.
BUT IT'S DIFFERENT AROUND HERE... THINGS ARE MORE SURREAL.
I'VE BEEN TOLD THE OTHER TERRITORIES ARE JUST AS DANGEROUS AS YOUR MANSION.
SO WHY NOT COME?
HOW DARING.
THEY DO SAY THAT OUTSIDERS ARE LOVED BY OUR CITIZENS.
SO YOU'RE NOT PUTTING YOUR LIFE IN DANGER... MUCH.
HAVE YOU MET ANOTHER OUTSIDER BEFORE, BLOOD?

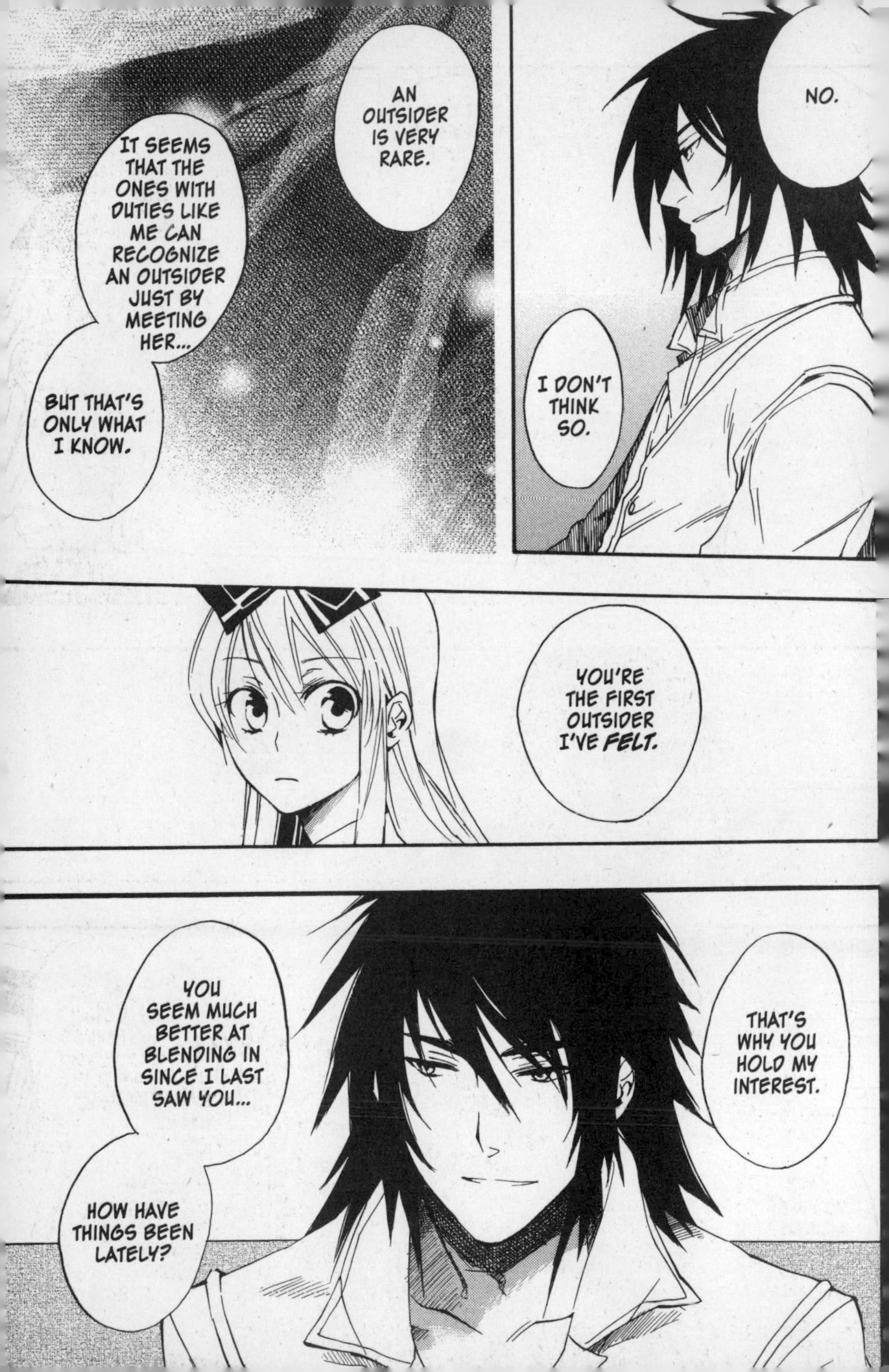
NO.
I DON'T THINK SO.
AN OUTSIDER IS VERY RARE.
IT SEEMS THAT THE ONES WITH DUTIES LIKE ME CAN RECOGNIZE AN OUTSIDER JUST BY MEETING HER...
BUT THAT'S ONLY WHAT I KNOW.
YOU'RE THE FIRST OUTSIDER I'VE *FELT.*
THAT'S WHY YOU HOLD MY INTEREST.
YOU SEEM MUCH BETTER AT BLENDING IN SINCE I LAST SAW YOU...
HOW HAVE THINGS BEEN LATELY?

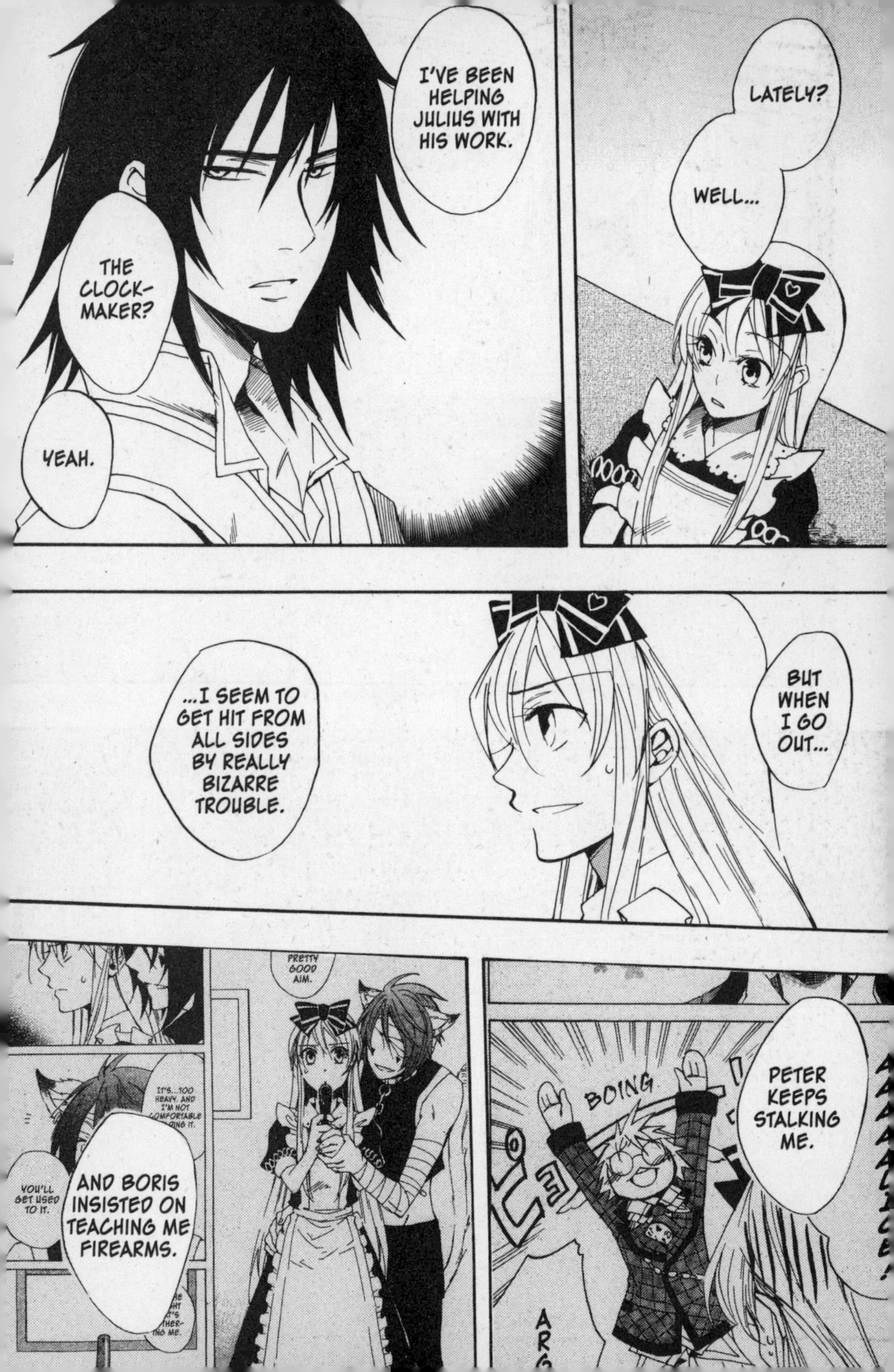
LATELY?
WELL...
I'VE BEEN HELPING JULIUS WITH HIS WORK.
THE CLOCK-MAKER?
YEAH.
BUT WHEN I GO OUT...
...I SEEM TO GET HIT FROM ALL SIDES BY REALLY BIZARRE TROUBLE.
AAAAALICE!
PETER KEEPS STALKING ME.
BOING
PRETTY GOOD AIM.
IT'S...TOO HEAVY. AND I'M NOT COMFORTABLE
AND BORIS INSISTED ON TEACHING ME FIREARMS.
YOU'LL GET USED TO IT.

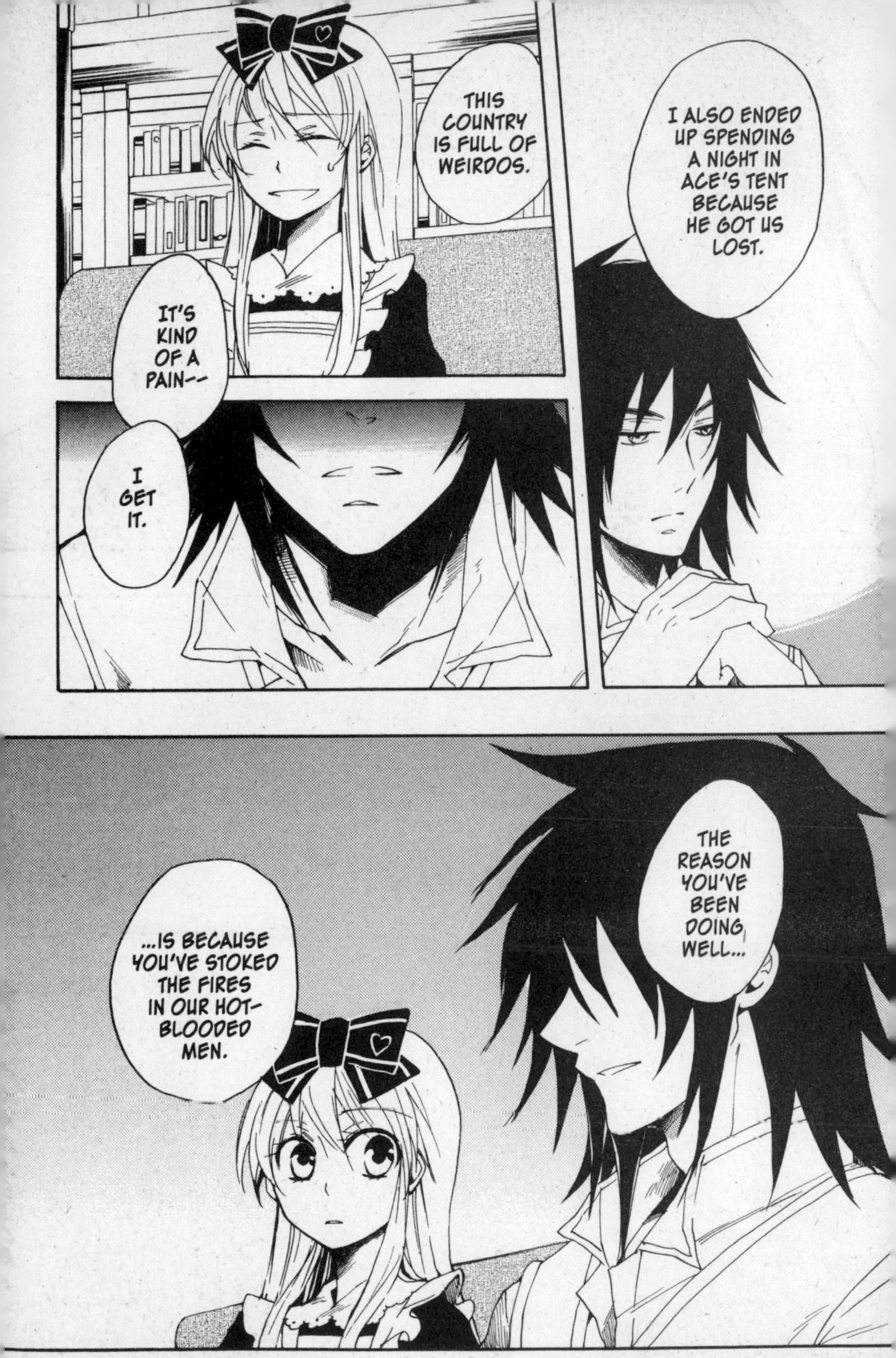
I ALSO ENDED UP SPENDING A NIGHT IN ACE'S TENT BECAUSE HE GOT US LOST.
THIS COUNTRY IS FULL OF WEIRDOS.
IT'S KIND OF A PAIN--
I GET IT.
THE REASON YOU'VE BEEN DOING WELL...
...IS BECAUSE YOU'VE STOKED THE FIRES IN OUR HOT-BLOODED MEN.

HMPH.

YOU'RE AWFULLY GOOD AT SPREADING YOUR HONEY.

EXCUSE ME?

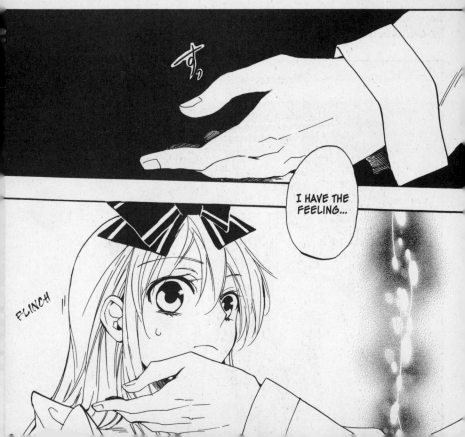

I HAVE THE FEELING...

FLINCH!!

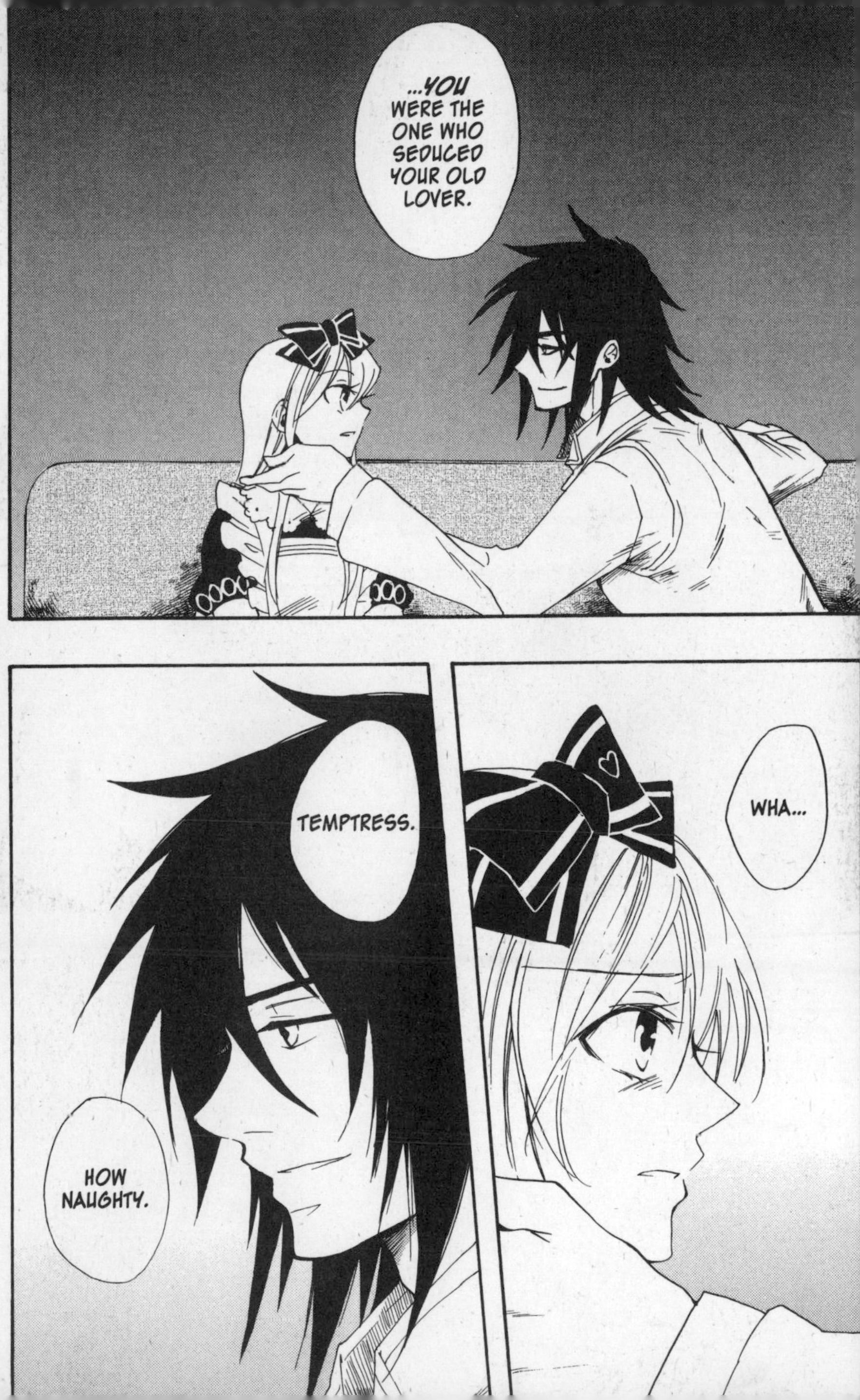
...YOU WERE THE ONE WHO SEDUCED YOUR OLD LOVER.
WHA...
TEMPTRESS.
HOW NAUGHTY.

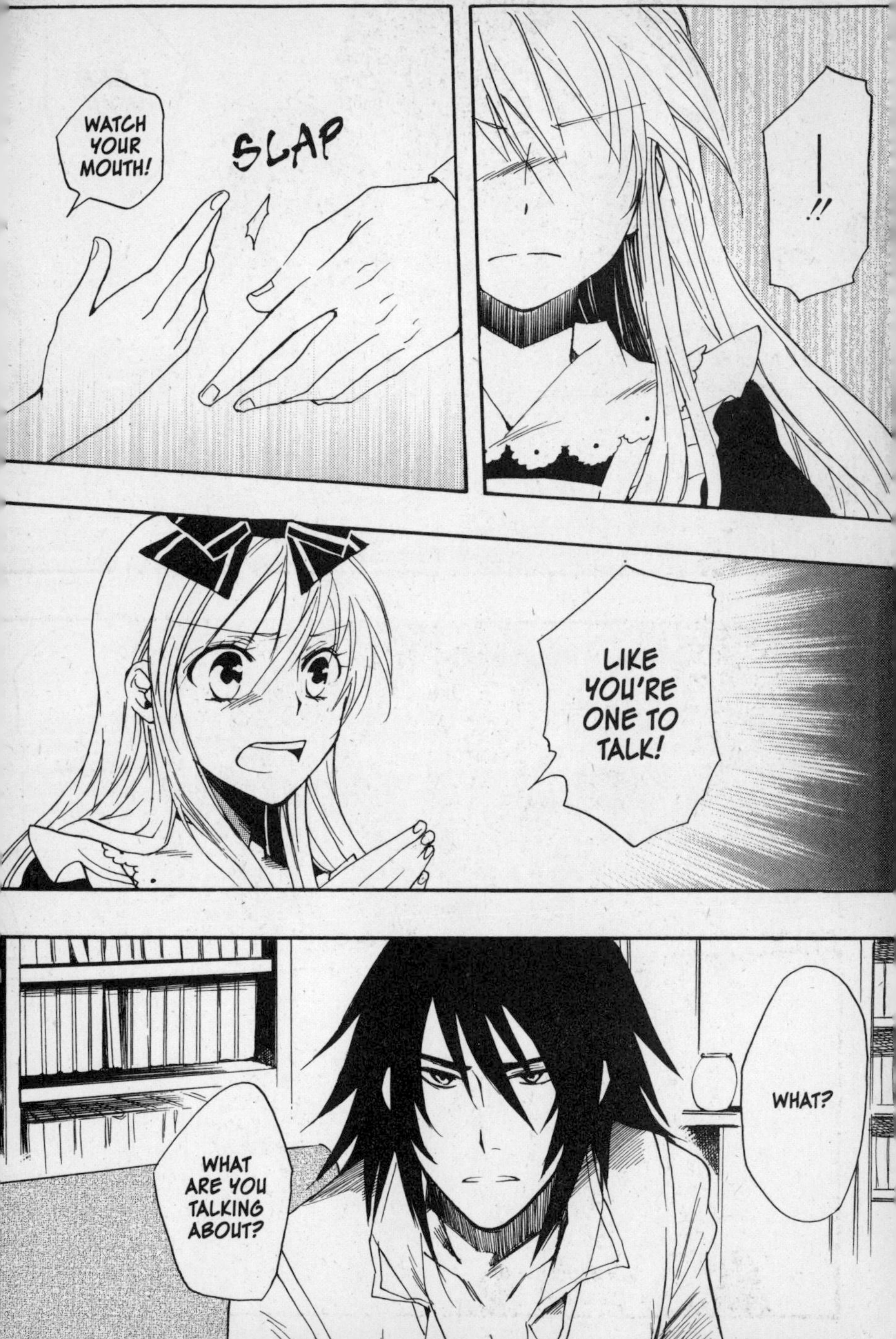
!!
SLAP
WATCH YOUR MOUTH!
LIKE YOU'RE ONE TO TALK!
WHAT?
WHAT ARE YOU TALKING ABOUT?

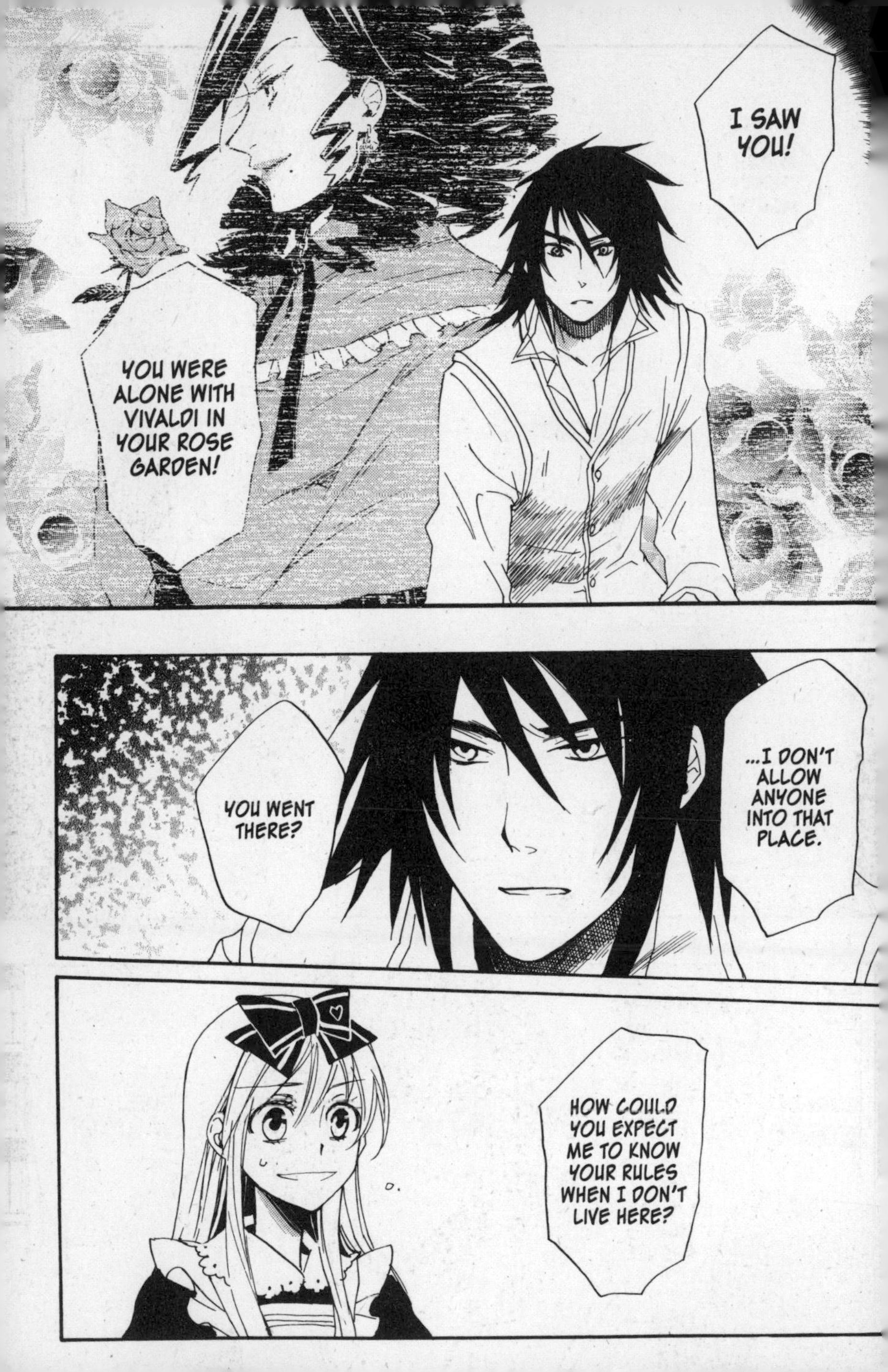
I SAW YOU!
YOU WERE ALONE WITH VIVALDI IN YOUR ROSE GARDEN!
...I DON'T ALLOW ANYONE INTO THAT PLACE.
YOU WENT THERE?
HOW COULD YOU EXPECT ME TO KNOW YOUR RULES WHEN I DON'T LIVE HERE?

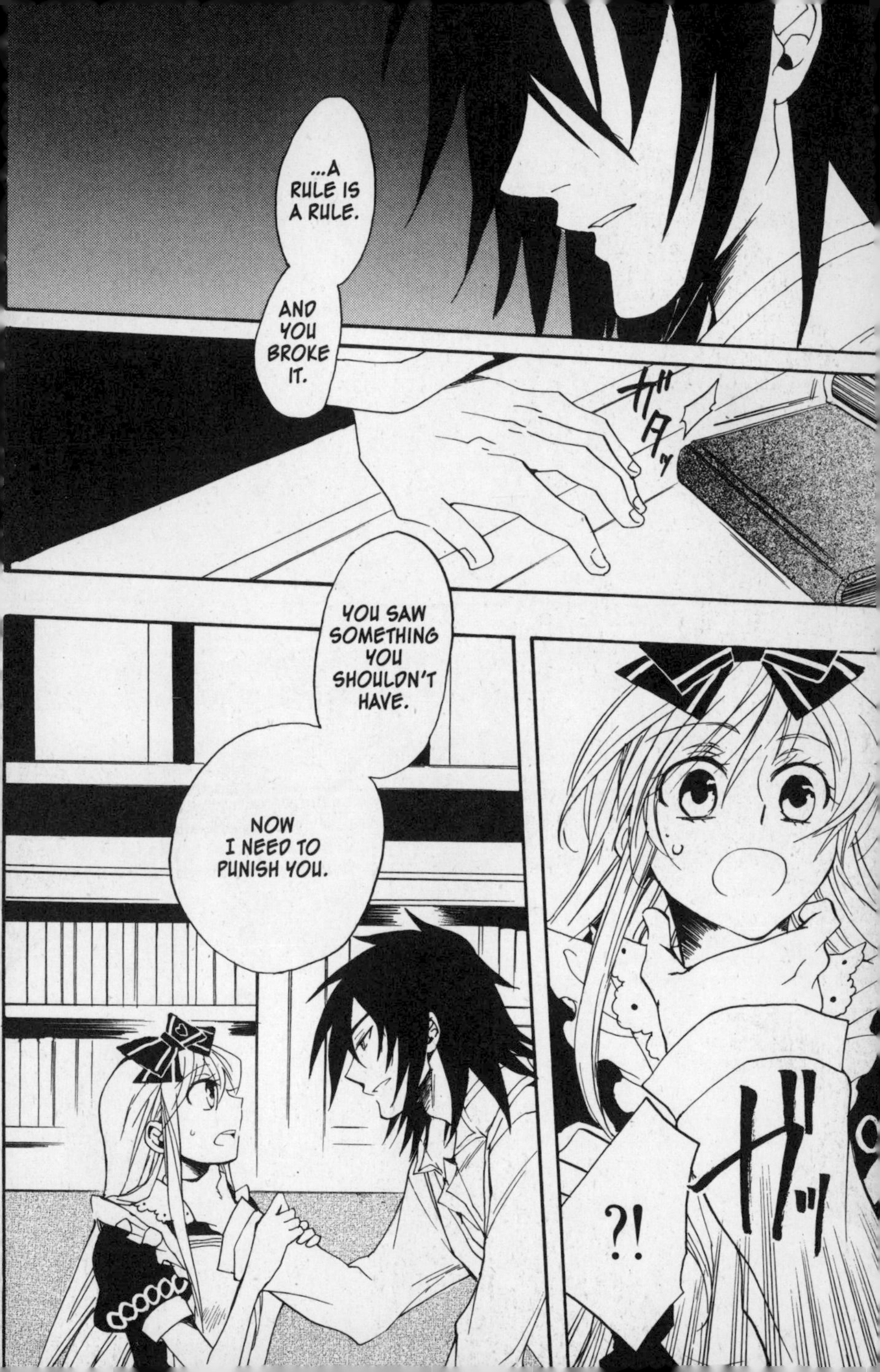
...A RULE IS A RULE.
AND YOU BROKE IT.
ガタッ
ガッ
?!
YOU SAW SOMETHING YOU SHOULDN'T HAVE.
NOW I NEED TO PUNISH YOU.

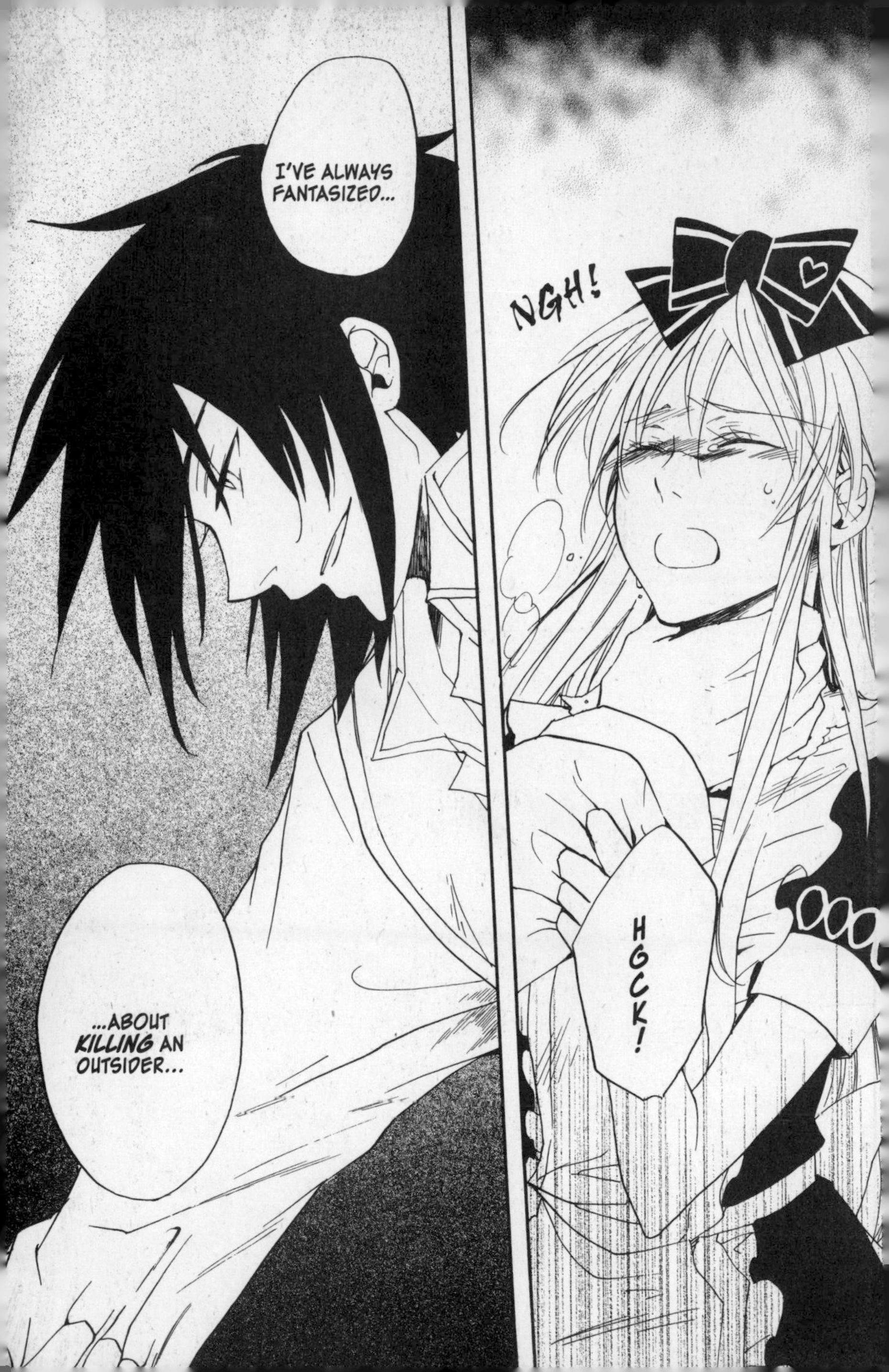
NGH!
HGCK!
I'VE ALWAYS FANTASIZED...
...ABOUT *KILLING* AN OUTSIDER...

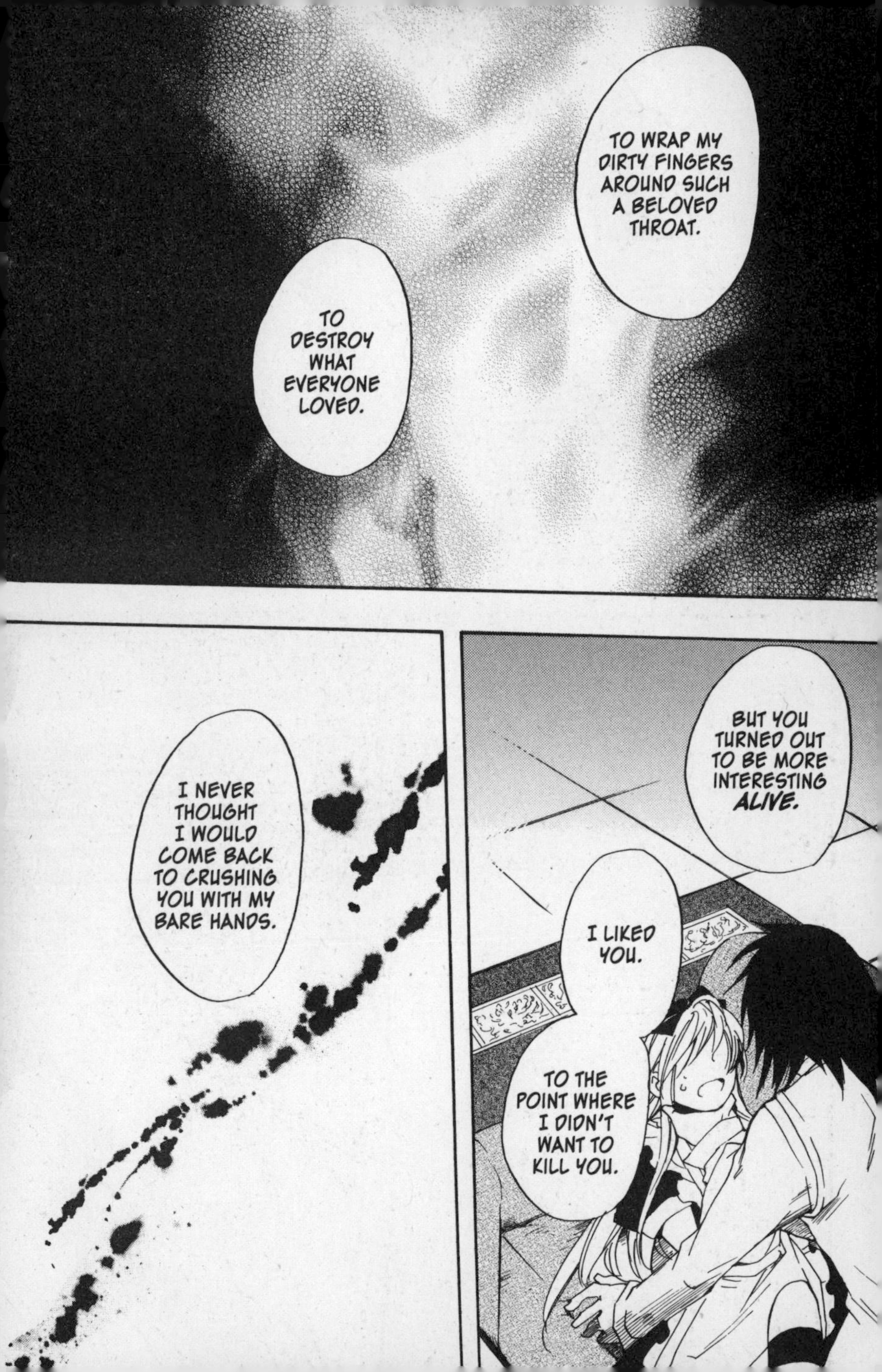
TO WRAP MY DIRTY FINGERS AROUND SUCH A BELOVED THROAT.
TO DESTROY WHAT EVERYONE LOVED.
BUT YOU TURNED OUT TO BE MORE INTERESTING *ALIVE.*
I LIKED YOU.
TO THE POINT WHERE I DIDN'T WANT TO KILL YOU.
I NEVER THOUGHT I WOULD COME BACK TO CRUSHING YOU WITH MY BARE HANDS.

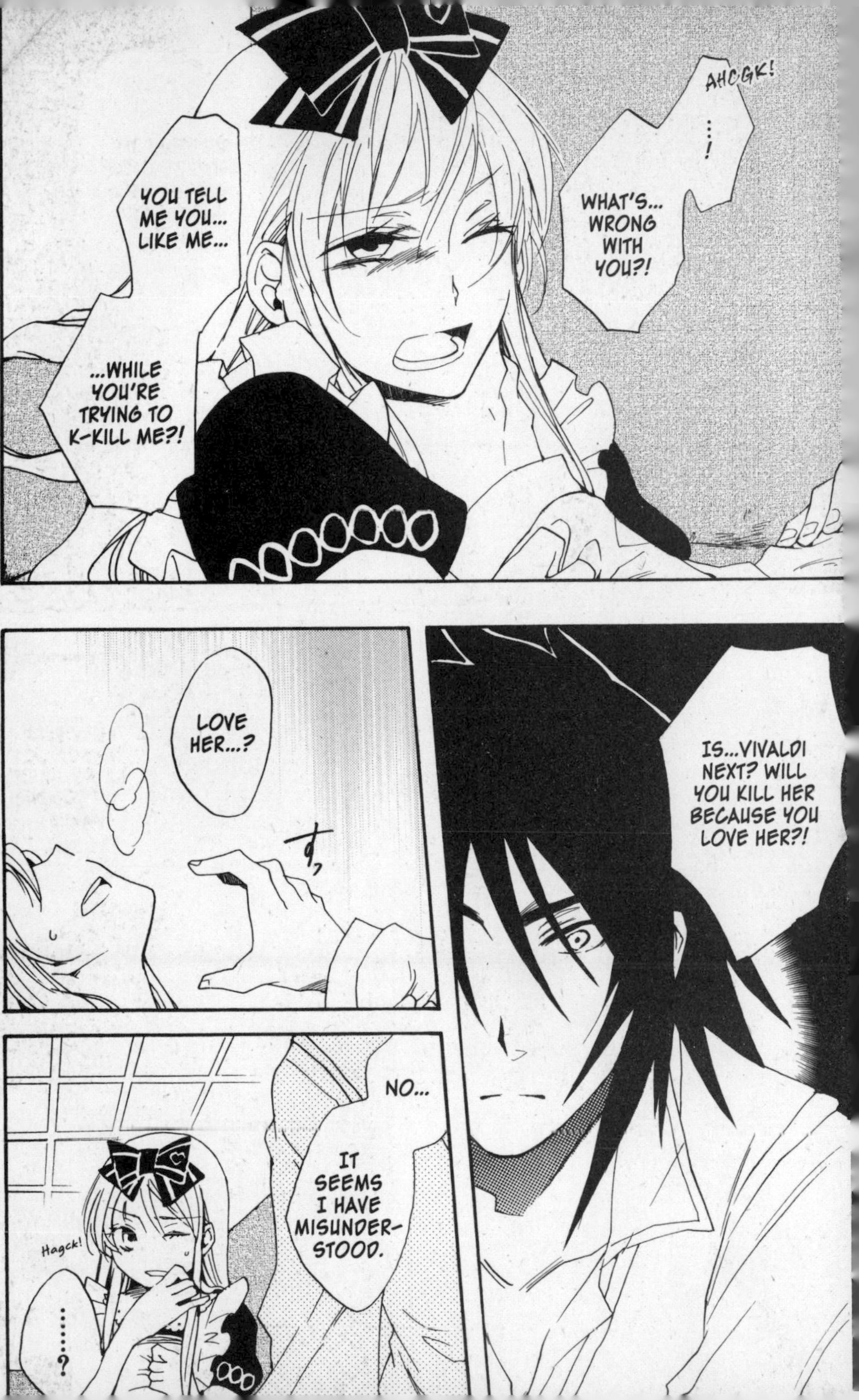
AHCGK!
...!
WHAT'S... WRONG WITH YOU?!
YOU TELL ME YOU... LIKE ME...
...WHILE YOU'RE TRYING TO K-KILL ME?!
IS...VIVALDI NEXT? WILL YOU KILL HER BECAUSE YOU LOVE HER?!
LOVE HER...?
NO...
IT SEEMS I HAVE MISUNDER-STOOD.
Hagck!
......?

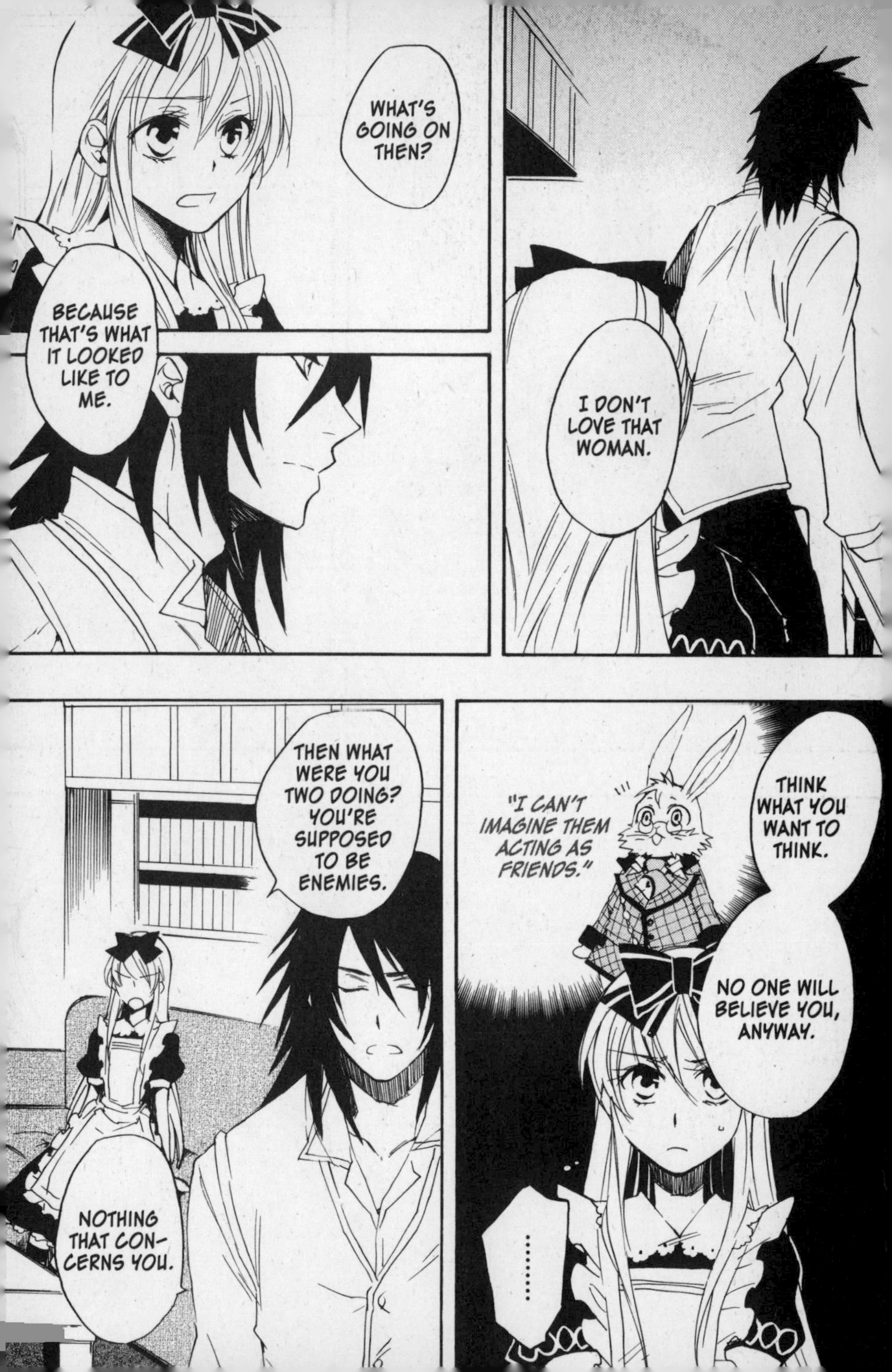
I DON'T LOVE THAT WOMAN.
WHAT'S GOING ON THEN?
BECAUSE THAT'S WHAT IT LOOKED LIKE TO ME.
THINK WHAT YOU WANT TO THINK.
"I CAN'T IMAGINE THEM ACTING AS FRIENDS."
NO ONE WILL BELIEVE YOU, ANYWAY.
......
THEN WHAT WERE YOU TWO DOING? YOU'RE SUPPOSED TO BE ENEMIES.
NOTHING THAT CONCERNS YOU.

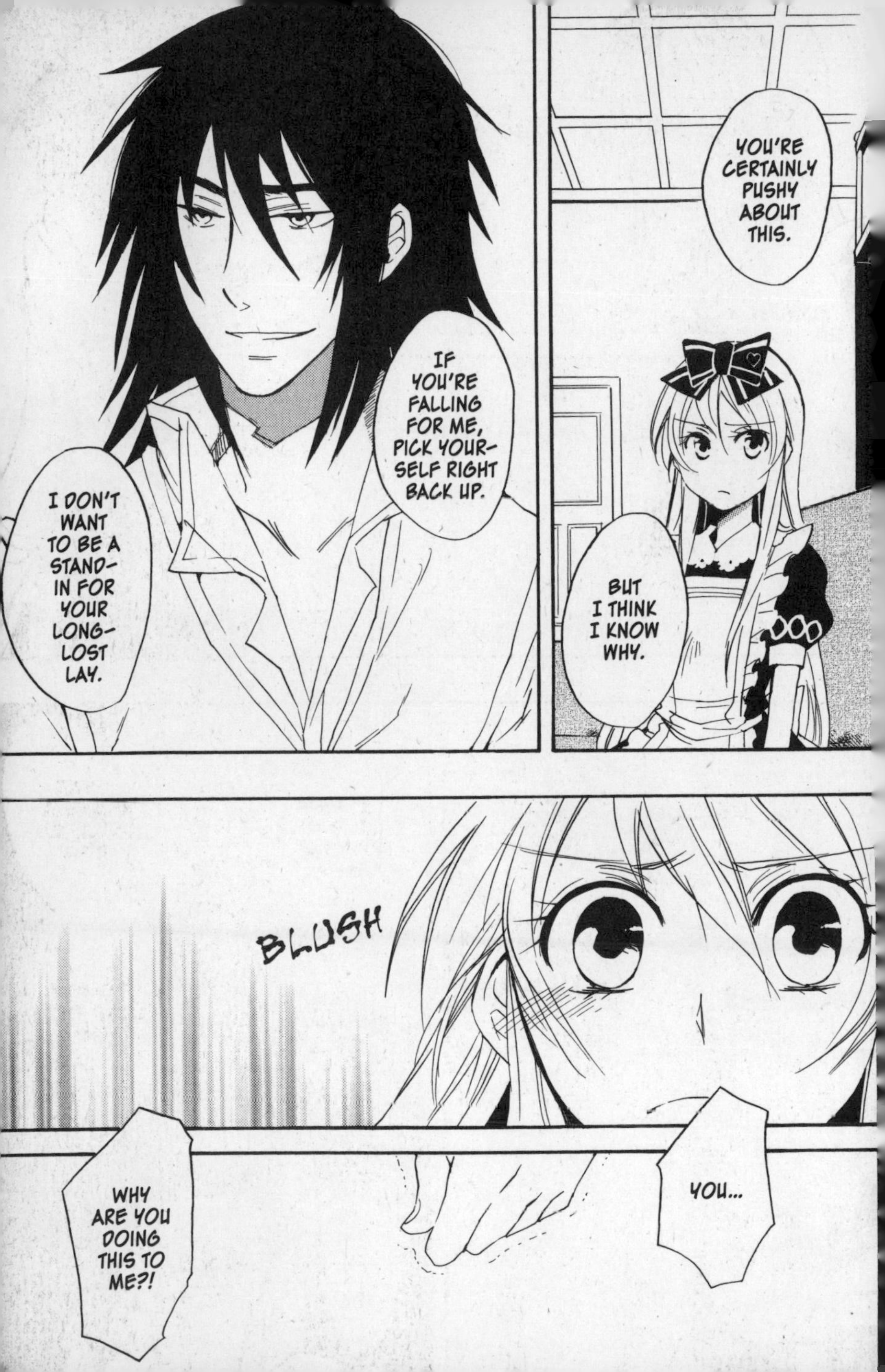
YOU'RE CERTAINLY PUSHY ABOUT THIS.
BUT I THINK I KNOW WHY.
IF YOU'RE FALLING FOR ME, PICK YOUR-SELF RIGHT BACK UP.
I DON'T WANT TO BE A STAND-IN FOR YOUR LONG-LOST LAY.
BLUSH
YOU...
WHY ARE YOU DOING THIS TO ME?!

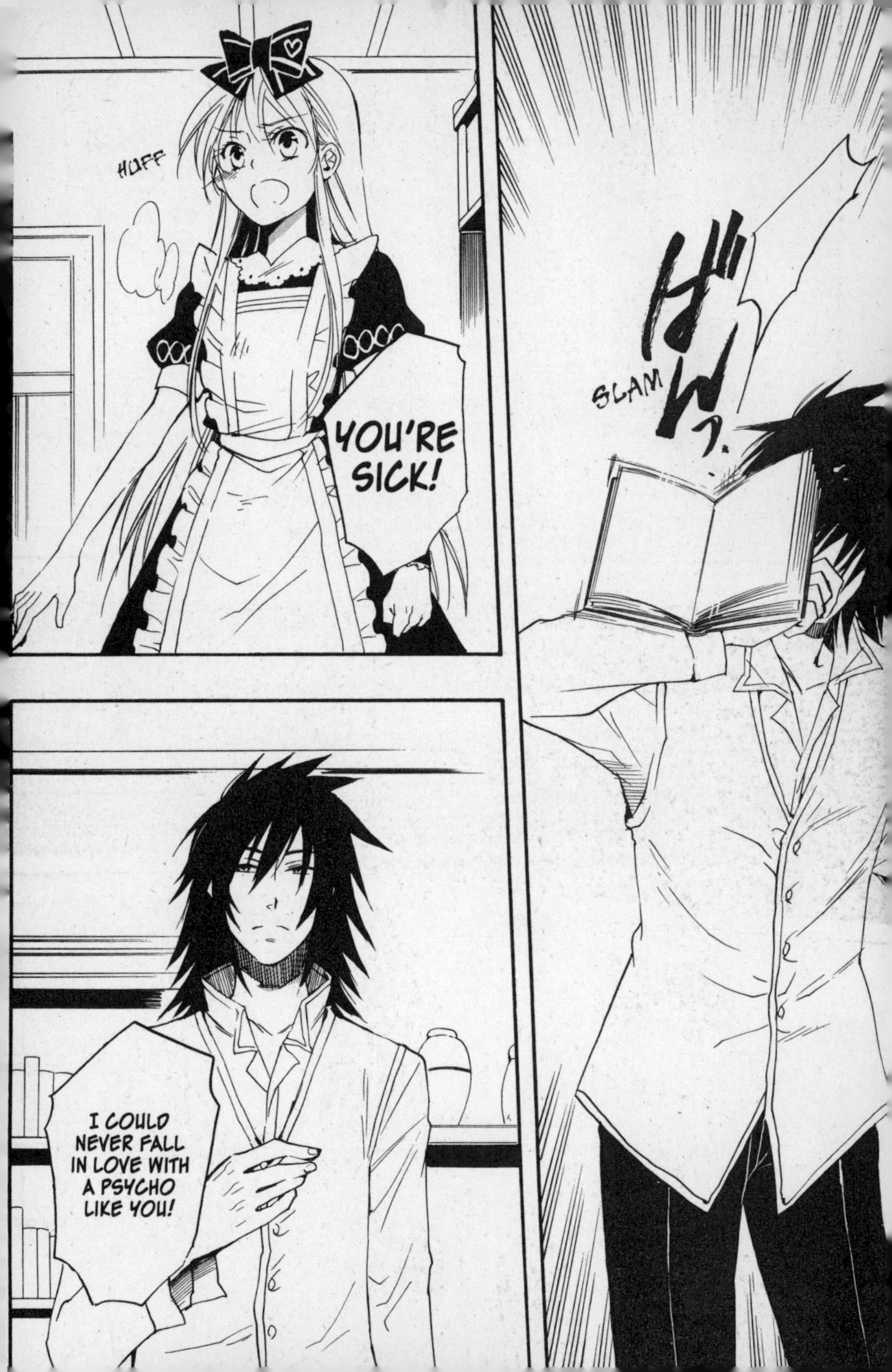
SLAM
HUFF
YOU'RE SICK!
I COULD NEVER FALL IN LOVE WITH A PSYCHO LIKE YOU!

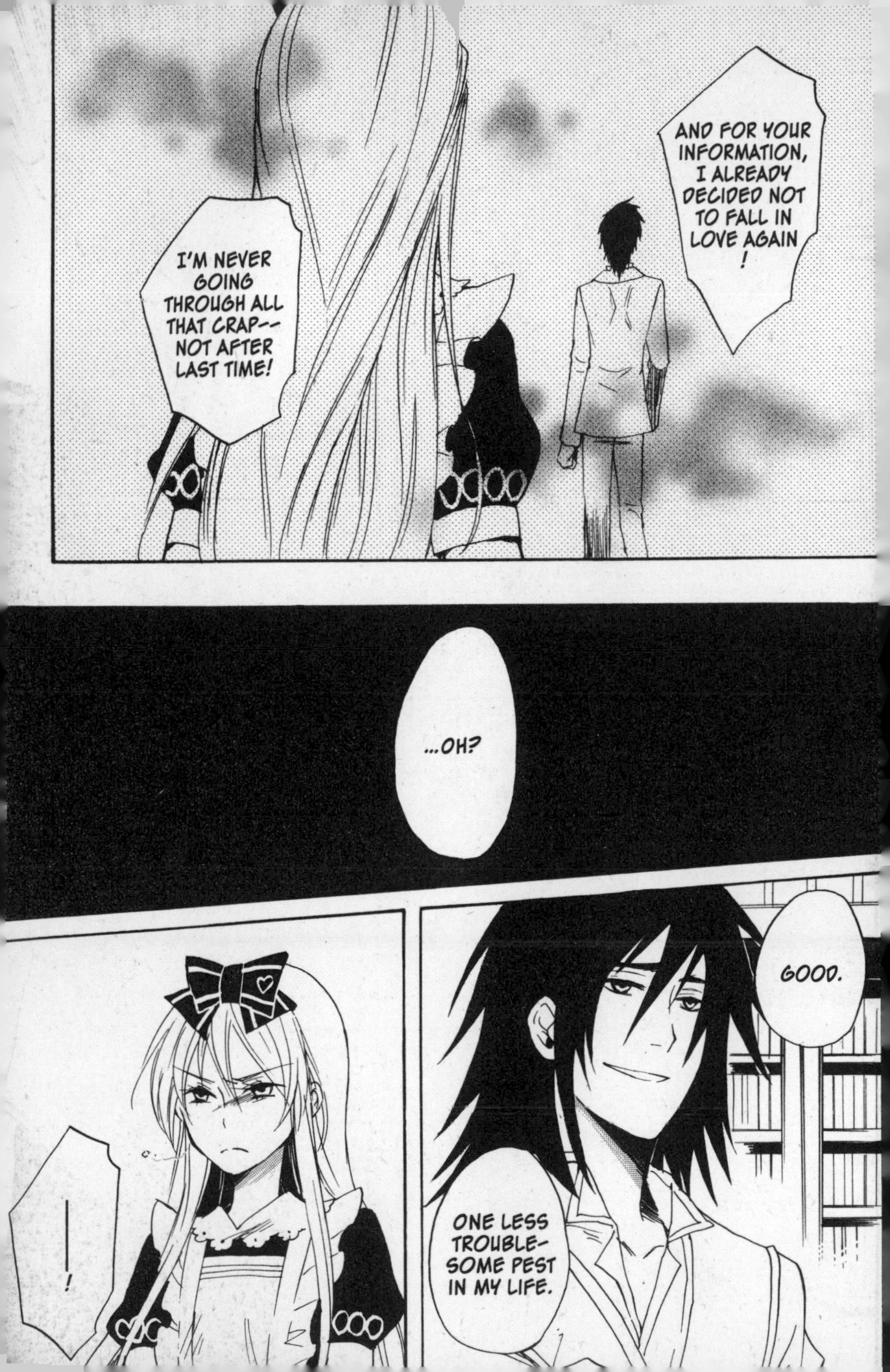
AND FOR YOUR INFORMATION, I ALREADY DECIDED NOT TO FALL IN LOVE AGAIN!
I'M NEVER GOING THROUGH ALL THAT CRAP--NOT AFTER LAST TIME!
...OH?
GOOD.
ONE LESS TROUBLE-SOME PEST IN MY LIFE.
--!

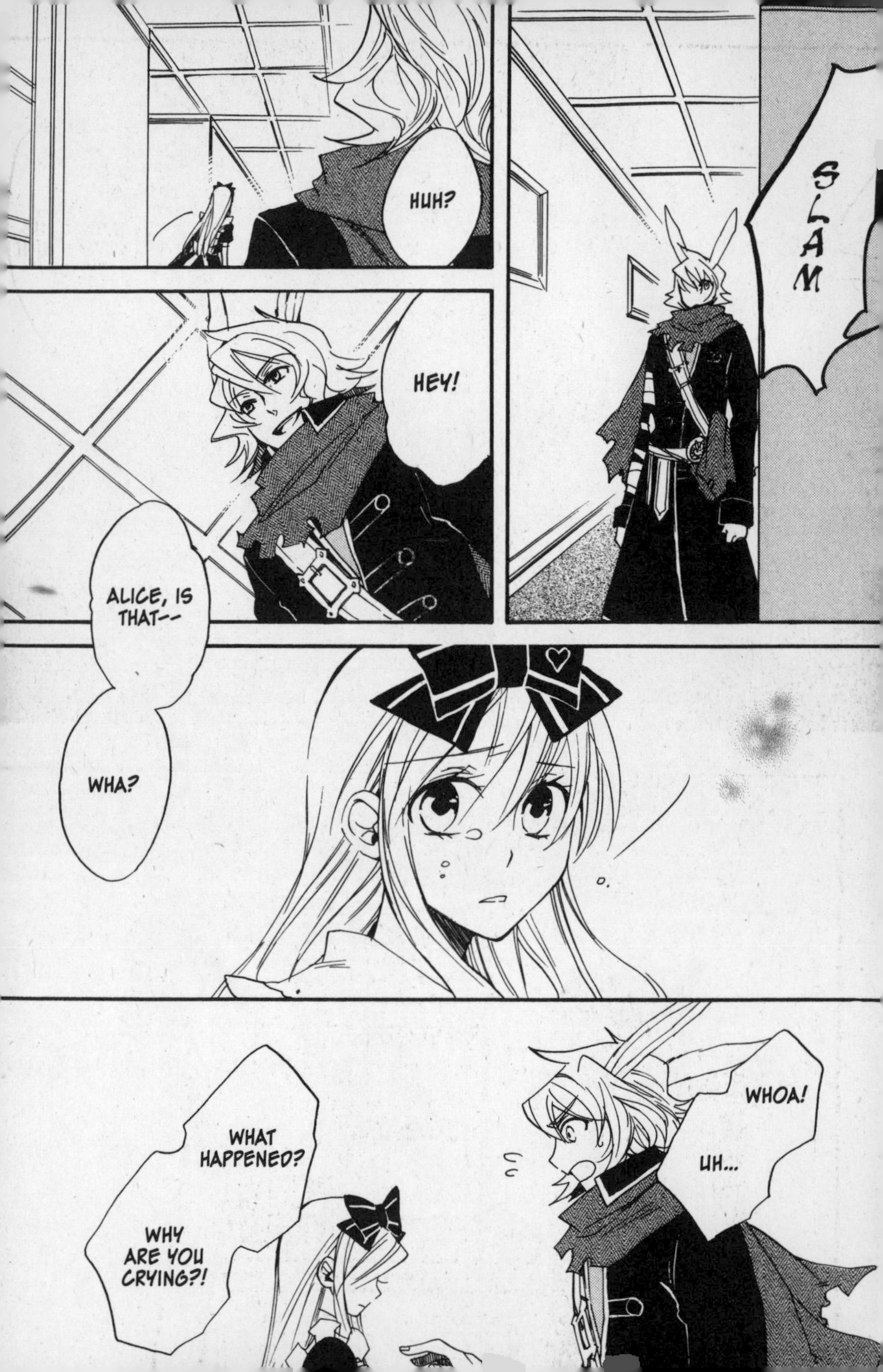
SLAM
HUH?
HEY!
ALICE, IS THAT--
WHA?
WHOA!
UH...
WHAT HAPPENED?
WHY ARE YOU CRYING?!

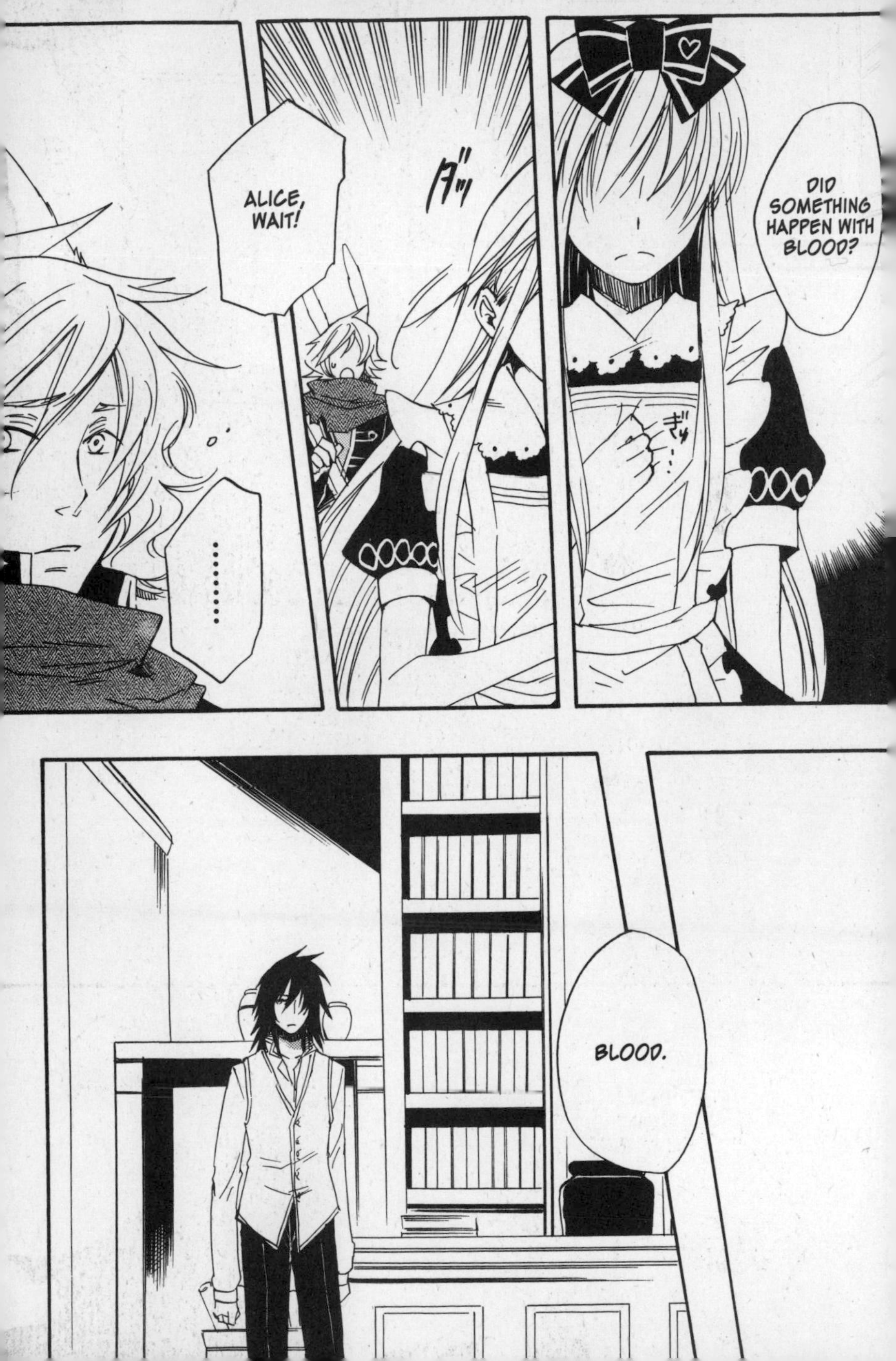
DID SOMETHING HAPPEN WITH BLOOD?
ぎゅ…
ダッ
ALICE, WAIT!
……
BLOOD.

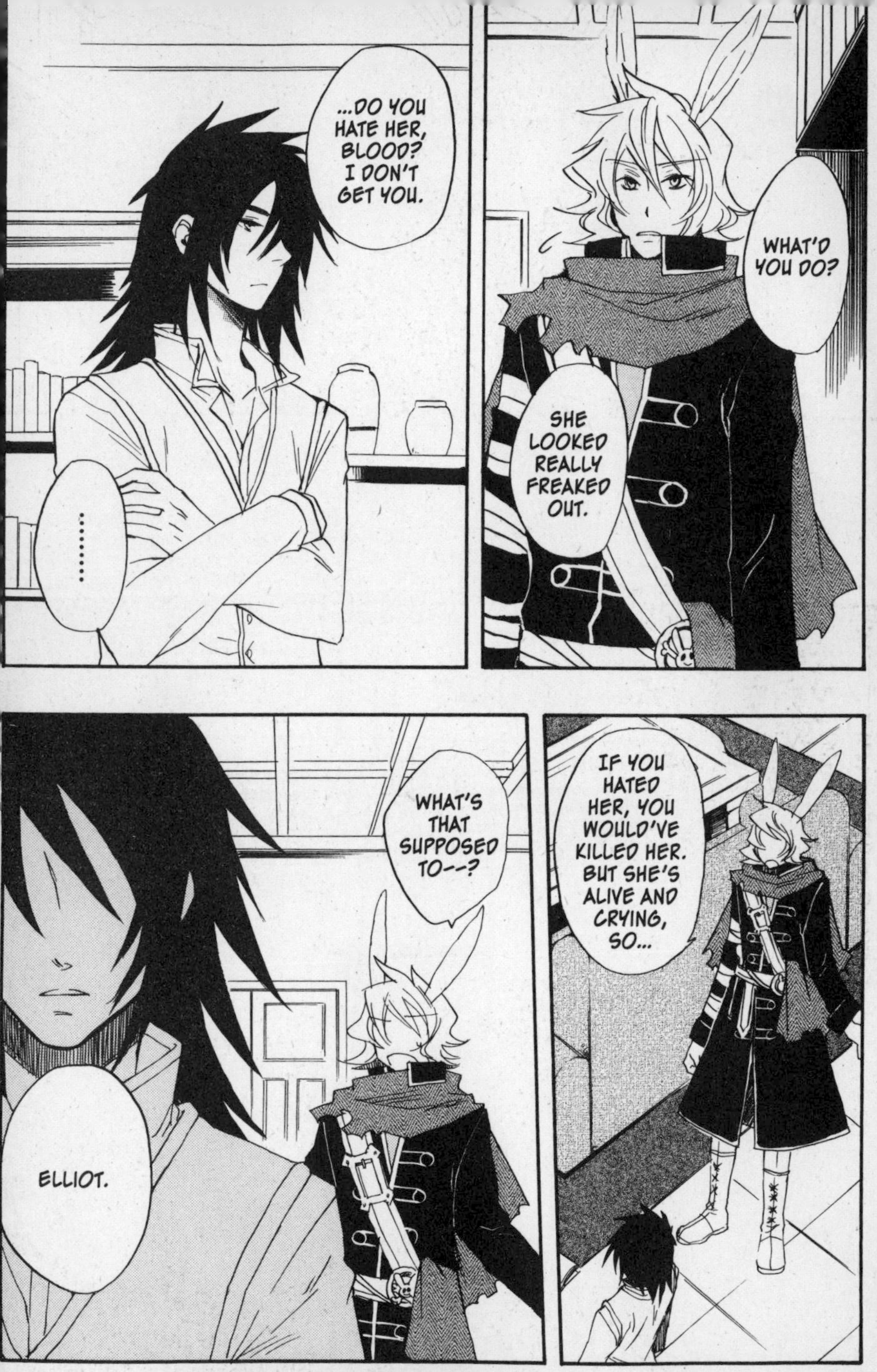
WHAT'D YOU DO?
SHE LOOKED REALLY FREAKED OUT.
...DO YOU HATE HER, BLOOD? I DON'T GET YOU.
......
IF YOU HATED HER, YOU WOULD'VE KILLED HER. BUT SHE'S ALIVE AND CRYING, SO...
WHAT'S THAT SUPPOSED TO--?
ELLIOT.

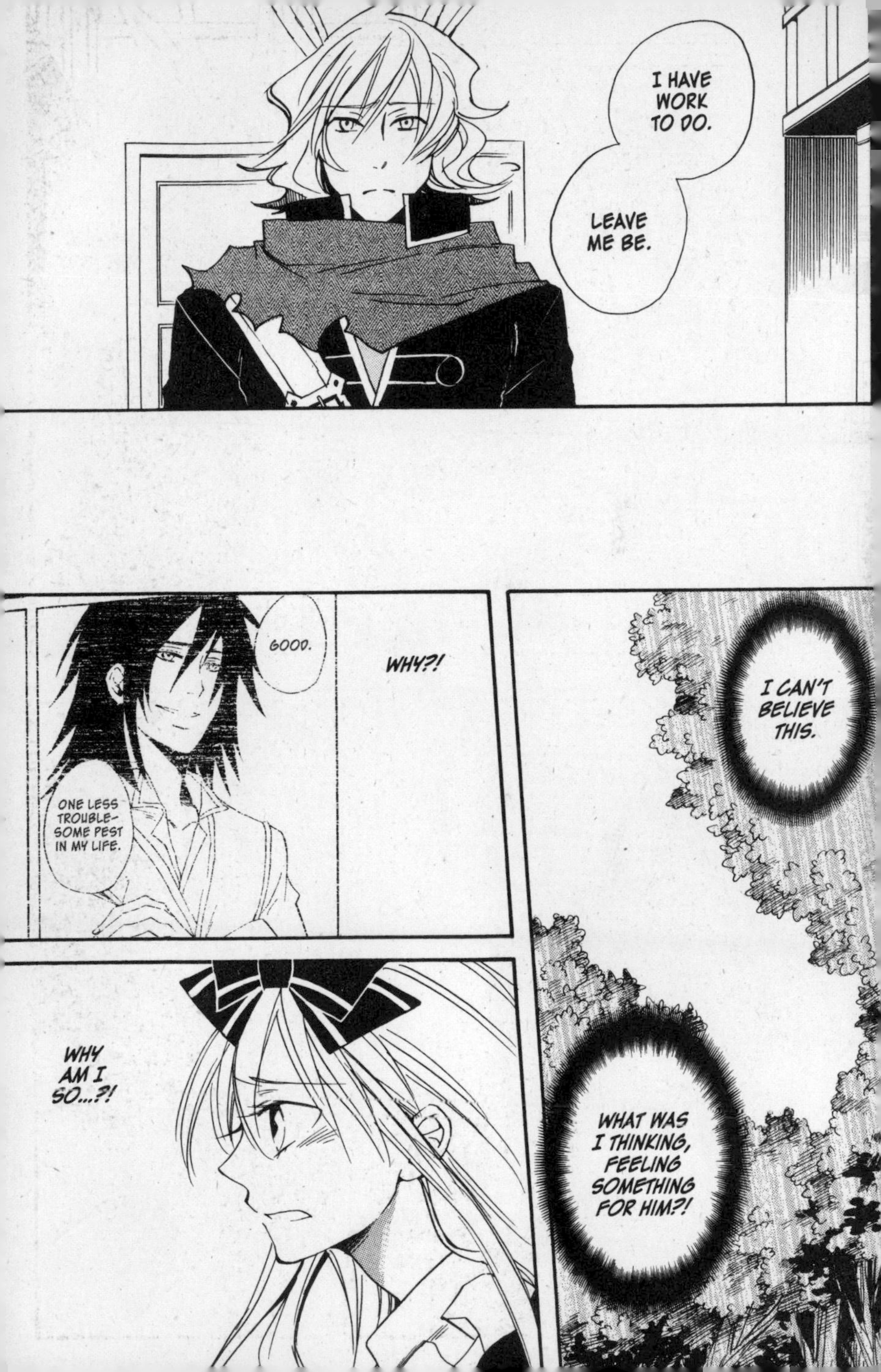
I HAVE WORK TO DO.
LEAVE ME BE.
I CAN'T BELIEVE THIS.
WHAT WAS I THINKING, FEELING SOMETHING FOR HIM?!
WHY?!
GOOD.
ONE LESS TROUBLE-SOME PEST IN MY LIFE.
WHY AM I SO...?!

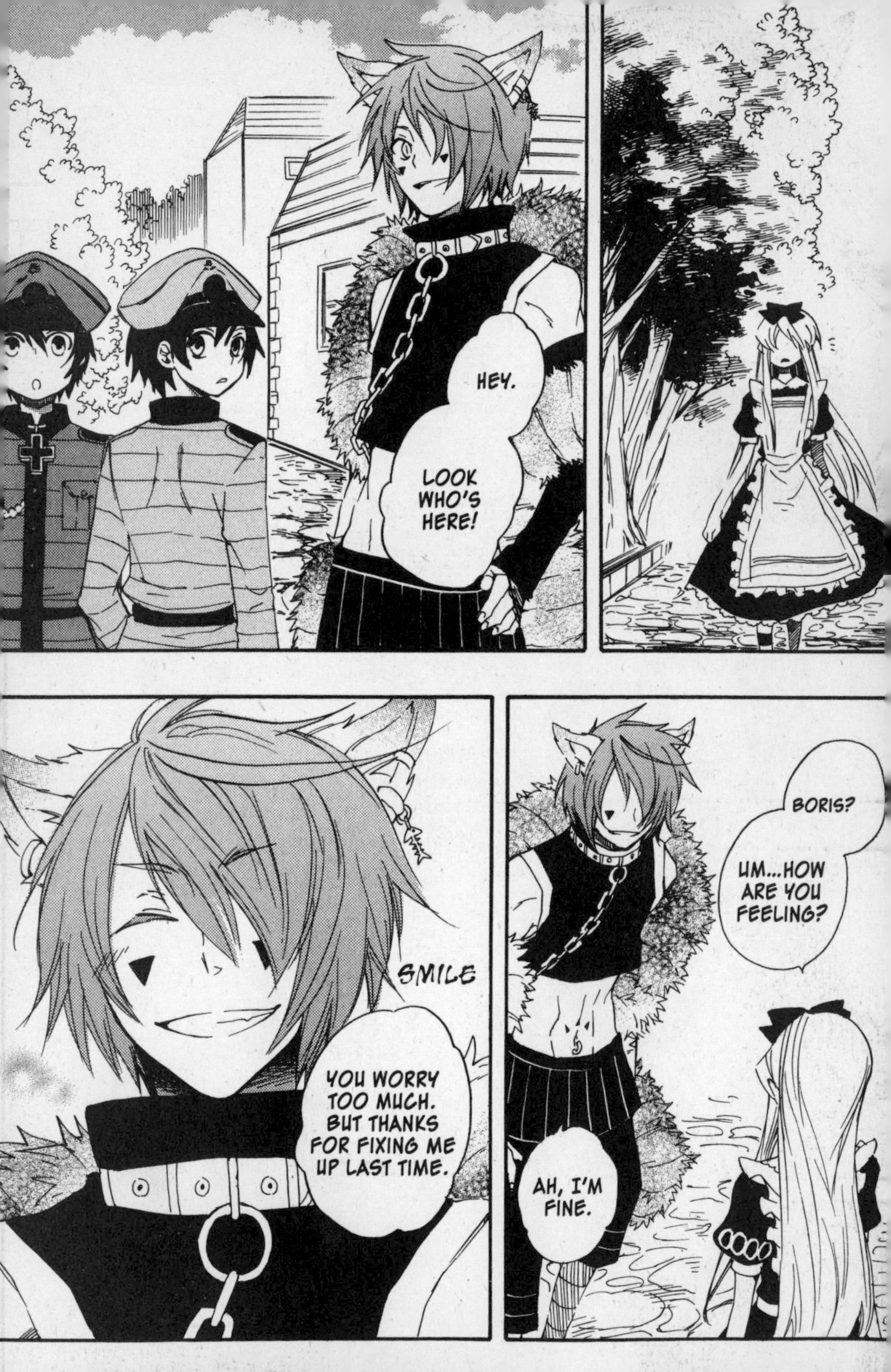
HEY.
LOOK WHO'S HERE!
BORIS?
UM...HOW ARE YOU FEELING?
AH, I'M FINE.
SMILE
YOU WORRY TOO MUCH. BUT THANKS FOR FIXING ME UP LAST TIME.

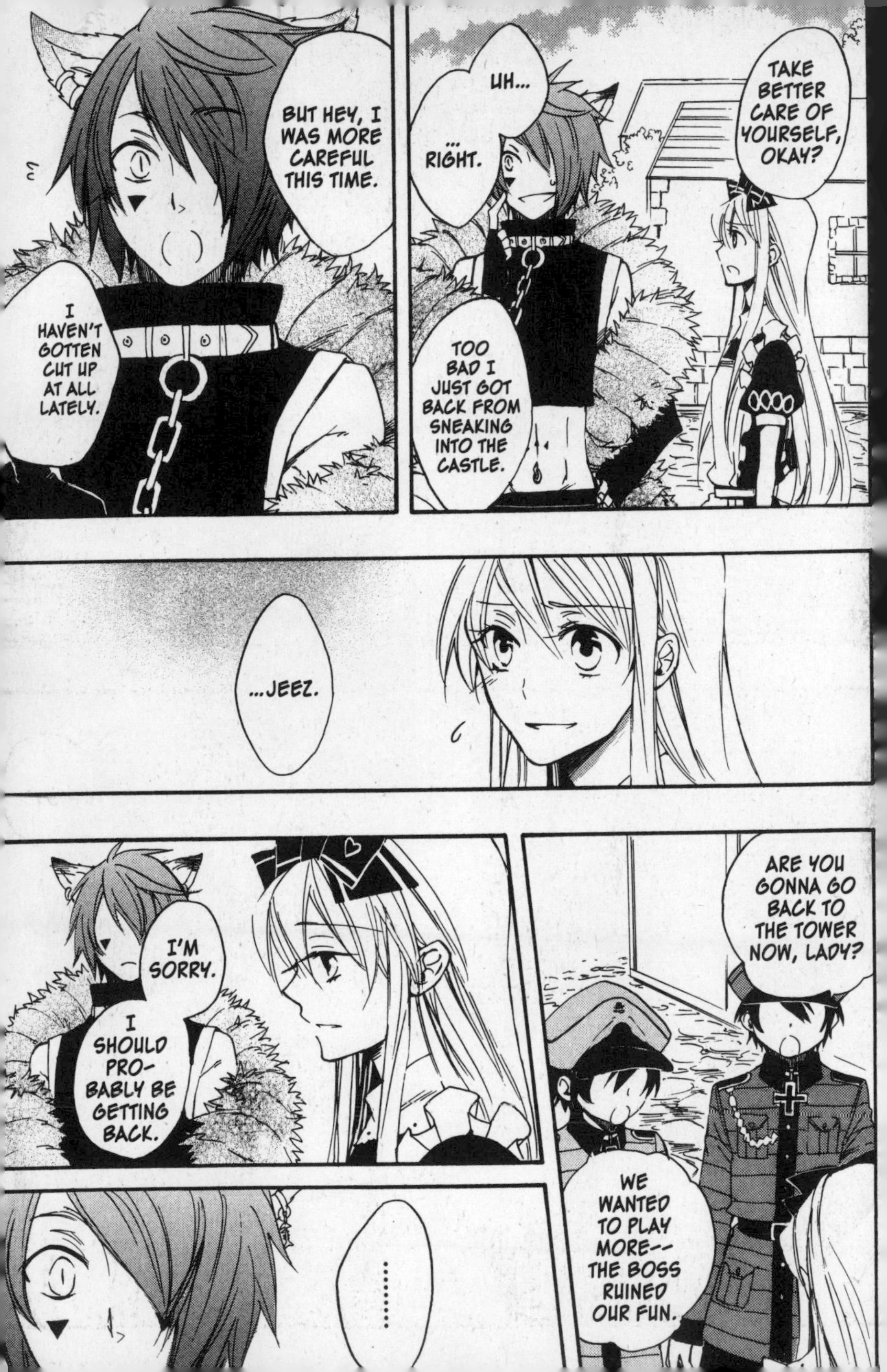

TAKE BETTER CARE OF YOURSELF, OKAY?
UH...
... RIGHT.
TOO BAD I JUST GOT BACK FROM SNEAKING INTO THE CASTLE.
BUT HEY, I WAS MORE CAREFUL THIS TIME.
I HAVEN'T GOTTEN CUT UP AT ALL LATELY.
...JEEZ.
ARE YOU GONNA GO BACK TO THE TOWER NOW, LADY?
WE WANTED TO PLAY MORE--THE BOSS RUINED OUR FUN.
I'M SORRY.
I SHOULD PRO-BABLY BE GETTING BACK.
......

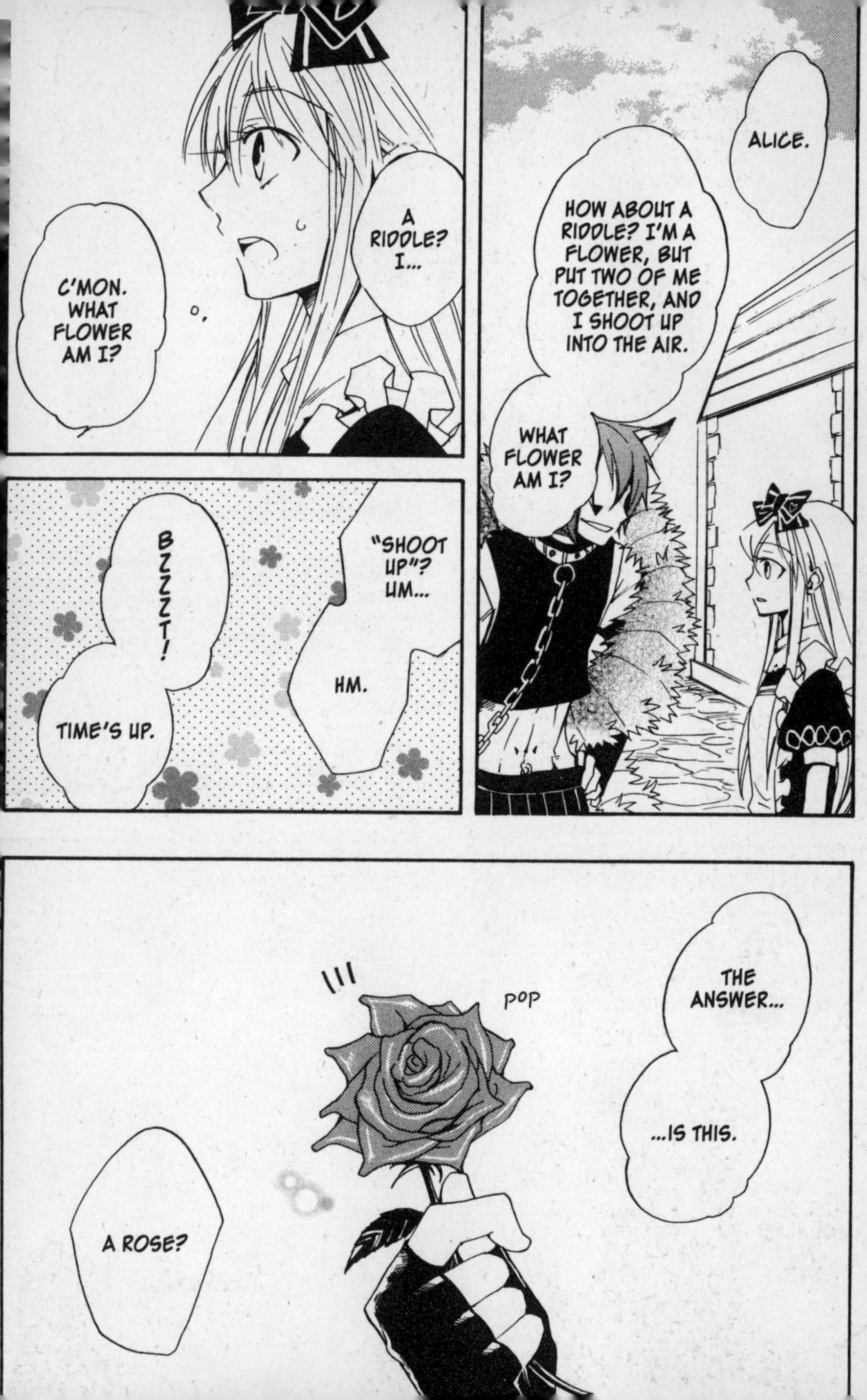
ALICE.
HOW ABOUT A RIDDLE? I'M A FLOWER, BUT PUT TWO OF ME TOGETHER, AND I SHOOT UP INTO THE AIR.
WHAT FLOWER AM I?
A RIDDLE? I...
C'MON. WHAT FLOWER AM I?
"SHOOT UP"? UM...
HM.
BZZZT!
TIME'S UP.
THE ANSWER...
...IS THIS.
POP
A ROSE?

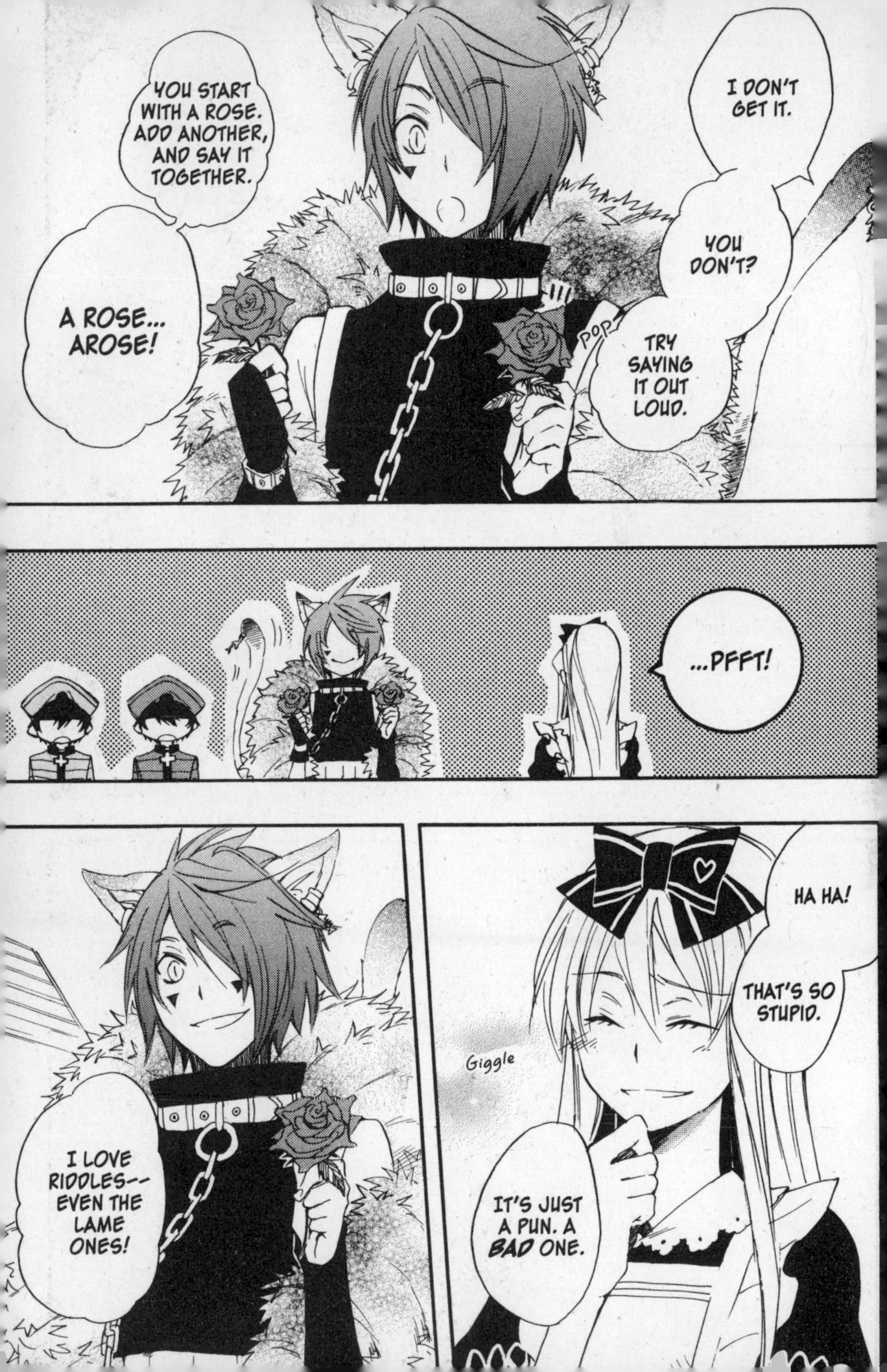
I DON'T GET IT.
YOU DON'T?
POP
TRY SAYING IT OUT LOUD.
YOU START WITH A ROSE. ADD ANOTHER, AND SAY IT TOGETHER.
A ROSE... AROSE!
...PFFT!
HA HA!
THAT'S SO STUPID.
Giggle
IT'S JUST A PUN. A *BAD* ONE.
I LOVE RIDDLES--EVEN THE LAME ONES!

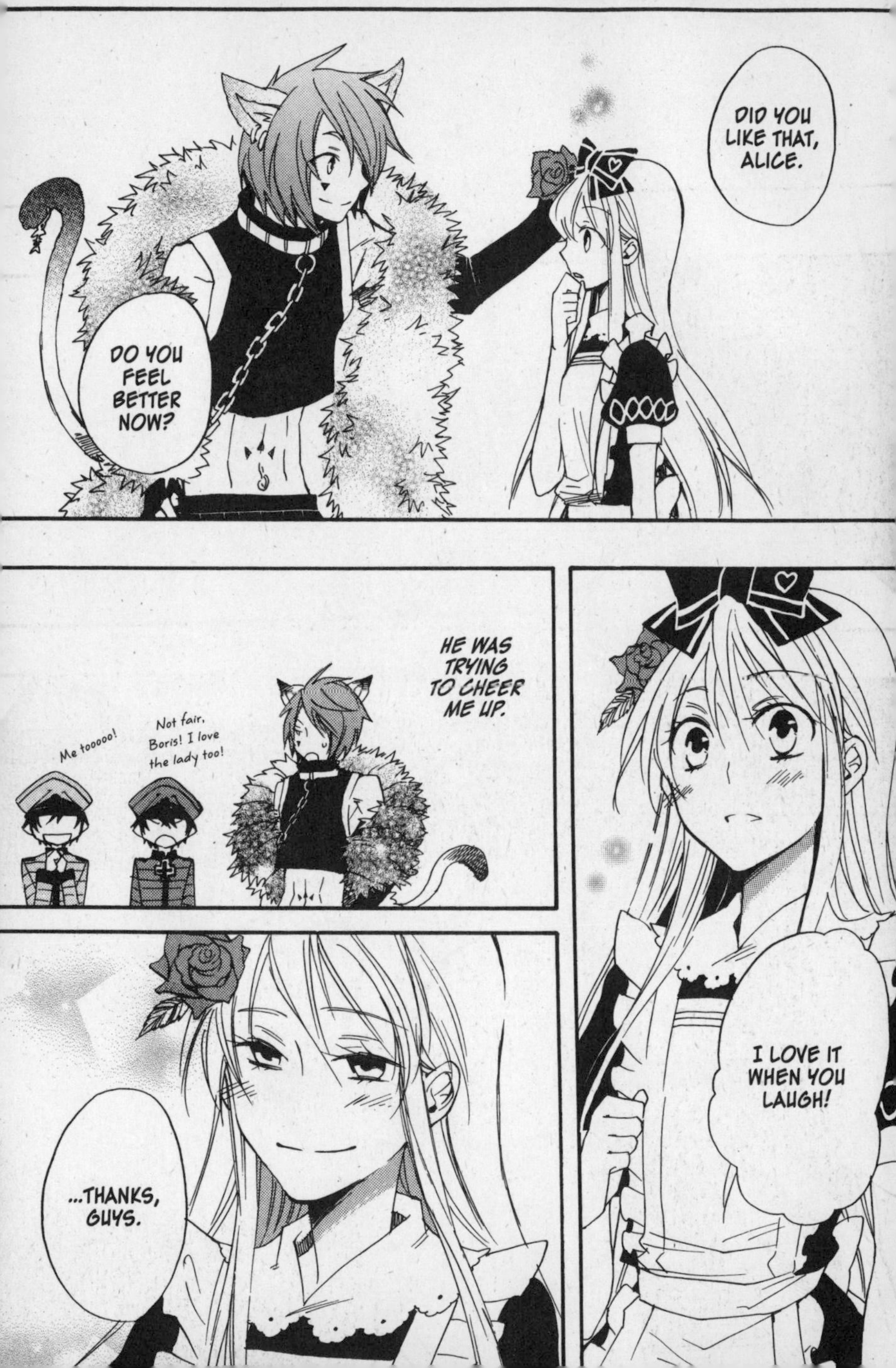
DID YOU LIKE THAT, ALICE.
DO YOU FEEL BETTER NOW?
I LOVE IT WHEN YOU LAUGH!
HE WAS TRYING TO CHEER ME UP.
Not fair, Boris! I love the lady too!
Me tooooo!
...THANKS, GUYS.

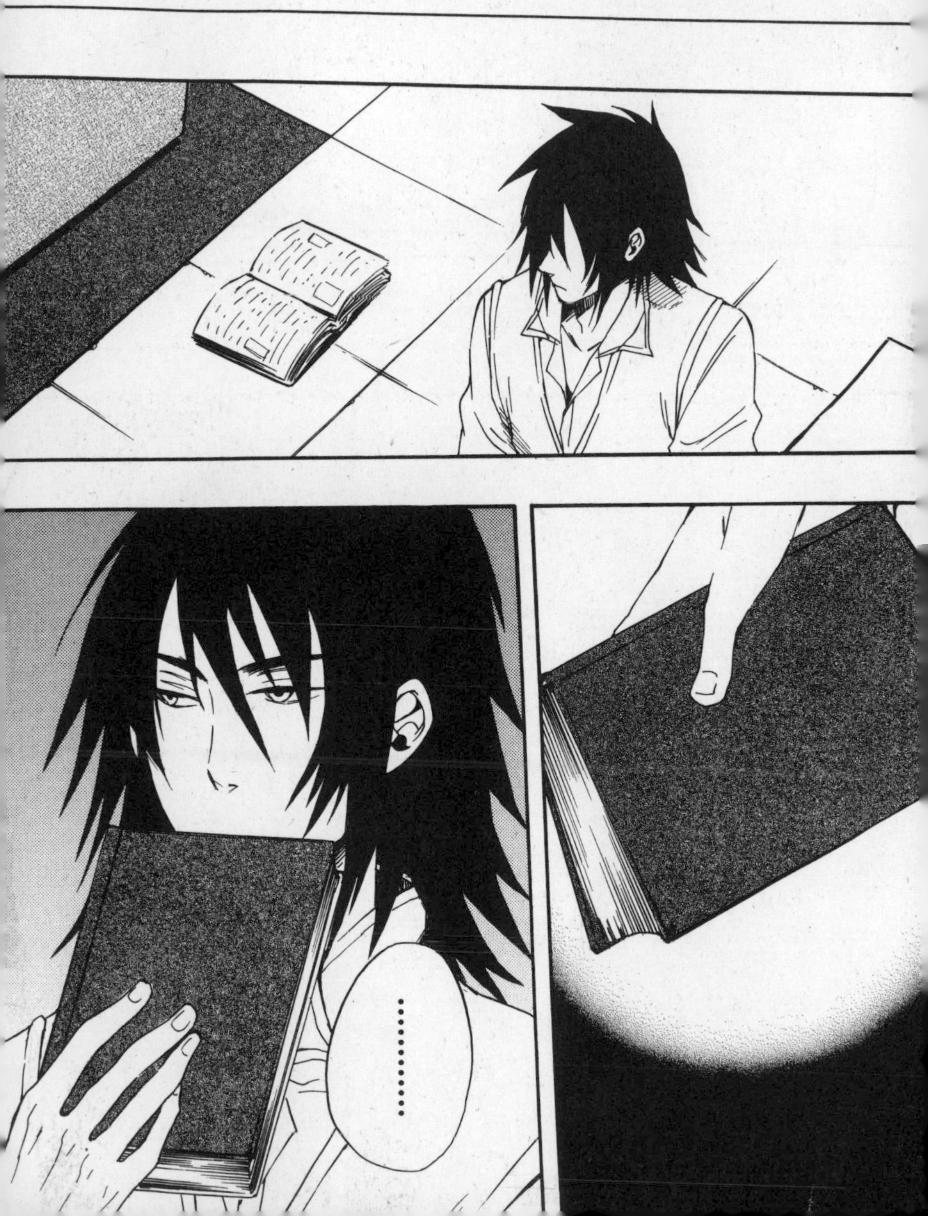
……

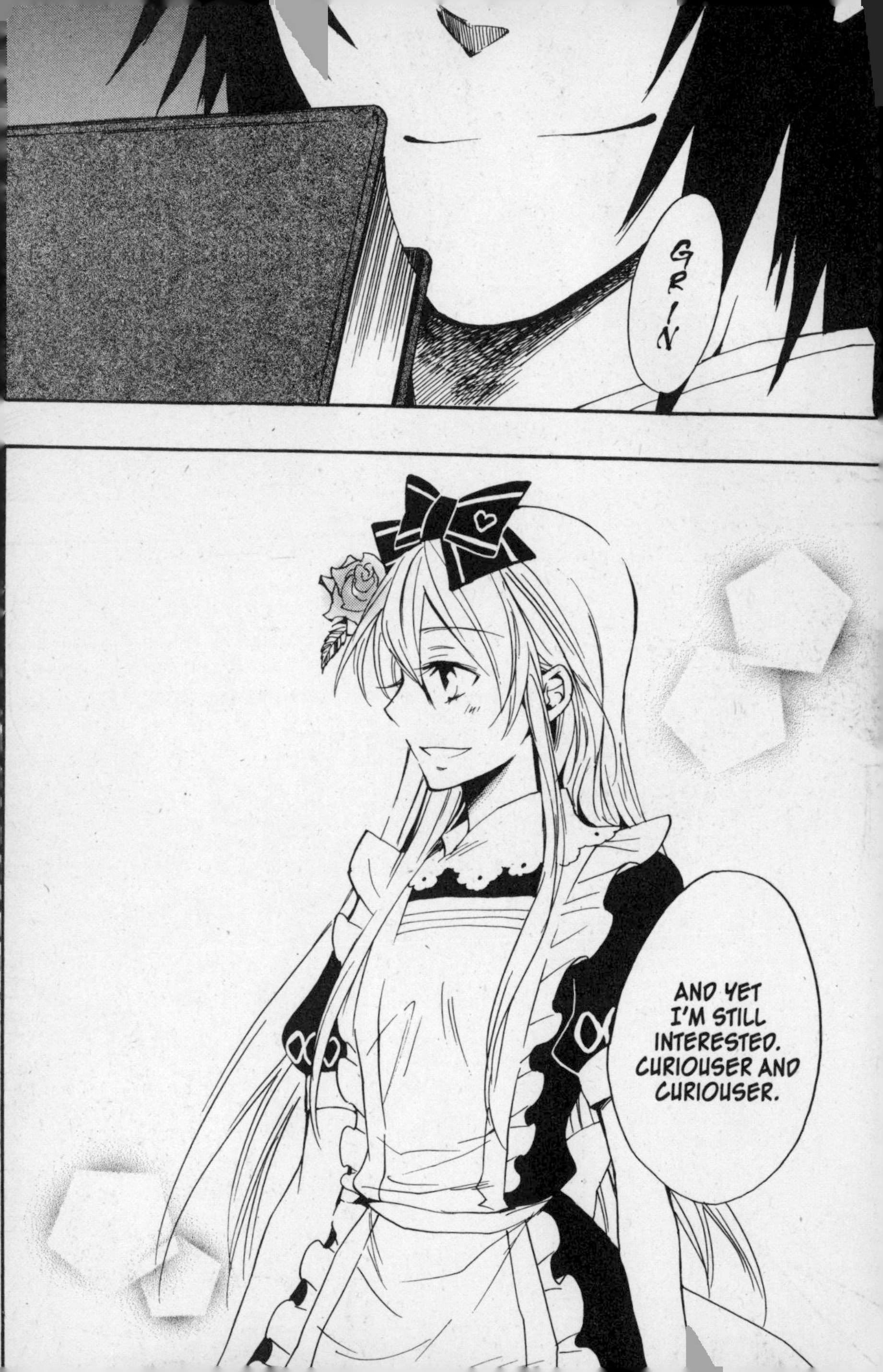
GRIN
AND YET I'M STILL INTERESTED. CURIOUSER AND CURIOUSER.

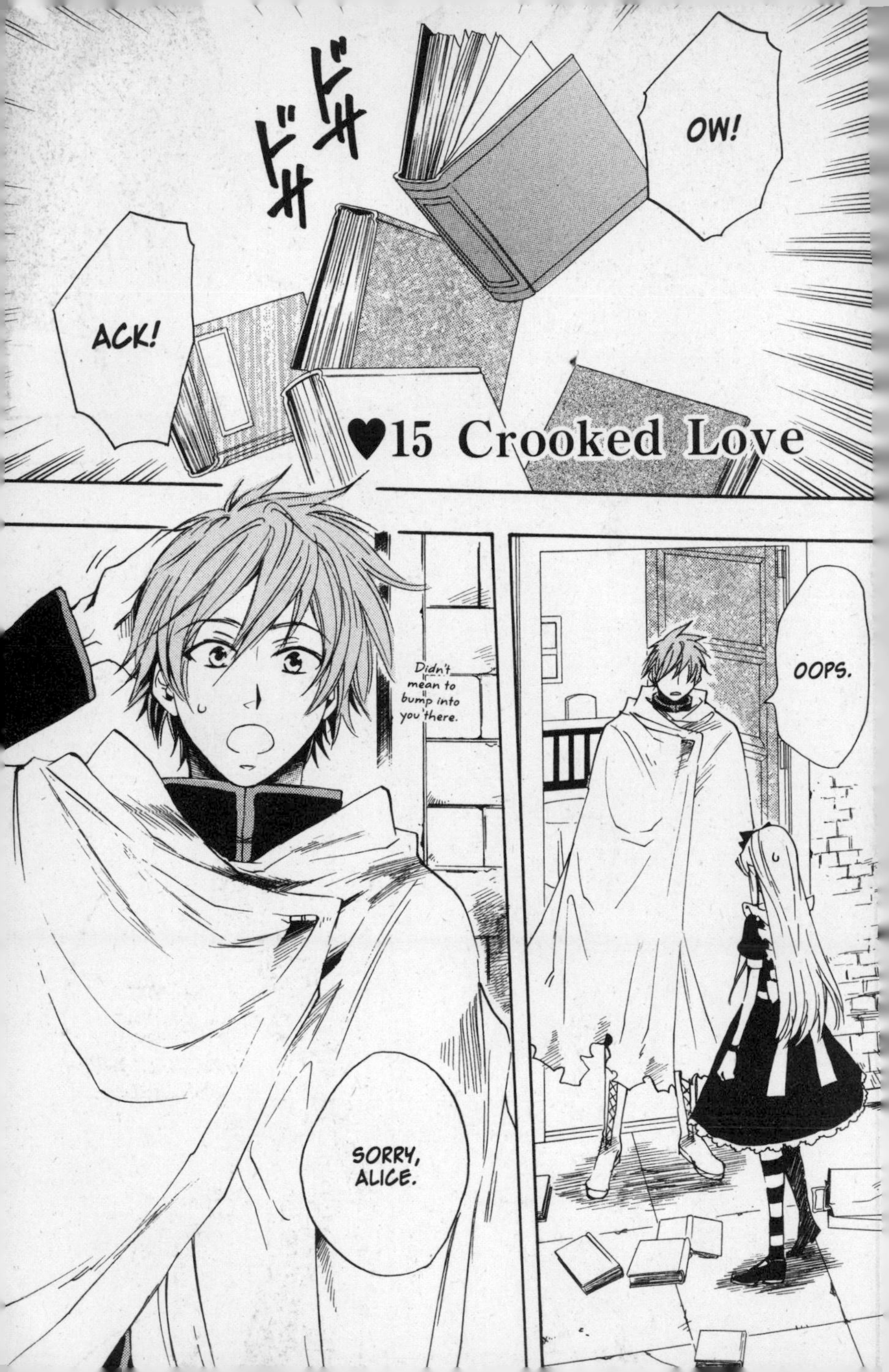
OW!
ドサ
ドサ
ACK!
♥15 Crooked Love
OOPS.
Didn't mean to bump into you there.
SORRY, ALICE.

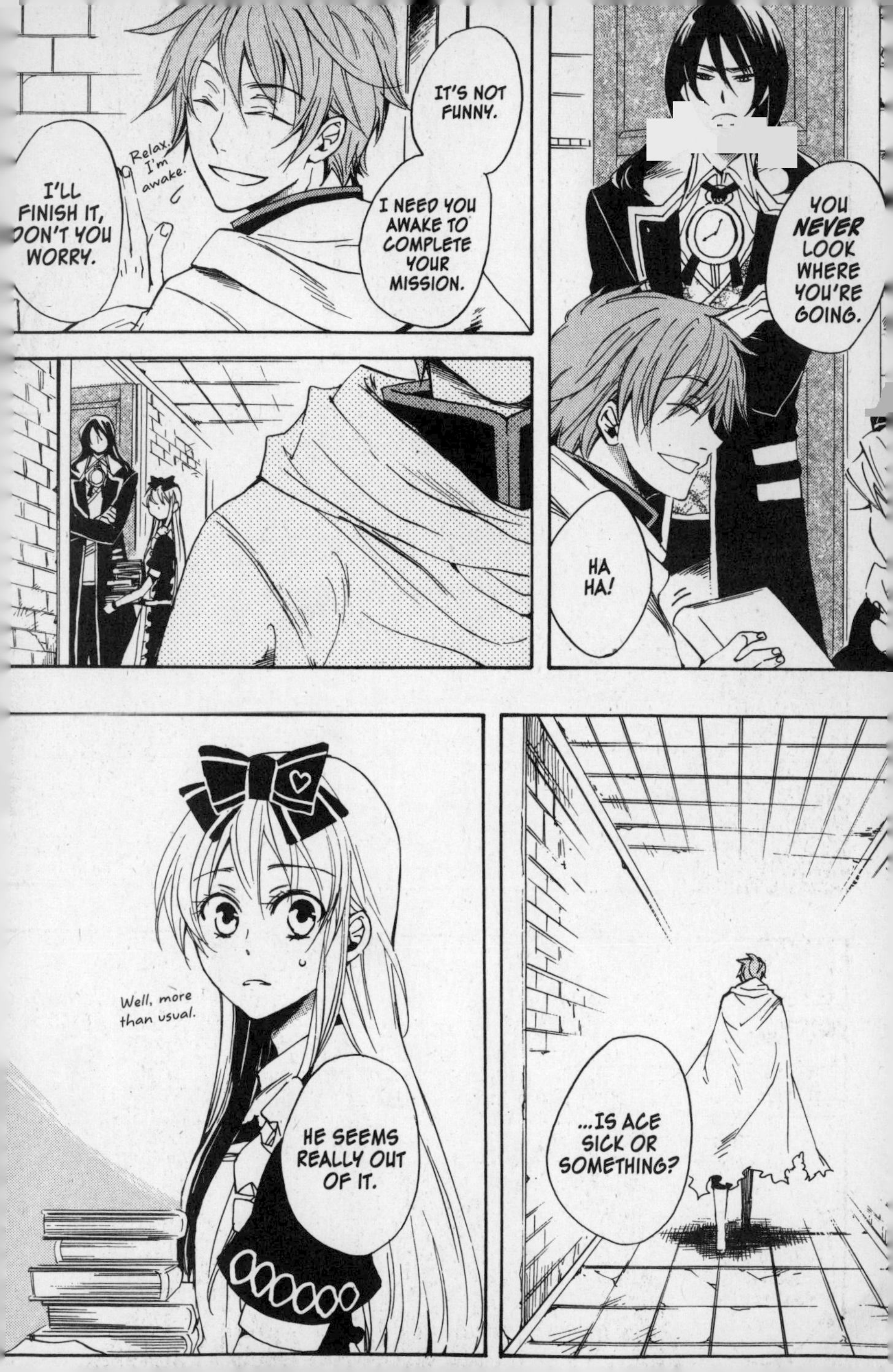
YOU NEVER LOOK WHERE YOU'RE GOING.
HA HA!
IT'S NOT FUNNY.
I NEED YOU AWAKE TO COMPLETE YOUR MISSION.
Relax. I'm awake.
I'LL FINISH IT, DON'T YOU WORRY.
...IS ACE SICK OR SOMETHING?
HE SEEMS REALLY OUT OF IT.
Well, more than usual.

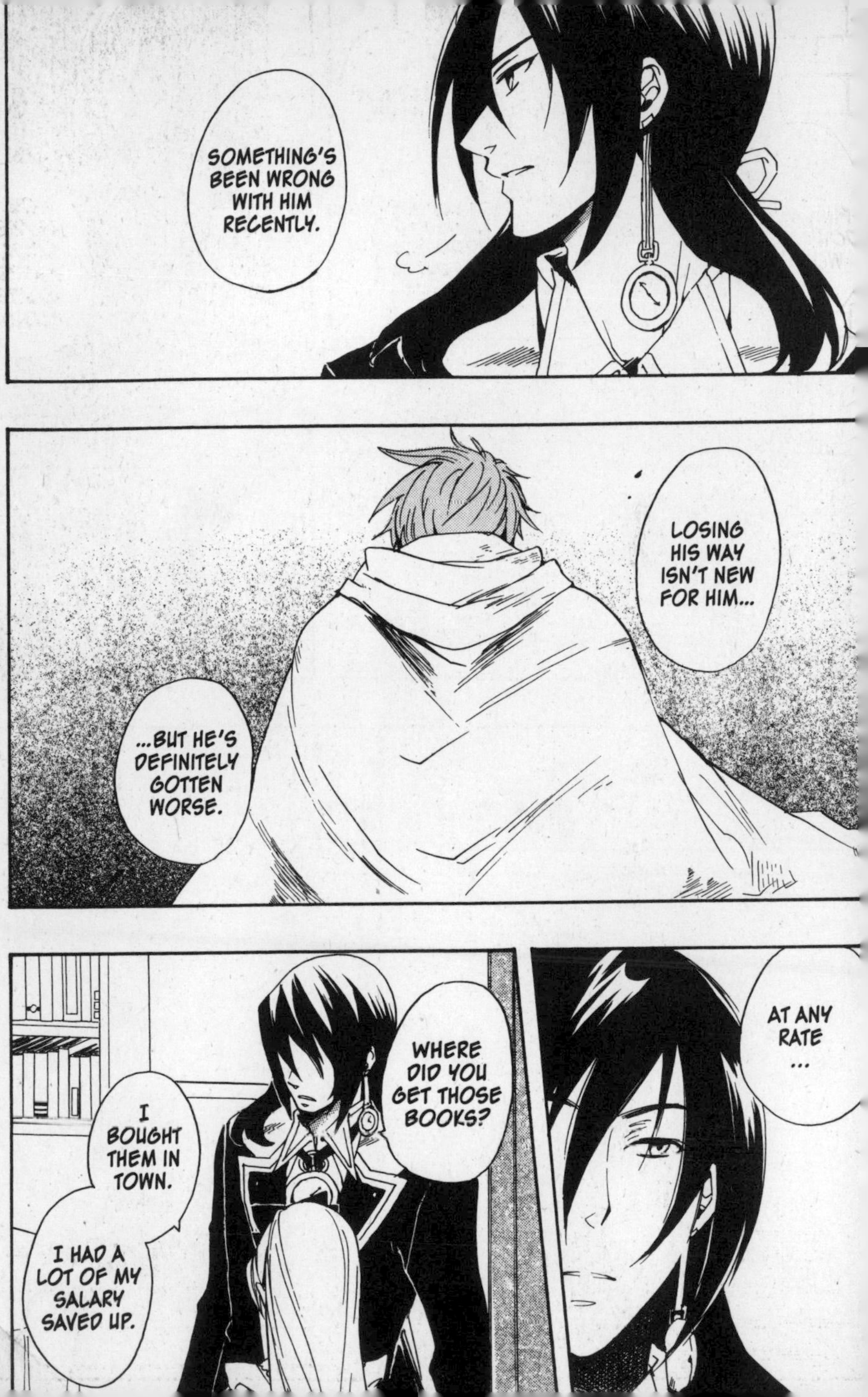
SOMETHING'S BEEN WRONG WITH HIM RECENTLY.
LOSING HIS WAY ISN'T NEW FOR HIM...
...BUT HE'S DEFINITELY GOTTEN WORSE.
AT ANY RATE ...
WHERE DID YOU GET THOSE BOOKS?
I BOUGHT THEM IN TOWN.
I HAD A LOT OF MY SALARY SAVED UP.

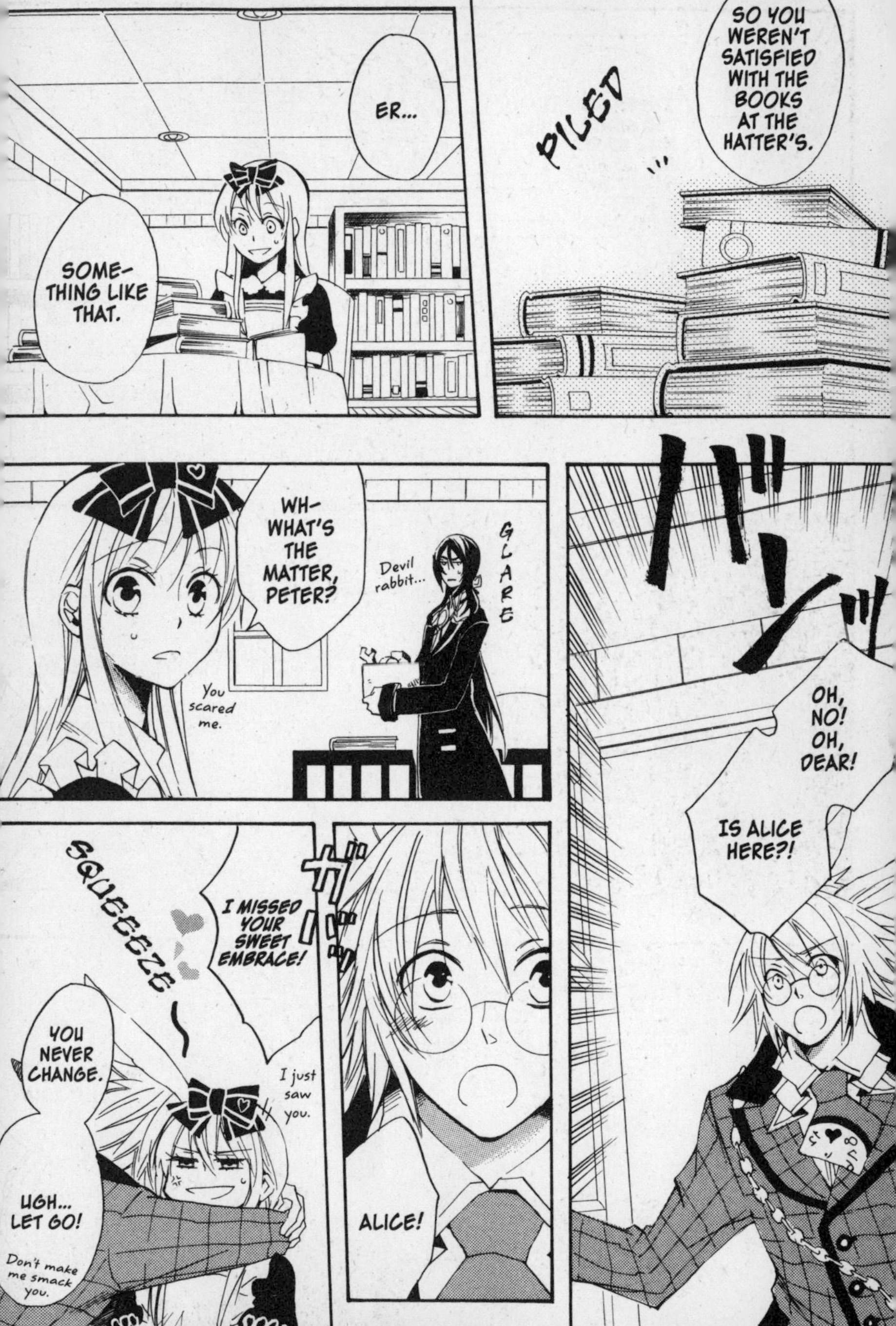
SO YOU WEREN'T SATISFIED WITH THE BOOKS AT THE HATTER'S.
PILED
...
ER...
SOME-THING LIKE THAT.
バンッ
OH, NO! OH, DEAR!
IS ALICE HERE?!
WH-WHAT'S THE MATTER, PETER?
Devil rabbit...
GLARE
You scared me.
ALICE!
I MISSED YOUR SWEET EMBRACE!
SQUEEEEZE
YOU NEVER CHANGE.
I just saw you.
UGH... LET GO!
Don't make me smack you.

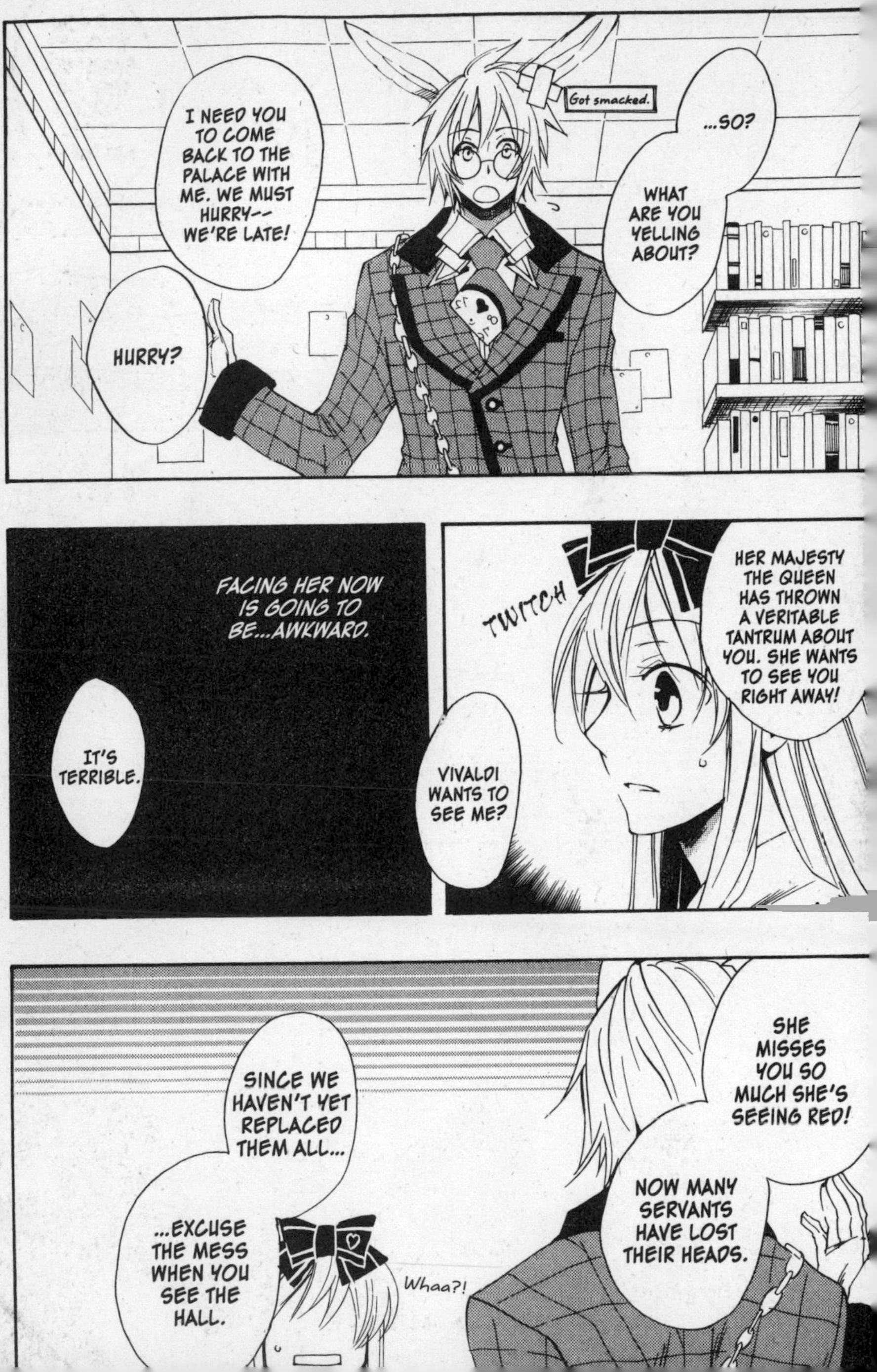
...SO?
WHAT ARE YOU YELLING ABOUT?
Got smacked.
I NEED YOU TO COME BACK TO THE PALACE WITH ME. WE MUST HURRY-- WE'RE LATE!
HURRY?
HER MAJESTY THE QUEEN HAS THROWN A VERITABLE TANTRUM ABOUT YOU. SHE WANTS TO SEE YOU RIGHT AWAY!
TWITCH
VIVALDI WANTS TO SEE ME?
FACING HER NOW IS GOING TO BE...AWKWARD.
IT'S TERRIBLE.
SHE MISSES YOU SO MUCH SHE'S SEEING RED!
NOW MANY SERVANTS HAVE LOST THEIR HEADS.
SINCE WE HAVEN'T YET REPLACED THEM ALL...
...EXCUSE THE MESS WHEN YOU SEE THE HALL.
Whaa?!

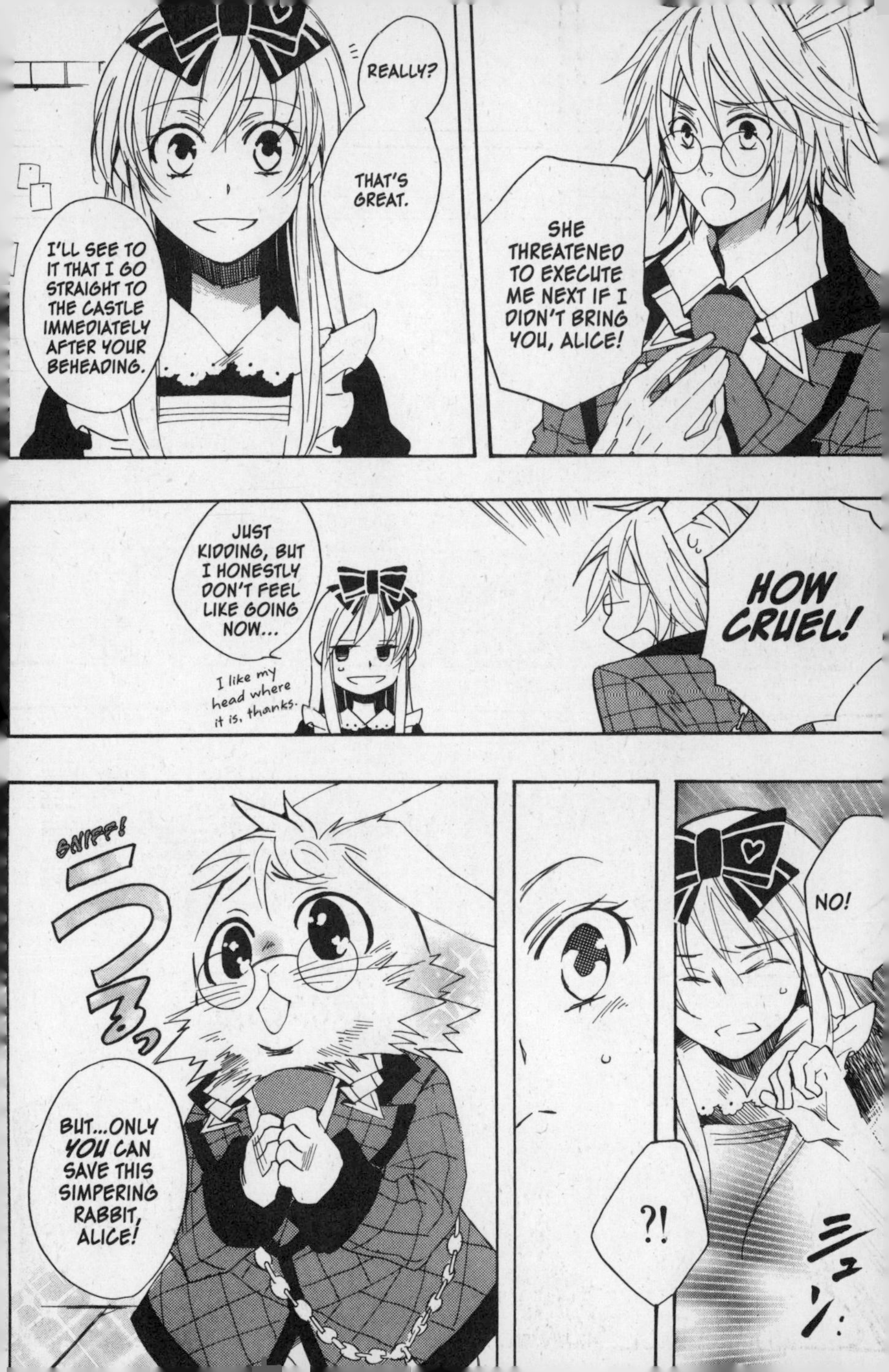
SHE THREATENED TO EXECUTE ME NEXT IF I DIDN'T BRING YOU, ALICE!
REALLY?
THAT'S GREAT.
I'LL SEE TO IT THAT I GO STRAIGHT TO THE CASTLE IMMEDIATELY AFTER YOUR BEHEADING.
HOW CRUEL!
JUST KIDDING, BUT I HONESTLY DON'T FEEL LIKE GOING NOW...
I like my head where it is, thanks.
NO!
?!
SNIFF!
BUT...ONLY YOU CAN SAVE THIS SIMPERING RABBIT, ALICE!

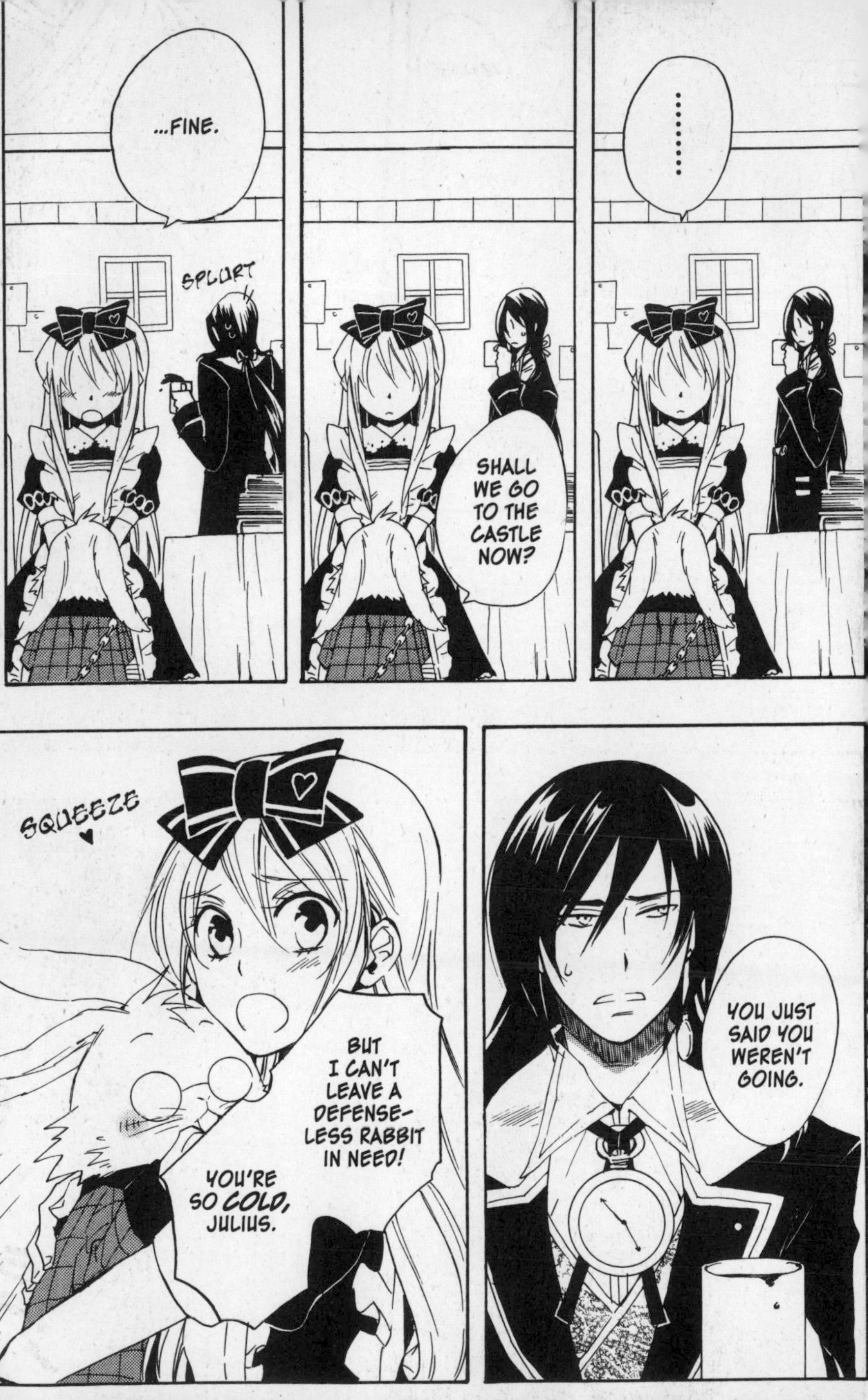
......
SHALL WE GO TO THE CASTLE NOW?
...FINE.
SPLURT
YOU JUST SAID YOU WEREN'T GOING.
SQUEEZE ♥
BUT I CAN'T LEAVE A DEFENSE-LESS RABBIT IN NEED!
YOU'RE SO COLD, JULIUS.

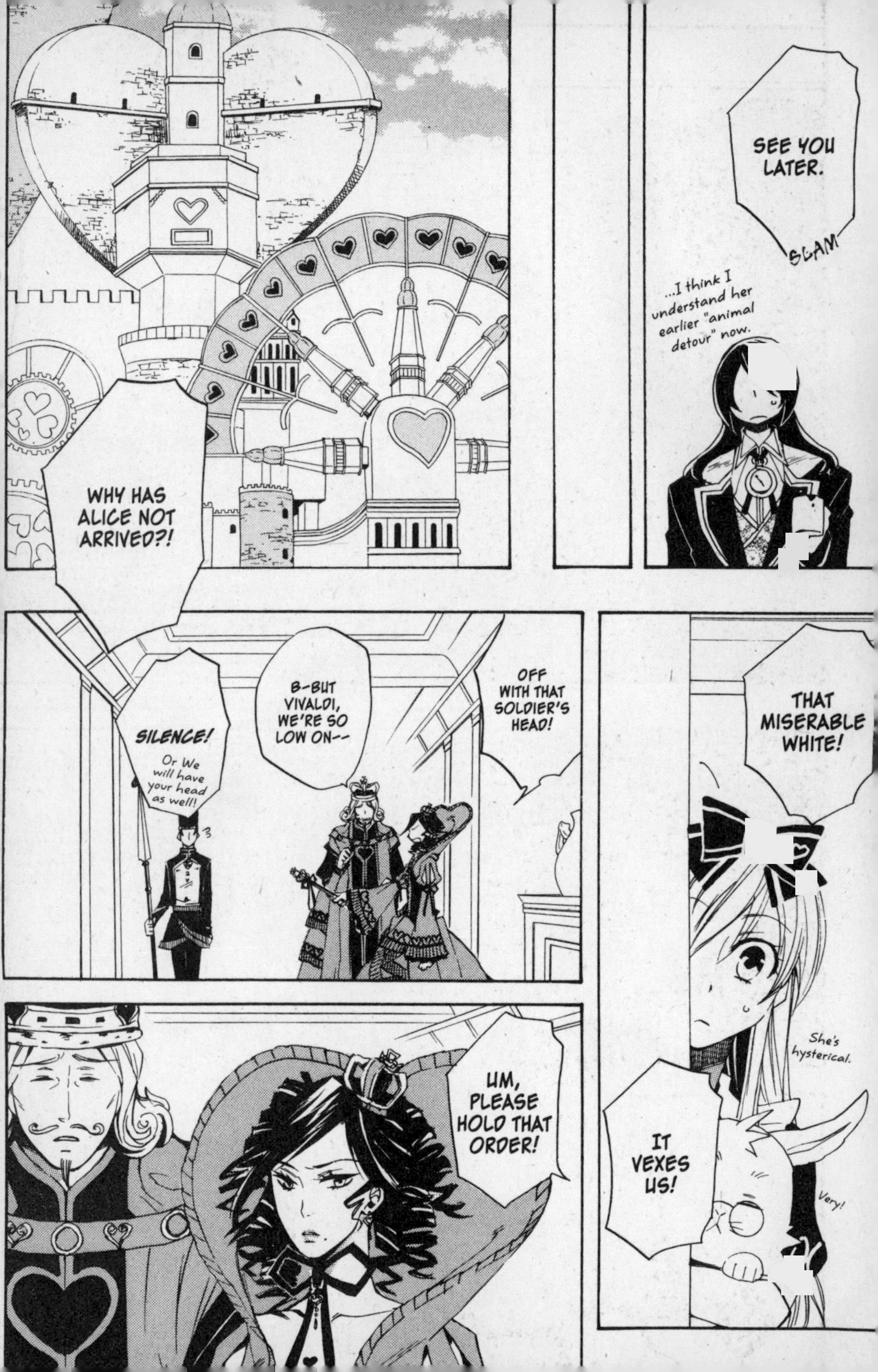
SEE YOU LATER.
SLAM
...I think I understand her earlier "animal detour" now.
WHY HAS ALICE NOT ARRIVED?!
THAT MISERABLE WHITE!
She's hysterical.
IT VEXES US!
Very!
OFF WITH THAT SOLDIER'S HEAD!
B-BUT VIVALDI, WE'RE SO LOW ON--
SILENCE!
Or We will have your head as well!
UM, PLEASE HOLD THAT ORDER!

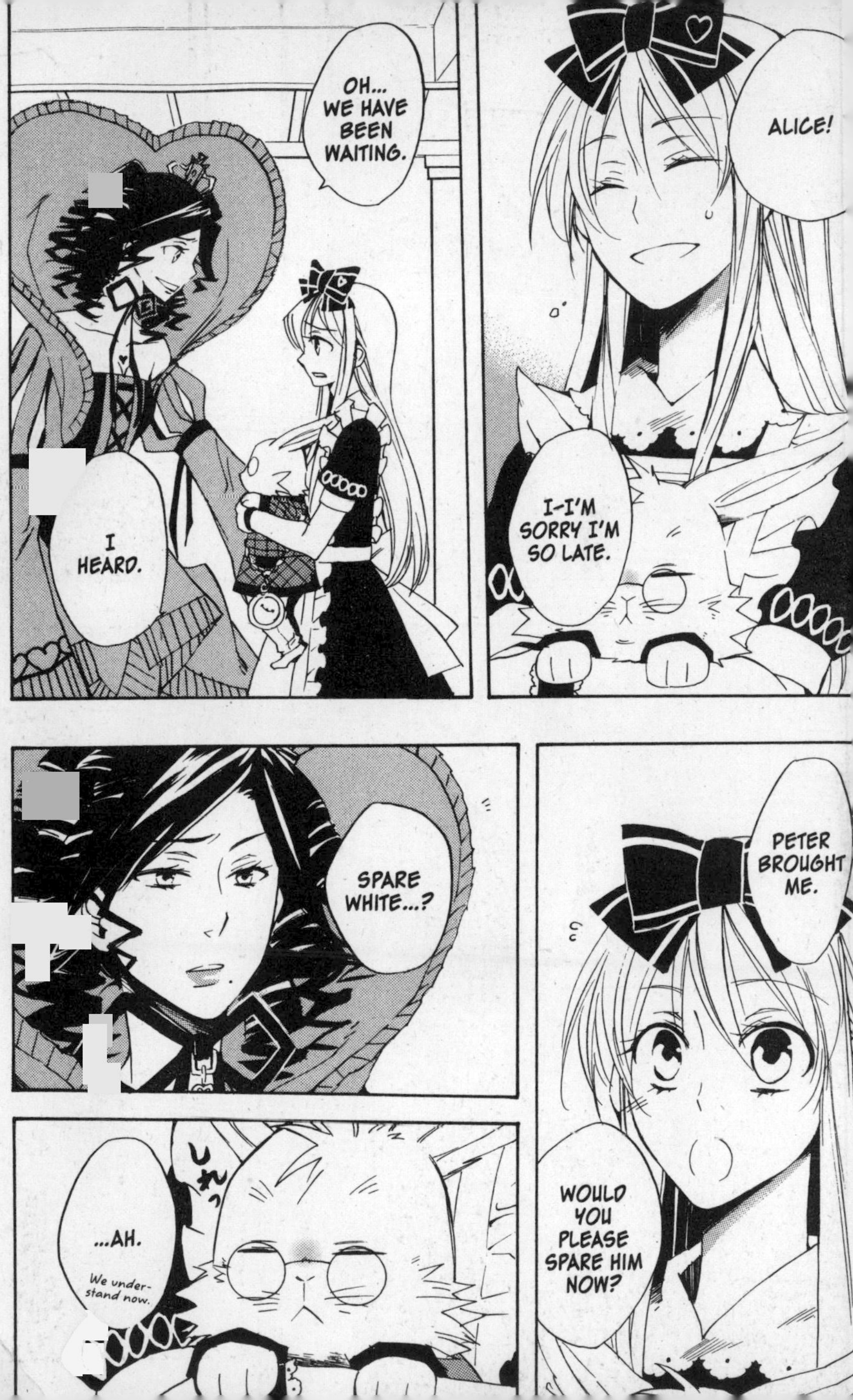
ALICE!
I-I'M SORRY I'M SO LATE.
OH... WE HAVE BEEN WAITING.
I HEARD.
PETER BROUGHT ME.
WOULD YOU PLEASE SPARE HIM NOW?
SPARE WHITE...?
しれっ
...AH.
We understand now.

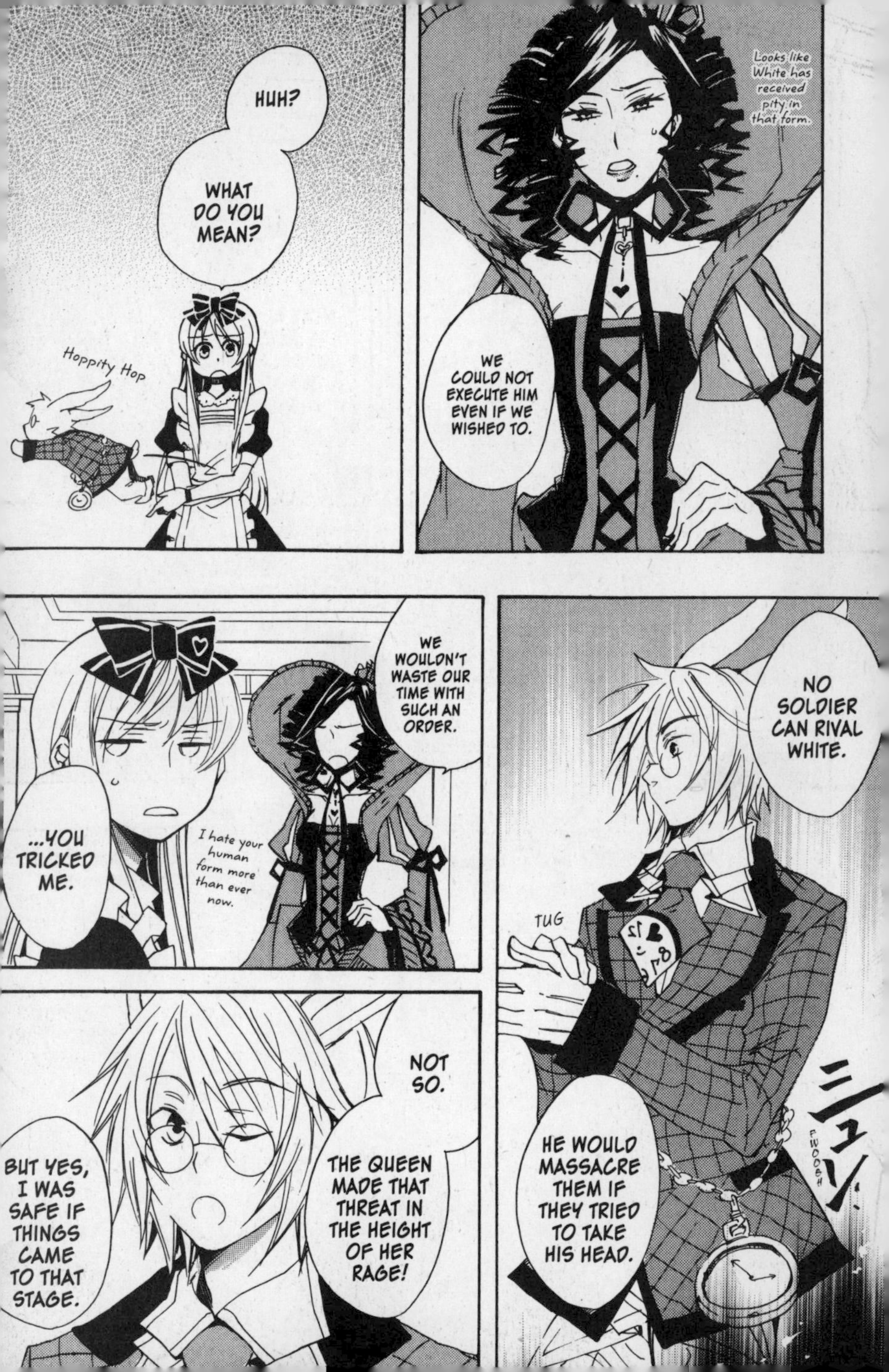
Looks like White has received pity in that form.
WE COULD NOT EXECUTE HIM EVEN IF WE WISHED TO.
HUH?
WHAT DO YOU MEAN?
Hoppity Hop
NO SOLDIER CAN RIVAL WHITE.
TUG
シュン
FWOOSH
HE WOULD MASSACRE THEM IF THEY TRIED TO TAKE HIS HEAD.
WE WOULDN'T WASTE OUR TIME WITH SUCH AN ORDER.
I hate your human form more than ever now.
...YOU TRICKED ME.
NOT SO.
THE QUEEN MADE THAT THREAT IN THE HEIGHT OF HER RAGE!
BUT YES, I WAS SAFE IF THINGS CAME TO THAT STAGE.

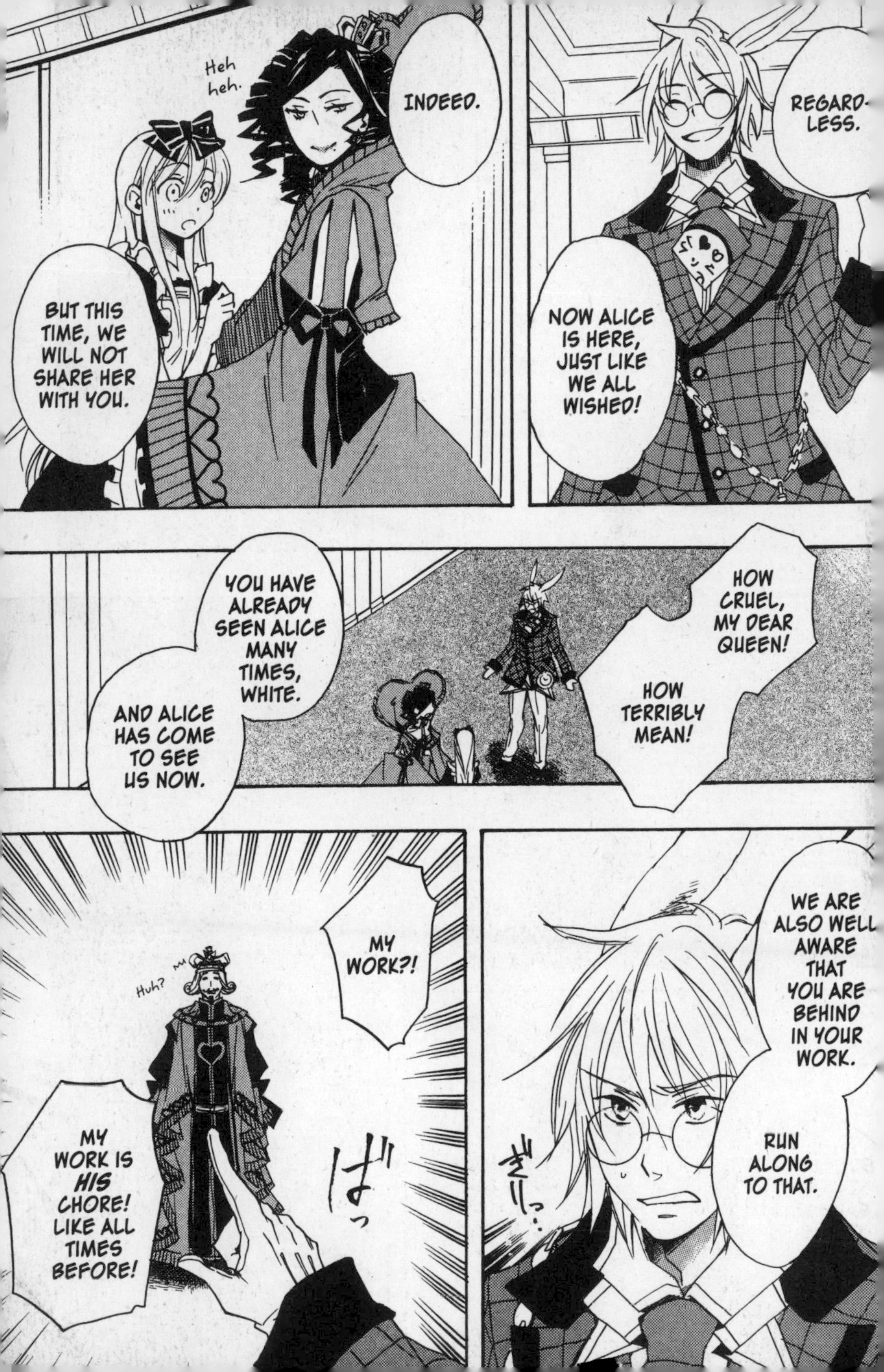
REGARDLESS.
NOW ALICE IS HERE, JUST LIKE WE ALL WISHED!
INDEED.
Heh heh.
BUT THIS TIME, WE WILL NOT SHARE HER WITH YOU.
HOW CRUEL, MY DEAR QUEEN!
HOW TERRIBLY MEAN!
YOU HAVE ALREADY SEEN ALICE MANY TIMES, WHITE.
AND ALICE HAS COME TO SEE US NOW.
WE ARE ALSO WELL AWARE THAT YOU ARE BEHIND IN YOUR WORK.
RUN ALONG TO THAT.
ぎりっ…
MY WORK?!
Huh?
MY WORK IS *HIS* CHORE! LIKE ALL TIMES BEFORE!
ばっ

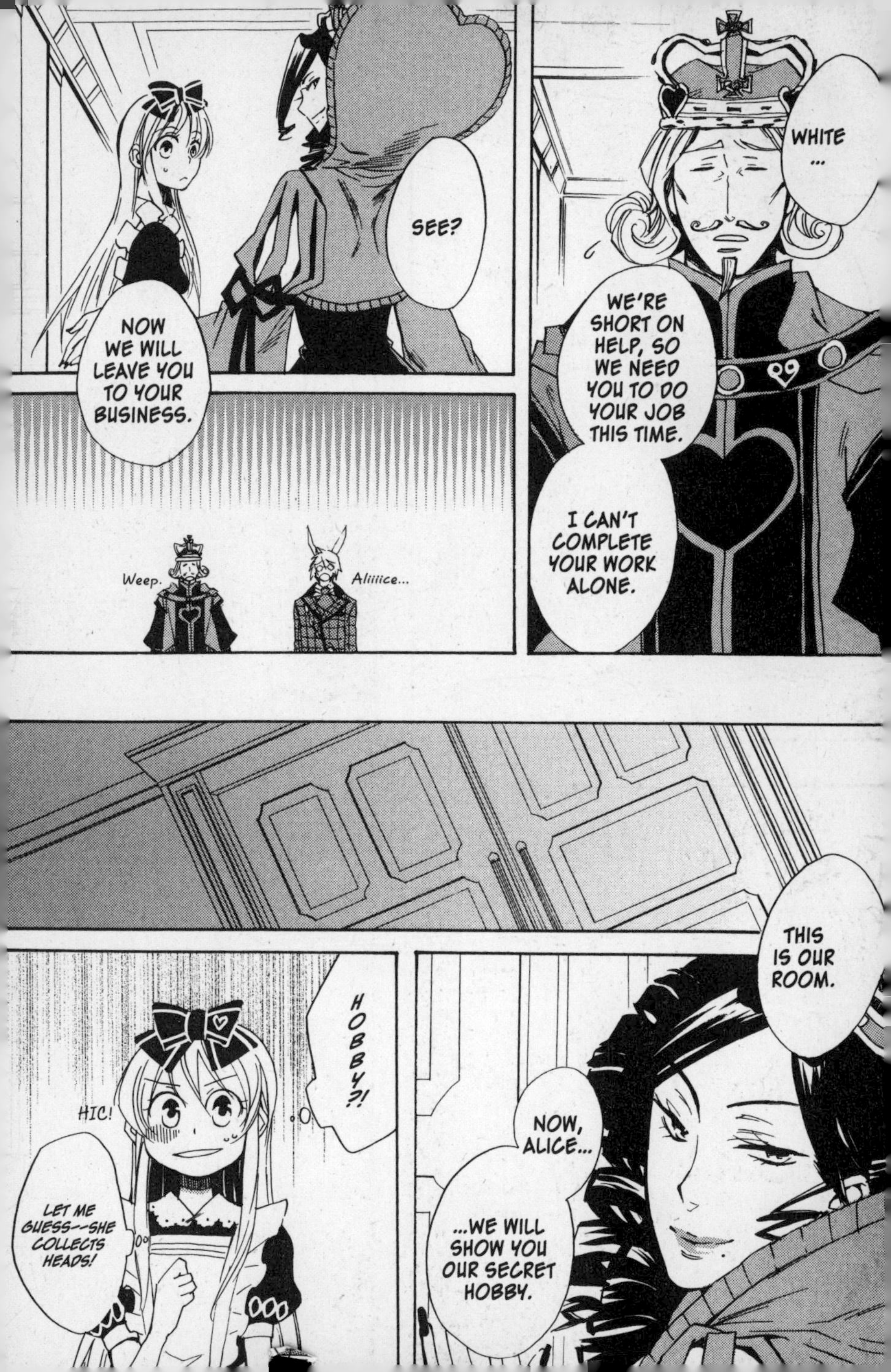
WHITE ...
WE'RE SHORT ON HELP, SO WE NEED YOU TO DO YOUR JOB THIS TIME.
I CAN'T COMPLETE YOUR WORK ALONE.
SEE?
NOW WE WILL LEAVE YOU TO YOUR BUSINESS.
Aliiiice...
Weep.
THIS IS OUR ROOM.
NOW, ALICE...
...WE WILL SHOW YOU OUR SECRET HOBBY.
HOBBY?!
HIC!
LET ME GUESS--SHE COLLECTS HEADS!

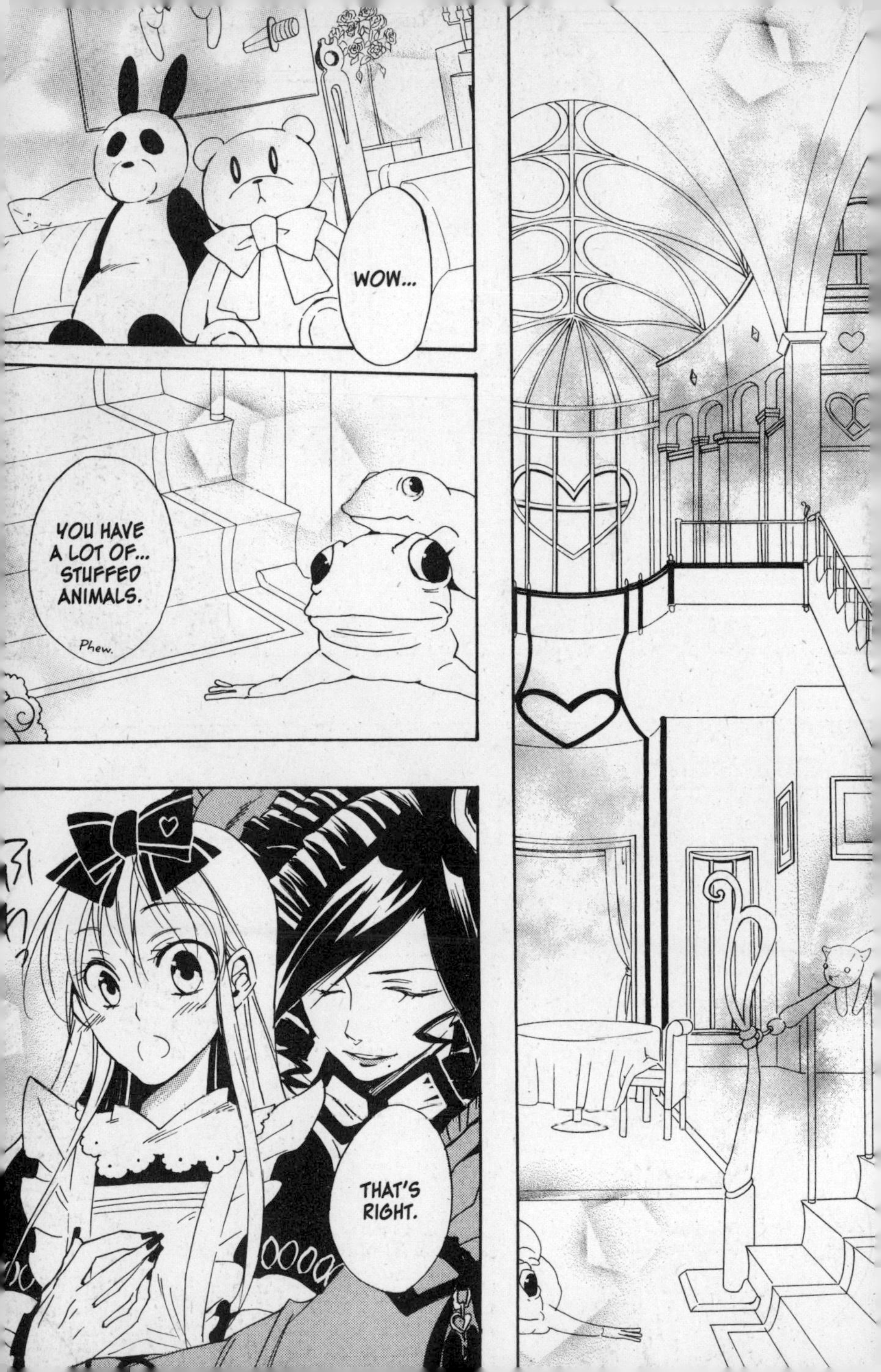
WOW...
YOU HAVE A LOT OF... STUFFED ANIMALS.
Phew.
THAT'S RIGHT.

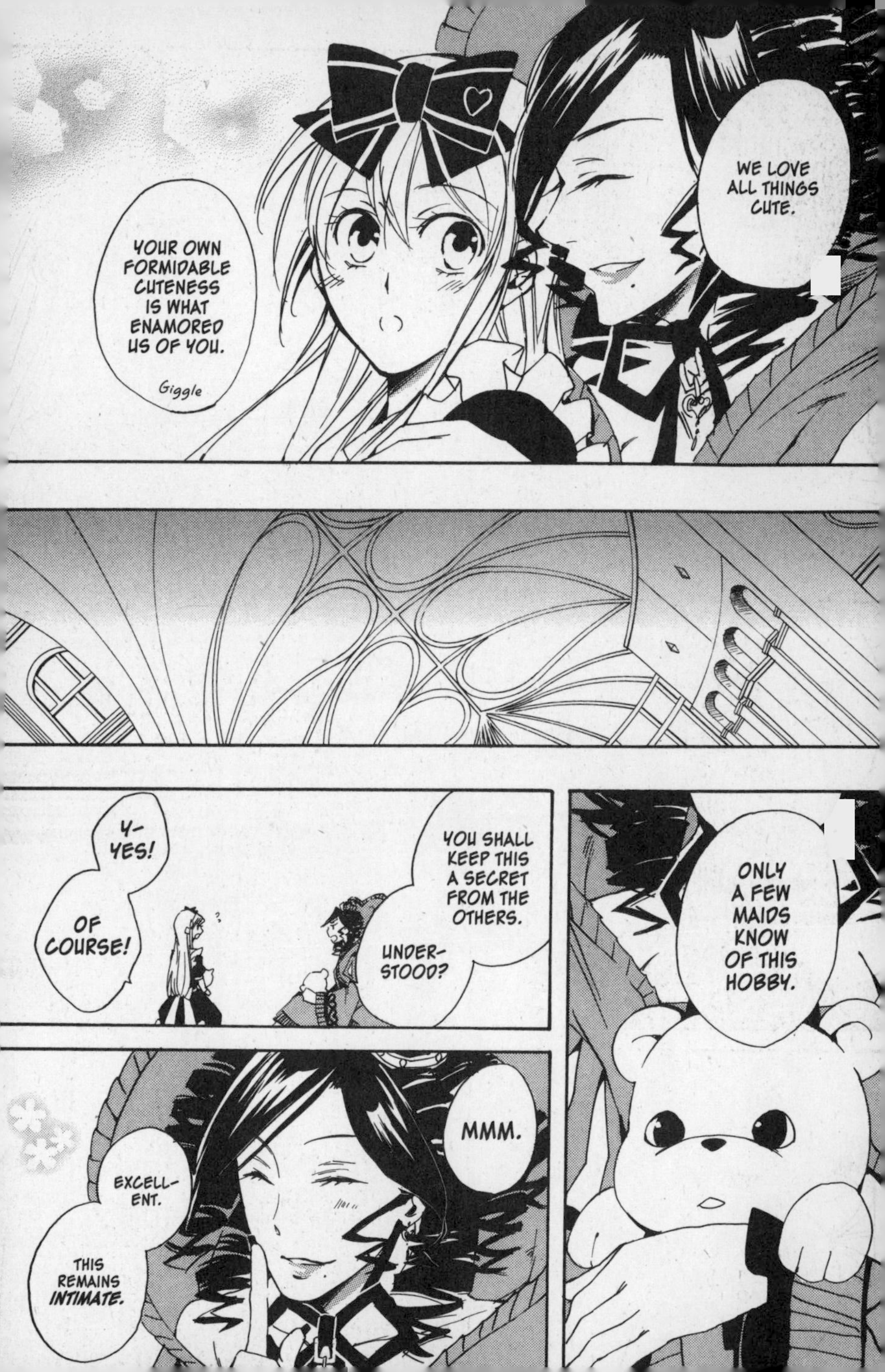
WE LOVE ALL THINGS CUTE.
YOUR OWN FORMIDABLE CUTENESS IS WHAT ENAMORED US OF YOU.
Giggle
ONLY A FEW MAIDS KNOW OF THIS HOBBY.
YOU SHALL KEEP THIS A SECRET FROM THE OTHERS.
UNDER-STOOD?
Y-YES!
OF COURSE!
MMM.
EXCELL-ENT.
THIS REMAINS INTIMATE.

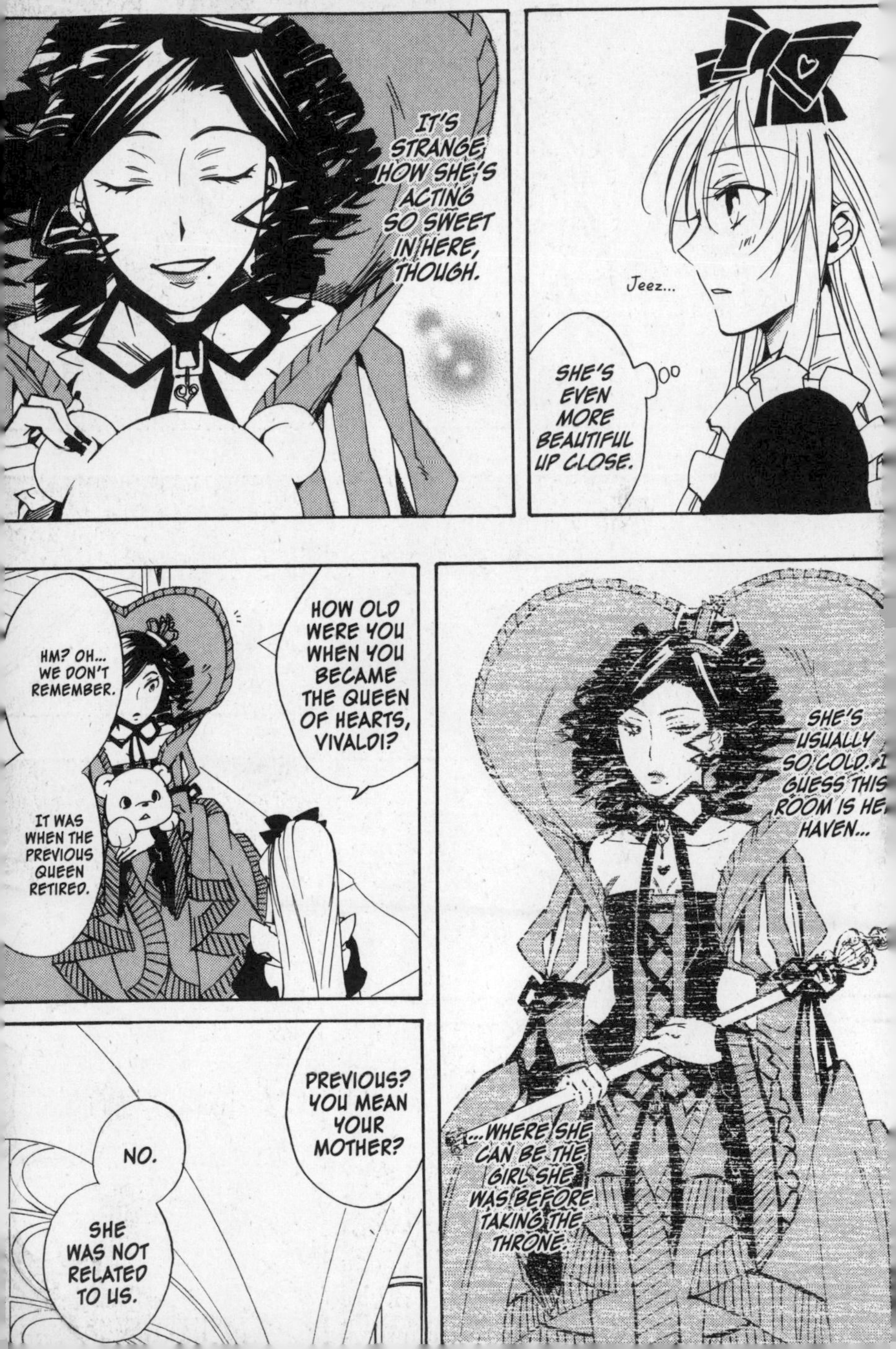

Jeez...
SHE'S EVEN MORE BEAUTIFUL UP CLOSE.
IT'S STRANGE, HOW SHE'S ACTING SO SWEET IN HERE, THOUGH.
SHE'S USUALLY SO COLD. I GUESS THIS ROOM IS HE HAVEN...
...WHERE SHE CAN BE THE GIRL SHE WAS BEFORE TAKING THE THRONE.
HOW OLD WERE YOU WHEN YOU BECAME THE QUEEN OF HEARTS, VIVALDI?
HM? OH... WE DON'T REMEMBER.
IT WAS WHEN THE PREVIOUS QUEEN RETIRED.
PREVIOUS? YOU MEAN YOUR MOTHER?
NO.
SHE WAS NOT RELATED TO US.

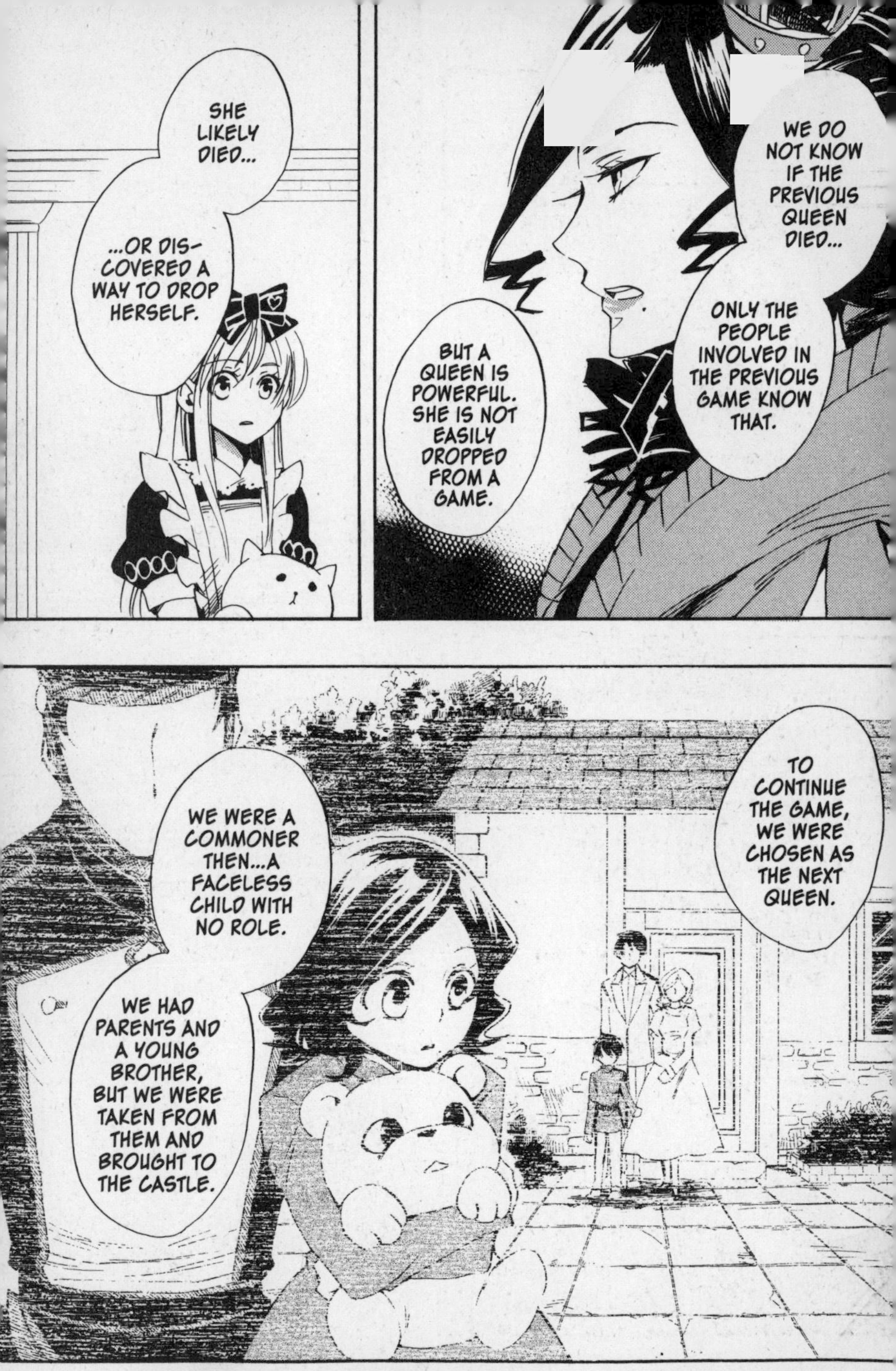
WE DO NOT KNOW IF THE PREVIOUS QUEEN DIED...
ONLY THE PEOPLE INVOLVED IN THE PREVIOUS GAME KNOW THAT.
BUT A QUEEN IS POWERFUL. SHE IS NOT EASILY DROPPED FROM A GAME.
SHE LIKELY DIED...
...OR DISCOVERED A WAY TO DROP HERSELF.
TO CONTINUE THE GAME, WE WERE CHOSEN AS THE NEXT QUEEN.
WE WERE A COMMONER THEN...A FACELESS CHILD WITH NO ROLE.
WE HAD PARENTS AND A YOUNG BROTHER, BUT WE WERE TAKEN FROM THEM AND BROUGHT TO THE CASTLE.

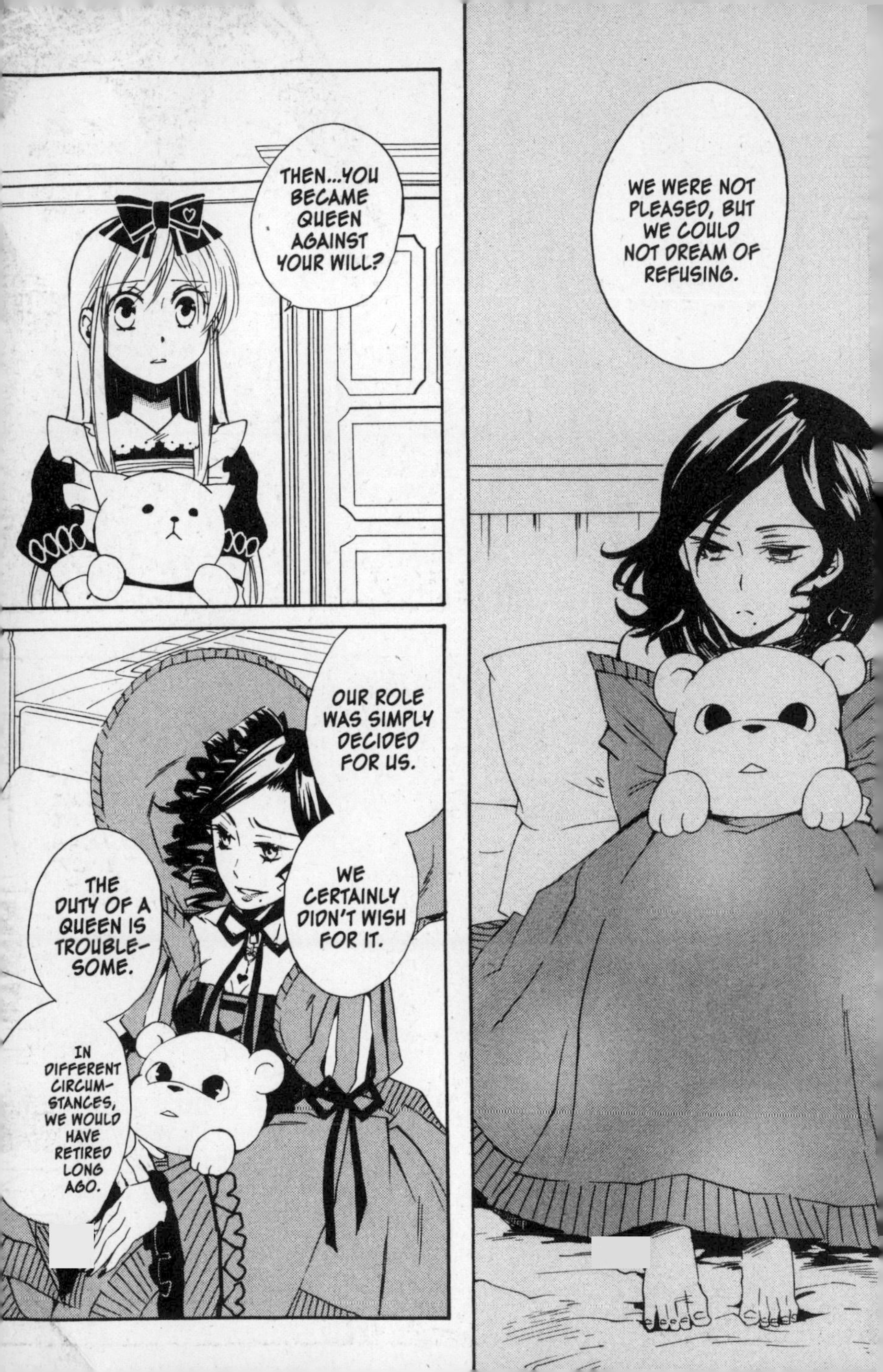
WE WERE NOT PLEASED, BUT WE COULD NOT DREAM OF REFUSING.
THEN...YOU BECAME QUEEN AGAINST YOUR WILL?
OUR ROLE WAS SIMPLY DECIDED FOR US.
WE CERTAINLY DIDN'T WISH FOR IT.
THE DUTY OF A QUEEN IS TROUBLE-SOME.
IN DIFFERENT CIRCUM-STANCES, WE WOULD HAVE RETIRED LONG AGO.

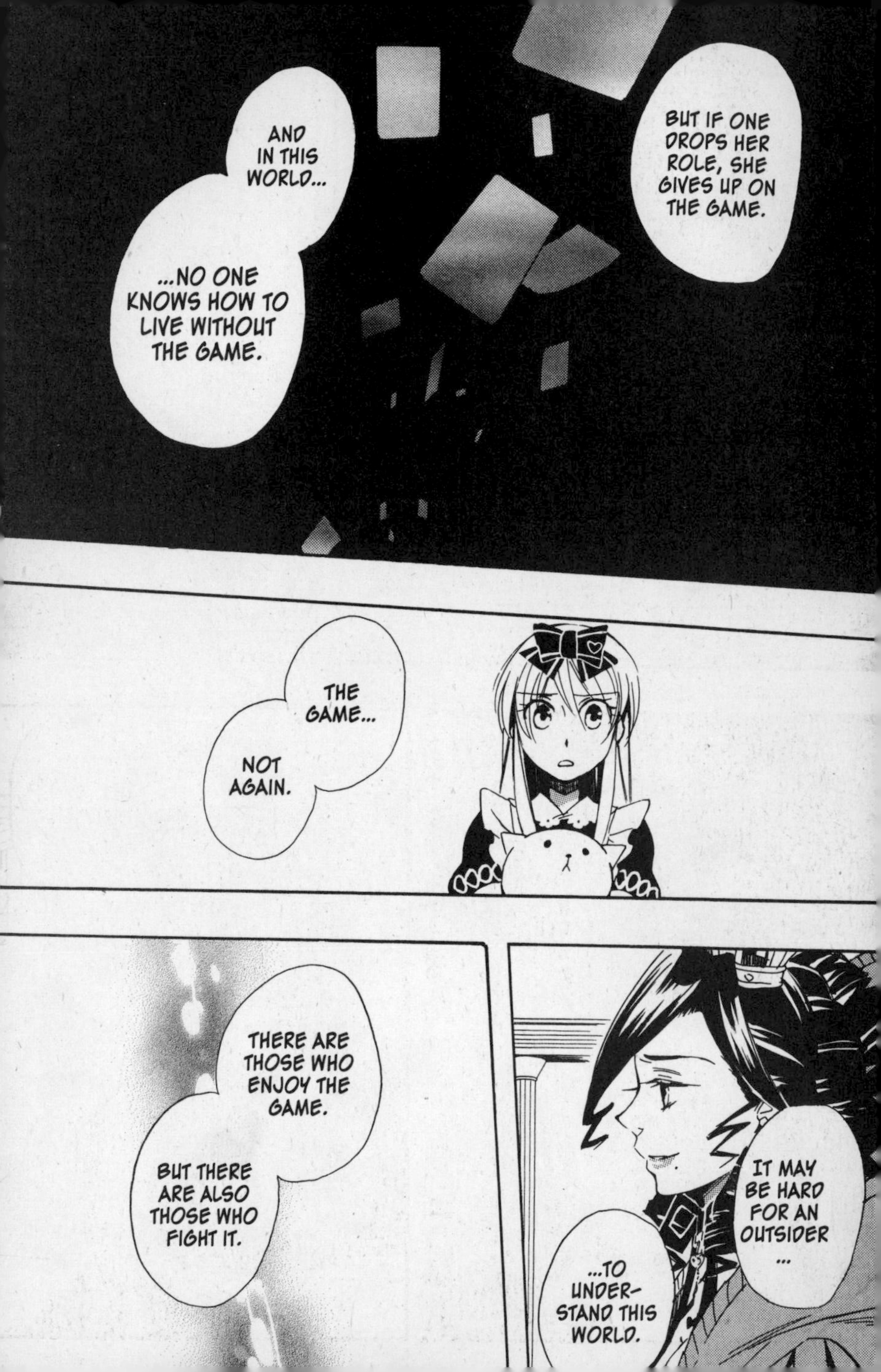
BUT IF ONE DROPS HER ROLE, SHE GIVES UP ON THE GAME.
AND IN THIS WORLD...
...NO ONE KNOWS HOW TO LIVE WITHOUT THE GAME.
THE GAME...
NOT AGAIN.
IT MAY BE HARD FOR AN OUTSIDER ...
...TO UNDER-STAND THIS WORLD.
THERE ARE THOSE WHO ENJOY THE GAME.
BUT THERE ARE ALSO THOSE WHO FIGHT IT.

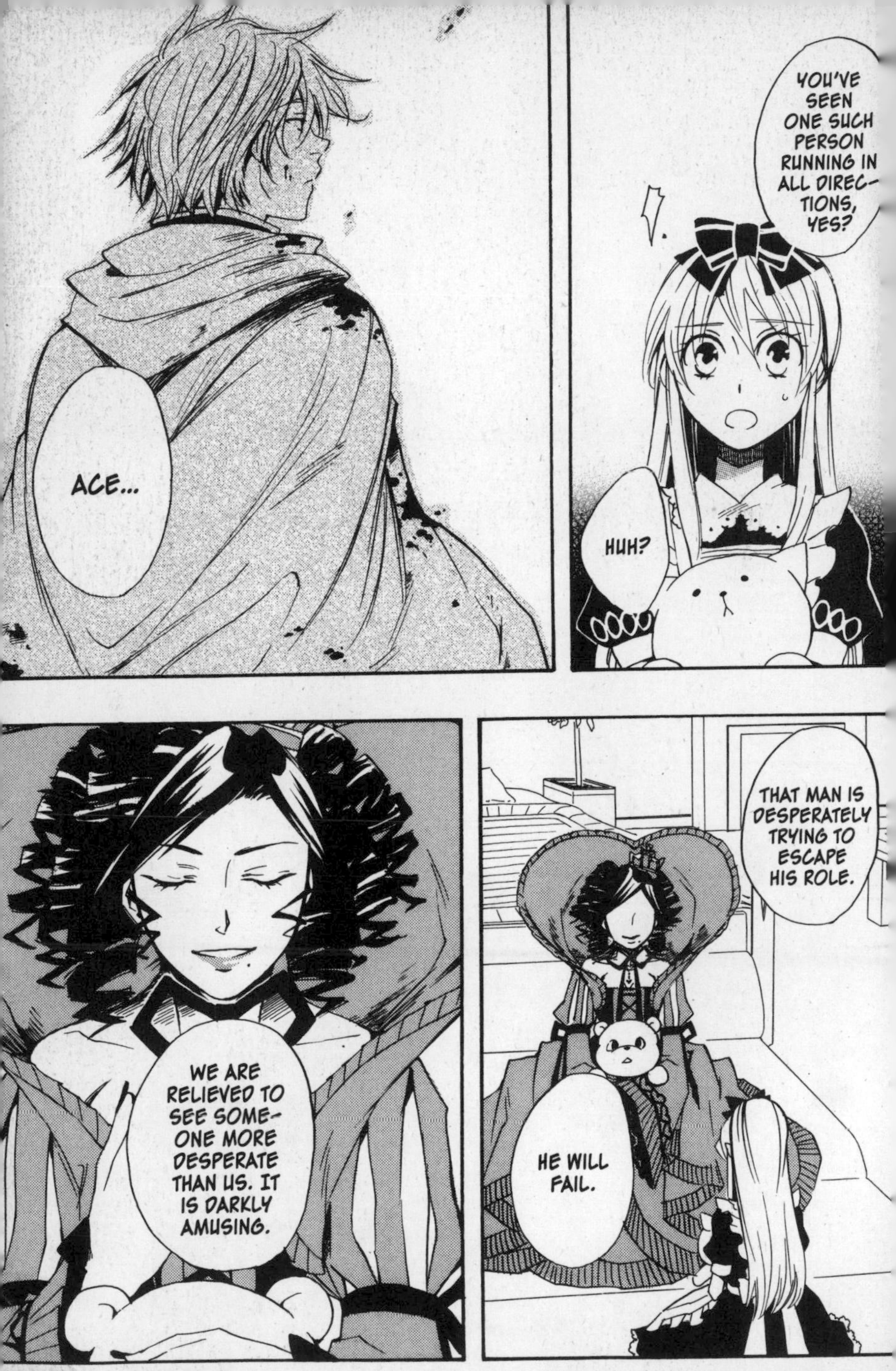
YOU'VE SEEN ONE SUCH PERSON RUNNING IN ALL DIRECTIONS, YES?
HUH?
ACE...
THAT MAN IS DESPERATELY TRYING TO ESCAPE HIS ROLE.
HE WILL FAIL.
WE ARE RELIEVED TO SEE SOME-ONE MORE DESPERATE THAN US. IT IS DARKLY AMUSING.

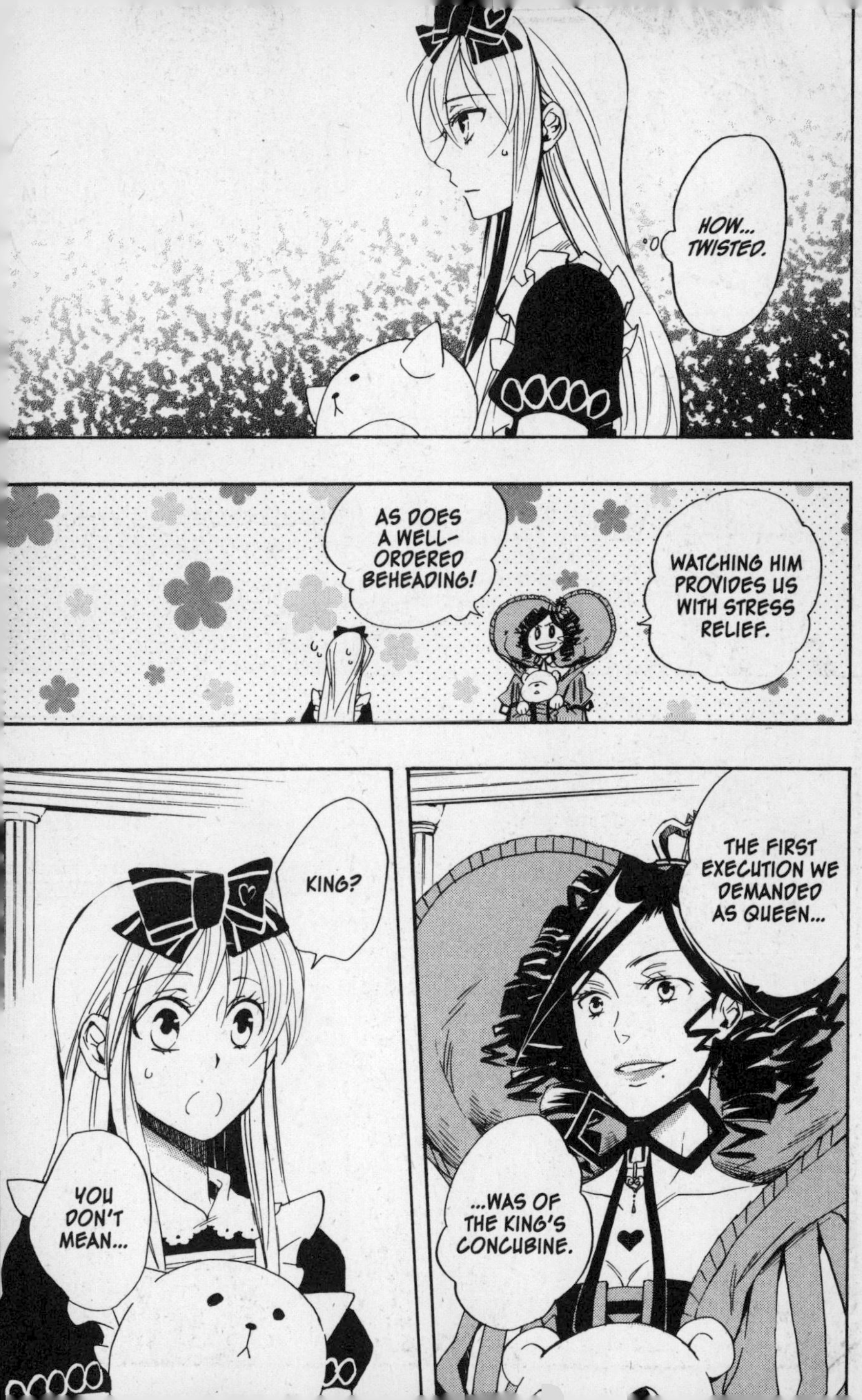
HOW... TWISTED.
WATCHING HIM PROVIDES US WITH STRESS RELIEF.
AS DOES A WELL-ORDERED BEHEADING!
THE FIRST EXECUTION WE DEMANDED AS QUEEN...
...WAS OF THE KING'S CONCUBINE.
KING?
YOU DON'T MEAN...

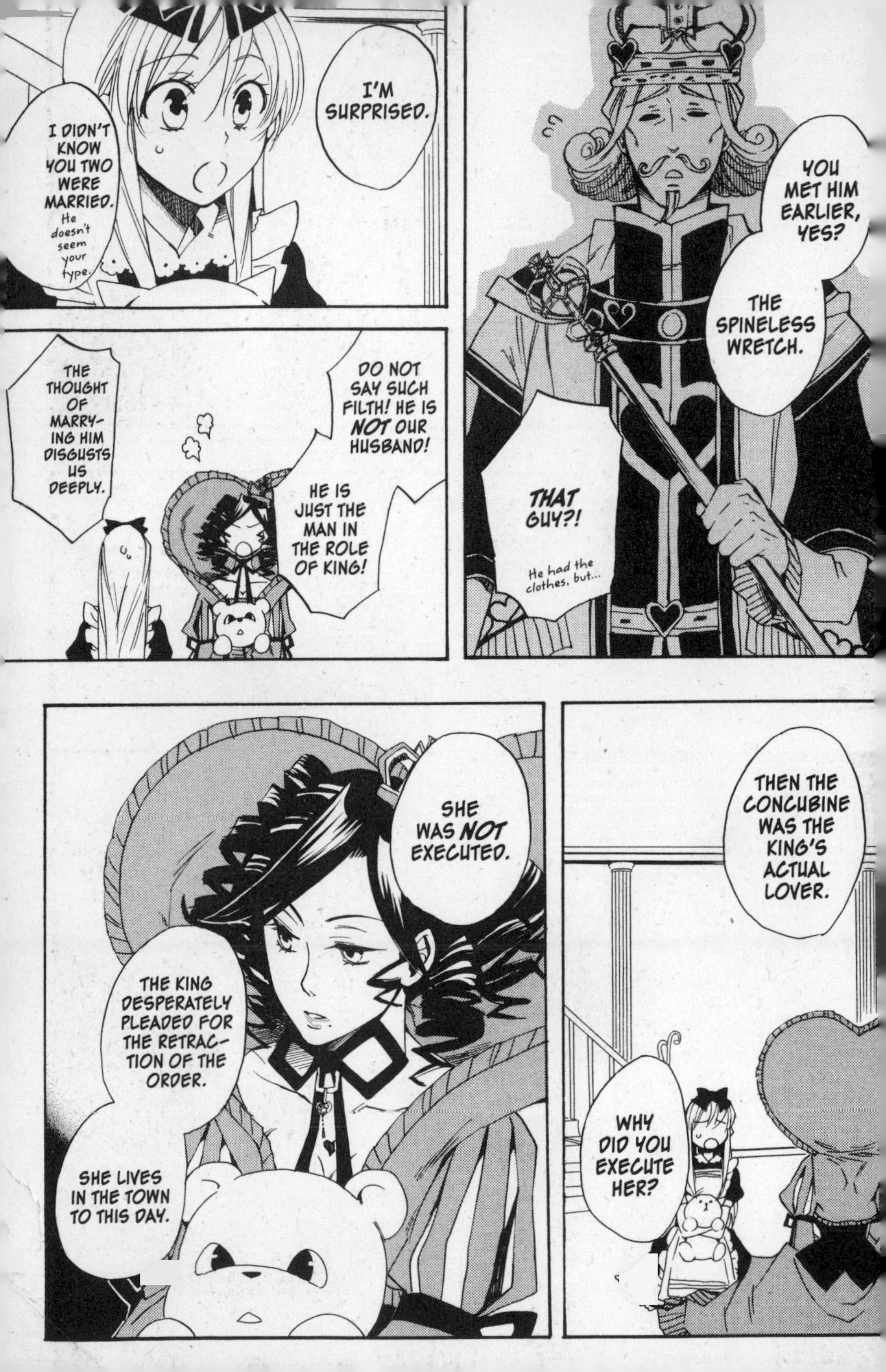
YOU MET HIM EARLIER, YES?
THE SPINELESS WRETCH.
THAT GUY?!
He had the clothes, but...
I'M SURPRISED.
I DIDN'T KNOW YOU TWO WERE MARRIED.
He doesn't seem your type.
DO NOT SAY SUCH FILTH! HE IS NOT OUR HUSBAND!
HE IS JUST THE MAN IN THE ROLE OF KING!
THE THOUGHT OF MARRY-ING HIM DISGUSTS US DEEPLY.
THEN THE CONCUBINE WAS THE KING'S ACTUAL LOVER.
WHY DID YOU EXECUTE HER?
SHE WAS NOT EXECUTED.
THE KING DESPERATELY PLEADED FOR THE RETRAC-TION OF THE ORDER.
SHE LIVES IN THE TOWN TO THIS DAY.

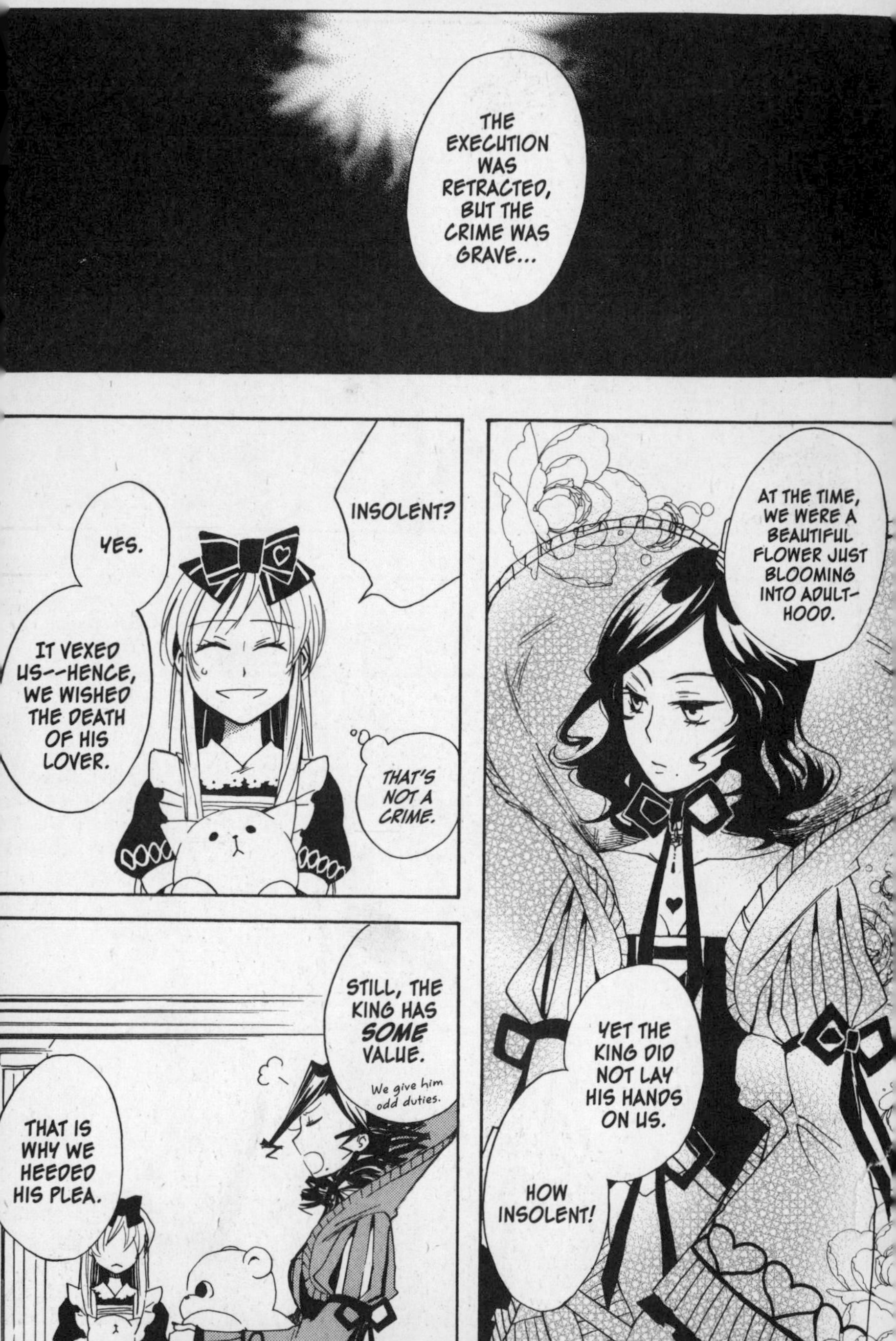
THE EXECUTION WAS RETRACTED, BUT THE CRIME WAS GRAVE...
AT THE TIME, WE WERE A BEAUTIFUL FLOWER JUST BLOOMING INTO ADULT-HOOD.
YET THE KING DID NOT LAY HIS HANDS ON US.
HOW INSOLENT!
INSOLENT?
YES.
IT VEXED US--HENCE, WE WISHED THE DEATH OF HIS LOVER.
THAT'S NOT A CRIME.
STILL, THE KING HAS SOME VALUE.
We give him odd duties.
THAT IS WHY WE HEEDED HIS PLEA.

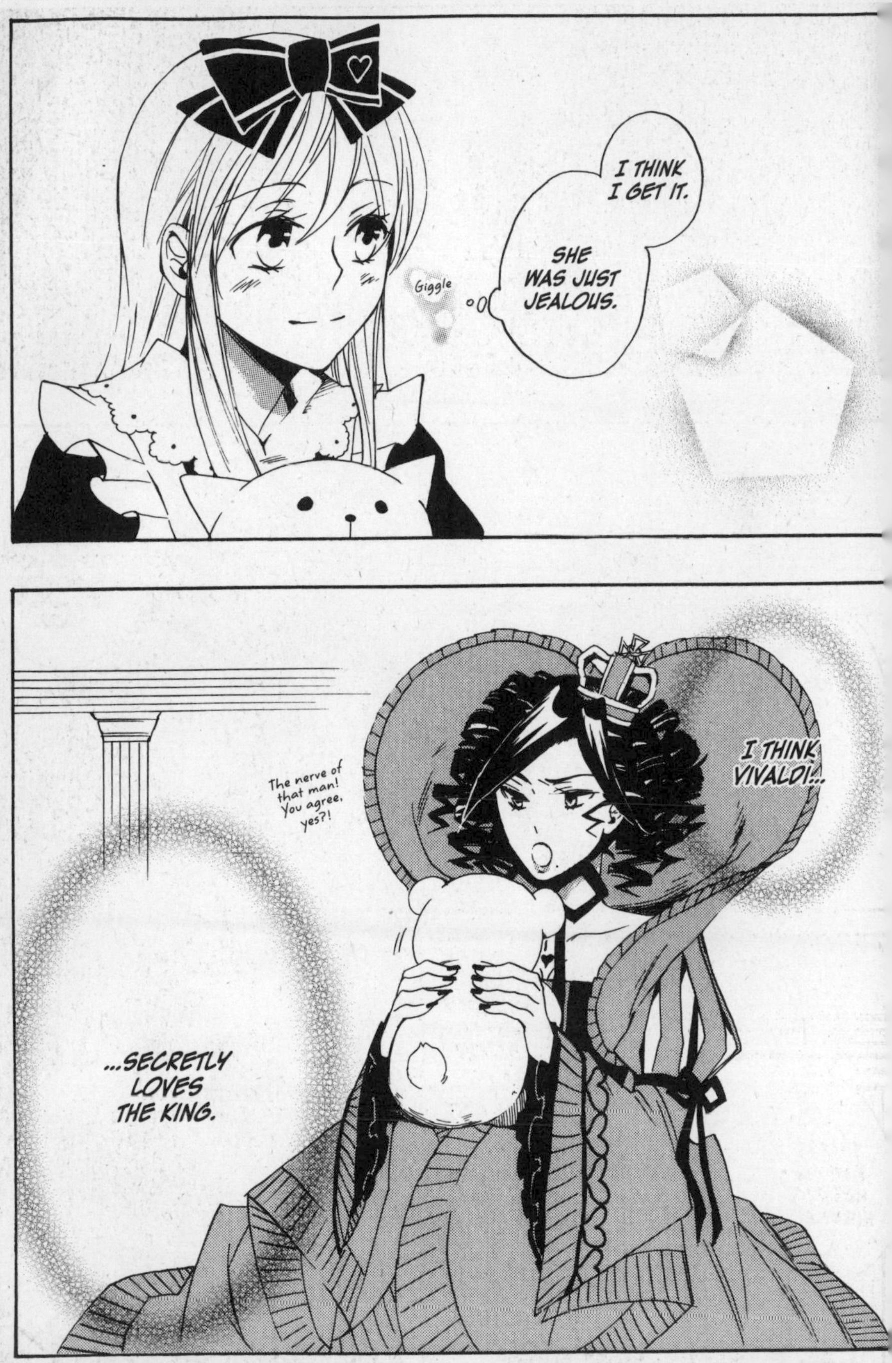
I THINK I GET IT.
SHE WAS JUST JEALOUS.
Giggle
I THINK VIVALDI...
The nerve of that man! You agree, yes?!
...SECRETLY LOVES THE KING.

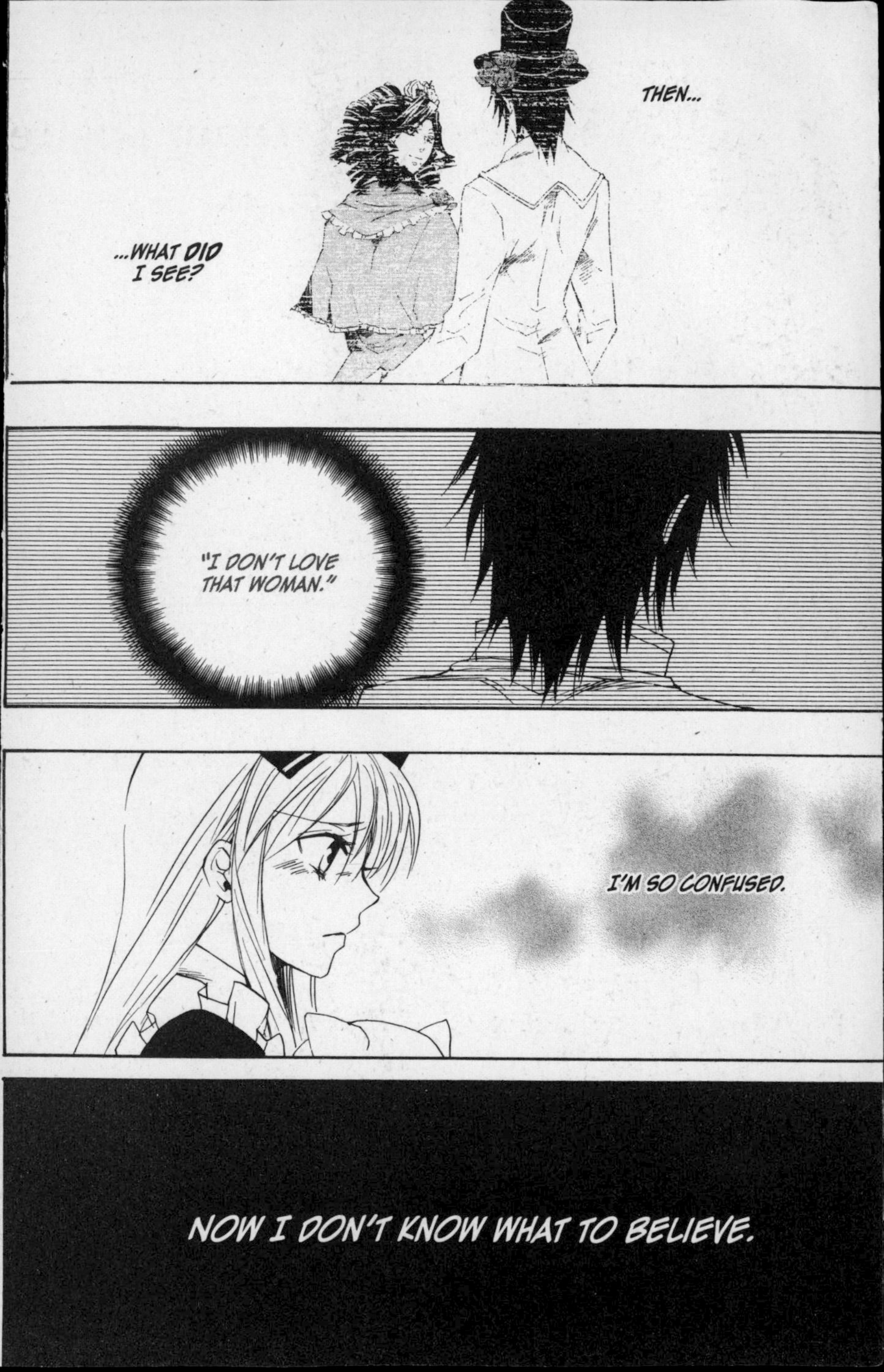
THEN...
...WHAT DID I SEE?
"I DON'T LOVE THAT WOMAN."
I'M SO CONFUSED.
NOW I DON'T KNOW WHAT TO BELIEVE.

♥16 Sweet Dream Taste

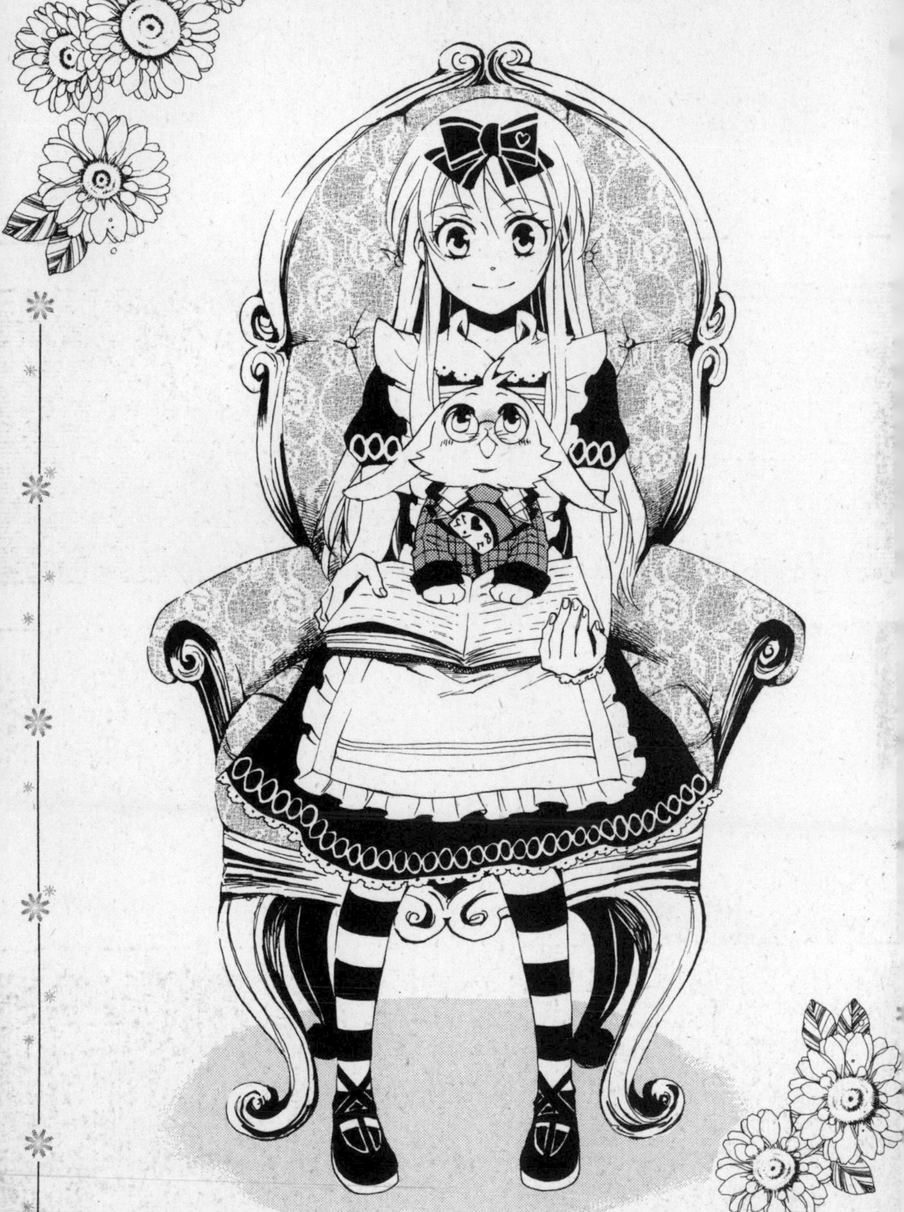

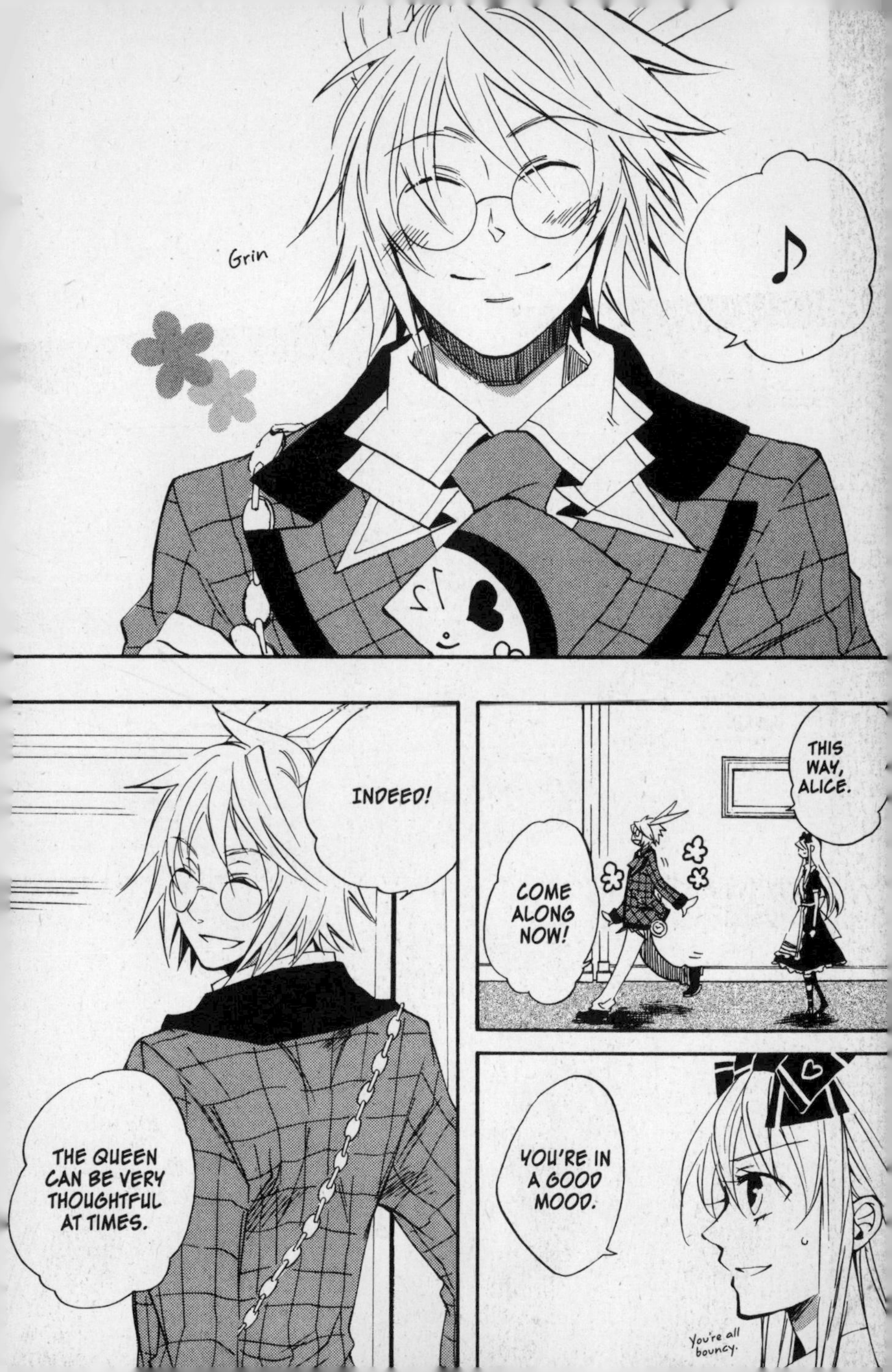
Grin
♪
THIS WAY, ALICE.
COME ALONG NOW!
YOU'RE IN A GOOD MOOD.
You're all bouncy.
INDEED!
THE QUEEN CAN BE VERY THOUGHTFUL AT TIMES.

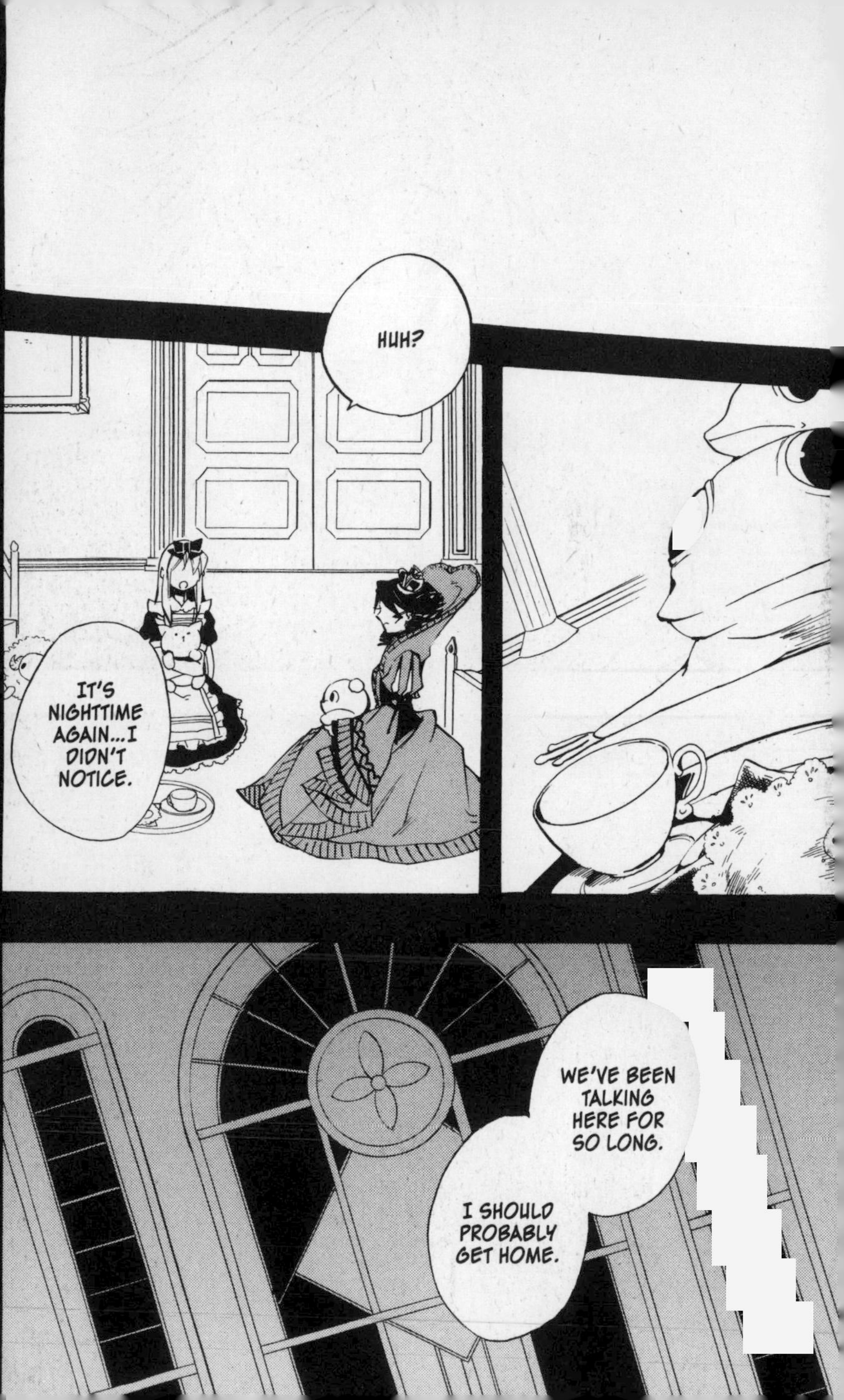
HUH?
IT'S NIGHTTIME AGAIN...I DIDN'T NOTICE.
WE'VE BEEN TALKING HERE FOR SO LONG.
I SHOULD PROBABLY GET HOME.

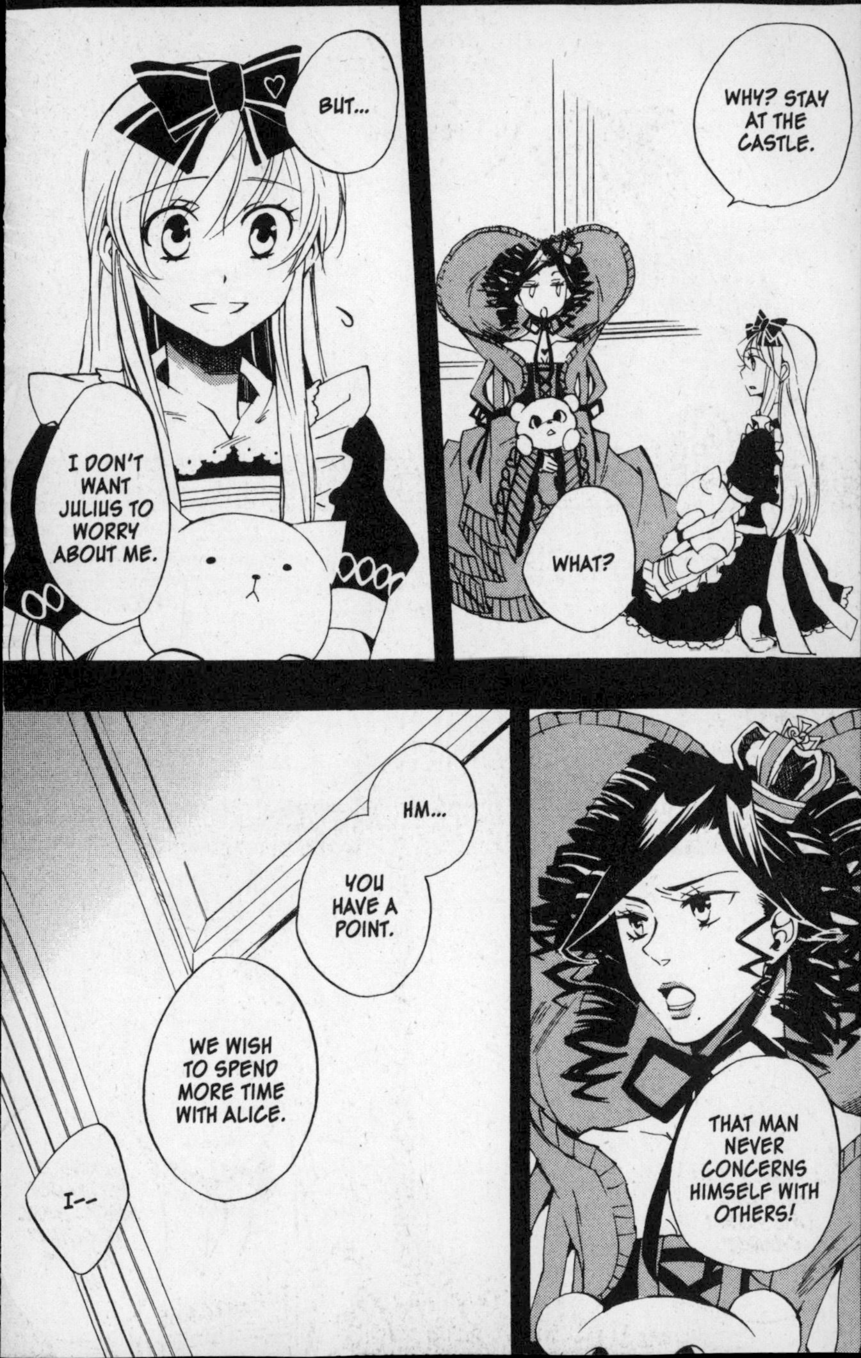
WHY? STAY AT THE CASTLE.
WHAT?
BUT...
I DON'T WANT JULIUS TO WORRY ABOUT ME.
THAT MAN NEVER CONCERNS HIMSELF WITH OTHERS!
HM...
YOU HAVE A POINT.
WE WISH TO SPEND MORE TIME WITH ALICE.
I--

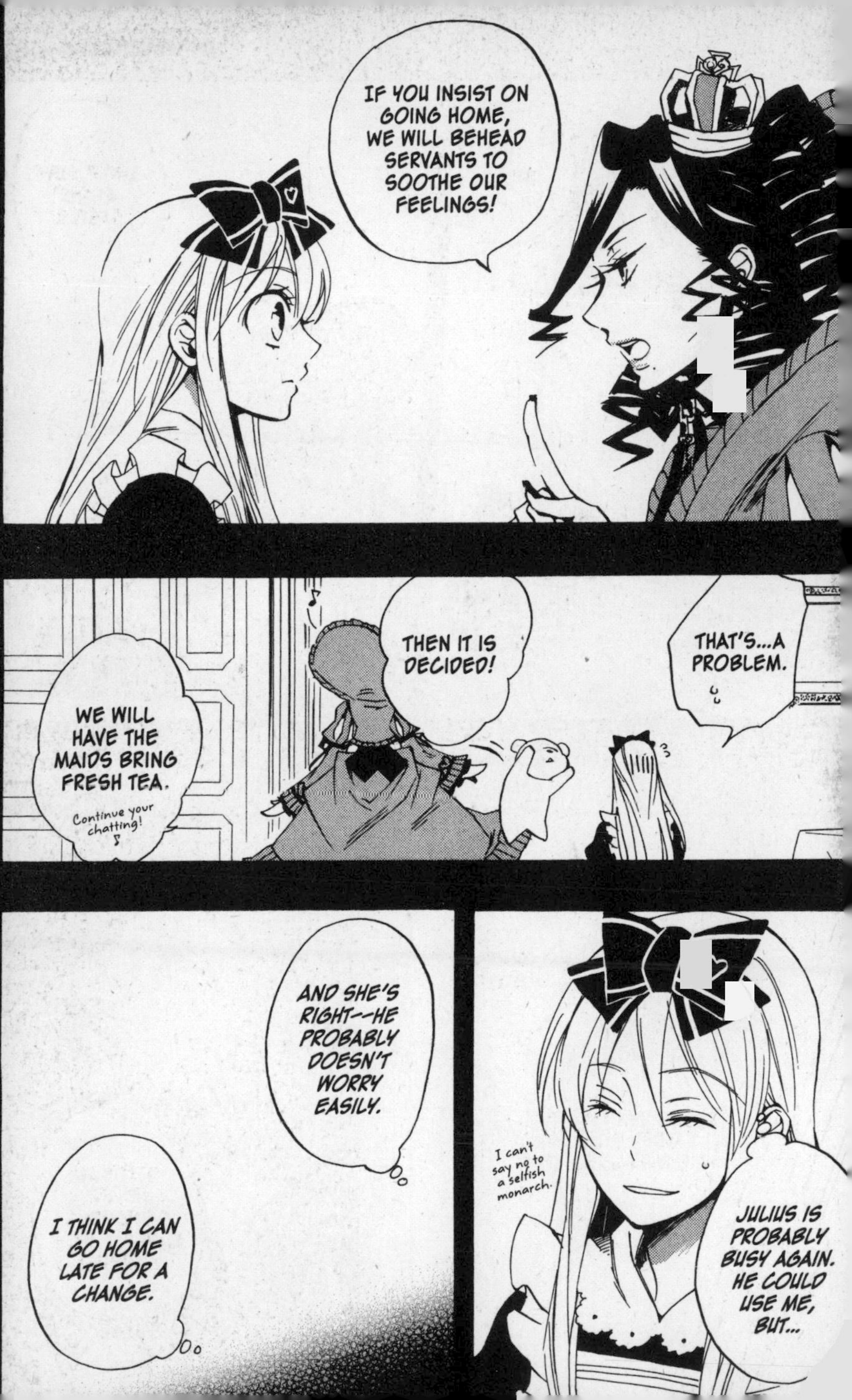
IF YOU INSIST ON GOING HOME, WE WILL BEHEAD SERVANTS TO SOOTHE OUR FEELINGS!
THAT'S...A PROBLEM.
THEN IT IS DECIDED!
WE WILL HAVE THE MAIDS BRING FRESH TEA.
Continue your chatting!
JULIUS IS PROBABLY BUSY AGAIN. HE COULD USE ME, BUT...
I can't say no to a selfish monarch.
AND SHE'S RIGHT--HE PROBABLY DOESN'T WORRY EASILY.
I THINK I CAN GO HOME LATE FOR A CHANGE.

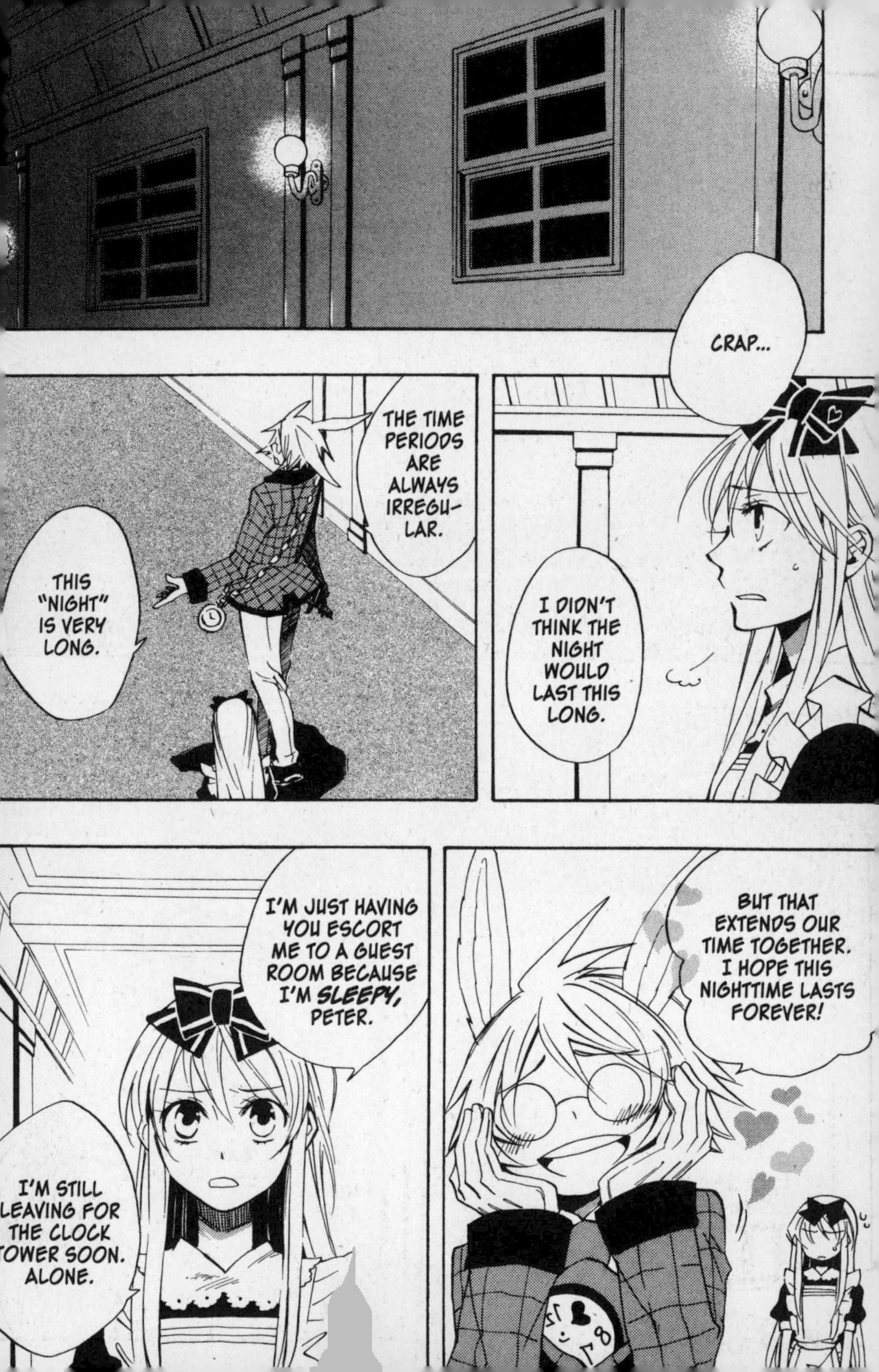
CRAP...
I DIDN'T THINK THE NIGHT WOULD LAST THIS LONG.
THE TIME PERIODS ARE ALWAYS IRREGU-LAR.
THIS "NIGHT" IS VERY LONG.
BUT THAT EXTENDS OUR TIME TOGETHER. I HOPE THIS NIGHTTIME LASTS FOREVER!
I'M JUST HAVING YOU ESCORT ME TO A GUEST ROOM BECAUSE I'M *SLEEPY,* PETER.
I'M STILL LEAVING FOR THE CLOCK TOWER SOON. ALONE.

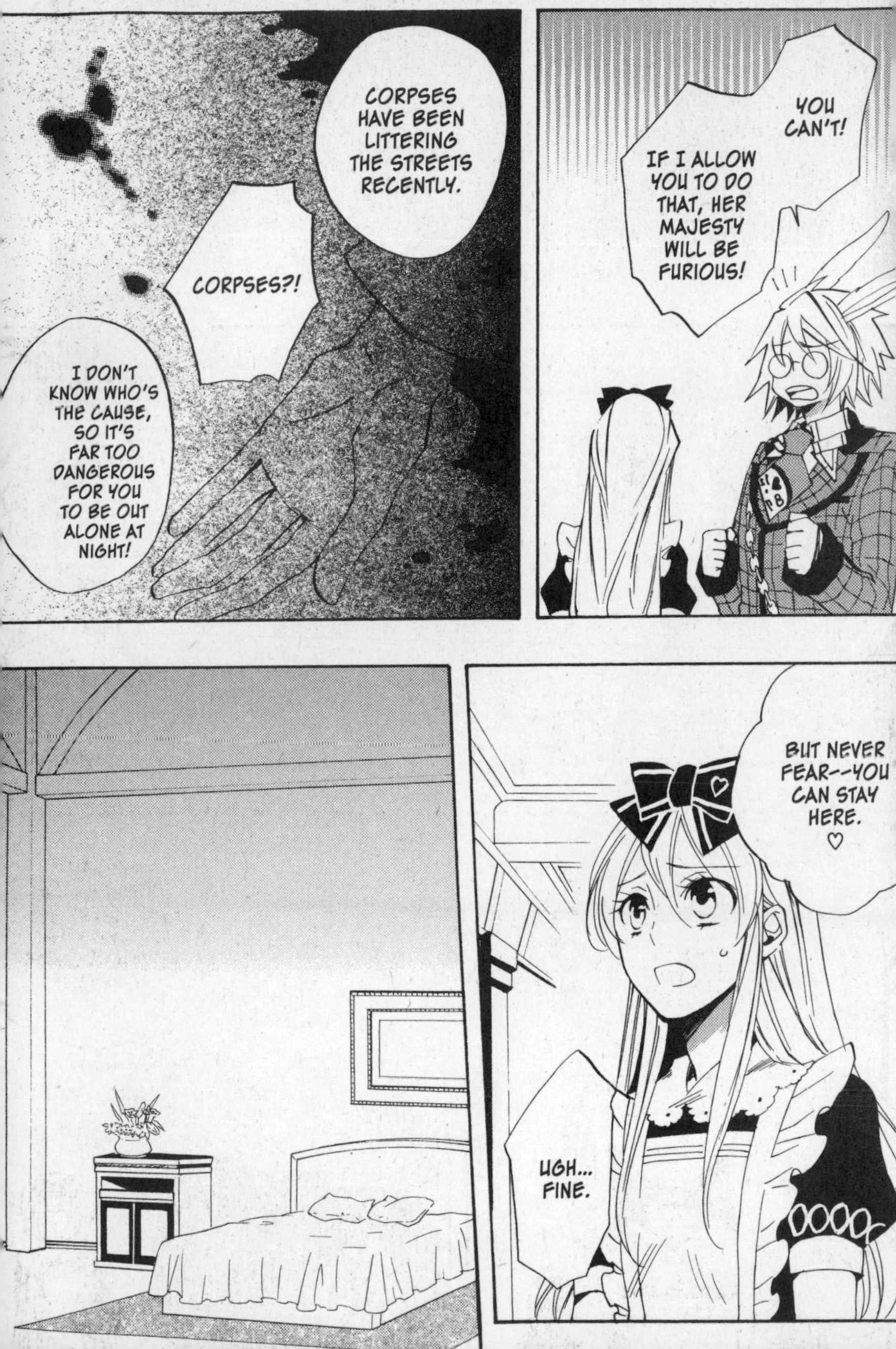
YOU CAN'T!
IF I ALLOW YOU TO DO THAT, HER MAJESTY WILL BE FURIOUS!
CORPSES HAVE BEEN LITTERING THE STREETS RECENTLY.
CORPSES?!
I DON'T KNOW WHO'S THE CAUSE, SO IT'S FAR TOO DANGEROUS FOR YOU TO BE OUT ALONE AT NIGHT!
BUT NEVER FEAR--YOU CAN STAY HERE. ♡
UGH... FINE.

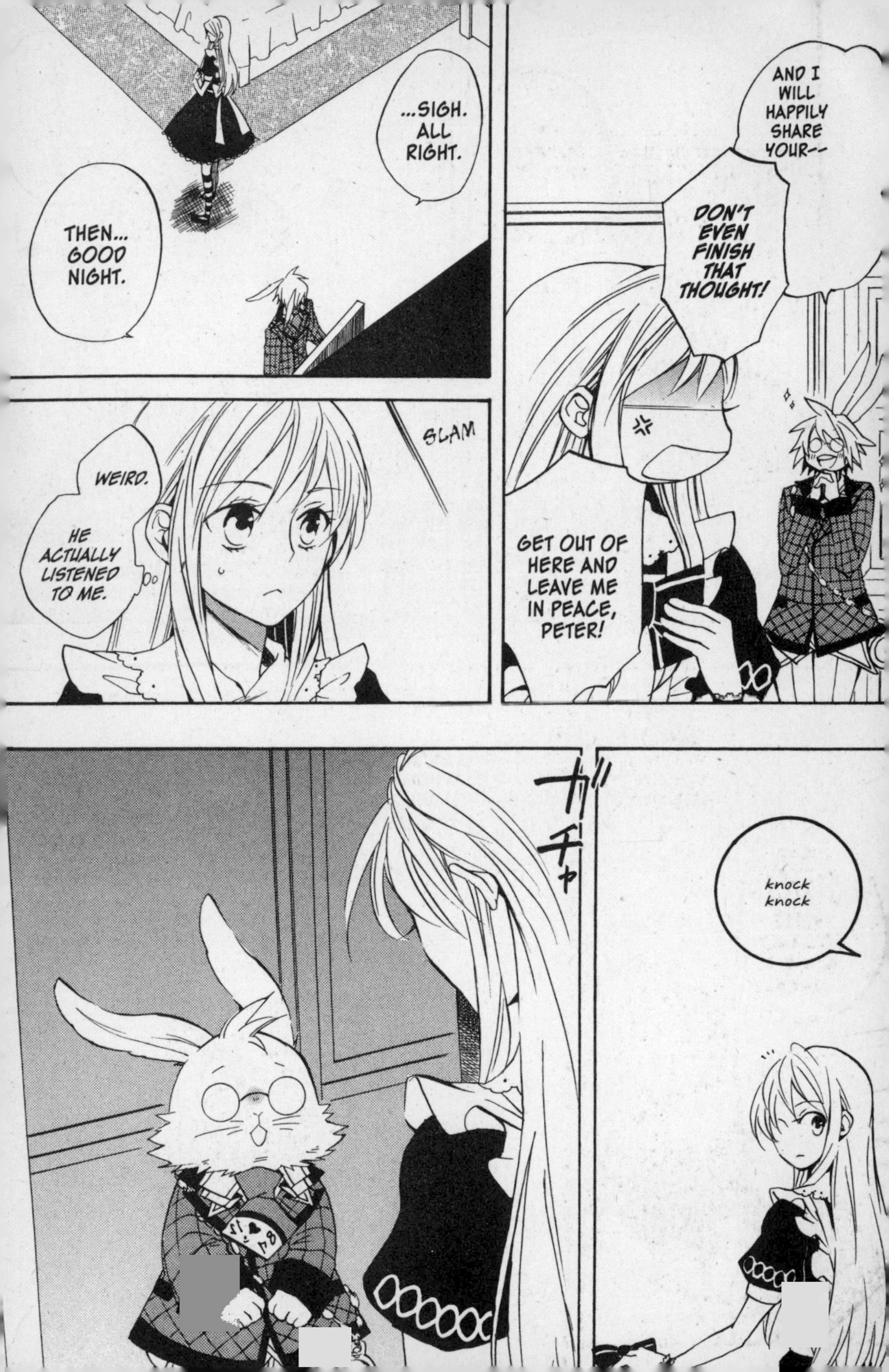
AND I WILL HAPPILY SHARE YOUR--
DON'T EVEN FINISH THAT THOUGHT!
GET OUT OF HERE AND LEAVE ME IN PEACE, PETER!
...SIGH. ALL RIGHT.
THEN... GOOD NIGHT.
SLAM
WEIRD.
HE ACTUALLY LISTENED TO ME.
knock knock
ガチャ

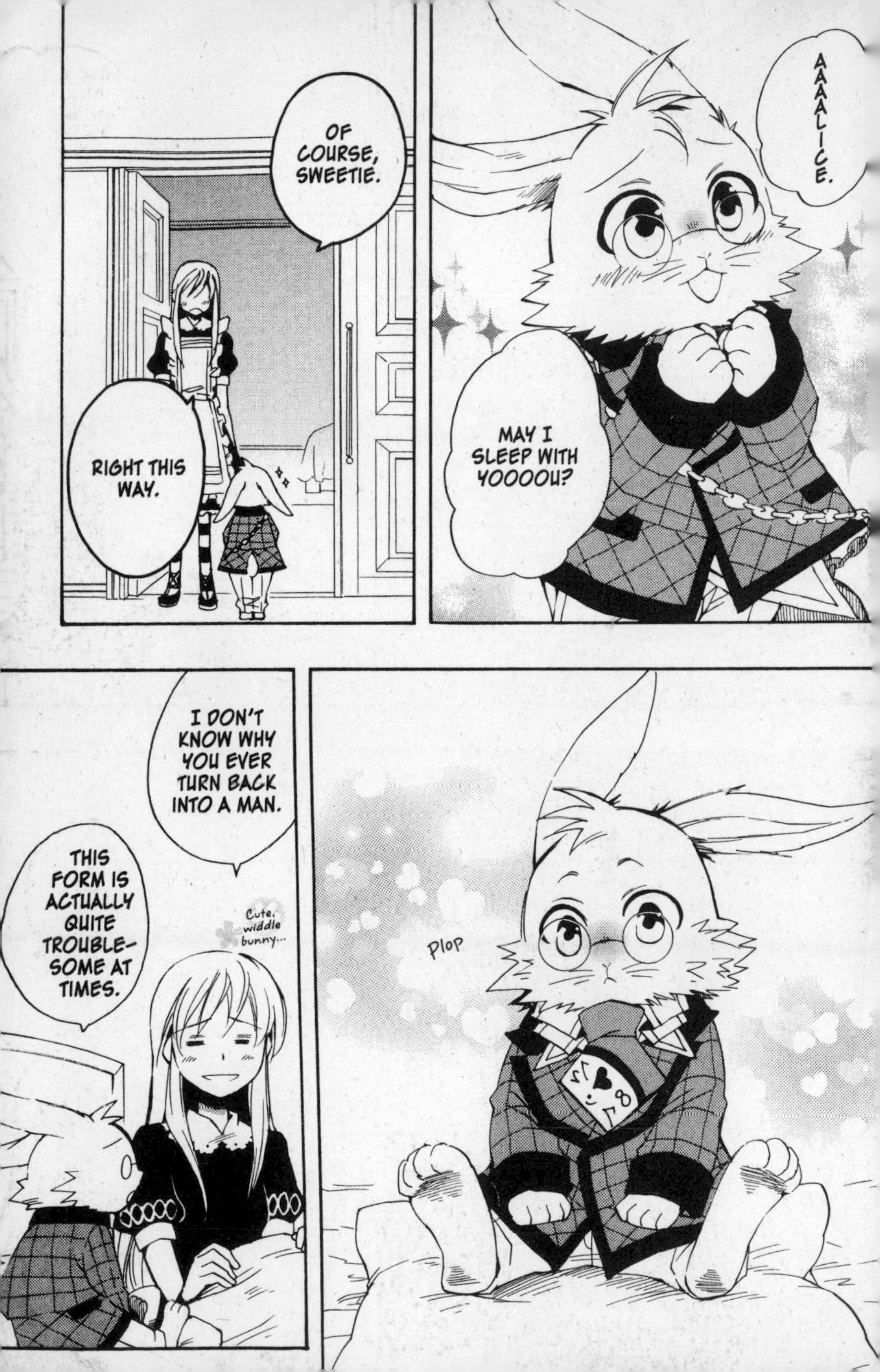
AAAALICE.
MAY I SLEEP WITH YOOOOU?
OF COURSE, SWEETIE.
RIGHT THIS WAY.
Plop
I DON'T KNOW WHY YOU EVER TURN BACK INTO A MAN.
THIS FORM IS ACTUALLY QUITE TROUBLE-SOME AT TIMES.
Cute, widdle bunny...

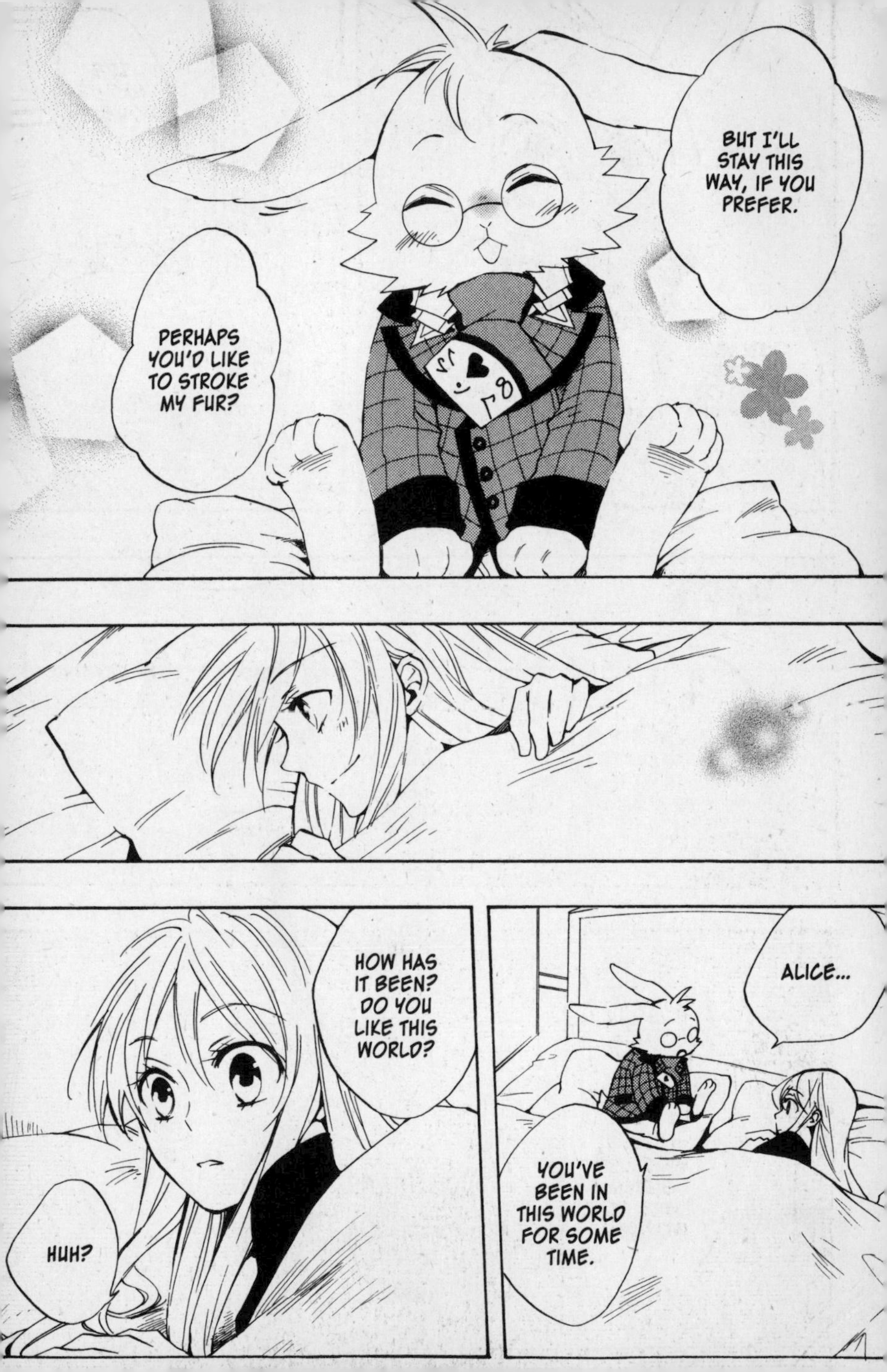
BUT I'LL STAY THIS WAY, IF YOU PREFER.
PERHAPS YOU'D LIKE TO STROKE MY FUR?
ALICE...
YOU'VE BEEN IN THIS WORLD FOR SOME TIME.
HOW HAS IT BEEN? DO YOU LIKE THIS WORLD?
HUH?

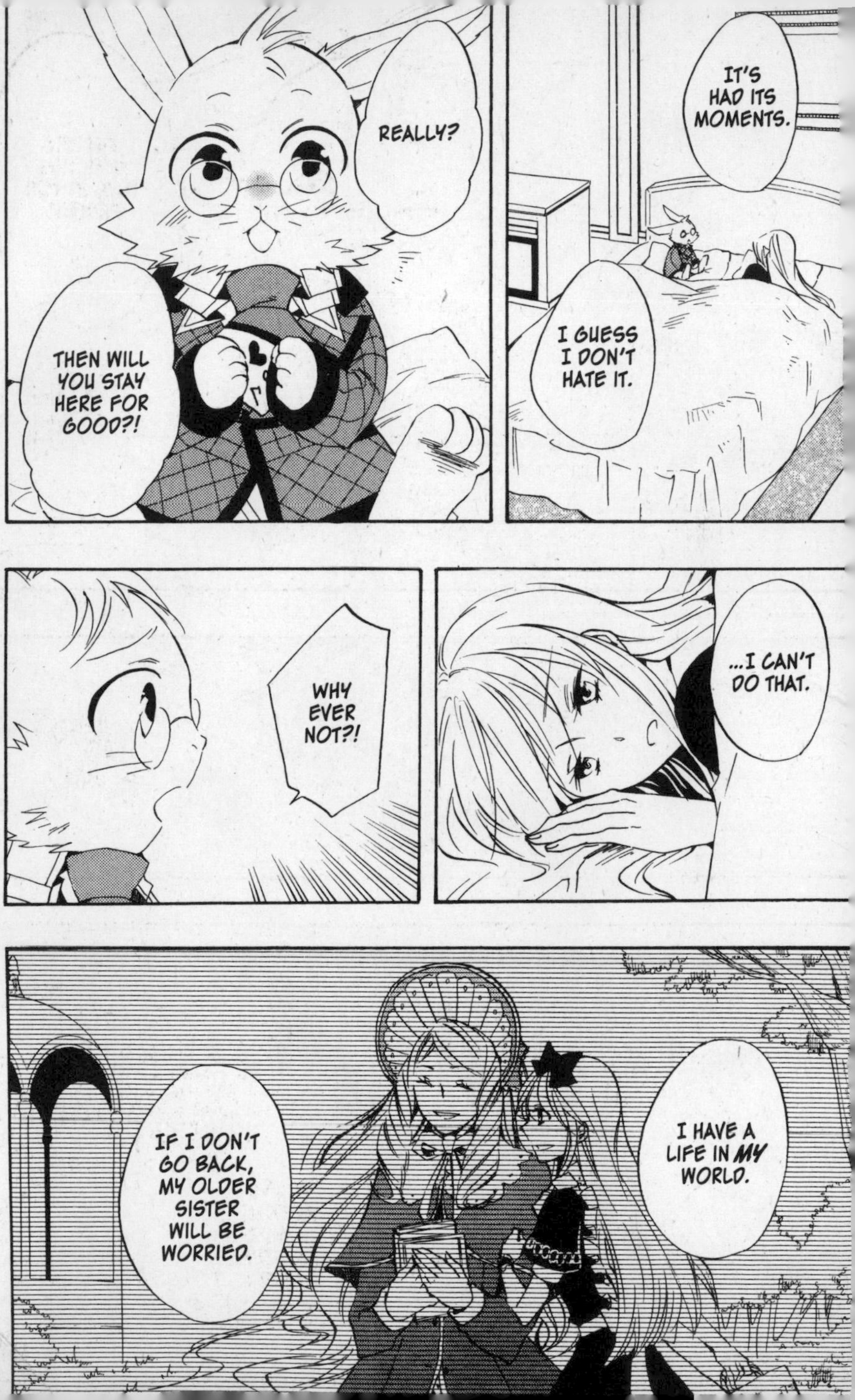
IT'S HAD ITS MOMENTS.
I GUESS I DON'T HATE IT.
REALLY?
THEN WILL YOU STAY HERE FOR GOOD?!
...I CAN'T DO THAT.
WHY EVER NOT?!
I HAVE A LIFE IN *MY* WORLD.
IF I DON'T GO BACK, MY OLDER SISTER WILL BE WORRIED.

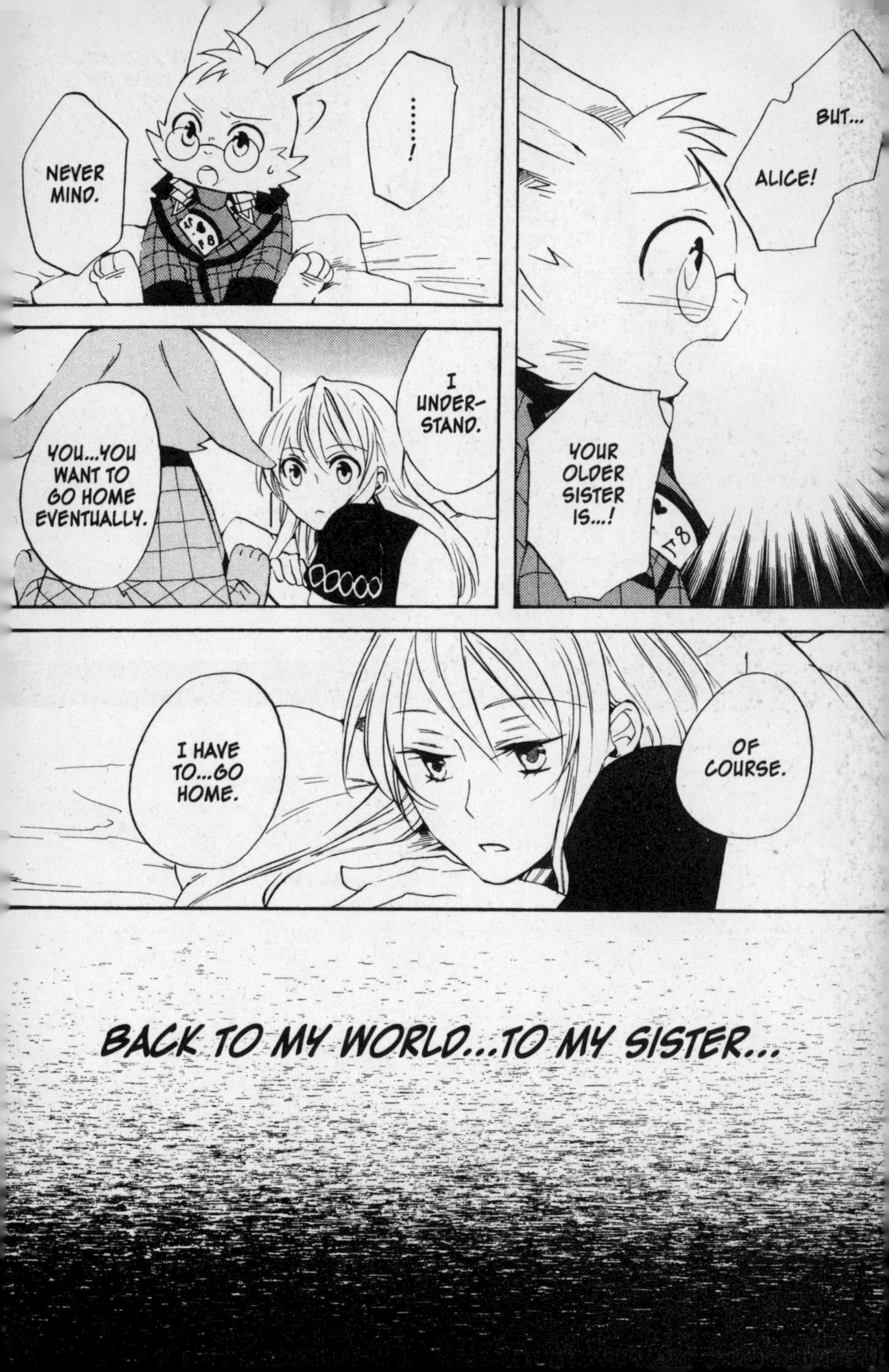
BUT...
ALICE!
YOUR OLDER SISTER IS...!
......!
NEVER MIND.
I UNDER-STAND.
YOU...YOU WANT TO GO HOME EVENTUALLY.
OF COURSE.
I HAVE TO...GO HOME.
BACK TO MY WORLD...TO MY SISTER...

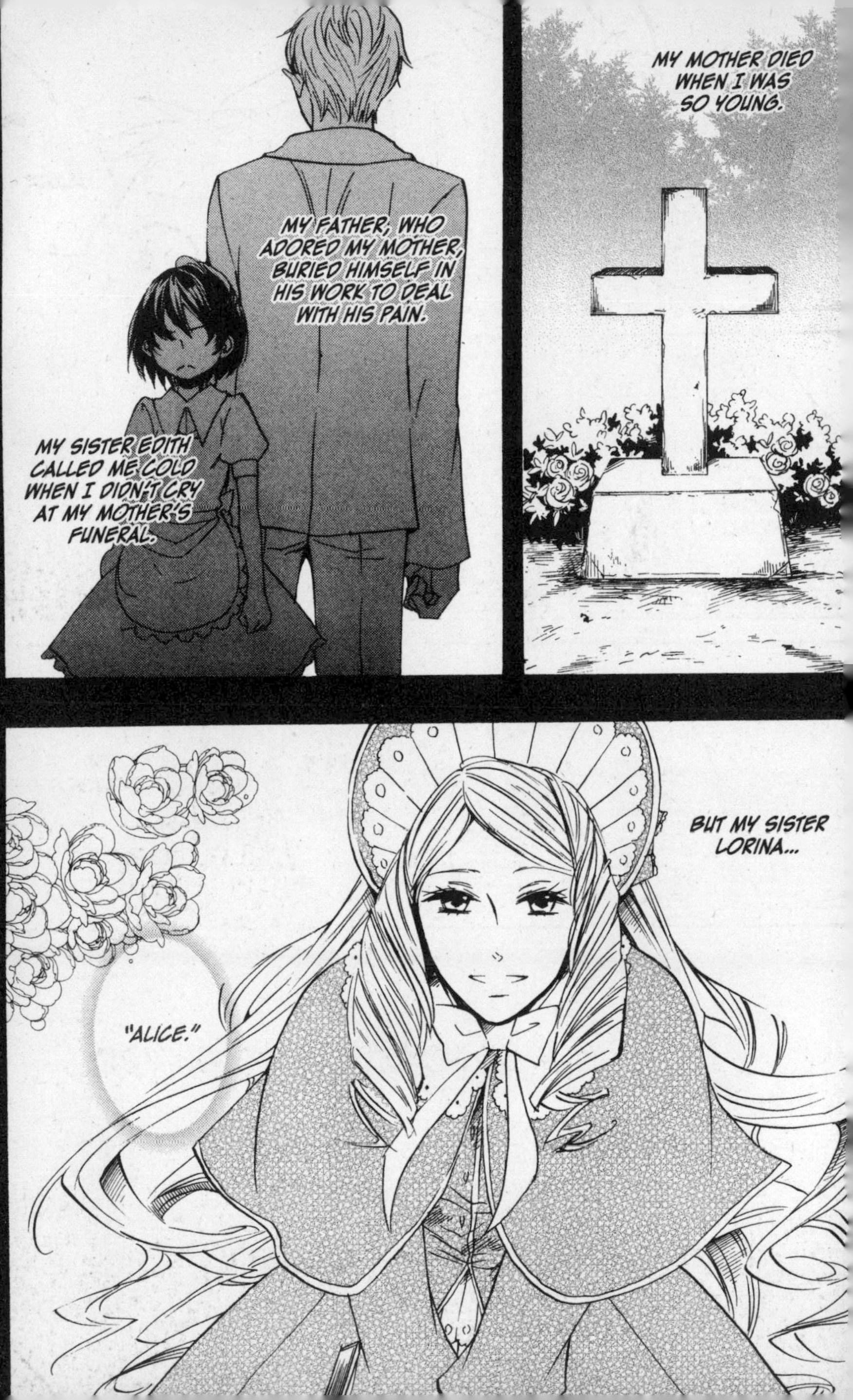
MY MOTHER DIED WHEN I WAS SO YOUNG.
MY FATHER, WHO ADORED MY MOTHER, BURIED HIMSELF IN HIS WORK TO DEAL WITH HIS PAIN.
MY SISTER EDITH CALLED ME COLD WHEN I DIDN'T CRY AT MY MOTHER'S FUNERAL.
BUT MY SISTER LORINA...
"ALICE."

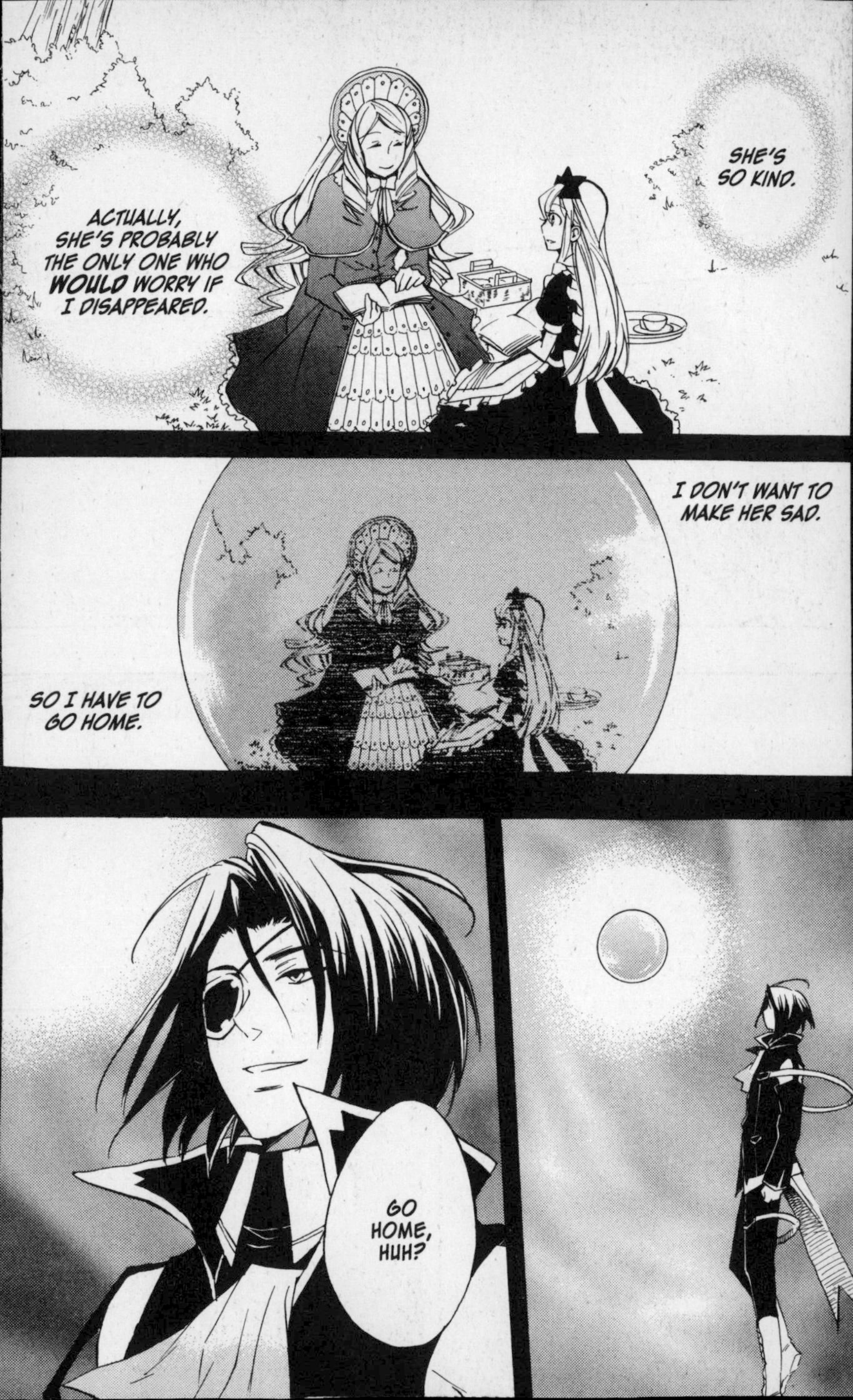
SHE'S SO KIND.
ACTUALLY, SHE'S PROBABLY THE ONLY ONE WHO **WOULD** WORRY IF I DISAPPEARED.
I DON'T WANT TO MAKE HER SAD.
SO I HAVE TO GO HOME.
GO HOME, HUH?

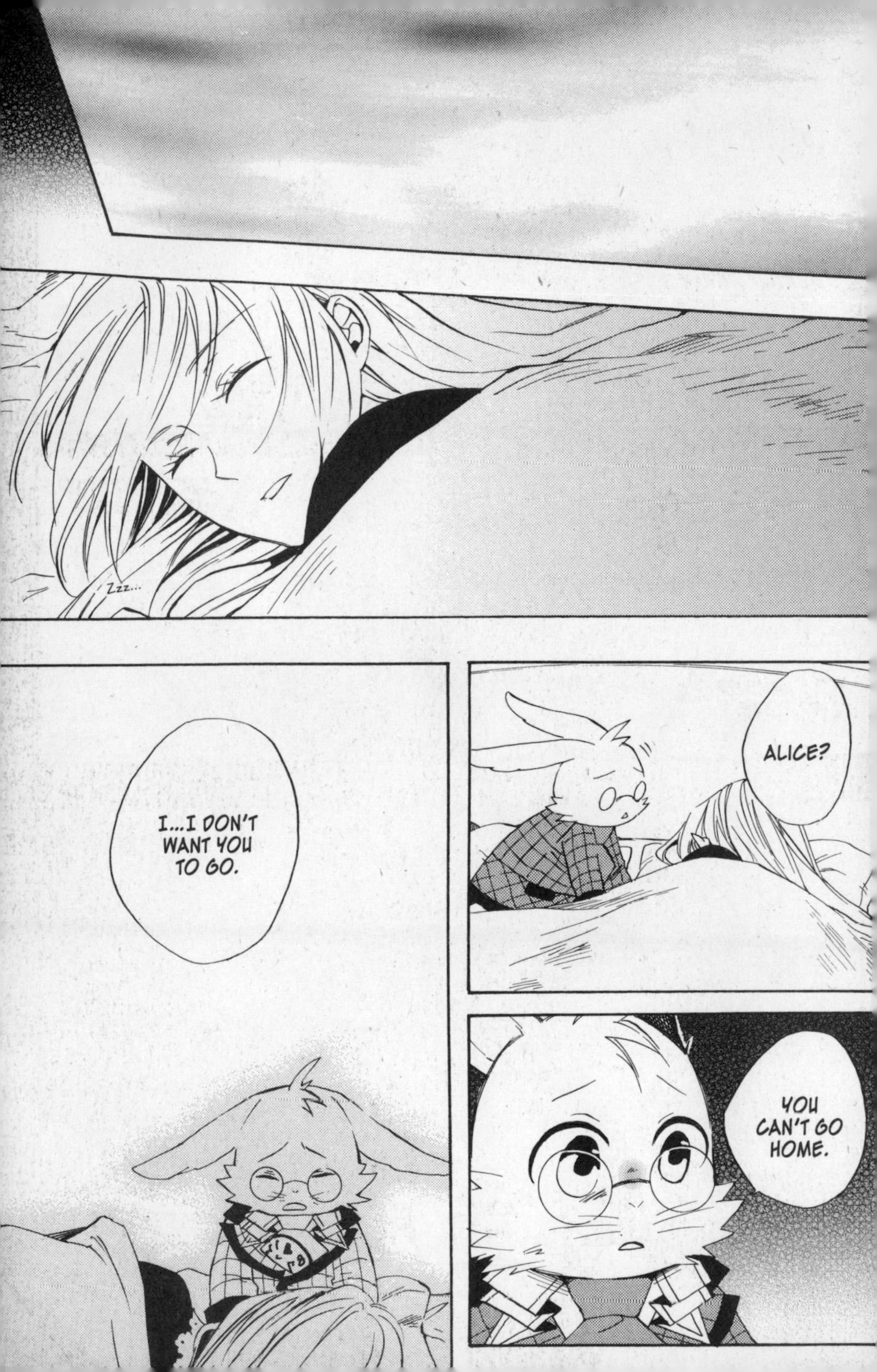
Zzz...
ALICE?
YOU CAN'T GO HOME.
I...I DON'T WANT YOU TO GO.

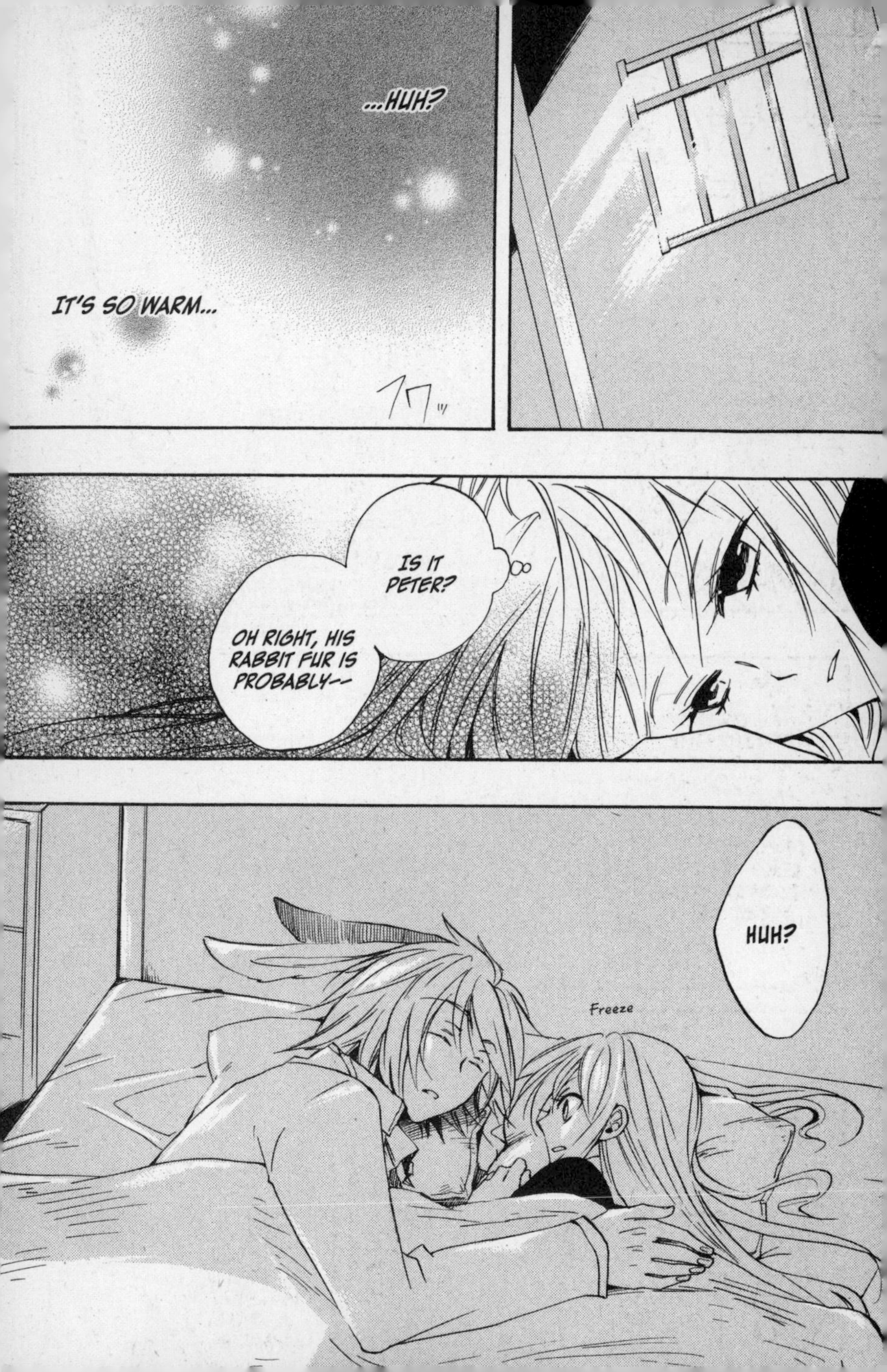
...HUH?
IT'S SO WARM...
フワッ
IS IT PETER?
OH RIGHT, HIS RABBIT FUR IS PROBABLY--
HUH?
Freeze

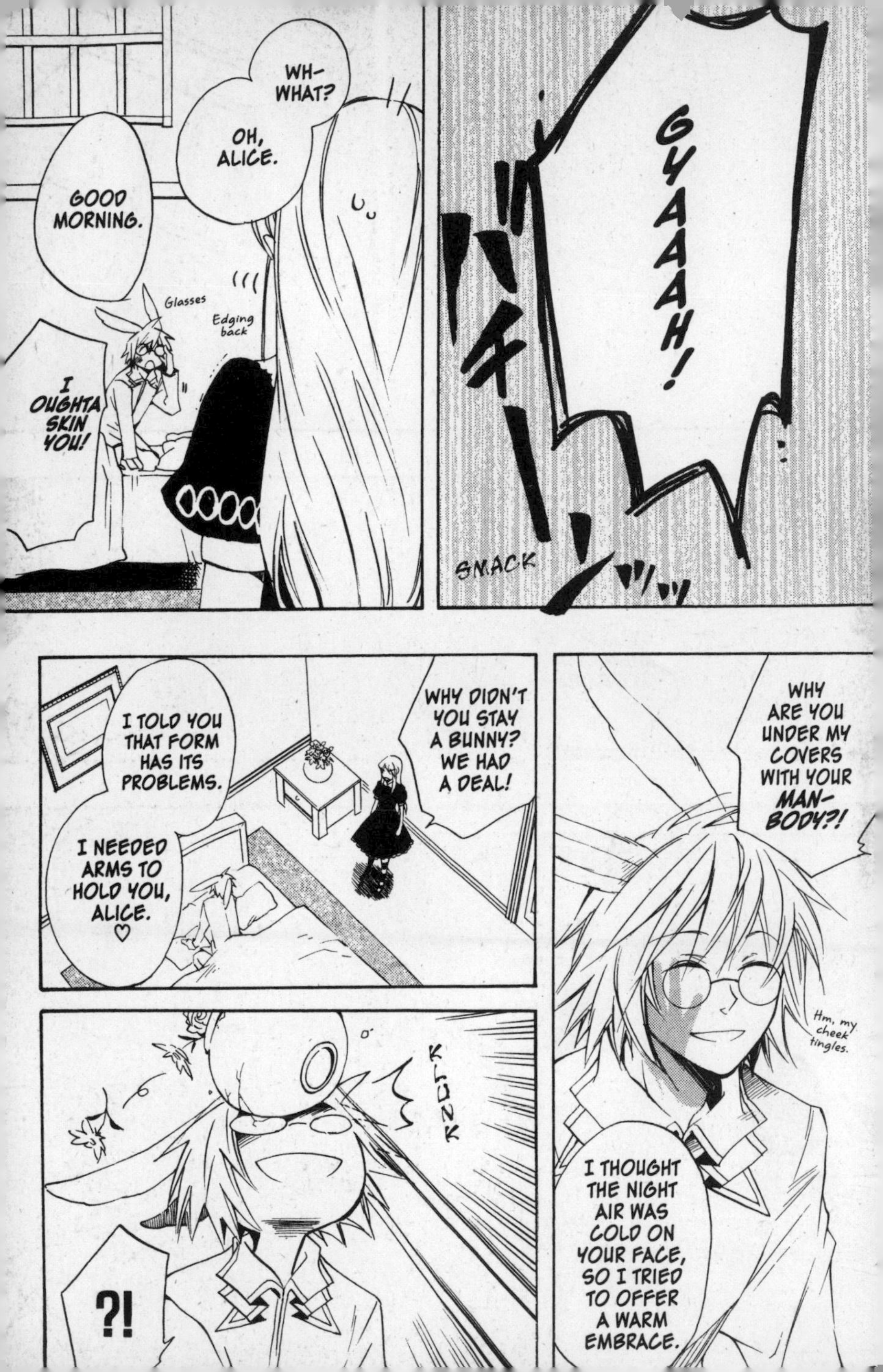
GYAAAH!
SMACK
WH- WHAT?
OH, ALICE.
GOOD MORNING.
Glasses
Edging back
I OUGHTA SKIN YOU!
WHY ARE YOU UNDER MY COVERS WITH YOUR MAN-BODY?!
Hm, my cheek tingles.
I THOUGHT THE NIGHT AIR WAS COLD ON YOUR FACE, SO I TRIED TO OFFER A WARM EMBRACE.
WHY DIDN'T YOU STAY A BUNNY? WE HAD A DEAL!
I TOLD YOU THAT FORM HAS ITS PROBLEMS.
I NEEDED ARMS TO HOLD YOU, ALICE. ♡
KLUNK
?!

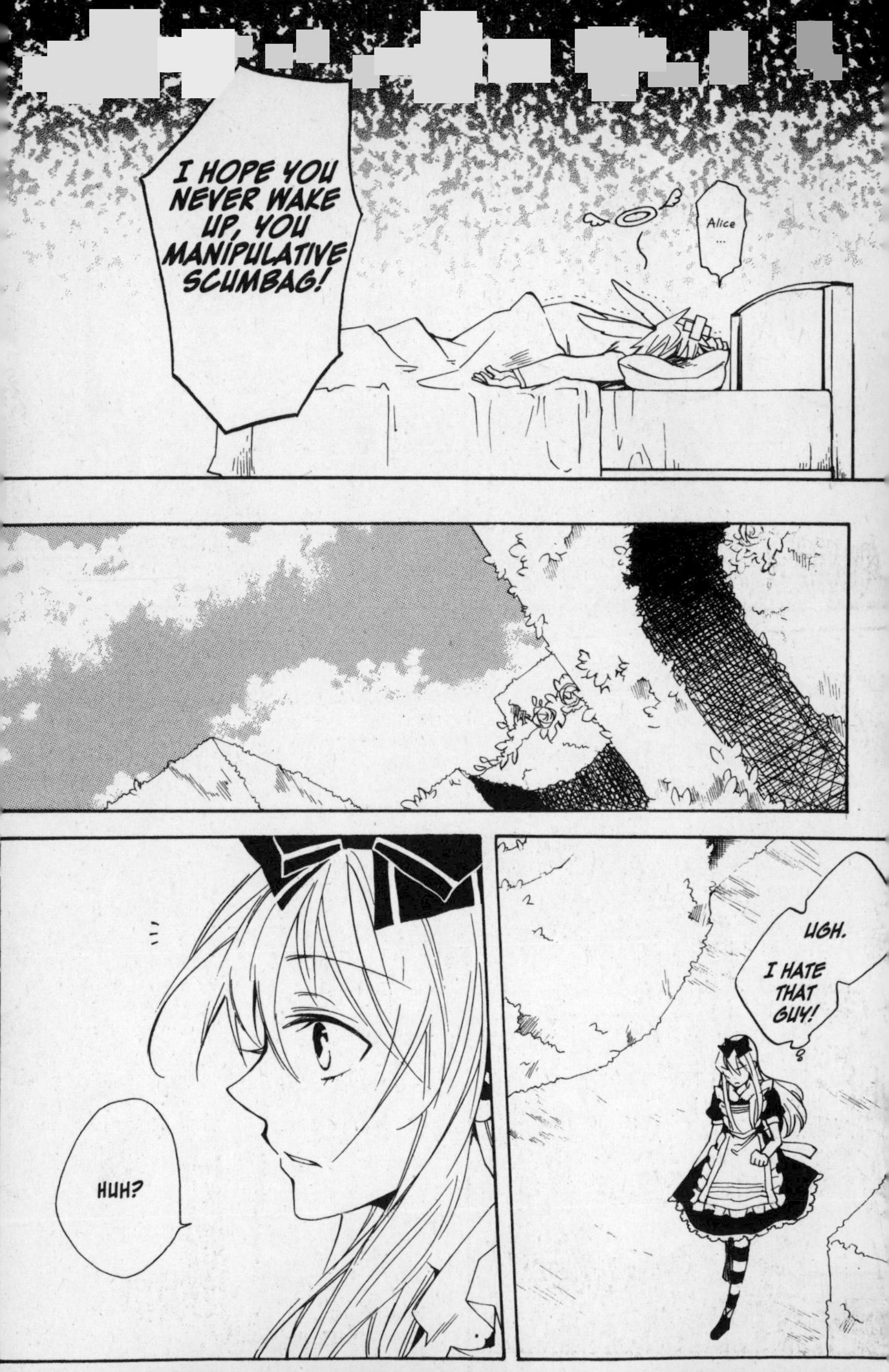
Alice ...
I HOPE YOU NEVER WAKE UP, YOU MANIPULATIVE SCUMBAG!
UGH.
I HATE THAT GUY!
HUH?

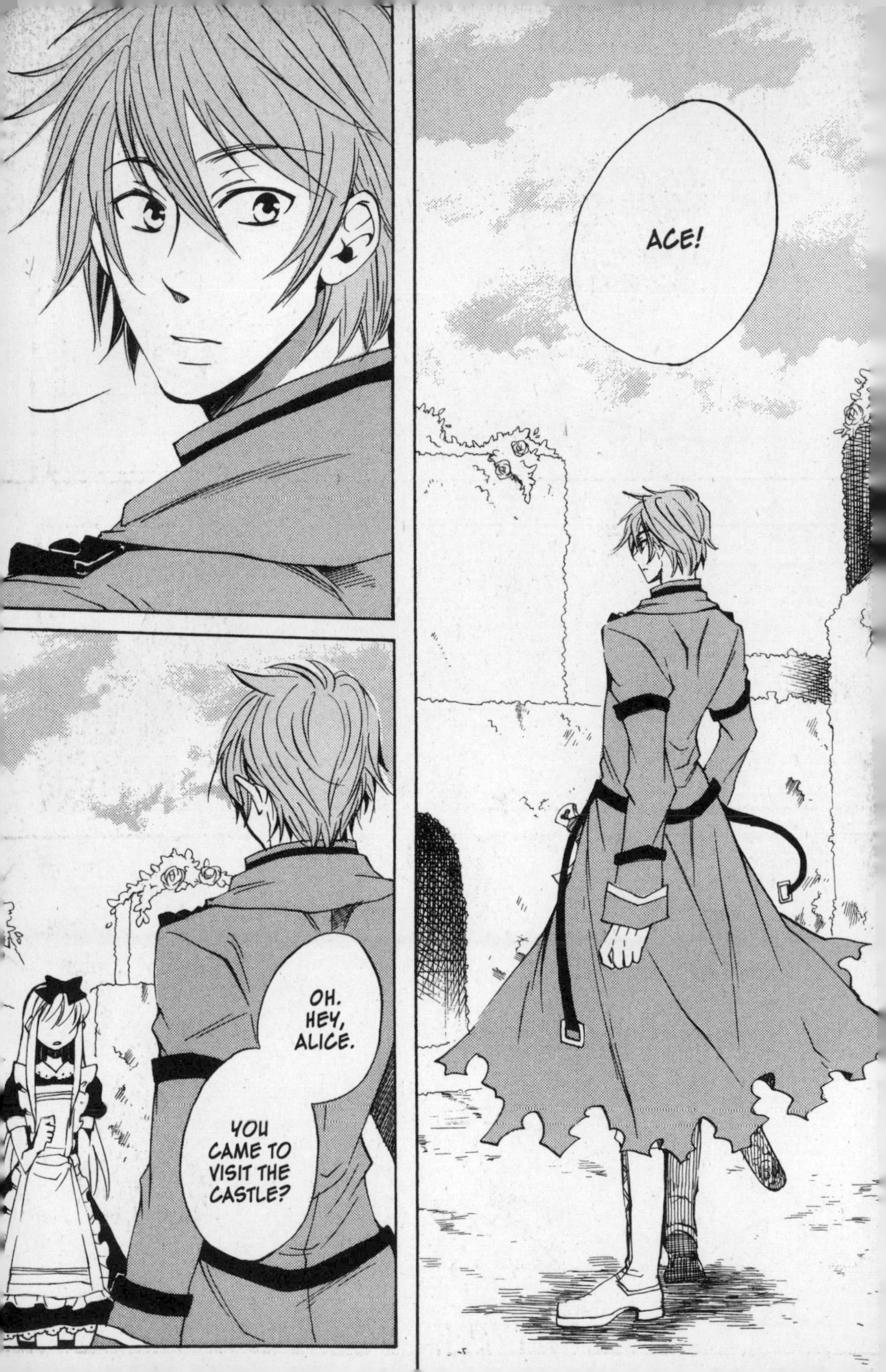
ACE!
OH. HEY, ALICE.
YOU CAME TO VISIT THE CASTLE?

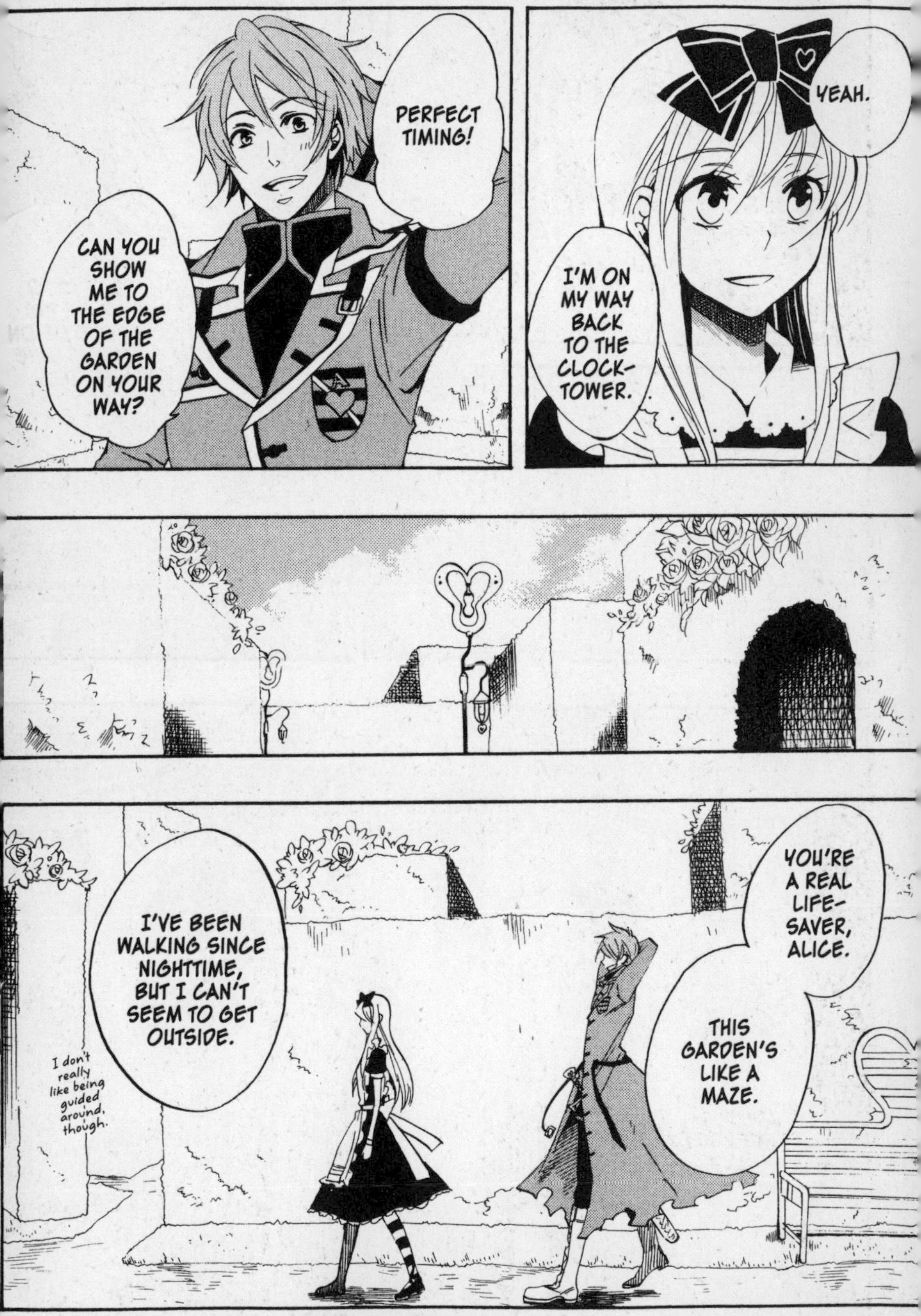
YEAH.
I'M ON MY WAY BACK TO THE CLOCK-TOWER.
PERFECT TIMING!
CAN YOU SHOW ME TO THE EDGE OF THE GARDEN ON YOUR WAY?
YOU'RE A REAL LIFE-SAVER, ALICE.
THIS GARDEN'S LIKE A MAZE.
I'VE BEEN WALKING SINCE NIGHTTIME, BUT I CAN'T SEEM TO GET OUTSIDE.
I don't really like being guided around, though.

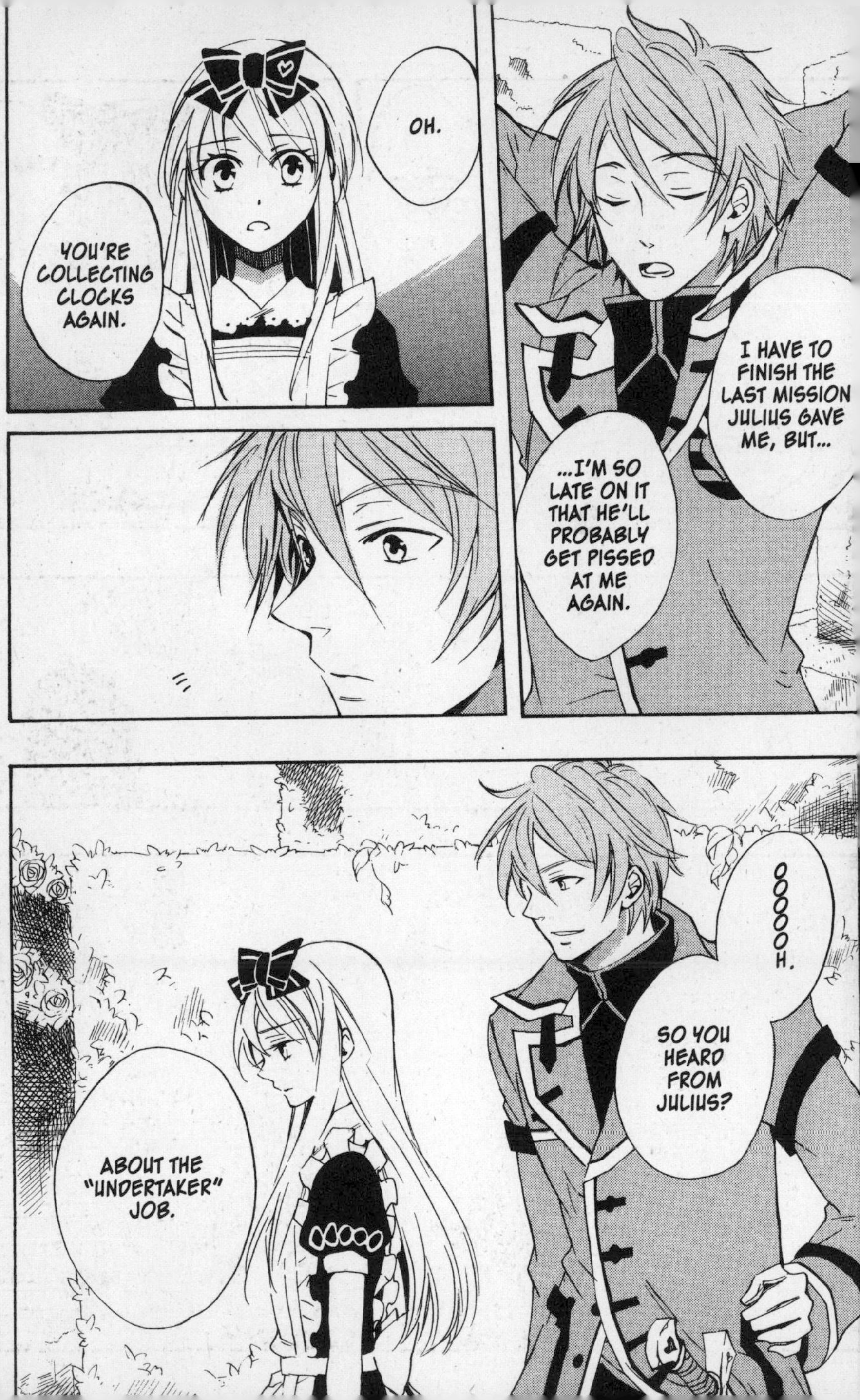
I HAVE TO FINISH THE LAST MISSION JULIUS GAVE ME, BUT...
...I'M SO LATE ON IT THAT HE'LL PROBABLY GET PISSED AT ME AGAIN.
OH.
YOU'RE COLLECTING CLOCKS AGAIN.
OOOOOOH.
SO YOU HEARD FROM JULIUS?
ABOUT THE "UNDERTAKER" JOB.

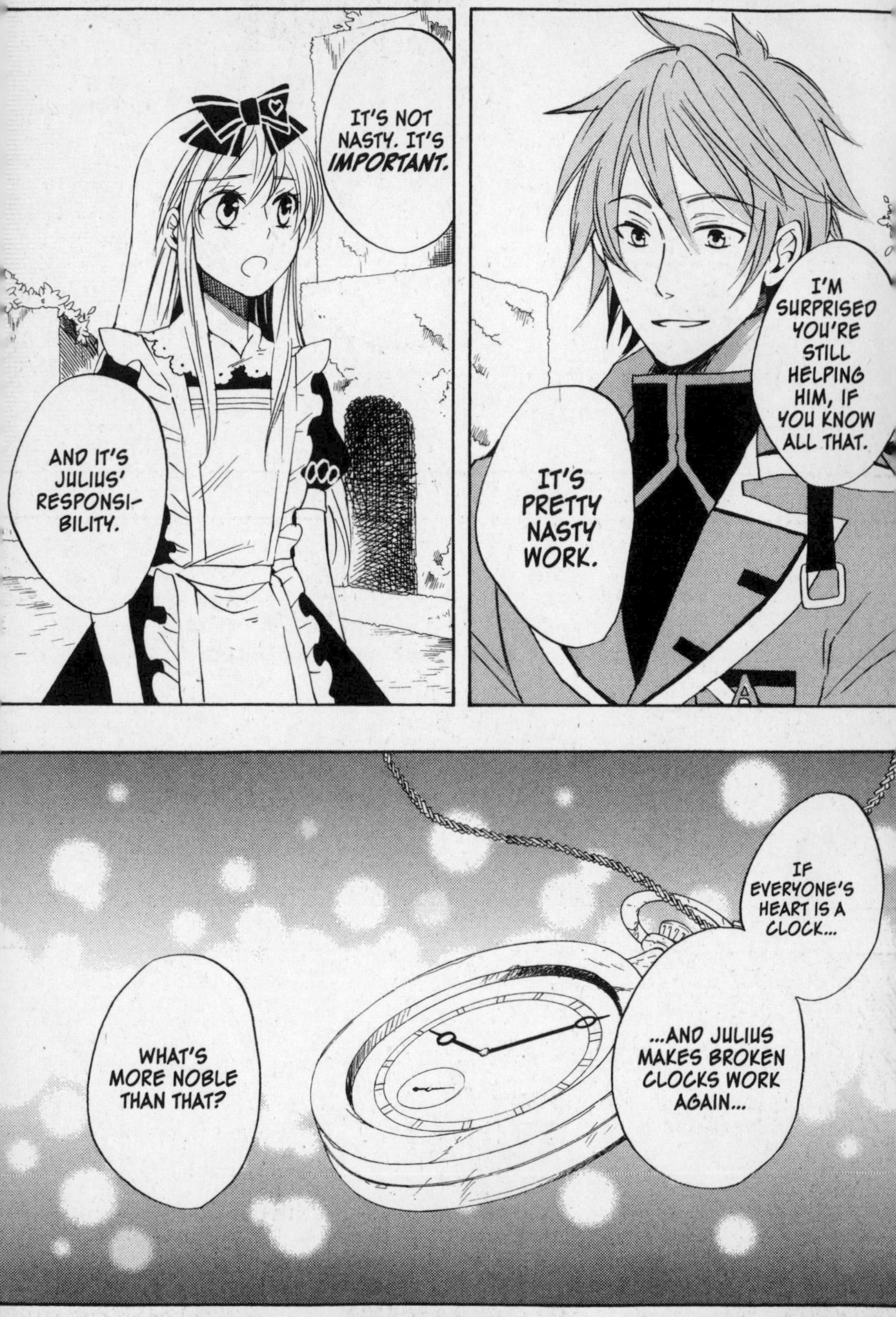
I'M SURPRISED YOU'RE STILL HELPING HIM, IF YOU KNOW ALL THAT.
IT'S PRETTY NASTY WORK.
IT'S NOT NASTY. IT'S *IMPORTANT.*
AND IT'S JULIUS' RESPONSI-BILITY.
IF EVERYONE'S HEART IS A CLOCK...
...AND JULIUS MAKES BROKEN CLOCKS WORK AGAIN...
WHAT'S MORE NOBLE THAN THAT?

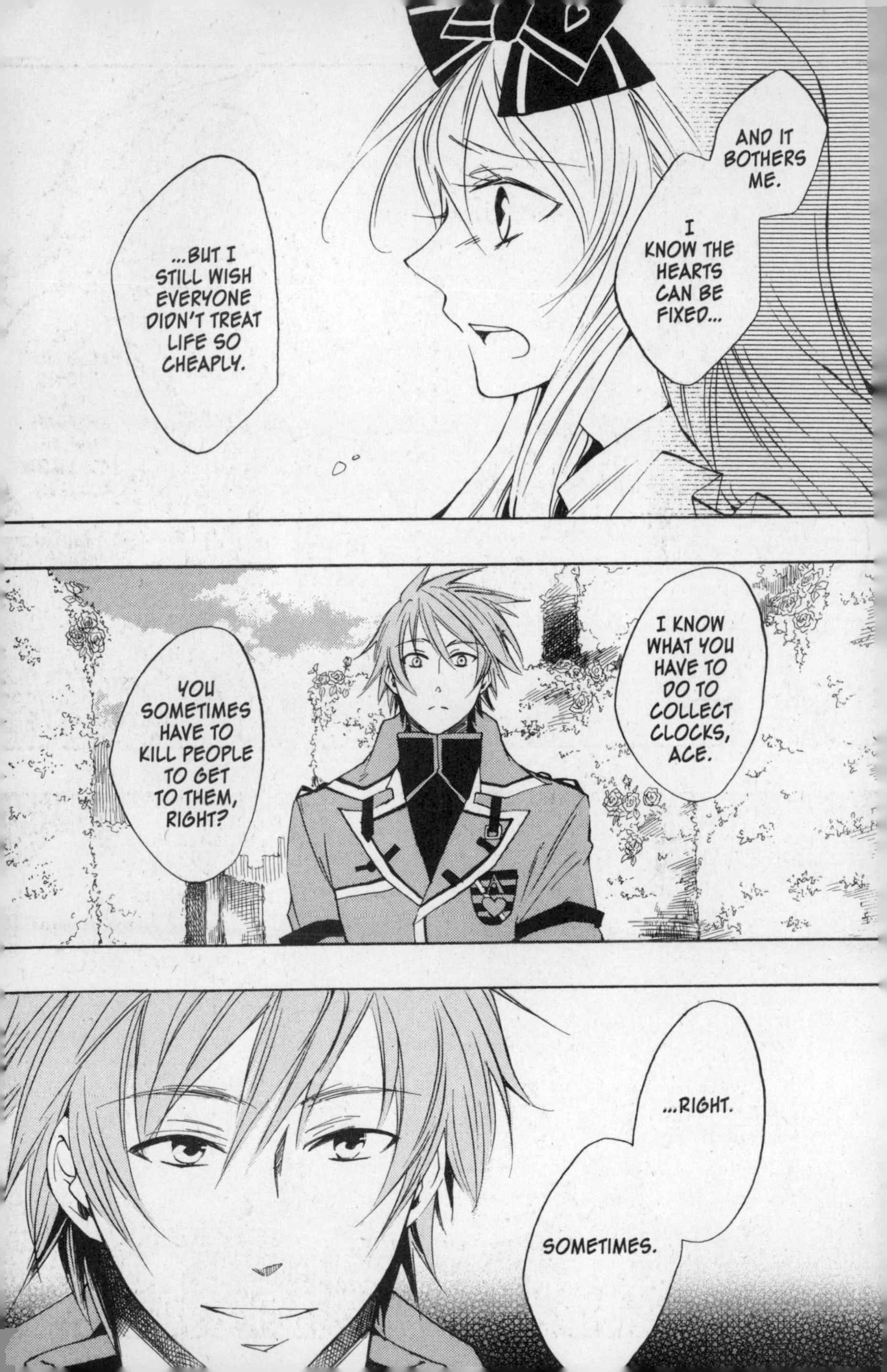
AND IT BOTHERS ME. I KNOW THE HEARTS CAN BE FIXED...
...BUT I STILL WISH EVERYONE DIDN'T TREAT LIFE SO CHEAPLY.
I KNOW WHAT YOU HAVE TO DO TO COLLECT CLOCKS, ACE.
YOU SOMETIMES HAVE TO KILL PEOPLE TO GET TO THEM, RIGHT?
...RIGHT. SOMETIMES.

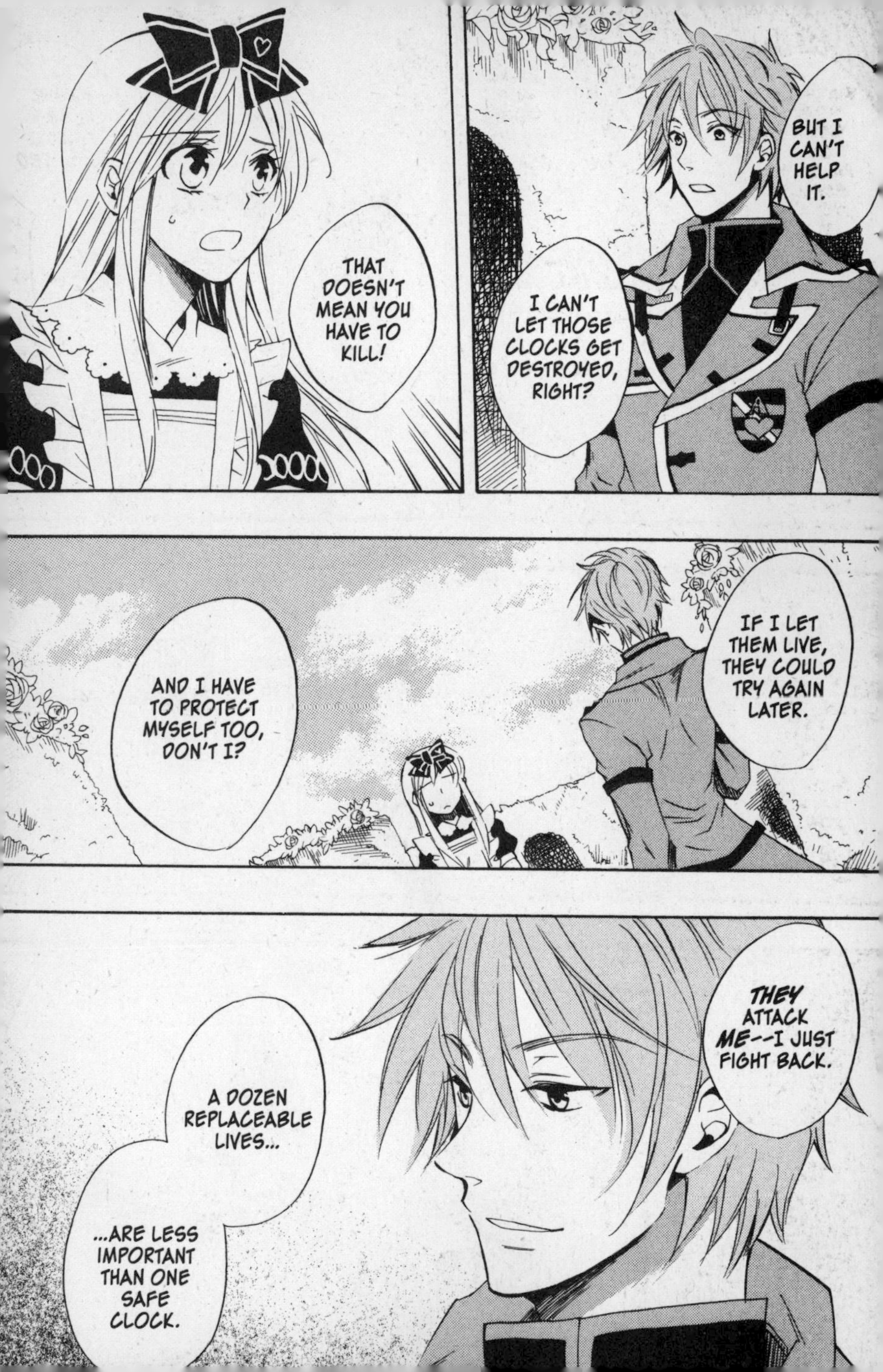
BUT I CAN'T HELP IT.
I CAN'T LET THOSE CLOCKS GET DESTROYED, RIGHT?
THAT DOESN'T MEAN YOU HAVE TO KILL!
IF I LET THEM LIVE, THEY COULD TRY AGAIN LATER.
AND I HAVE TO PROTECT MYSELF TOO, DON'T I?
THEY ATTACK *ME*--I JUST FIGHT BACK.
A DOZEN REPLACEABLE LIVES...
...ARE LESS IMPORTANT THAN ONE SAFE CLOCK.

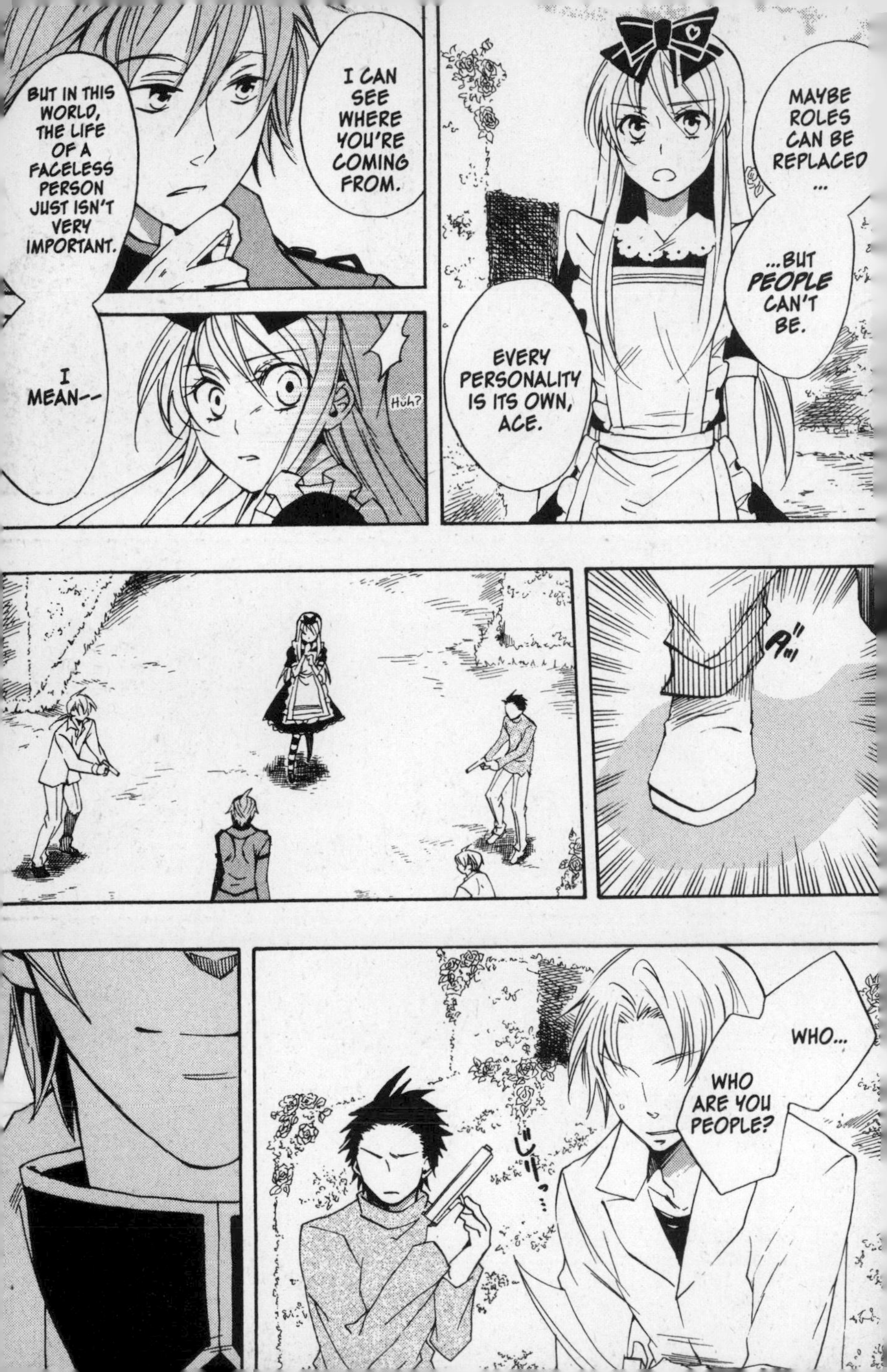
MAYBE ROLES CAN BE REPLACED ...
...BUT PEOPLE CAN'T BE.
EVERY PERSONALITY IS ITS OWN, ACE.
I CAN SEE WHERE YOU'RE COMING FROM.
BUT IN THIS WORLD, THE LIFE OF A FACELESS PERSON JUST ISN'T VERY IMPORTANT.
Huh?
I MEAN--
WHO...
WHO ARE YOU PEOPLE?

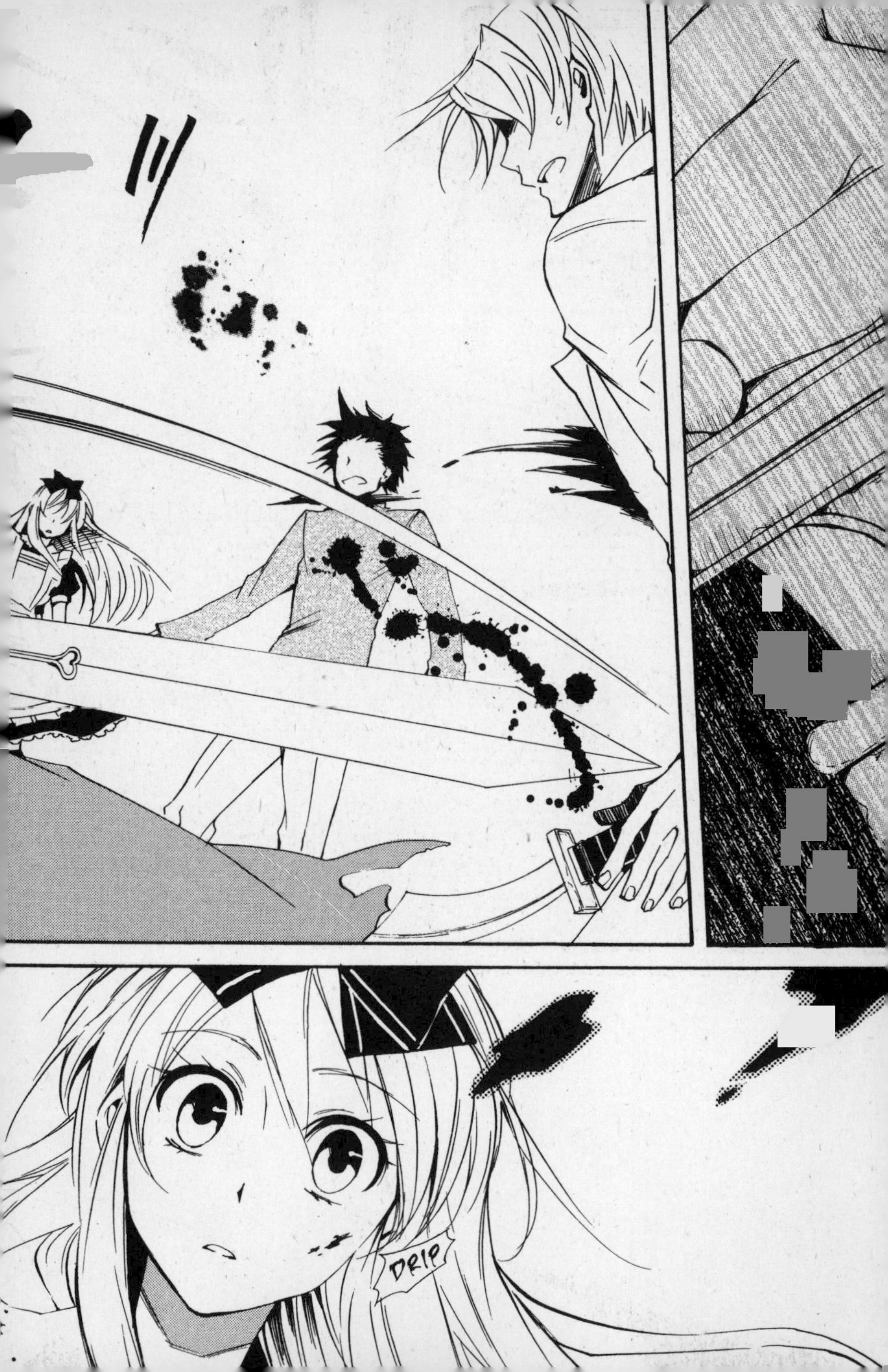
DRIP

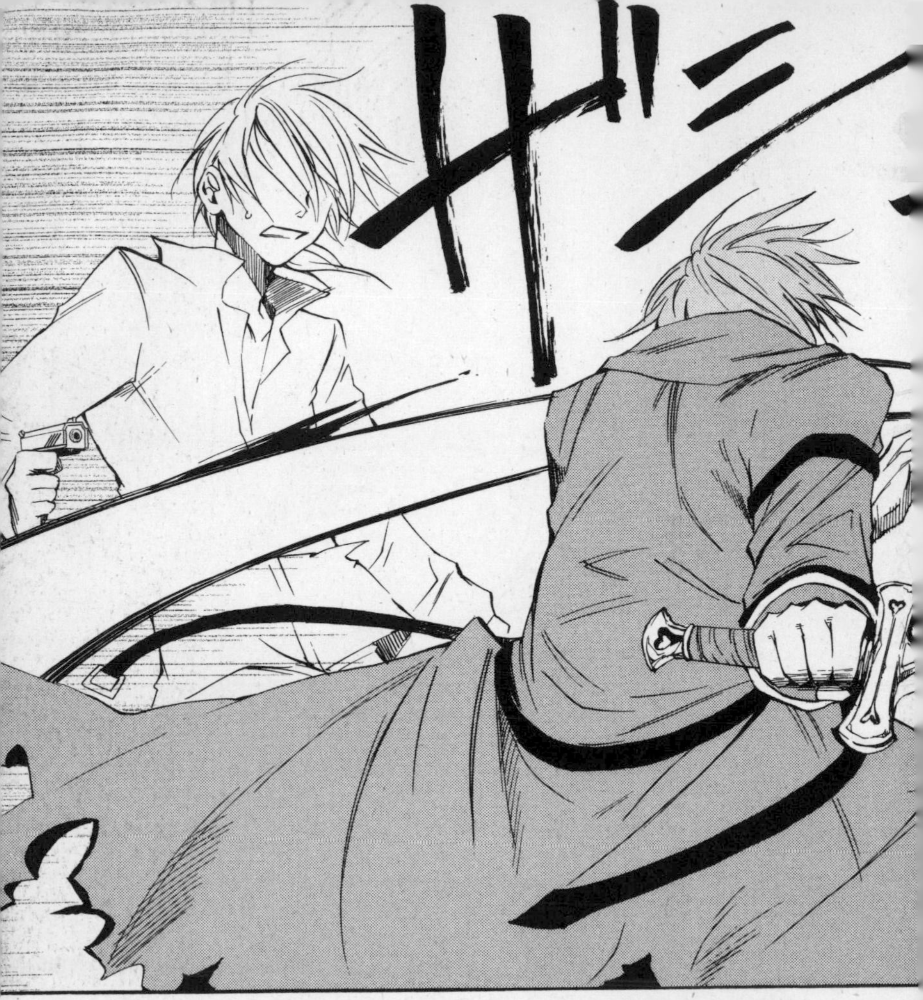
ザシ

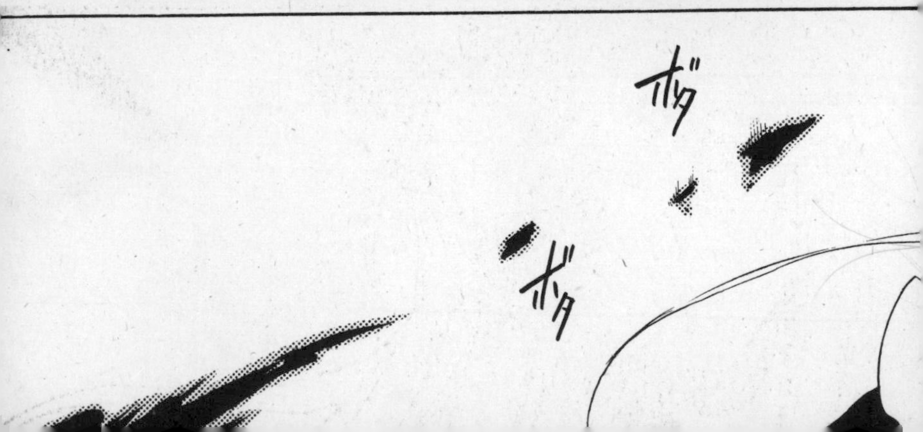
ボタ
ボタ

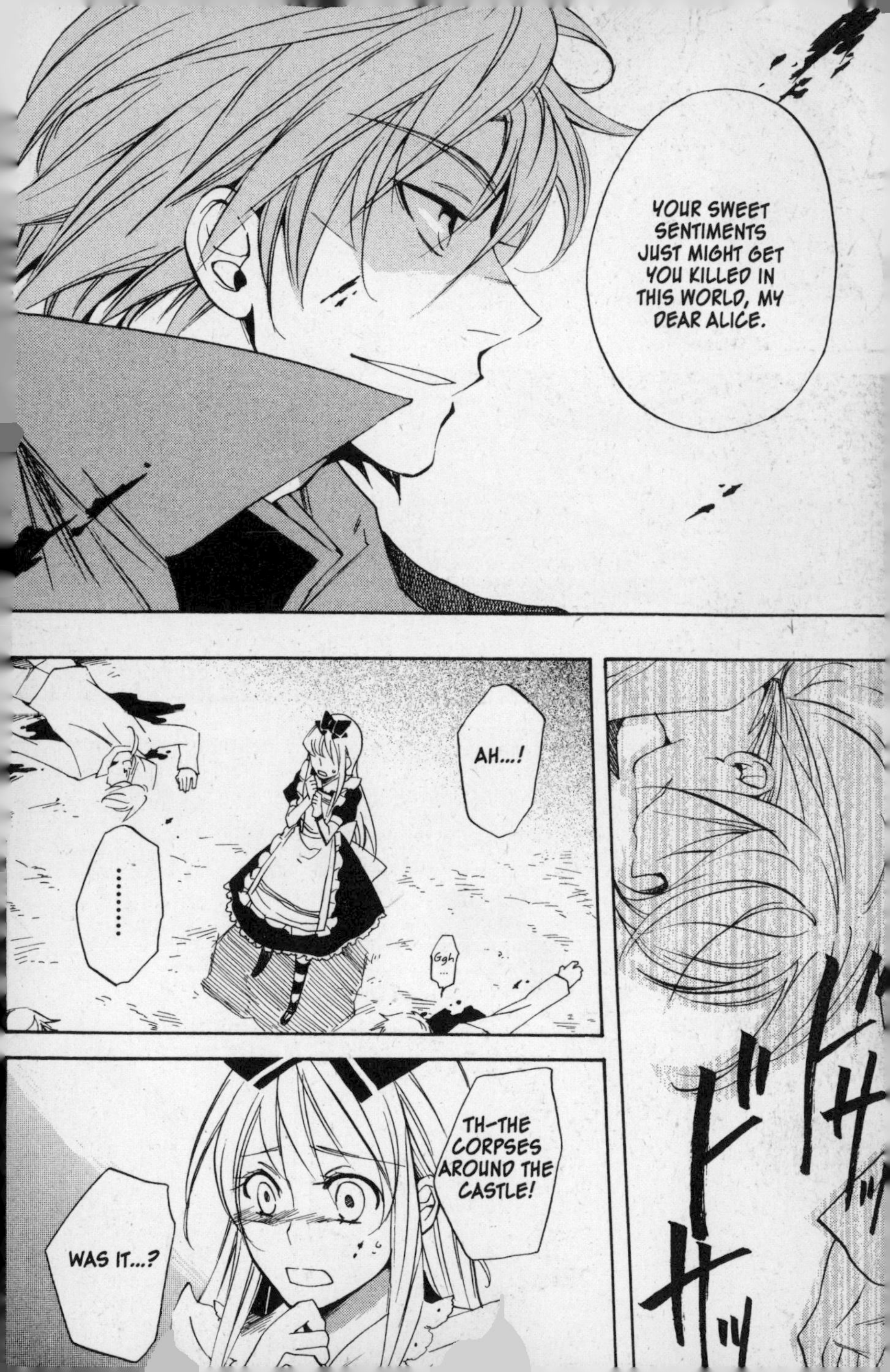
YOUR SWEET SENTIMENTS JUST MIGHT GET YOU KILLED IN THIS WORLD, MY DEAR ALICE.
ドサッ
サッ
AH...!
......
Ggh...
TH-THE CORPSES AROUND THE CASTLE!
WAS IT...?

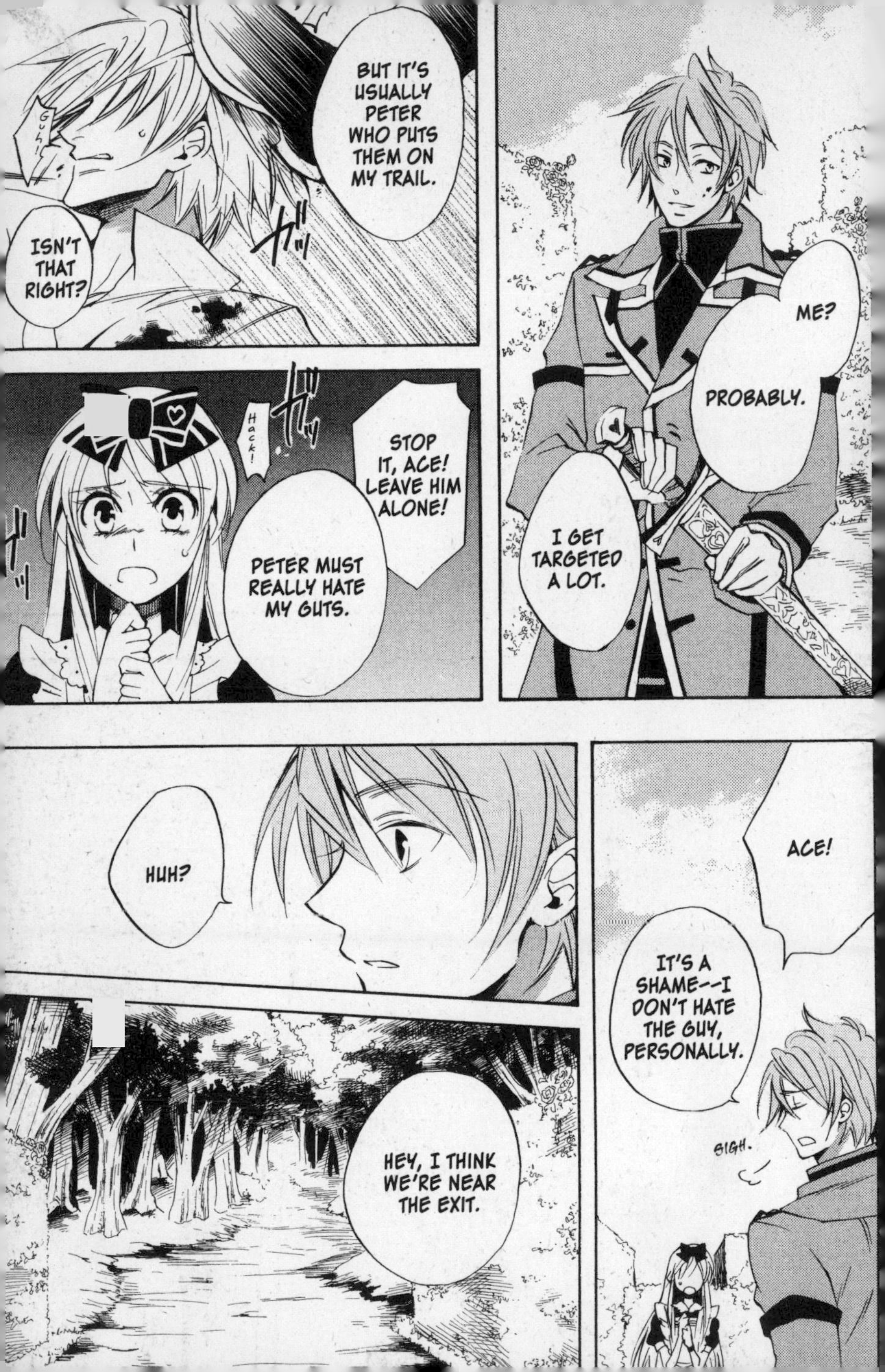
ME?
PROBABLY.
I GET TARGETED A LOT.
BUT IT'S USUALLY PETER WHO PUTS THEM ON MY TRAIL.
Guh!
ガッ
ISN'T THAT RIGHT?
ガッ
STOP IT, ACE! LEAVE HIM ALONE!
Hack!
PETER MUST REALLY HATE MY GUTS.
ガッ
ACE!
IT'S A SHAME--I DON'T HATE THE GUY, PERSONALLY.
SIGH.
HUH?
HEY, I THINK WE'RE NEAR THE EXIT.

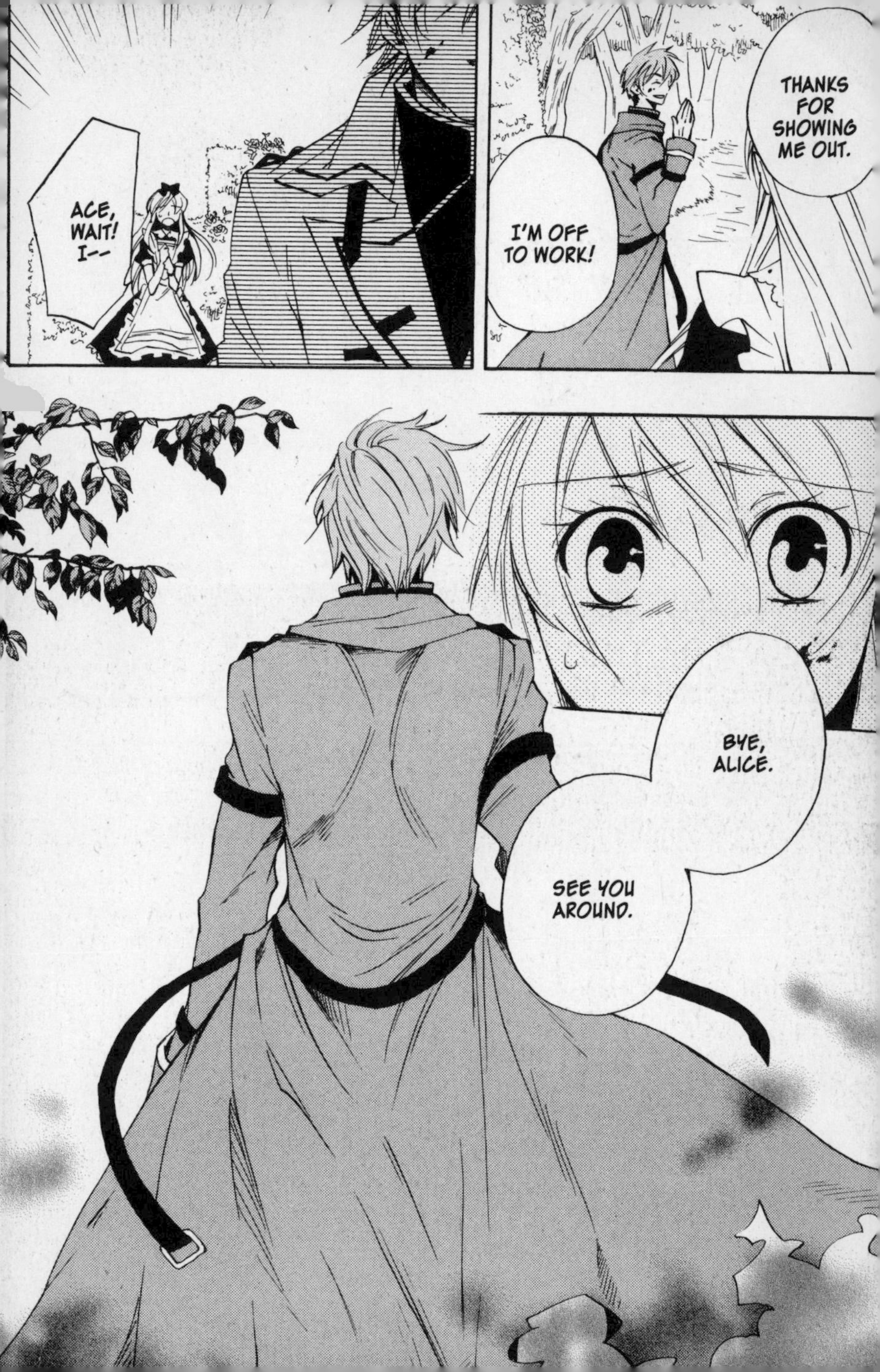
THANKS FOR SHOWING ME OUT.
I'M OFF TO WORK!
ACE, WAIT! I--
BYE, ALICE.
SEE YOU AROUND.

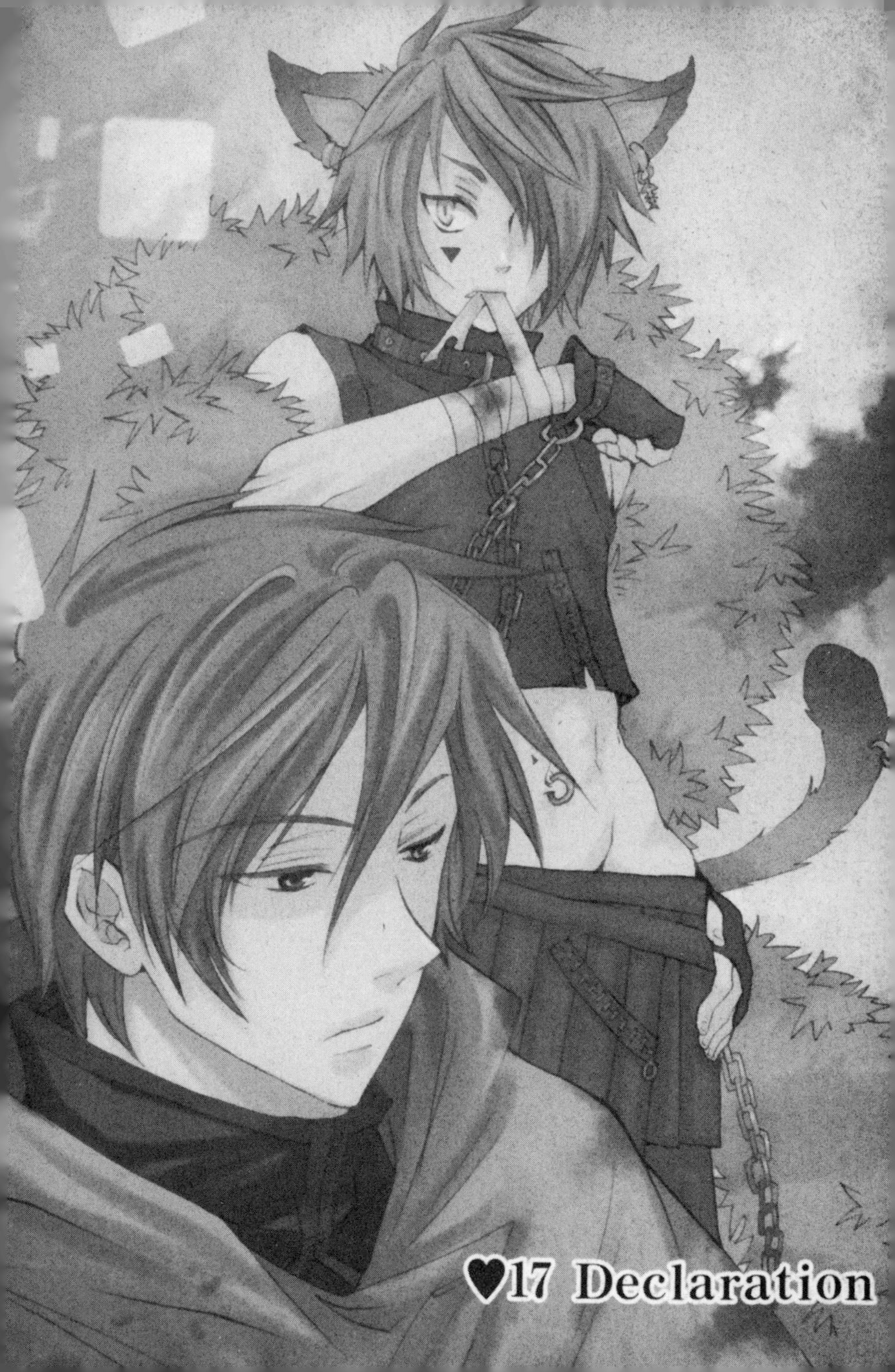
♥17 Declaration

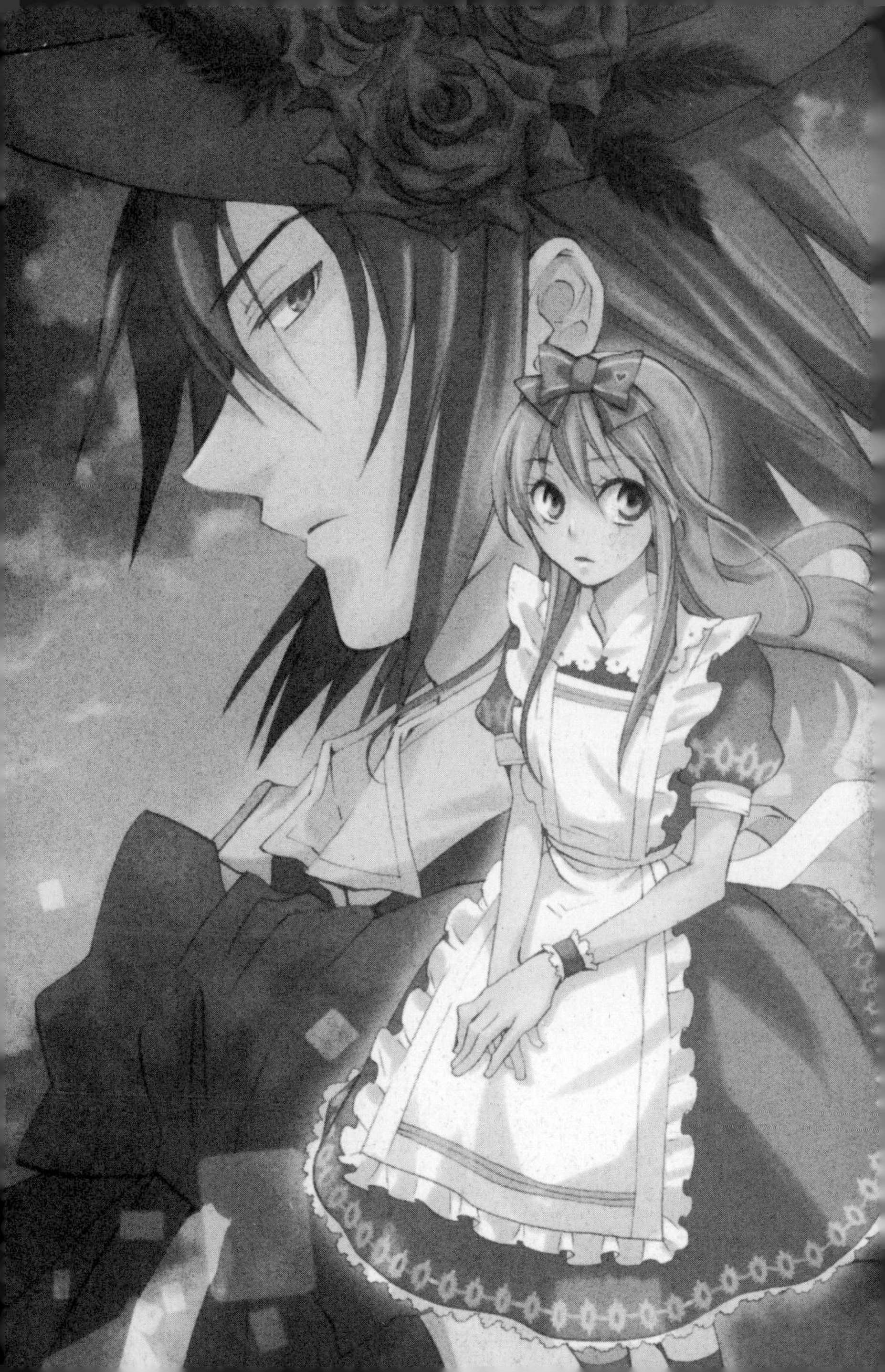

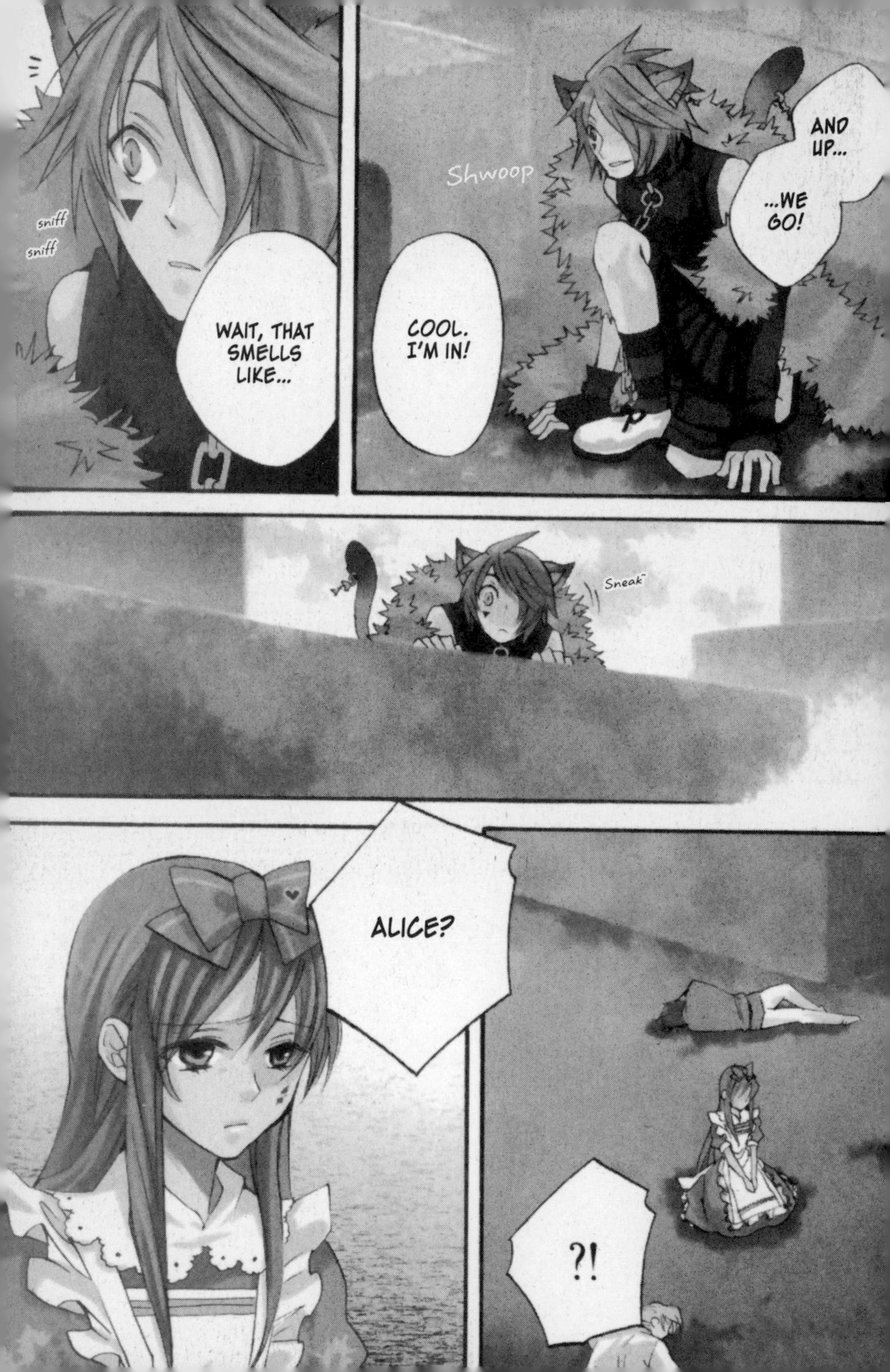
AND UP...
...WE GO!
Shwoop
COOL. I'M IN!
sniff
sniff
WAIT, THAT SMELLS LIKE...
Sneak~
?!
ALICE?

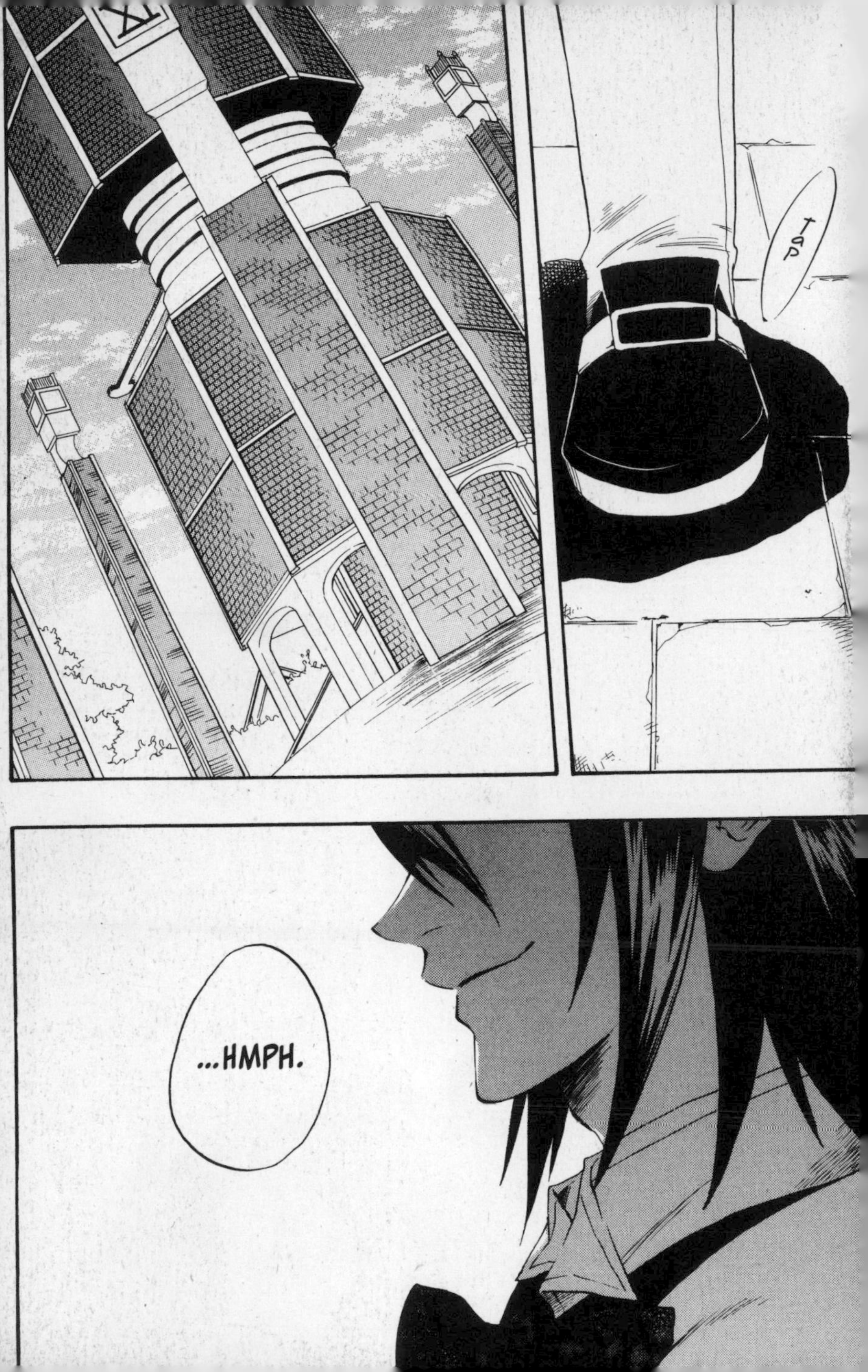
Tap
...HMPH.

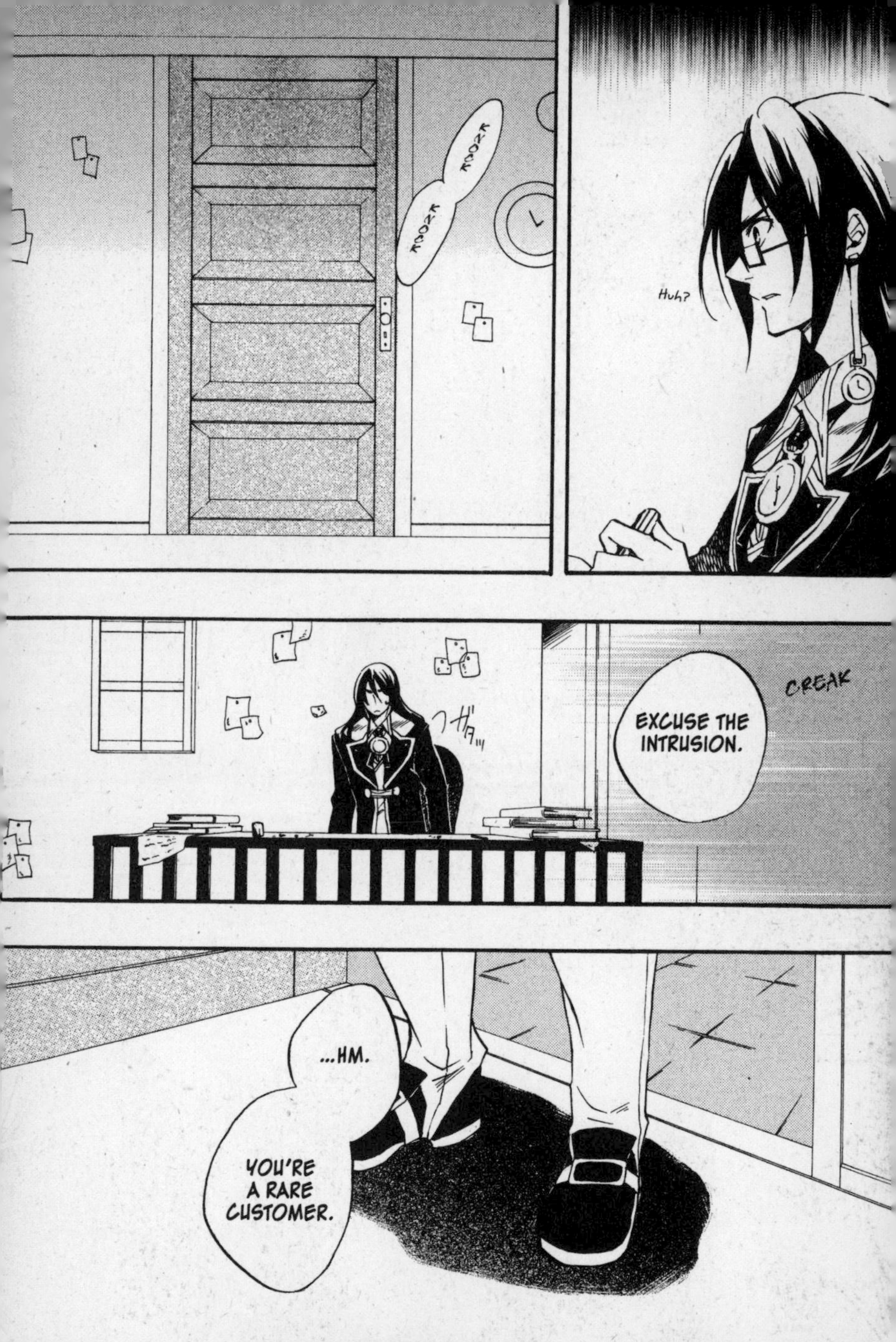
Huh?
KNOCK KNOCK
CREAK
EXCUSE THE INTRUSION.
ガタッ
...HM.
YOU'RE A RARE CUSTOMER.

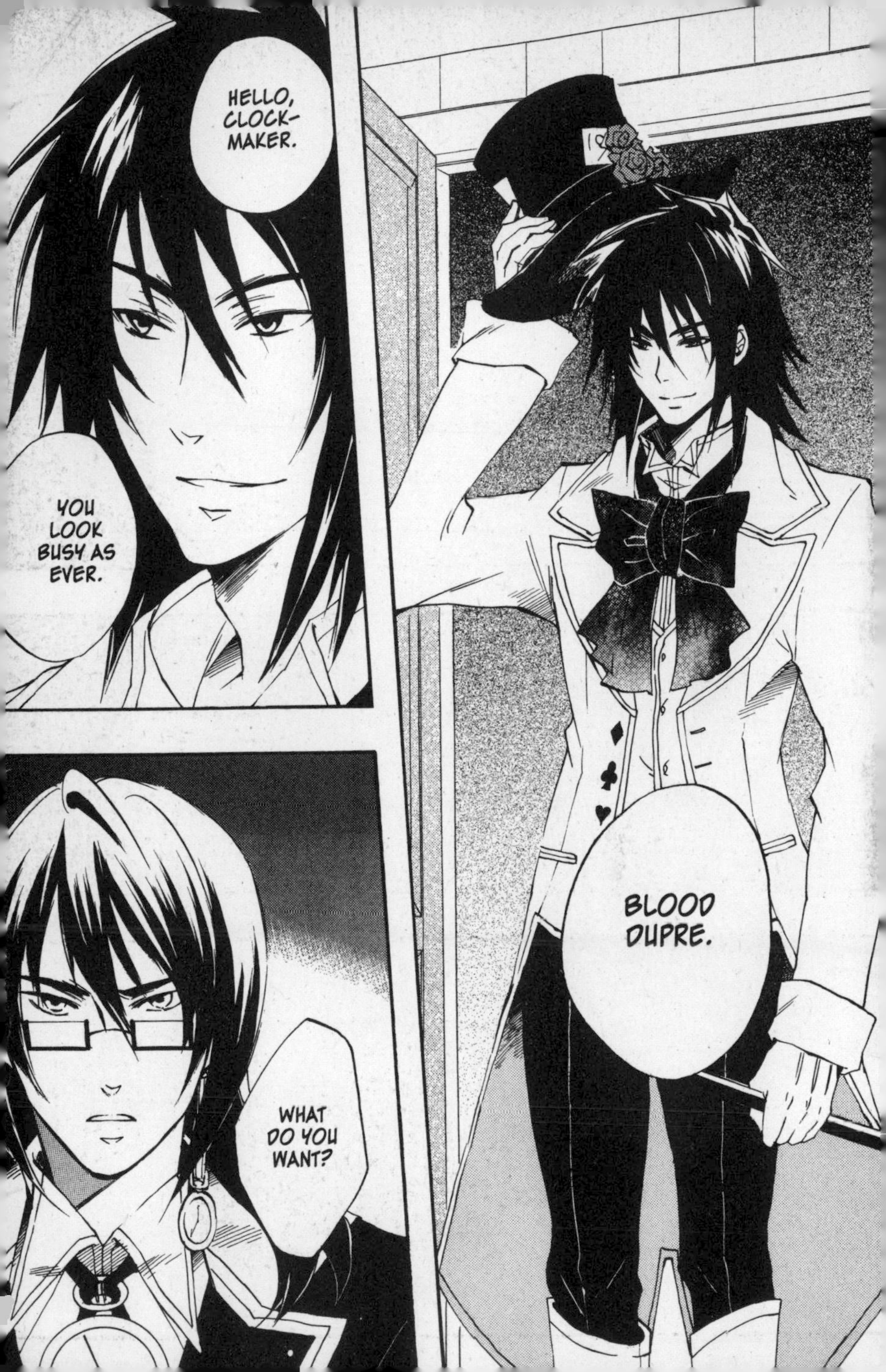
BLOOD DUPRE.
HELLO, CLOCK-MAKER.
YOU LOOK BUSY AS EVER.
WHAT DO YOU WANT?

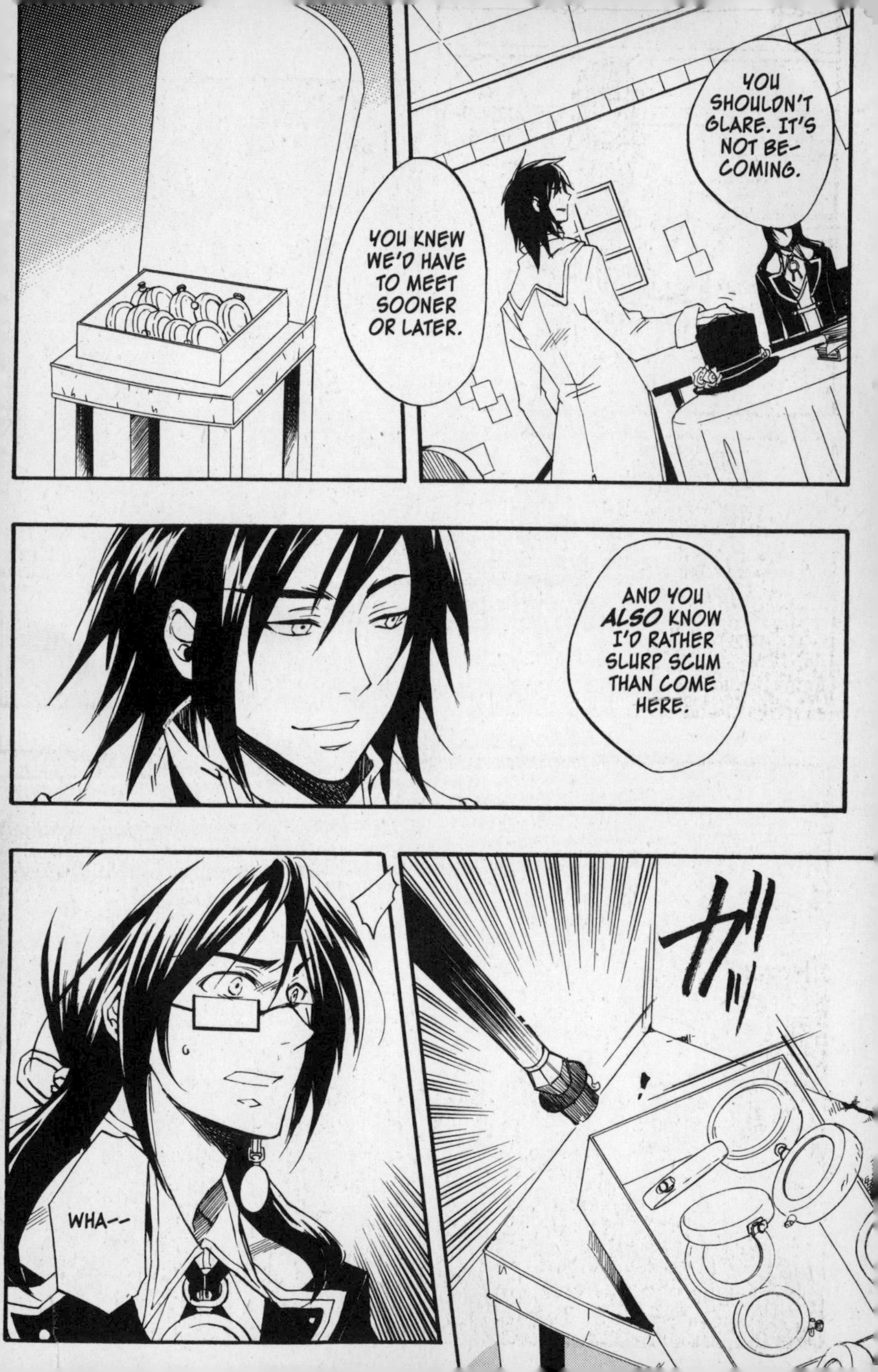
YOU SHOULDN'T GLARE. IT'S NOT BE-COMING.
YOU KNEW WE'D HAVE TO MEET SOONER OR LATER.
AND YOU ALSO KNOW I'D RATHER SLURP SCUM THAN COME HERE.
ガッ
WHA--

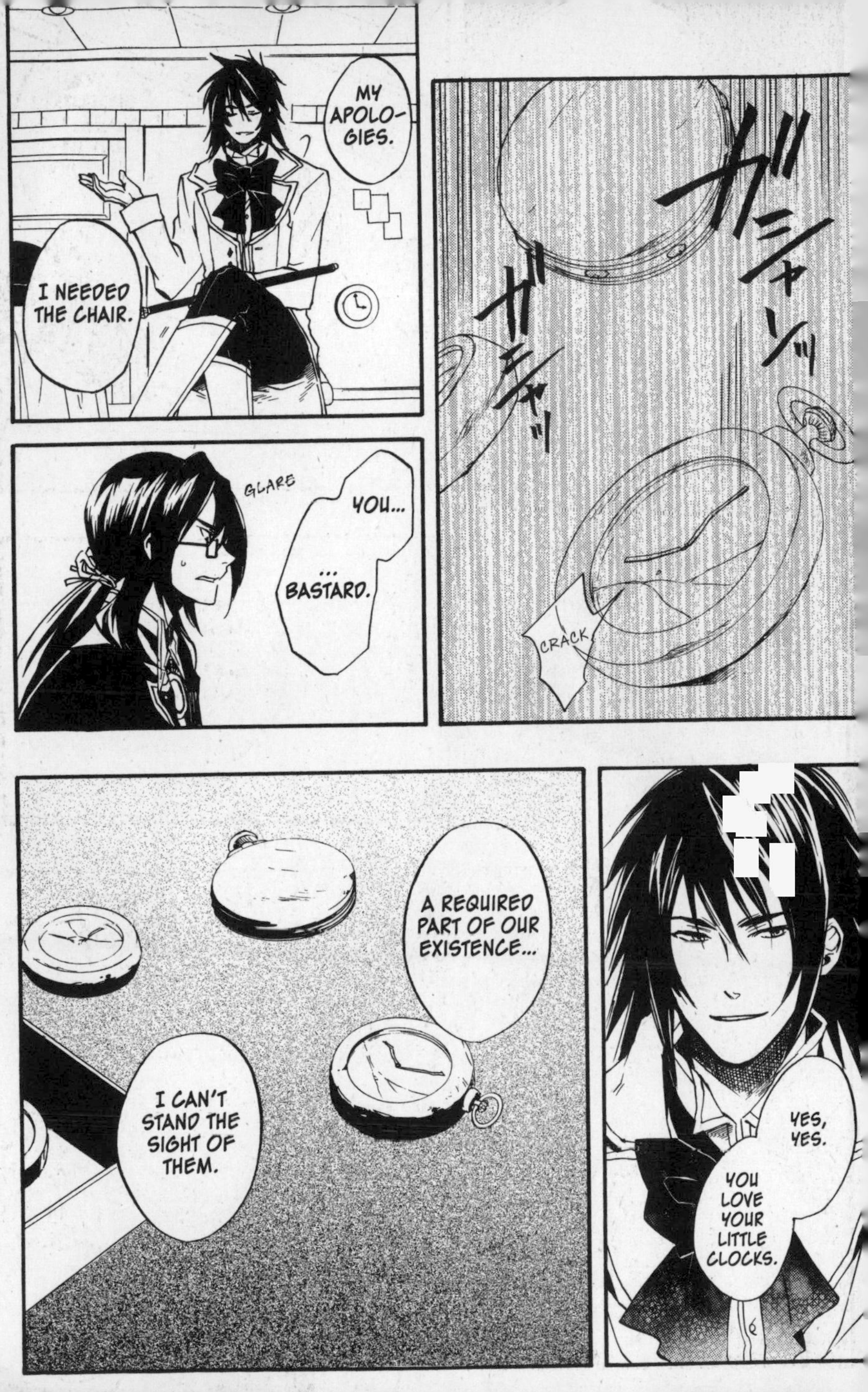
ガシャーンッ
ガシャッ
CRACK
MY APOLOGIES.
I NEEDED THE CHAIR.
GLARE
YOU...
...BASTARD.
YES, YES.
YOU LOVE YOUR LITTLE CLOCKS.
A REQUIRED PART OF OUR EXISTENCE...
I CAN'T STAND THE SIGHT OF THEM.

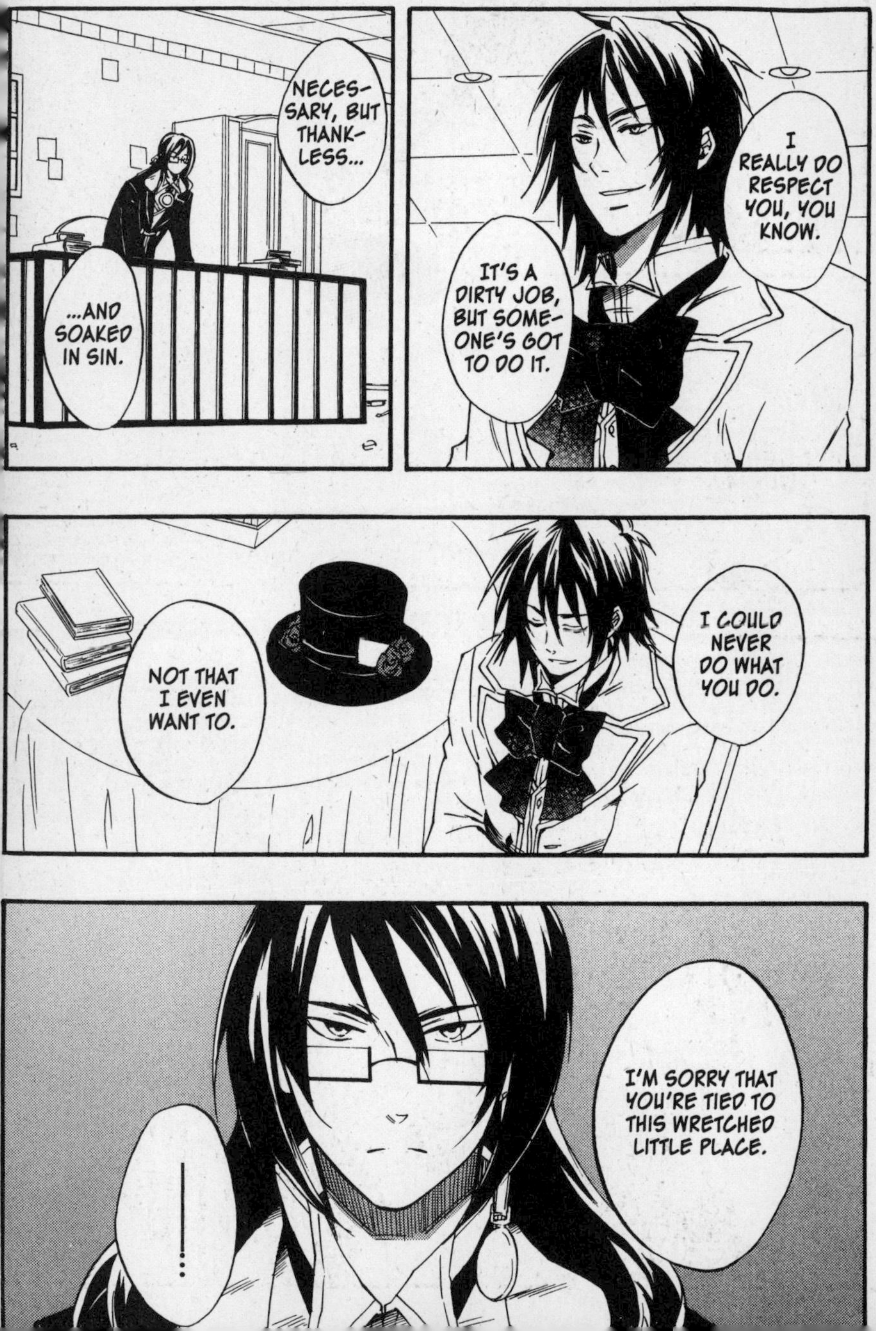
I REALLY DO RESPECT YOU, YOU KNOW.
IT'S A DIRTY JOB, BUT SOMEONE'S GOT TO DO IT.
NECESSARY, BUT THANKLESS...
...AND SOAKED IN SIN.
I COULD NEVER DO WHAT YOU DO.
NOT THAT I EVEN WANT TO.
I'M SORRY THAT YOU'RE TIED TO THIS WRETCHED LITTLE PLACE.
......

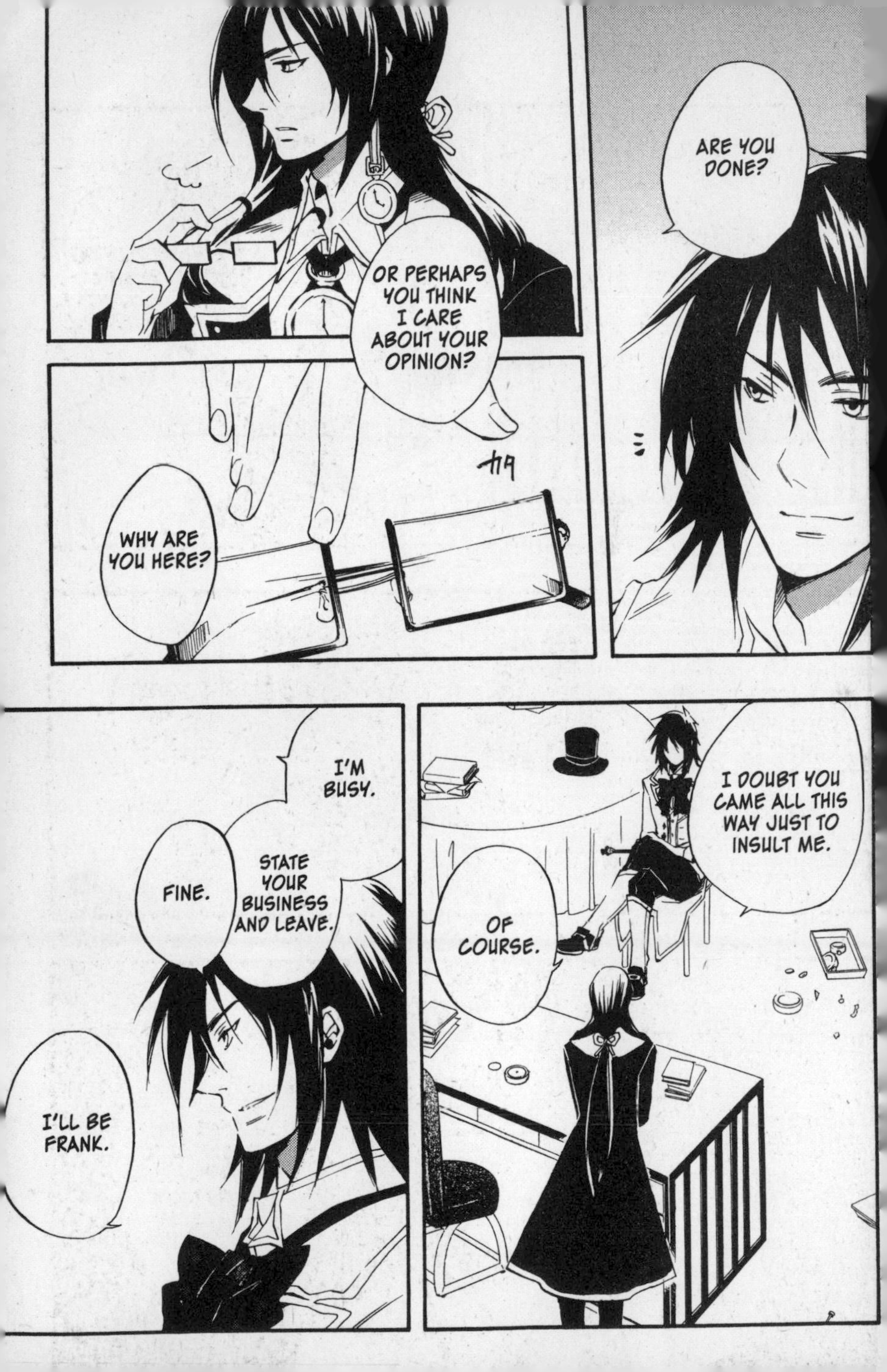
ARE YOU DONE?
OR PERHAPS YOU THINK I CARE ABOUT YOUR OPINION?
カタ
WHY ARE YOU HERE?
I DOUBT YOU CAME ALL THIS WAY JUST TO INSULT ME.
OF COURSE.
I'M BUSY.
STATE YOUR BUSINESS AND LEAVE.
FINE.
I'LL BE FRANK.

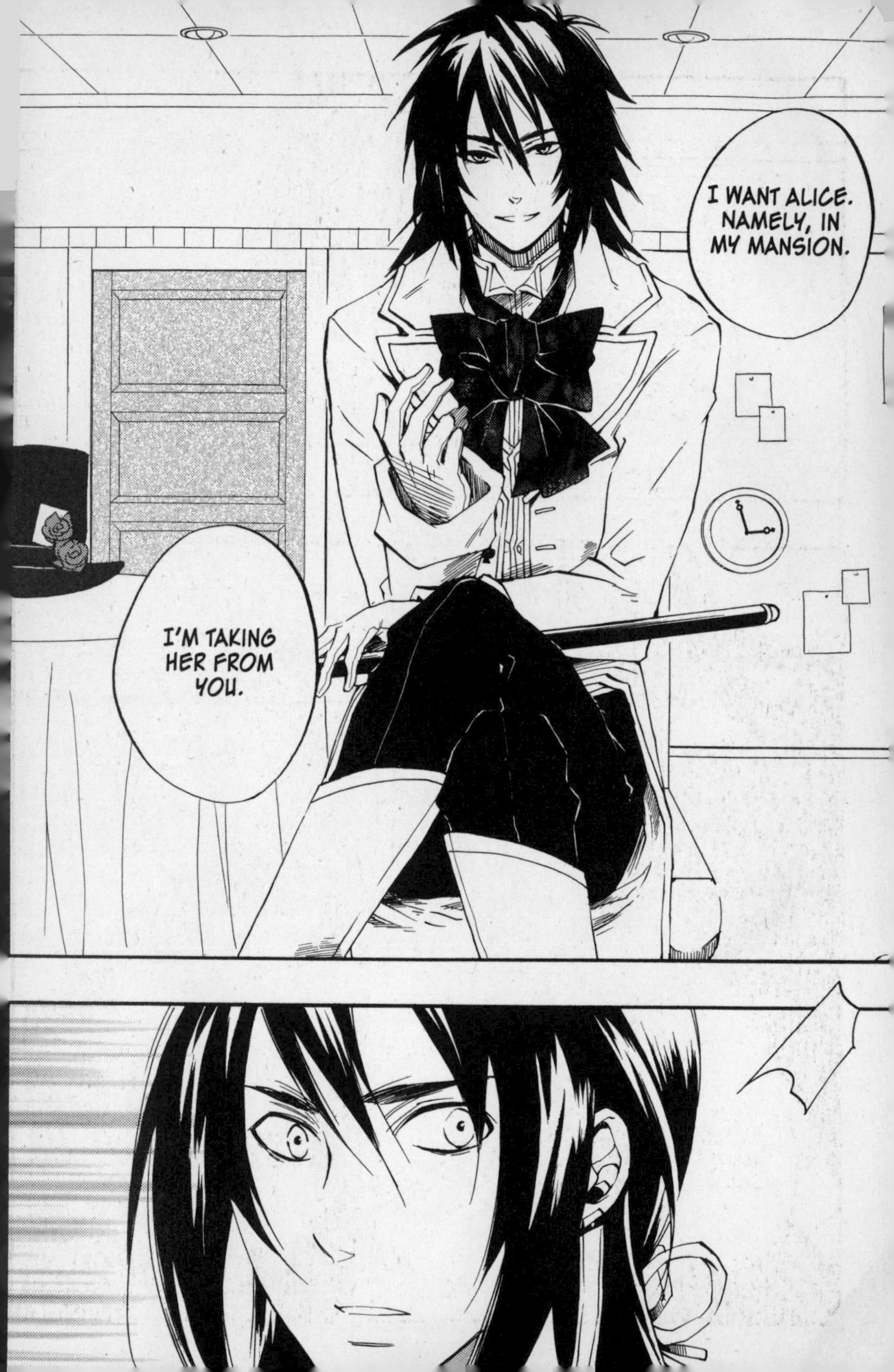
I WANT ALICE. NAMELY, IN MY MANSION.
I'M TAKING HER FROM YOU.

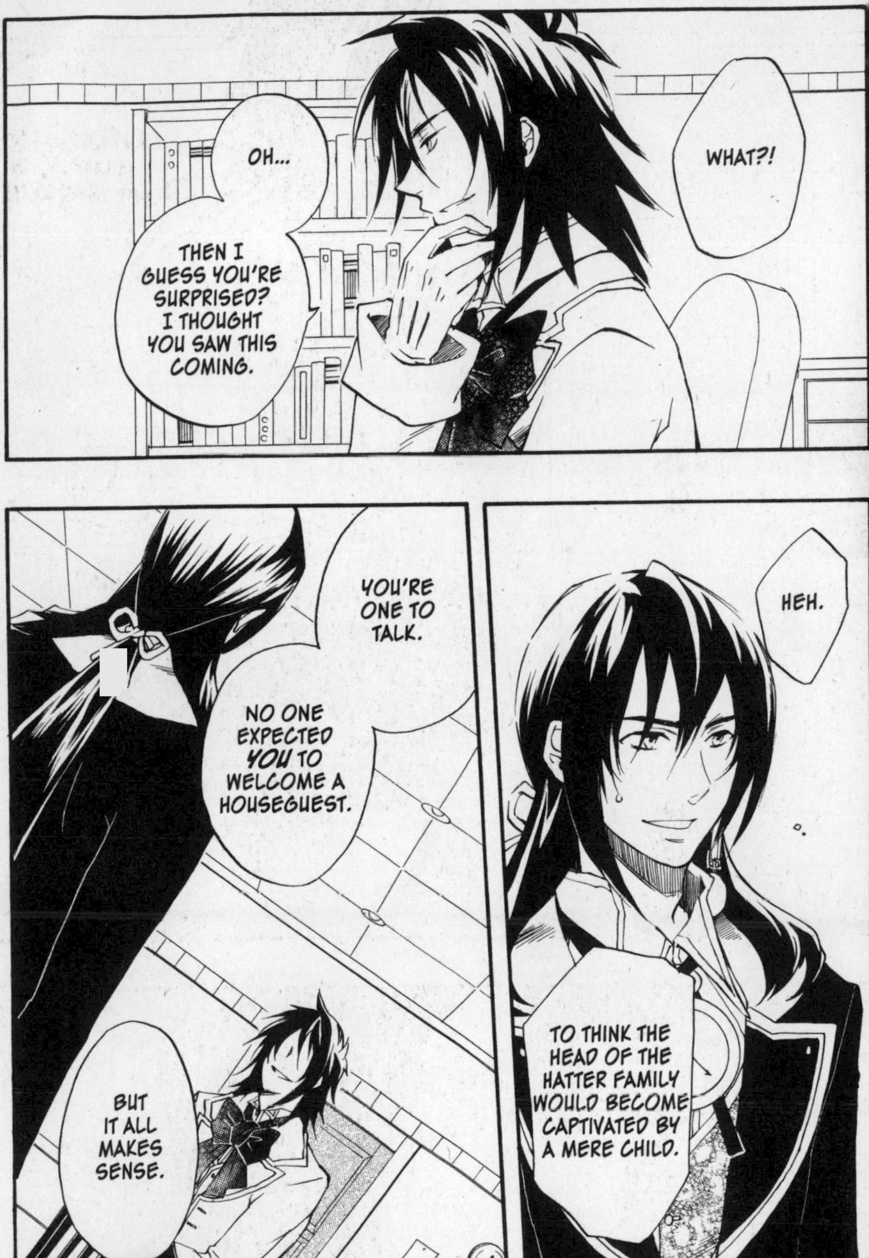
WHAT?!
OH...
THEN I GUESS YOU'RE SURPRISED? I THOUGHT YOU SAW THIS COMING.
HEH.
TO THINK THE HEAD OF THE HATTER FAMILY WOULD BECOME CAPTIVATED BY A MERE CHILD.
YOU'RE ONE TO TALK.
NO ONE EXPECTED *YOU* TO WELCOME A HOUSEGUEST.
BUT IT ALL MAKES SENSE.

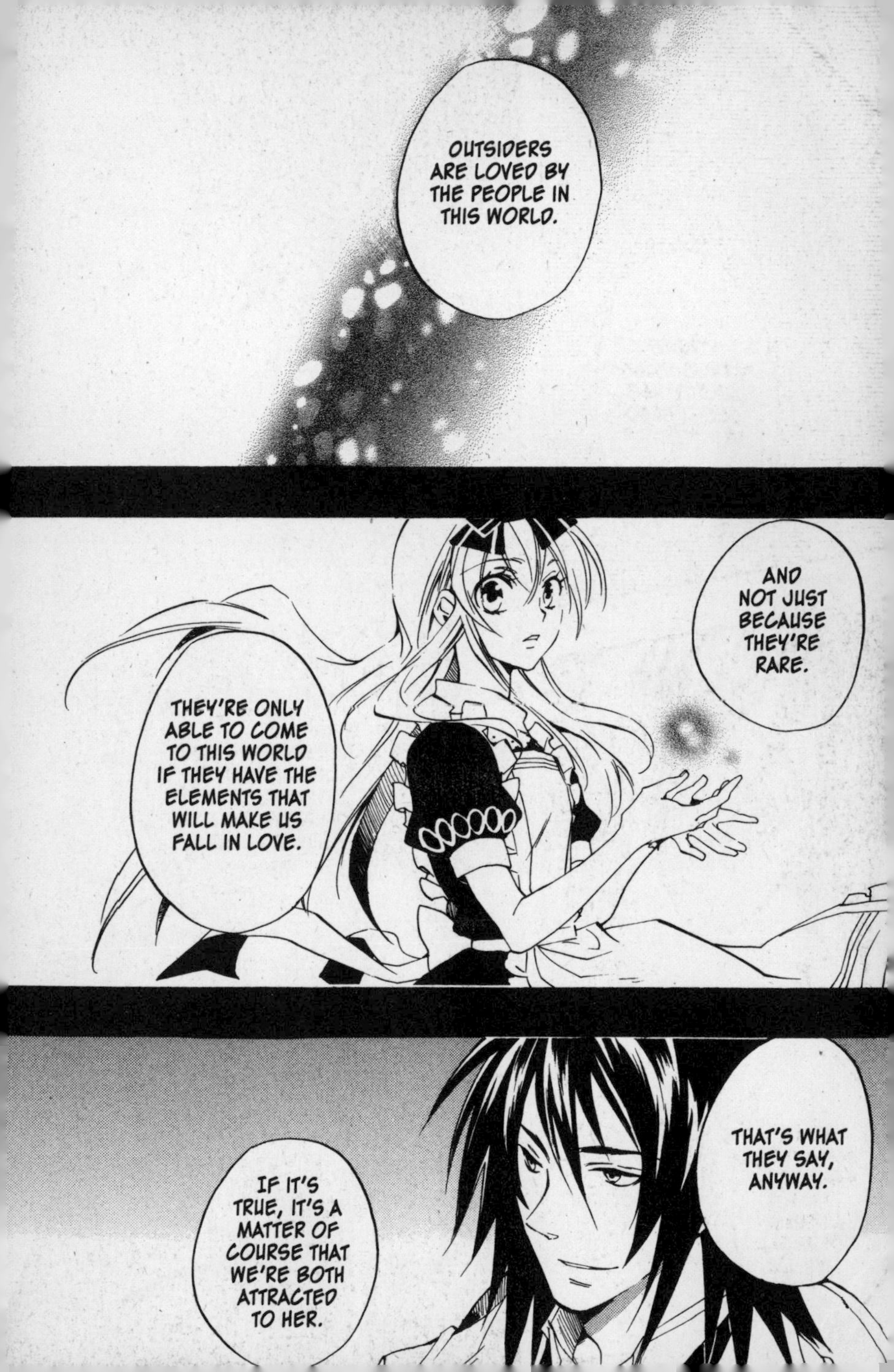
OUTSIDERS ARE LOVED BY THE PEOPLE IN THIS WORLD.
AND NOT JUST BECAUSE THEY'RE RARE.
THEY'RE ONLY ABLE TO COME TO THIS WORLD IF THEY HAVE THE ELEMENTS THAT WILL MAKE US FALL IN LOVE.
THAT'S WHAT THEY SAY, ANYWAY.
IF IT'S TRUE, IT'S A MATTER OF COURSE THAT WE'RE BOTH ATTRACTED TO HER.

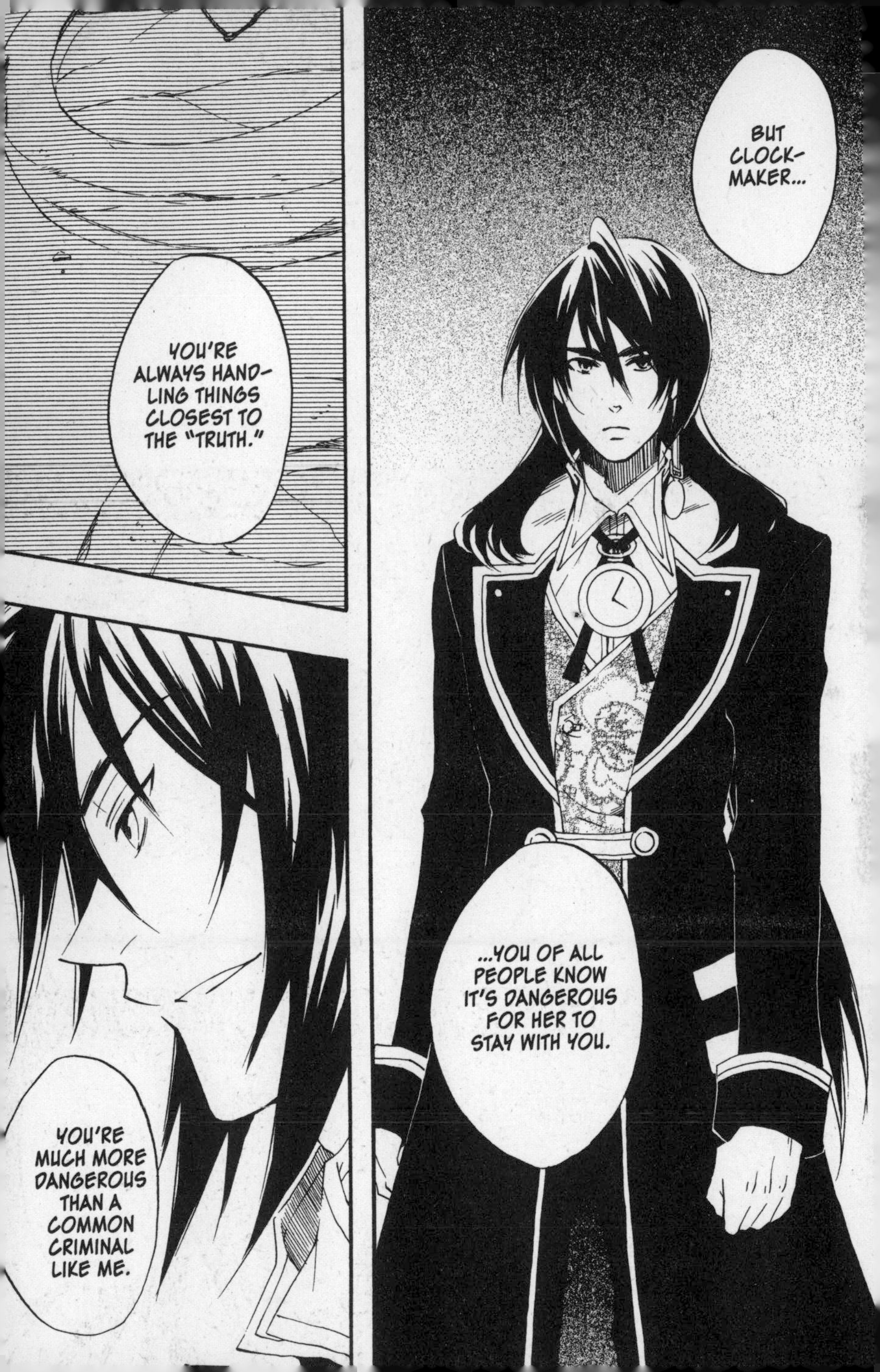
BUT CLOCK-MAKER...
...YOU OF ALL PEOPLE KNOW IT'S DANGEROUS FOR HER TO STAY WITH YOU.
YOU'RE ALWAYS HAND-LING THINGS CLOSEST TO THE "TRUTH."
YOU'RE MUCH MORE DANGEROUS THAN A COMMON CRIMINAL LIKE ME.

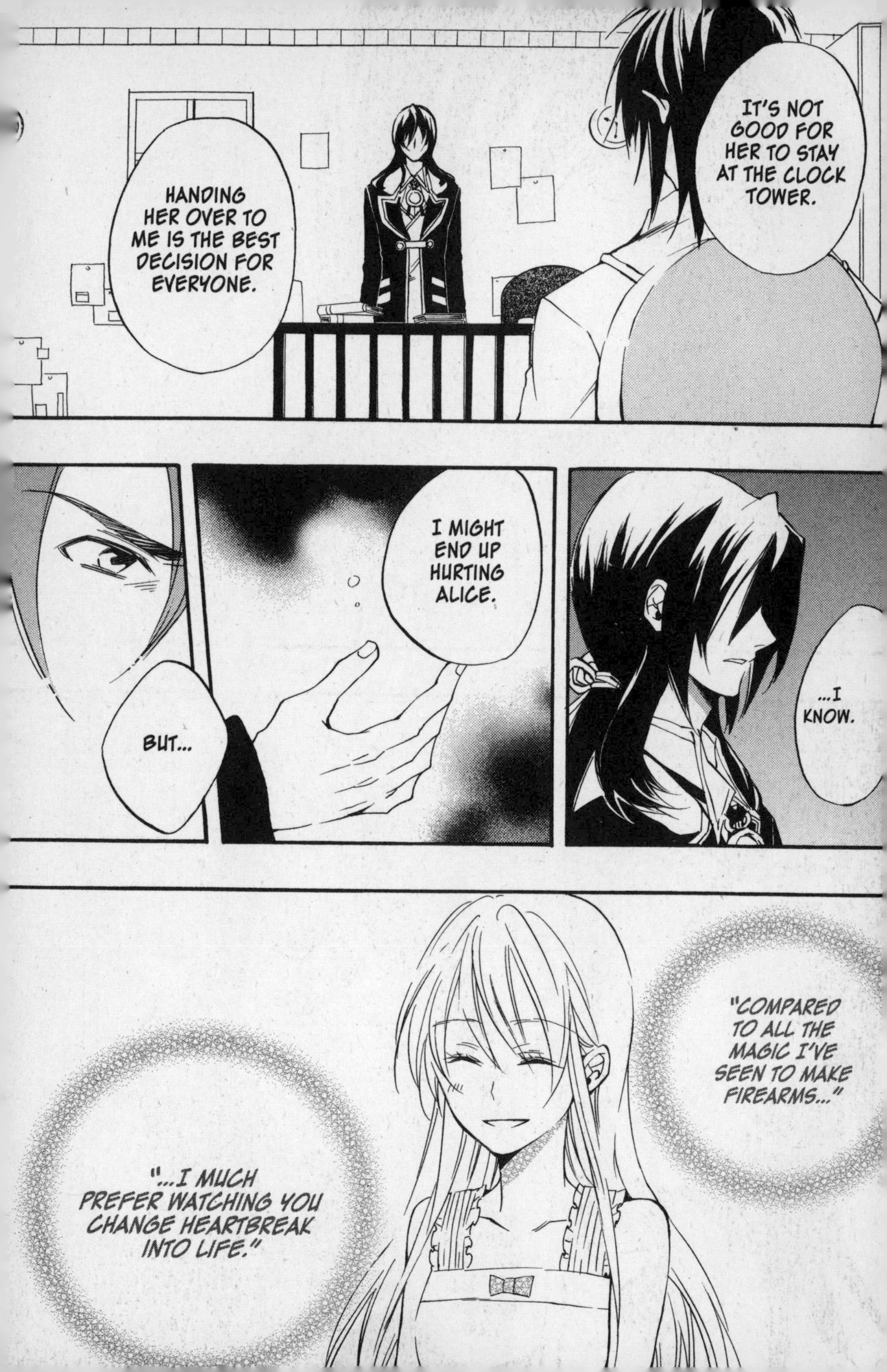
IT'S NOT GOOD FOR HER TO STAY AT THE CLOCK TOWER.
HANDING HER OVER TO ME IS THE BEST DECISION FOR EVERYONE.
...I KNOW.
I MIGHT END UP HURTING ALICE.
BUT...
"COMPARED TO ALL THE MAGIC I'VE SEEN TO MAKE FIREARMS..."
"...I MUCH PREFER WATCHING YOU CHANGE HEARTBREAK INTO LIFE."

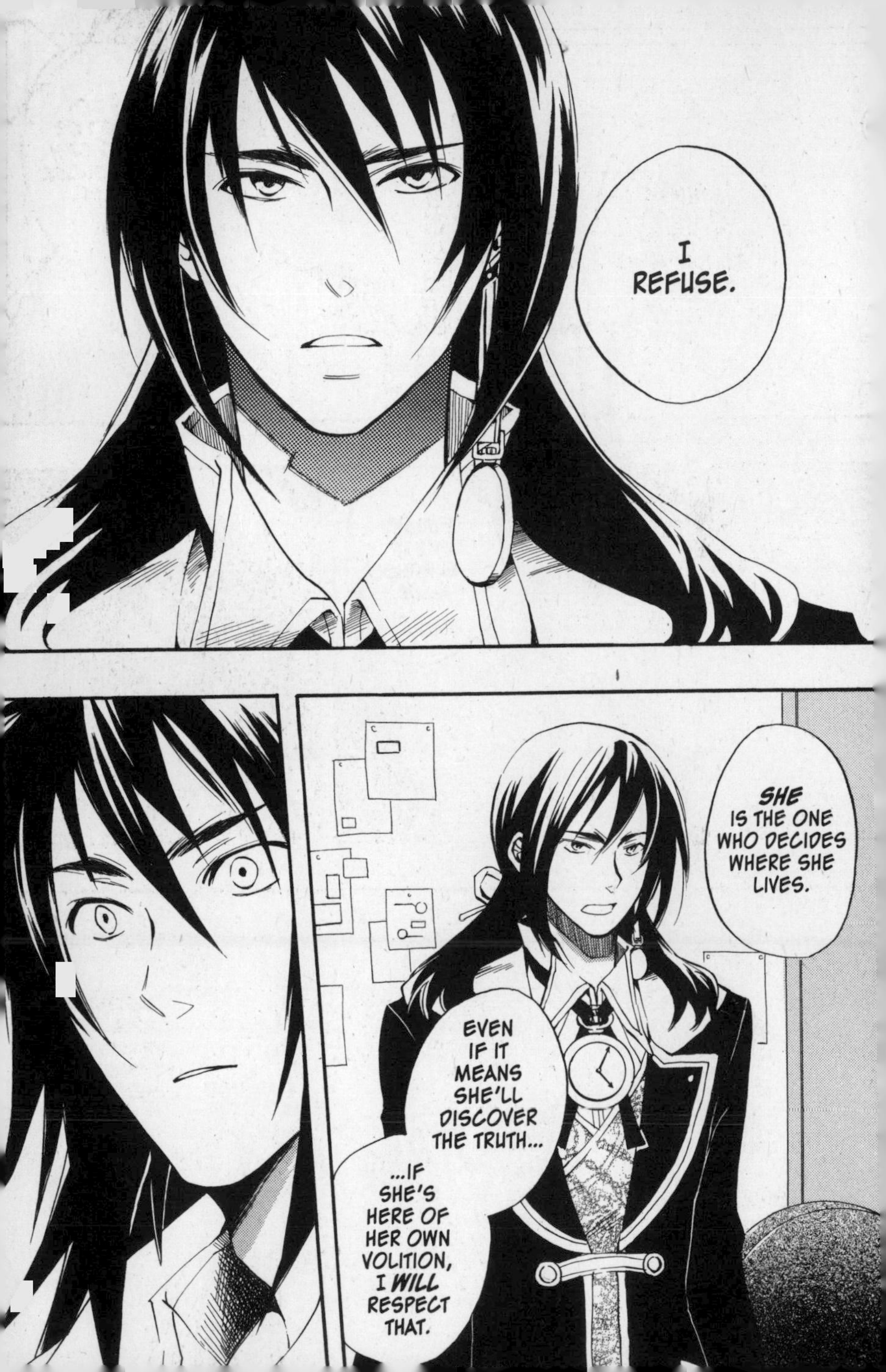
I REFUSE.
SHE IS THE ONE WHO DECIDES WHERE SHE LIVES.
EVEN IF IT MEANS SHE'LL DISCOVER THE TRUTH...
...IF SHE'S HERE OF HER OWN VOLITION, I *WILL* RESPECT THAT.

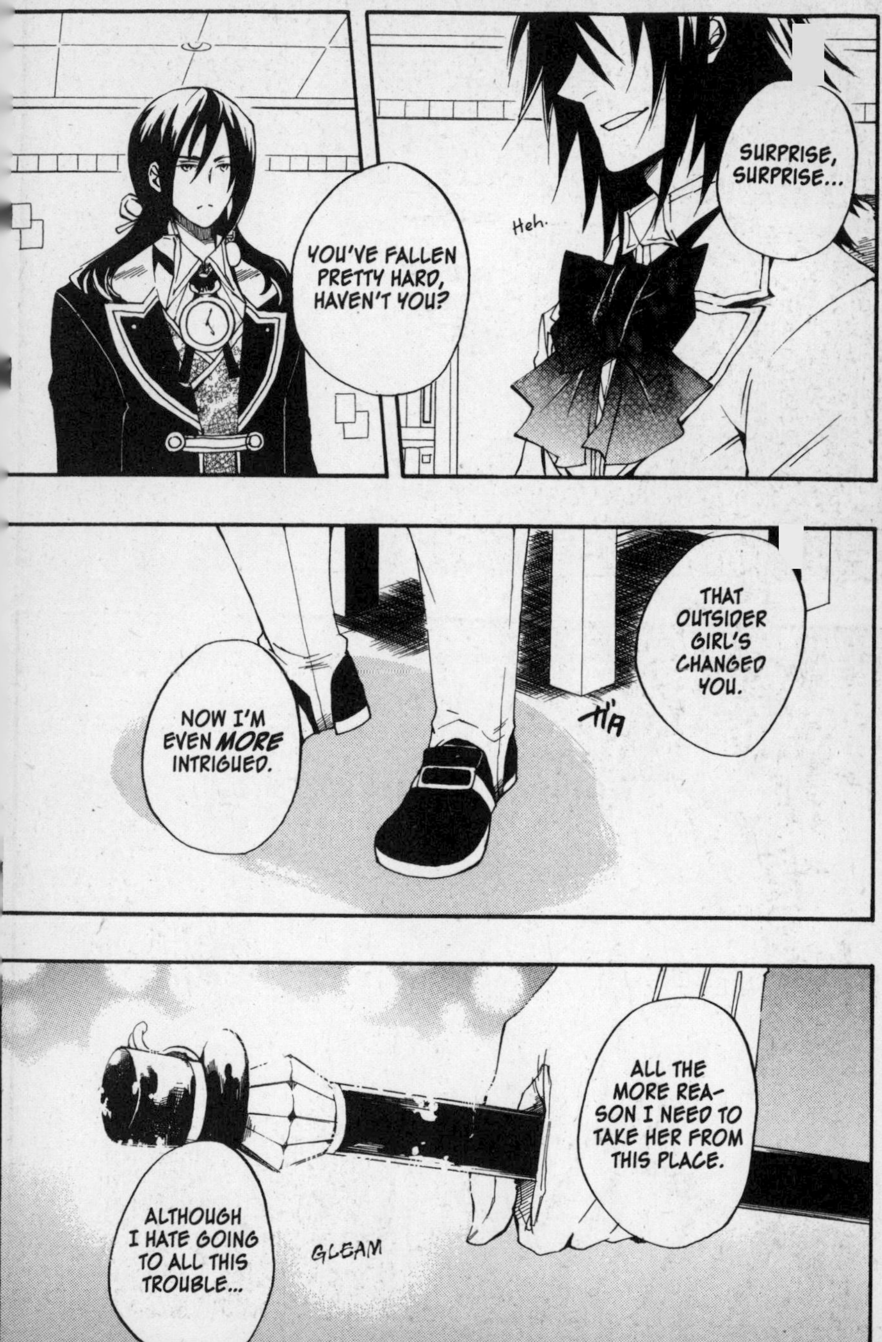
SURPRISE, SURPRISE...
Heh.
YOU'VE FALLEN PRETTY HARD, HAVEN'T YOU?
THAT OUTSIDER GIRL'S CHANGED YOU.
HA
NOW I'M EVEN *MORE* INTRIGUED.
ALL THE MORE REA-SON I NEED TO TAKE HER FROM THIS PLACE.
ALTHOUGH I HATE GOING TO ALL THIS TROUBLE...
GLEAM

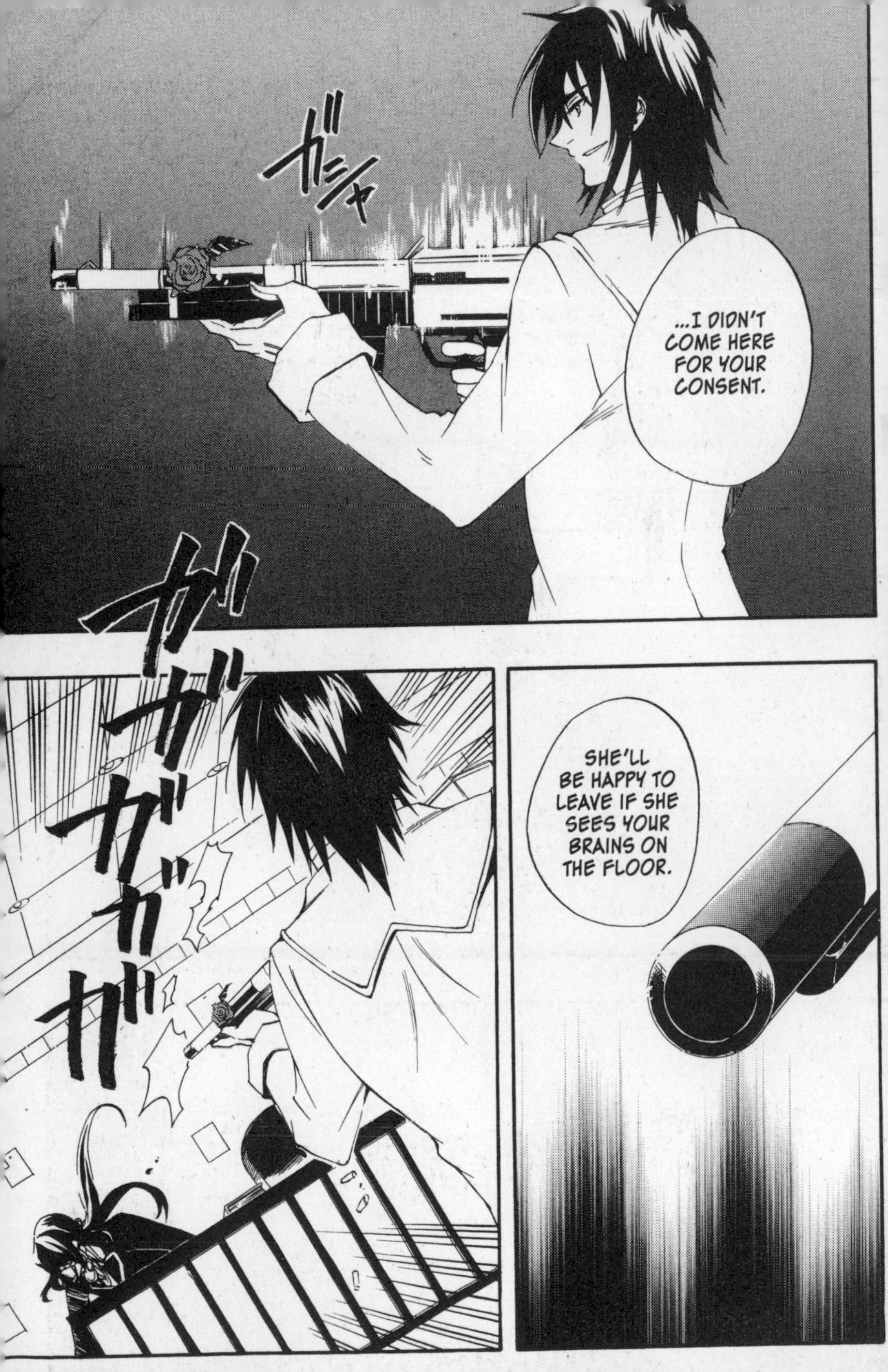
ガシャ
...I DIDN'T COME HERE FOR YOUR CONSENT.
SHE'LL BE HAPPY TO LEAVE IF SHE SEES YOUR BRAINS ON THE FLOOR.
ガガガガ

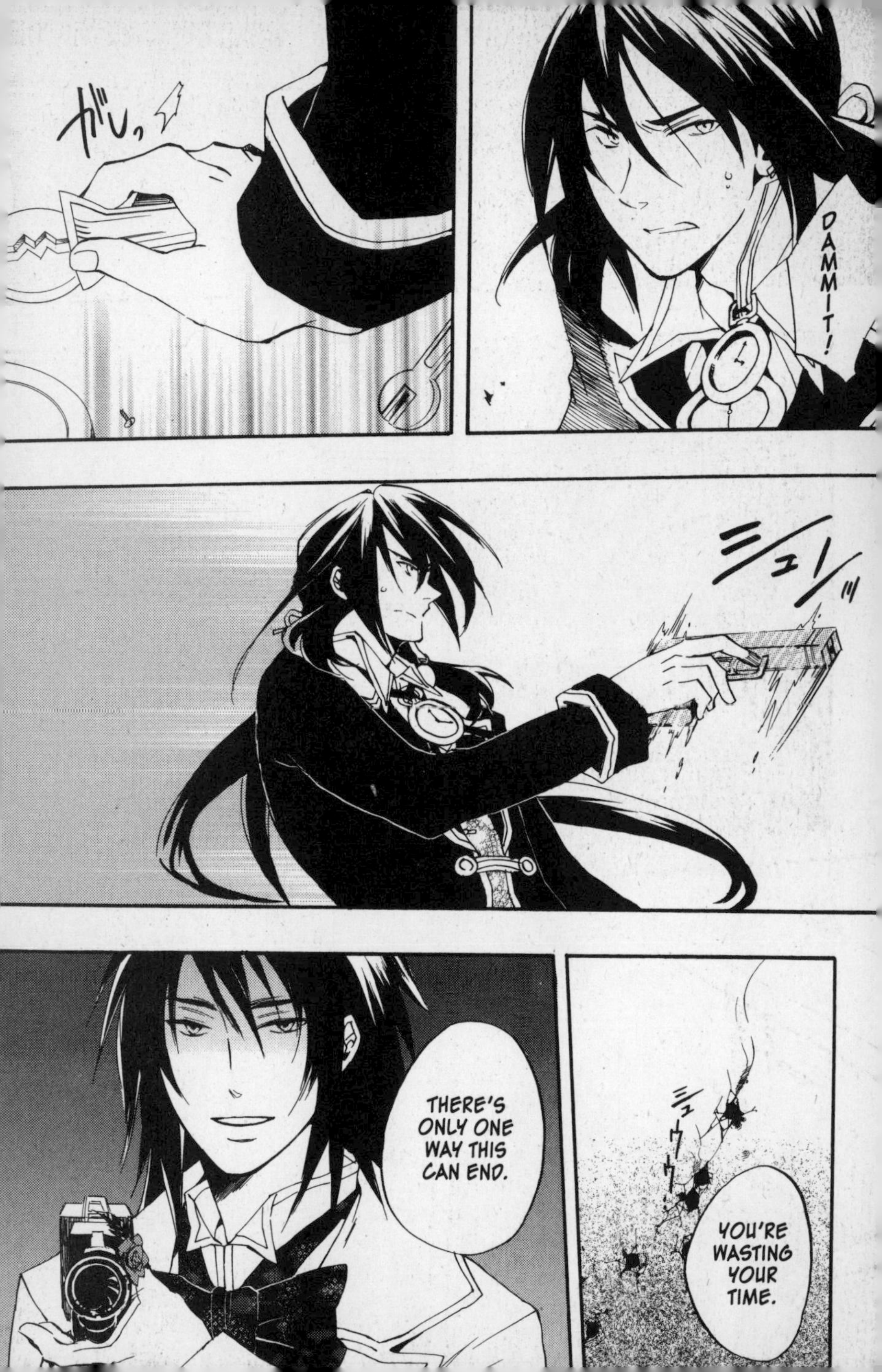
DAMMIT!
がしっ
シュン
シュウウ
YOU'RE WASTING YOUR TIME.
THERE'S ONLY ONE WAY THIS CAN END.

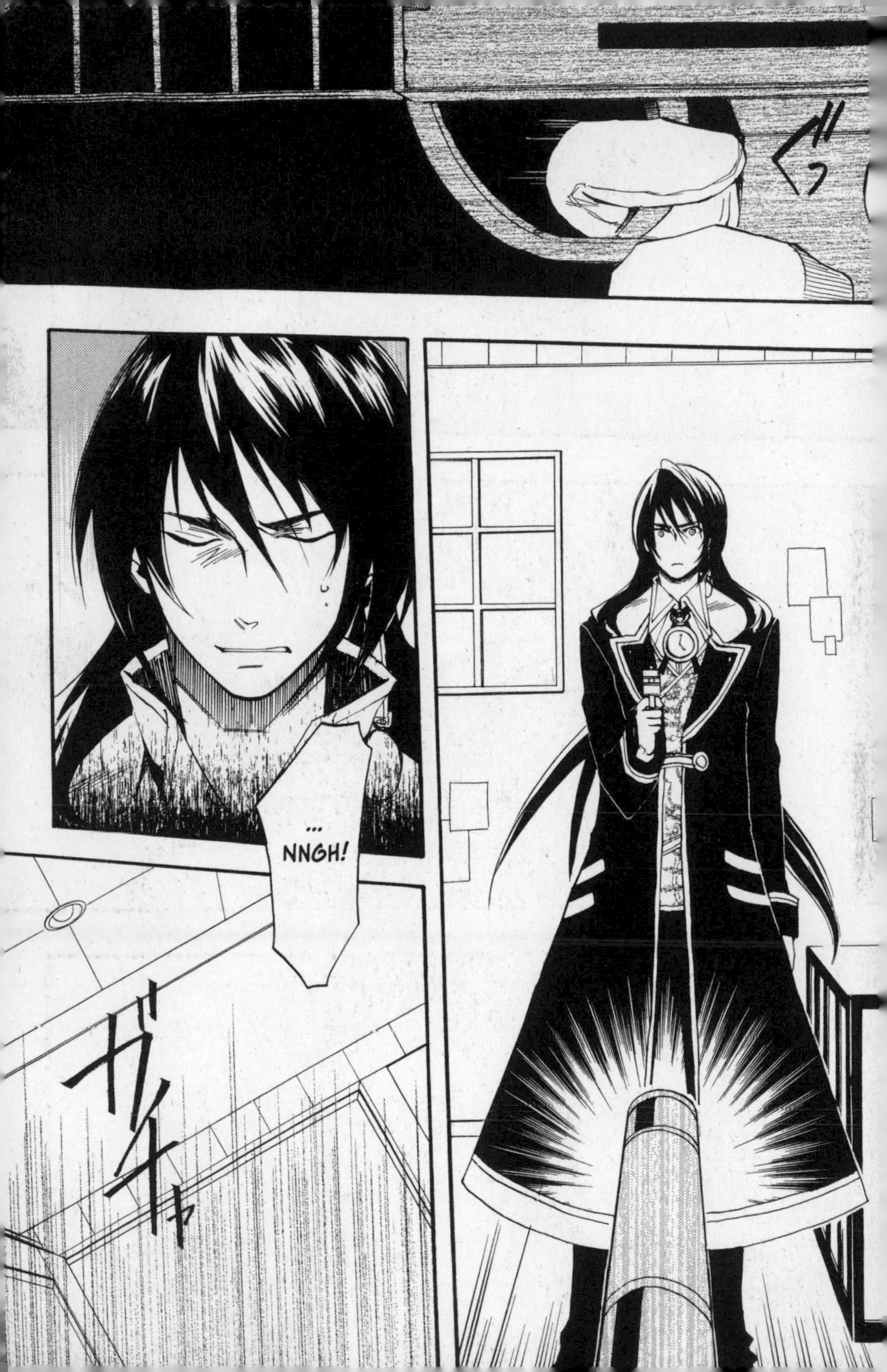
ぐっ
... NNGH!
ガチャ

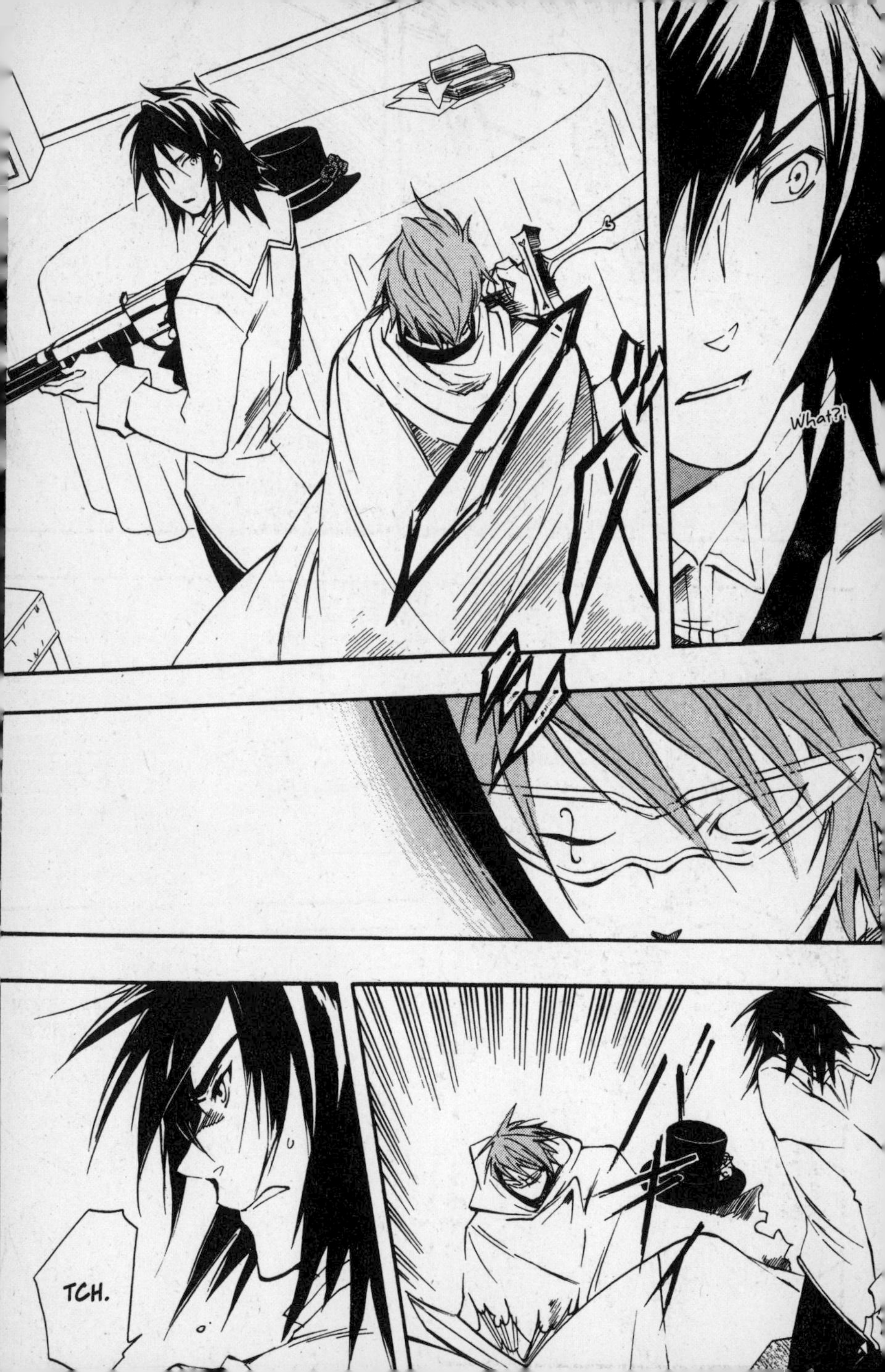
What?!
TCH.

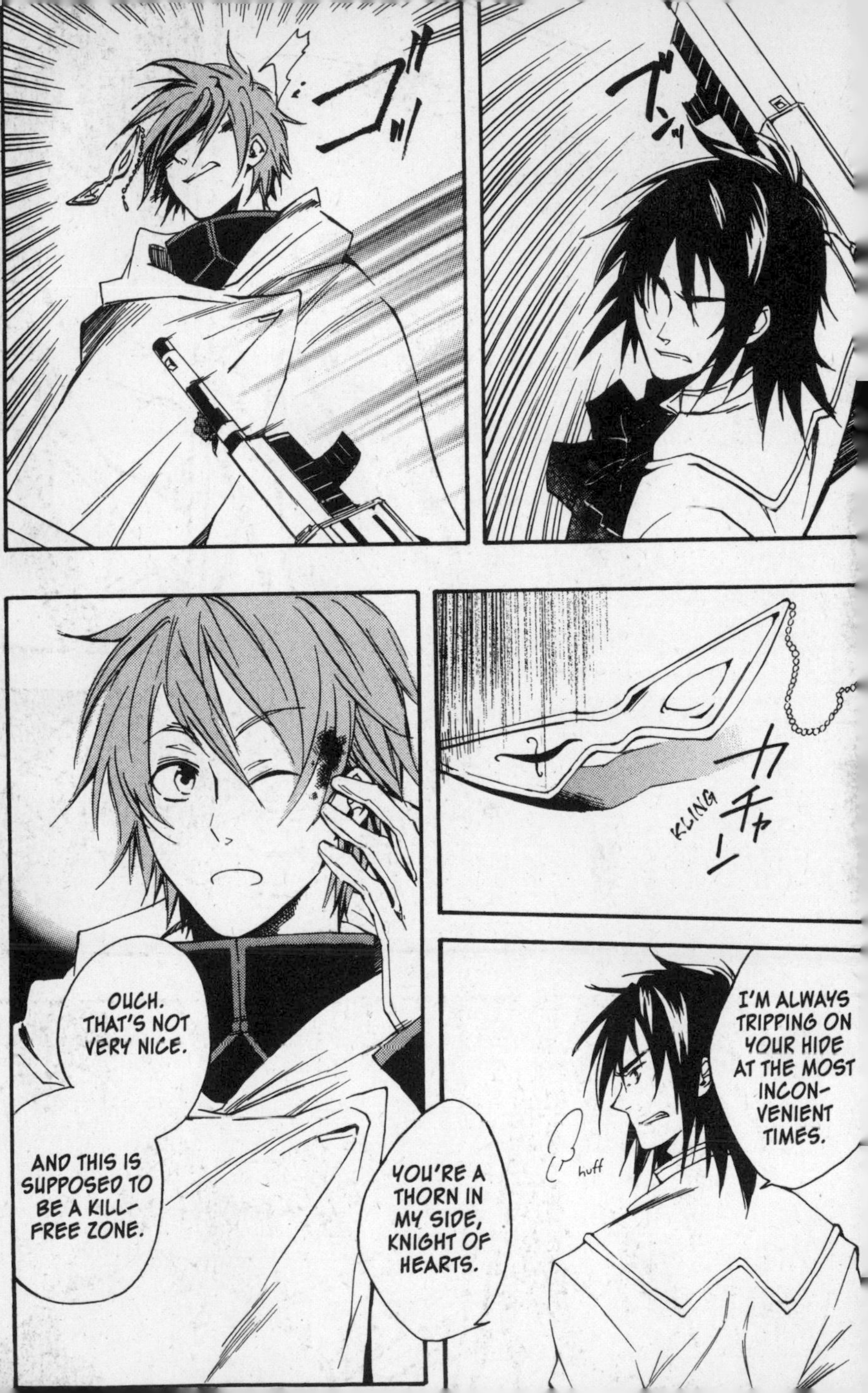
ズンッ
ゴッ
カチャン
KLING
I'M ALWAYS TRIPPING ON YOUR HIDE AT THE MOST INCON-VENIENT TIMES.
huff
OUCH. THAT'S NOT VERY NICE.
YOU'RE A THORN IN MY SIDE, KNIGHT OF HEARTS.
AND THIS IS SUPPOSED TO BE A KILL-FREE ZONE.

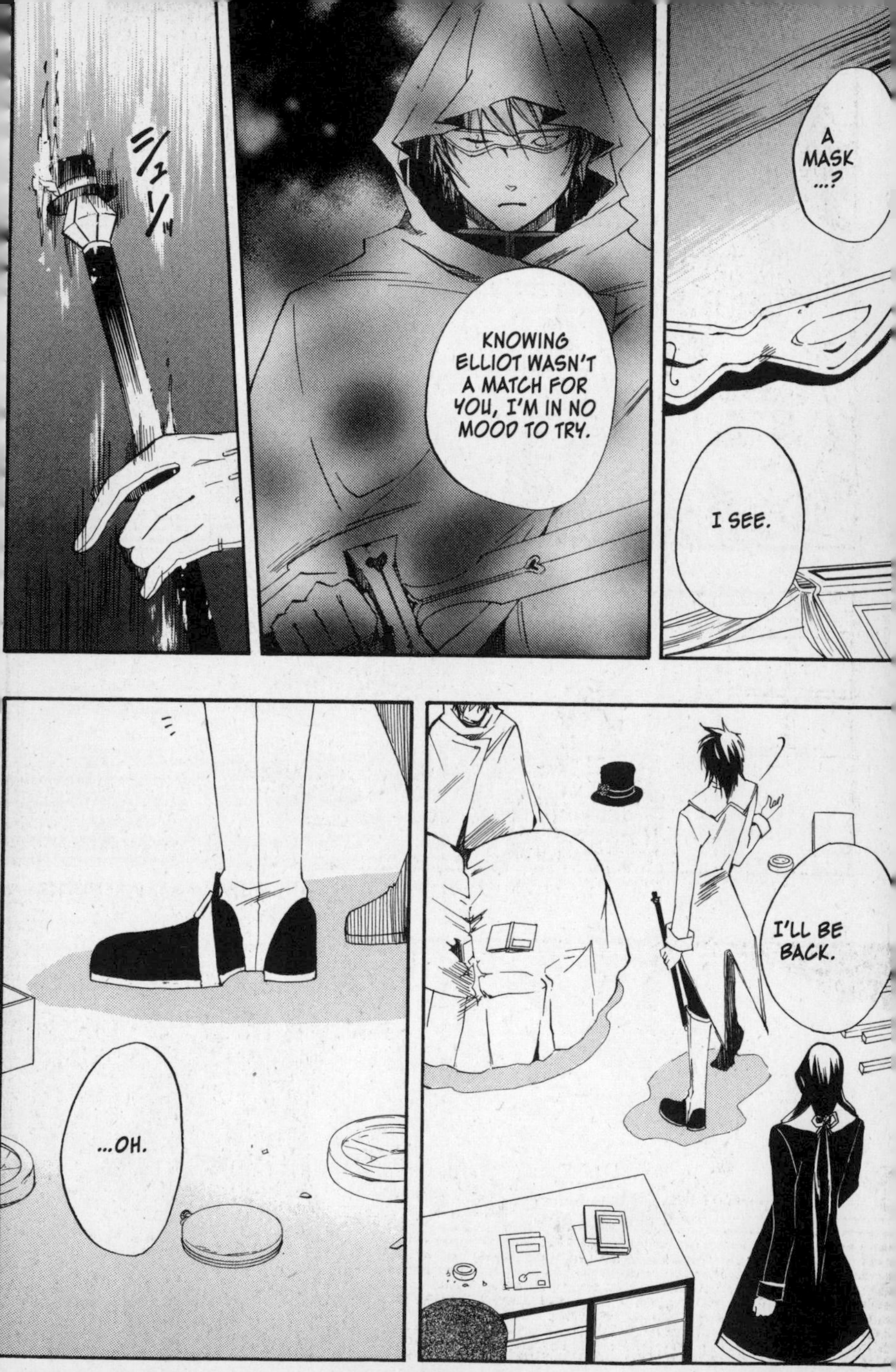
A MASK ...?
I SEE.
KNOWING ELLIOT WASN'T A MATCH FOR YOU, I'M IN NO MOOD TO TRY.
I'LL BE BACK.
...OH.

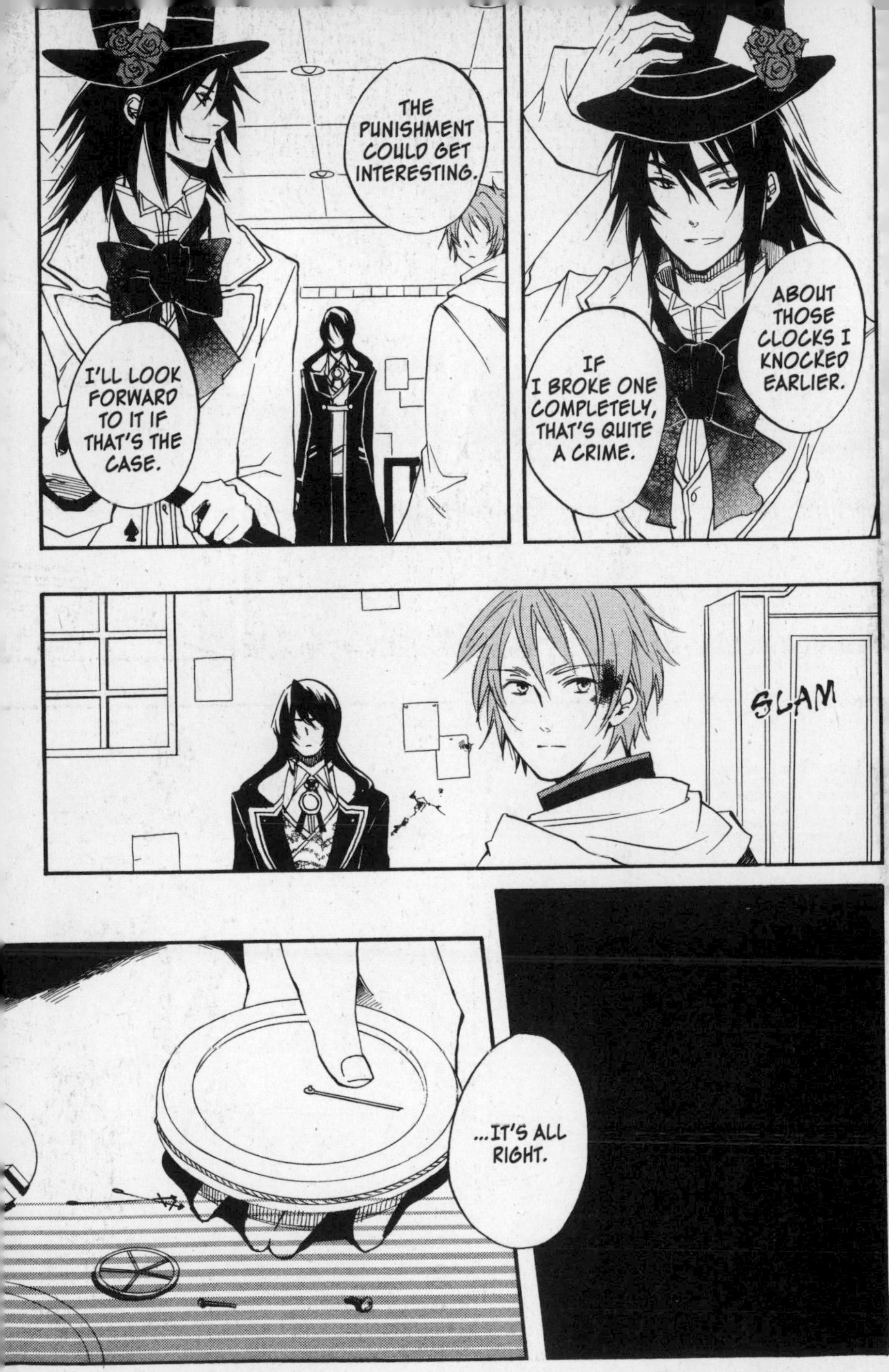
ABOUT THOSE CLOCKS I KNOCKED EARLIER.
IF I BROKE ONE COMPLETELY, THAT'S QUITE A CRIME.
THE PUNISHMENT COULD GET INTERESTING.
I'LL LOOK FORWARD TO IT IF THAT'S THE CASE.
SLAM
...IT'S ALL RIGHT.

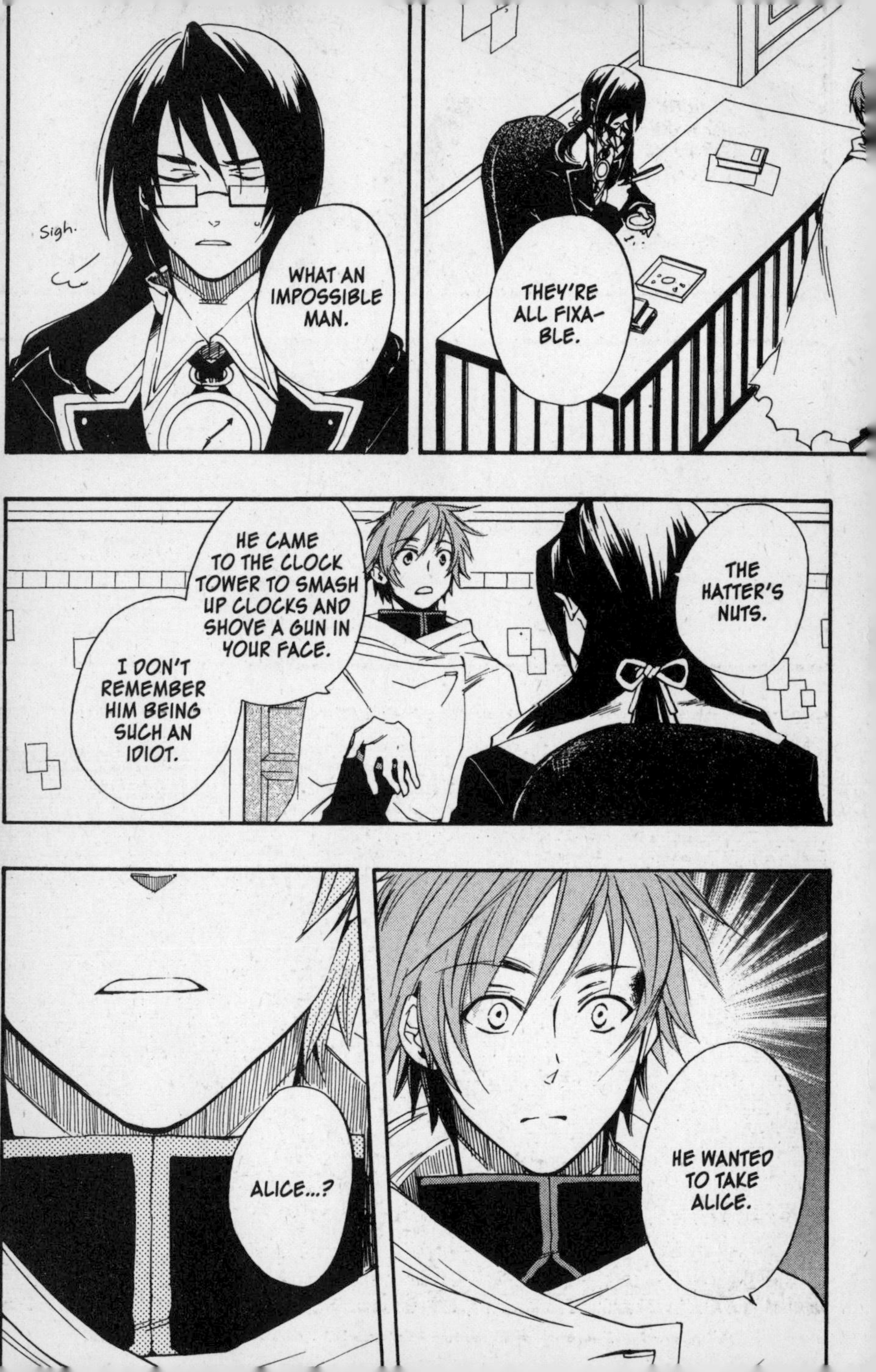
THEY'RE ALL FIXA-BLE.
Sigh.
WHAT AN IMPOSSIBLE MAN.
THE HATTER'S NUTS.
HE CAME TO THE CLOCK TOWER TO SMASH UP CLOCKS AND SHOVE A GUN IN YOUR FACE.
I DON'T REMEMBER HIM BEING SUCH AN IDIOT.
HE WANTED TO TAKE ALICE.
ALICE...?

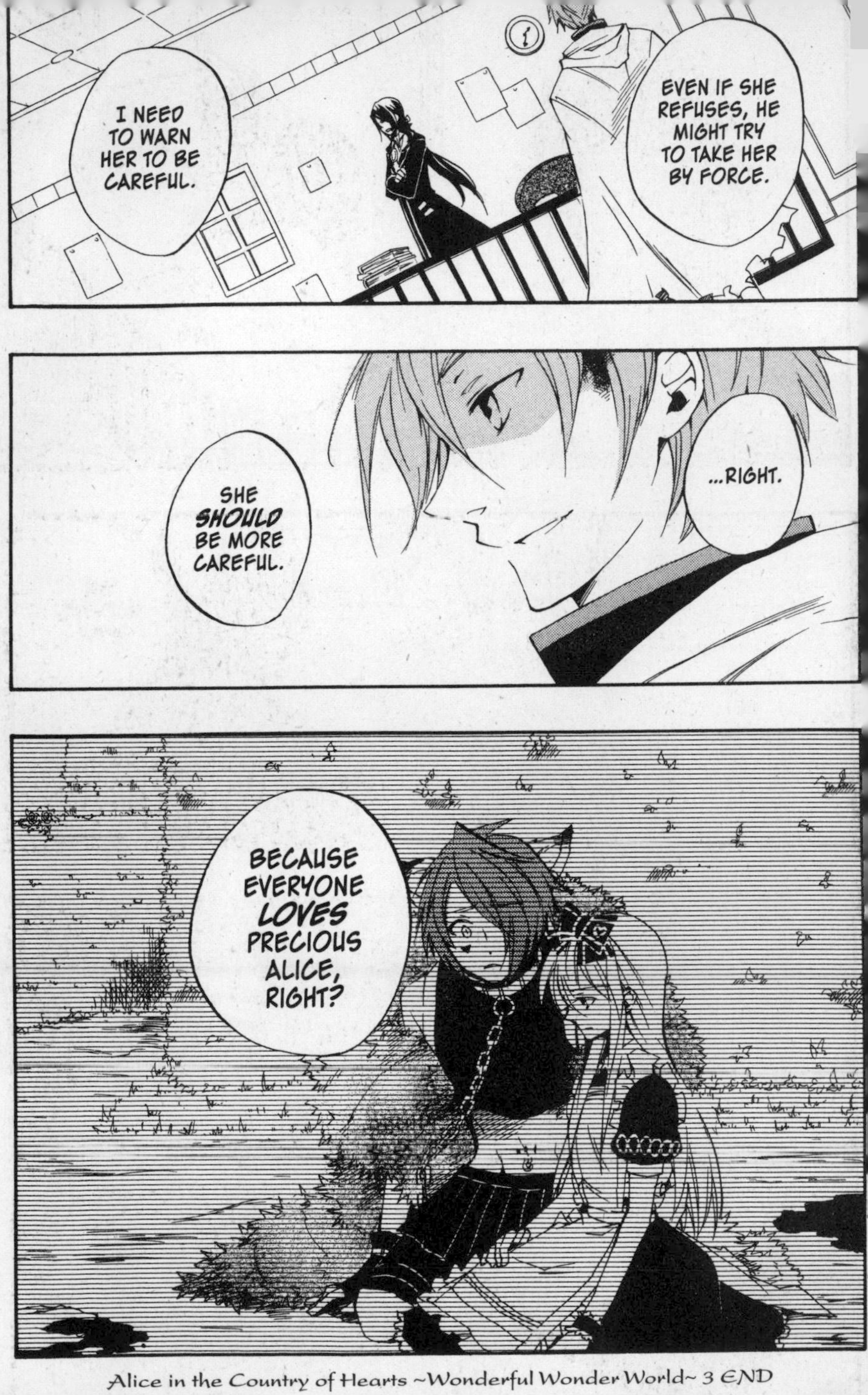
EVEN IF SHE REFUSES, HE MIGHT TRY TO TAKE HER BY FORCE.
I NEED TO WARN HER TO BE CAREFUL.
...RIGHT.
SHE SHOULD BE MORE CAREFUL.
BECAUSE EVERYONE LOVES PRECIOUS ALICE, RIGHT?

Alice in the Country of Hearts ~Wonderful Wonder World~ 3 END

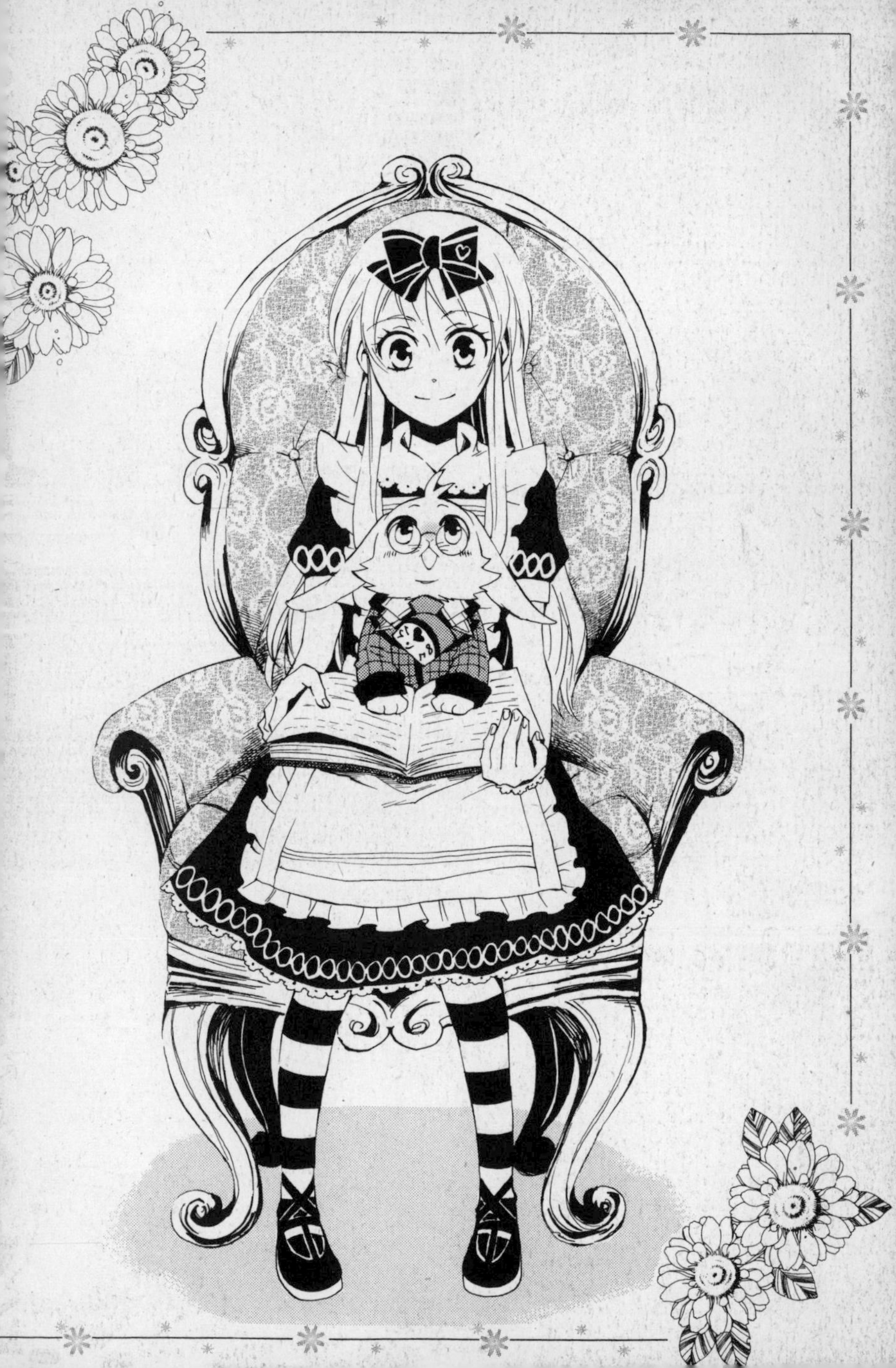

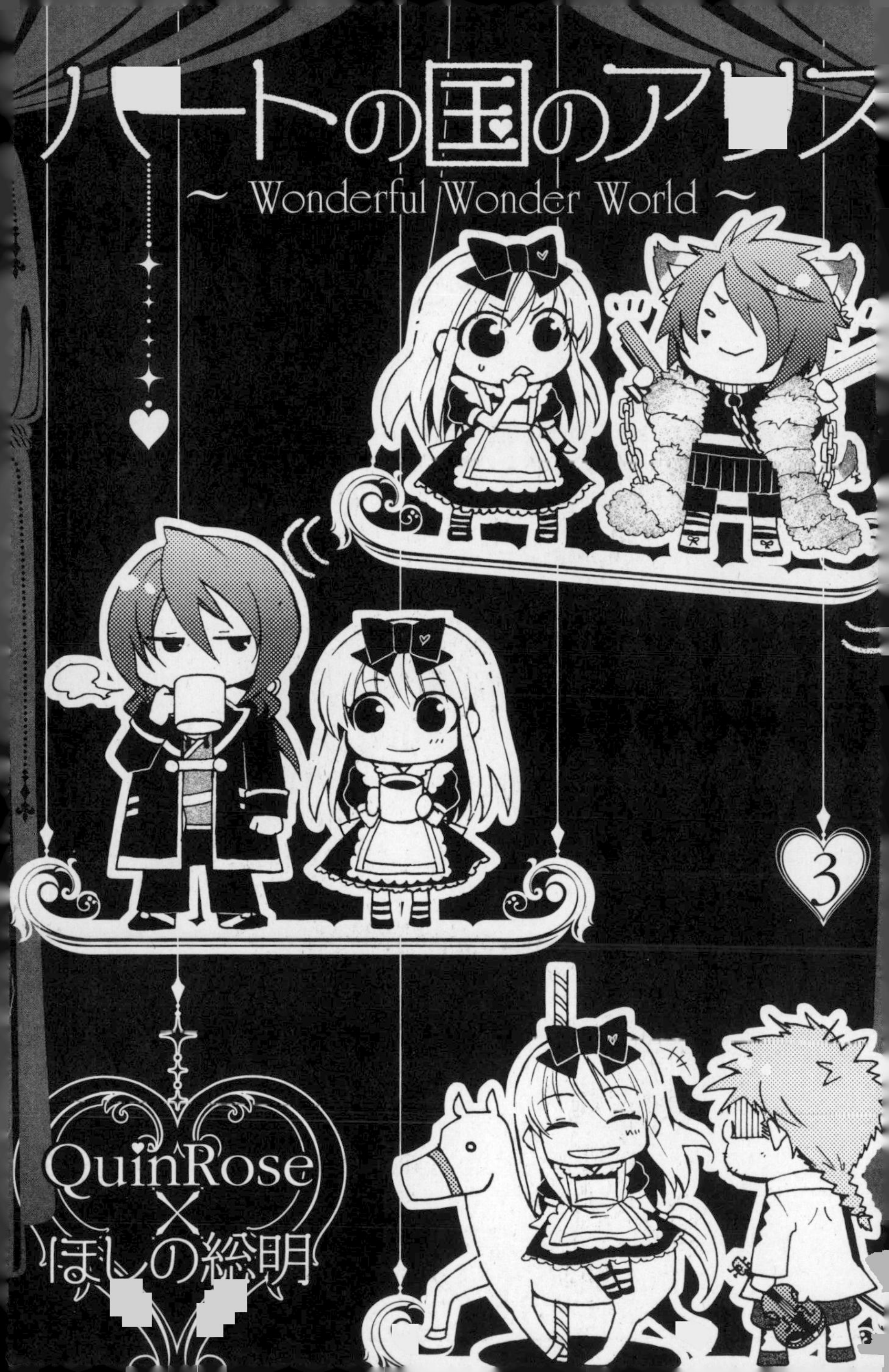
ハ トの国のア ス
~ Wonderful Wonder World ~
3
QuinRose
×
ほしの総明

In the next volume of...

Alice IN THE COUNTRY OF Hearts

Sadness looms over Alice after Ace shows how life is treated in Wonderland. To cheer her up, Boris takes Alice to the amusement park, but when she comes home, Julius asks her if she wants to leave the clock tower. Where will Alice choose to live? Then, Peter brings Alice an invitation to a mysterious ball where even enemies must come together to socialize. What kind of deadly dances will take place at this strange party?

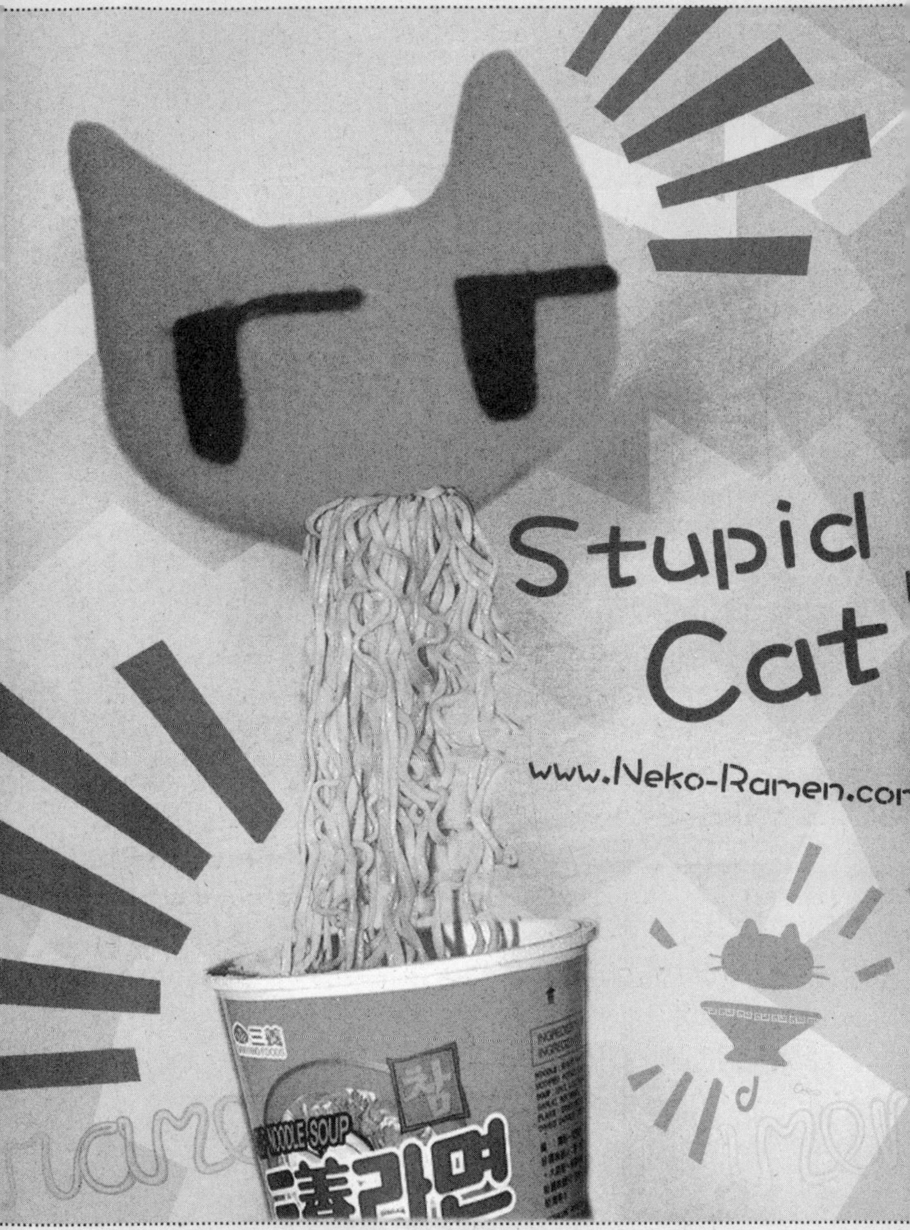
Stupid
Cat
www.Neko-Ramen.cor

THE SMALLEST HERO!?
RATMAN
ラットマン

THE SMALLEST HERO!?
RATMAN
ラットマン
TOKYOPOP

Shuto Katsuragi is a superhero otaku. Only problem is, he's a shrimp always getting teased for his height...especially when he tries to emulate his favorite superhero! To make matters worse, Shuto suddenly gets abducted by his classmate and tricked into participating in some rather sketchy and super-villainous experiments! Why is it always one step forward and a hundred steps back for this little guy?

ACTION

OT
OLDER TEEN
AGE 16+

STOP!

This is the back of the book.
You wouldn't want to spoil a great ending!

This book is printed "manga-style," in the authentic Japanese right-to-left format. Since none of the artwork has been flipped or altered, readers get to experience the story just as the creator intended. You've been asking for it, so TOKYOPOP® delivered: authentic, hot-off-the-press, and far more fun!

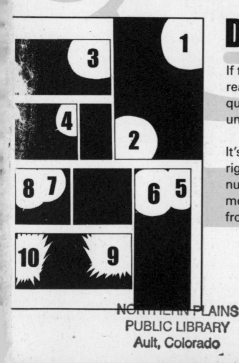

DIRECTIONS

If this is your first time reading manga-style, here's a quick guide to help you understand how it works.

It's easy... just start in the top right panel and follow the numbers. Have fun, and look for more 100% authentic manga from TOKYOPOP®!

THE MANGA REVOLUTION · LEADING · THE MANGA REVOLUTION · LEADING

漫画
革命